Financial and Monetary Policy Studies

Volume 42

Series Editor
Ansgar Belke, Essen, Germany

More information about this series at
http://www.springer.com/series/5982

Beniamino Moro • Victor A. Beker

Modern Financial Crises

Argentina, United States and Europe

Springer

Beniamino Moro
Department of Economics
and Business
University of Cagliari
Cagliari, Italy

Victor A. Beker
Department of Economics
University of Belgrano and University
of Buenos Aires
Buenos Aires, Argentina

ISSN 0921-8580 ISSN 2197-1889 (electronic)
Financial and Monetary Policy Studies
ISBN 978-3-319-20990-6 ISBN 978-3-319-20991-3 (eBook)
DOI 10.1007/978-3-319-20991-3

Library of Congress Control Number: 2015946316

Springer Cham Heidelberg New York Dordrecht London

Printed on acid-free paper

Springer International Publishing AG Switzerland is part of Springer Science+Business Media (www.springer.com)

Preface

This book is devoted to the analysis of the three main financial crises which happened in the present century. The first one was the 2001 Argentina's default on its external debt; the second was the American subprime crisis; and the third was the European public debt and banking crisis. In fact, the recent Great Crisis has extended over two periods: the first one covered the 2007–2009 subprime crisis in the USA, while the second took the form of a twin sovereign debt and banking crisis in Europe after 2010 and in some respects persists in 2015.

These events have led to increasing interest on the subject of financial crises, to which economists had paid almost no attention during the optimistic years of the so-called Great Moderation, which cover the last two decades of the twentieth century following the two oil crises that happened in the 1970s. However, as Reinhart and Rogoff exhaustively show, financial crises and sovereign debt defaults are far from strange events in economic history, in both less developed as well as developed countries.

While in 2003, Padma Desai, from Columbia University, could still assert that there was a big difference in the debt management between developed and emerging countries, events after 2007 show that this is no longer valid. In spite of being endowed with a sophisticated network of financial institutions and supervisory regulatory agencies, the US economy was hit by a financial crisis that has much in common with previous episodes in emerging countries. The same has happened in the European Union in the last years. Moreover, the policies being undertaken by crisis-hit countries are similar to those Argentina tried in 2001 in its desperate effort to save the peso-dollar peg.

Undoubtedly, the financial crisis damaged the reputation of economics. The institutional changes that made the 2007–2008 crisis possible were inspired by the mainstream belief based on the self-reliance of utter competition, rationality, and efficiency; the same origins had the analytical models used to build the subprime mortgage securitization pyramid that nearly blew up the financial system in the USA.

The purpose of this book is threefold. First, to give a picture of three episodes of modern financial crises. Second, to analyze what went wrong with mainstream economic theory, which not even took into consideration the possibility of such a kind of economic turmoil. Third, to review macroeconomic theory, by reevaluating Keynes's original contribution, on one side, and by taking account of the most insightful analysis of Neoclassical theory, on the other. We point out the need to rebuilt macroeconomics with a view on studying economic illness of modern economies, rather than trying to prove their long run tendency to equilibrium.

Studying economic pathologies and how to cure them should be encouraged in both Keynesian and Neoclassical schools of thought, while fewer resources should be devoted to merely showing why an economy is in good health. It is time to recover the contributions on economic crises by authors like John Kenneth Galbraith, Charles Kindleberger, John Maynard Keynes, and Milton Friedman. They cannot be ignored by any economist nowadays.

The book is organized as follows. Part I, which contains only Chap. 1, introduces on the main characteristics of financial crises. It is the combination of asymmetric information and illiquidity that gives rise to the possibility of a banking crisis, a situation whereby all depositors want their cash back. A securities-based financial system has the same attributes as the classic banking business model. In both cases, a financial crisis is associated with an increase in demand for liquidity or more liquid securities. This puts strain on the balance sheets of those intermediaries who provide liquidity in financial markets: their assets fall in value, including sovereign bonds of troubled countries, and their liabilities increase in value. To restore their own financial equilibrium, those intermediaries sell their assets in a situation where buyers are relatively fewer. Securities prices fall further, and this causes "panic," the "flight to quality," the "run," or whatever one chooses to call it. Short-term credit dries up, including the normally straightforward repurchase agreement ("the run on repo"), interbank lending, and commercial paper markets. This panic is usually followed by a very sharp recession.

Part II, which contains Chap. 2, is devoted to the analysis of the 2001 Argentine default. A detailed presentation is made of the events which led to Argentina's external debt repudiation. In particular, the role of the IMF is pointed out and the lessons which emerge from this experience are emphasized. In fact, it is very difficult to understand how Argentina's external debt largely increased in the 1990s despite just coming out from default without taking into account that in the 1990s Argentina was considered the best pupil of the IMF, the World Bank, and the US government. The IMF played a key role in restoring confidence in Argentina by capital markets. So, it seems to be clear that a primary responsibility in the 2001 public sector debt crisis was played by the IMF endorsement of an economic scheme which was doomed to fail.

Part III is devoted to the American 2007–2009 subprime crisis. It contains two chapters. Chapter 3 discusses the American subprime meltdown. The role of banks and rating agencies that created and certified as almost risk-free securities assets that were actually highly risky—as the events after 2007 overwhelmingly showed—is pointed out. Credit rating agencies played in the American crisis the same role as the IMF played in the Argentine case: to induce lenders to put their money into buying securities of doubtful collectability. In particular, the role of the so-called shadow banking system which emerged during the last 30 years is highlighted as well as its responsibility in creating the conditions for a panic.

Chapter 4 explains that this time the panic firstly took place in the repo market, which suffered a run when "depositors" required increasing haircuts. Fears of insolvency reduced interbank lending, and this so-called "run on repo" caused temporary disruptions in the pricing system of short-term debt markets. The subsequent crisis reduced the pool of assets considered acceptable as collateral, resulting in a liquidity shortage. With declining asset values and increasing haircuts, the US banking system was effectively insolvent for the first time since the Great Depression.

Part IV is devoted to the European debt crisis. It contains three chapters. Chapter 5 analyzes how, via the banking system, the financial contagion was extended from the USA to Europe. In fact, we observe the extension of the Great Crisis from the international banking system to the European sovereign debts. The problem is that the expansionary fiscal policies of deficit spending implemented by most States to tackle the crisis have created very large public deficits. To save banks, private debt became public debt. At the same time, with deteriorating public finances, sovereign risk has increased and worsened bank's balance sheets. In fact, it is really a sequence of interactions between sovereign problems and banking problems. The full explanation of these interactions also focuses on the imbalances of European Monetary Union (EMU) countries balance-of-payments. The European crisis has shown that it can spread quickly among closely integrated economies, either through the trade channel or the financial channel, or both.

Chapter 6 explains why, in the European crisis, TARGET2 payment system of EMU countries became crucial, reflecting funding stress in the banking systems of most crisis-hit countries. In this context, the ECB has assumed a crucial role to overcome the financial crisis. Anyway, a deep depression followed the financial turmoil. To promote a full economic recovery in Europe, a strict interconnection between single countries fiscal policies and the ECB's autonomous monetary policy is necessary. In this regard, in the medium term, a successful crisis resolution requires more political integration of EMU countries, which should include a fiscal union and a banking union. However, in the short run, a prompt recovery is essential to get out of trouble, and this requires that surplus countries (specially Germany) expand aggregate demand and let domestic wages and the ensuing internal inflation rate increase.

Chapter 7 makes a distinction between a first group of European countries whose debt problems have roots before 2007, but did not worsen significantly after that year, and a second one of new highly indebted countries. Among them, Spain appears as a special case. The development of the indebtedness process in these three different types of countries allows isolating the factors which were determinant in each case. The conclusion is that the European indebtedness process does not accept a unique explanation and that its solution will necessarily require resource transfers from the richer to the poorer countries of the Eurozone.

Part V is devoted to the impact of the Great Crisis on economic thought. It also contains three chapters. Chapter 8 deals with the theoretical debate on the Great Crisis, which contrast Keynesian to Neoclassical economists. According to Keynesians, the central cause of the profession's failure to forecast the recent Great Crisis is the abandoning of Keynesian theory, and the prevailing of monetarism and neoclassical vision that whatever happens in a market economy must be right. According to Neoclassicals, instead, economic models do not just fail to predict the timing of financial crises, they say that we cannot. Keynesians suggest that deficit spending is the right policy to put the economic system in a full employment equilibrium path, while Neoclassicals think that fiscal stimulus is only a bad way to transfer money from taxpayers to inefficient bureaucrats, policymakers, and zombie firms. Anyway, Keynesians and Neoclassicals share the opinion that we need a more tightening regulation of financial markets. Commercial banks, who are allowed to manage systemic contracts like bank deposits, and for that reason they have access to the lender of last resort, should be kept strictly separated from investment banks, hedge funds, and other financial speculative institutions, none of which should be considered too big to fail.

The purpose of Chap. 9 is threefold. First, it seeks to clarify what economics is guilty of; second, to spell out what sort of science economics is, what is legitimate to expect from it and what is not; and, third, to discuss the flaws of economics and how to correct them. It is argued that what happened with the crisis was a case of malpractice by hundreds of professionals in banks and rating agencies that created and certified as virtually risk-free securities assets that were actually highly risky, as the events after 2007 overwhelmingly demonstrated. Such a massive case of malpractice exposed deep failures in the regulatory system.

Chapter 10 discusses the impact of the US financial crisis on economic theory. An analysis is made of the responsibility of economics and economists in the crisis and how to redirect economics research agenda to address real economic problems instead of building elegant models with little, if any, relationship with policy and practical issues. In particular, the predictability capability of standard economic models is discussed. Suggestions in economic theorizing are made so as to prevent the crisis from happening again. What this implies for macroeconomics is emphasized. Readers are reminded of the origin of macroeconomics as a branch of economics; a claim is made to reevaluate Keynes' original contribution to economic analysis and to return to Keynes' thoughts, which have been ignored or misstated during the past 40 years.

Finally, Part VI contains two chapters. Chapter 11 deals with current issues and policies regarding the last updated developments of the three crises dealt with in this book: in Argentina, United States, and Europe. Argentina restructured its debt in 2005 with a significant reduction, which was accepted by 76 % of the creditors and resumed payment to them. In 2010, a second debt swap was offered which was accepted by another 17 % of the creditors. So, only 7 % of the bondholders rejected the terms of the debt exchanges, which anyway poses some open questions. In the USA, the consequences of the Dodd–Frank Act are analyzed, while in the EMU it still remains unsolved a near-defaulting situation for Greece. For all the other

EMU's countries, the recent quantitative easing monetary policy implemented by the ECB succeeded to calm financial markets and created the right environment necessary to promote a new European economic recovery.

Chapter 12 concludes with policy recommendations to avoid crises from happening again as well as on the economic theory research agenda. The role in the crises of institutions like the IMF, the banking system, and ratings agencies is underlined as well as the need for reform of the financial system regulatory and supervisory architecture. Studying economic pathologies and how to cure them should be the core of the economics research agenda in the coming years, while fewer resources should be devoted to merely showing why an economy is in good health.

Buenos Aires, Argentina
Cagliari, Italy
June 2015

Victor A. Beker
Beniamino Moro

Acknowledgements

This book is the result of the joint effort of both authors, who share the responsibility of the whole content from the scientific point of view. Anyway, the chapters have been written following a criterion of specialization. Therefore, Chaps. 2, 3, 7, 9, 10, 12, and Sects. 11.2 and 11.3 have been written by Victor A. Beker, while Chaps. 1, 4, 5, 6, 8, and Sects. 11.1 and 11.4 have been written by Beniamino Moro. We thank Miguel Leon-Ledesma, Vincenzo Merella, and Galo Nuño Barrau for their comments on the manuscript of the book. Usual disclaimers apply.

Contents

Part I
Introduction

Chapter 1
The Core Characteristics of Financial Crises

Beniamino Moro

1.1 Introduction

In the nineteenth century, before deposit insurance, financial shocks caused depositors to be anxious about their deposits, in which case they would run to their banks en masse demanding cash. In January 2006, in the USA, there was a shock in that house prices began to fall. One year and a half later, in August 2007, a financial crisis began with a shock in the subprime mortgage market, with firms withdrawing credit from other firms. So, a banking panic occurred due to the shock to subprime mortgage values caused by house prices falling, which confirmed that uninsured bank debt is vulnerable to panic.

This caused the first part of the recent Great Crisis, occurred in the USA in 2007–2009 (Chaps. 3 and 4), while the second one began in Europe after 2010 (Chaps. 5, 6, and 7) and for some aspects persists until 2015. Understanding that the current crisis, both for the USA and for Europe, is originated, as in the past, by a banking panic is essential to understand the dynamics of financial crises and to design regulation of the financial system.

In 2010–2013, the new focus of turbulence was Europe, which faced a severe economic and financial crisis. However, the origin of the European crisis can be directly traced back to the American crisis of 2007–2009, which spilled over into a sovereign debt crisis in several euro area countries. Although this is usually described as a sovereign debt crisis, in fact it is really a sequence of interactions between sovereign debt problems and banking problems. In fact, with deteriorating public finances, sovereign risk has increased and worsened bank's balance sheets. Therefore, the European situation in this period is best described as twin sovereign

B. Moro (✉)
Department of Economics and Business, University of Cagliari, Viale San Ignazio 17, 09123 Cagliari, Italy
e-mail: moro@unica.it

B. Moro, V.A. Beker, *Modern Financial Crises*, Financial and Monetary Policy Studies 42, DOI 10.1007/978-3-319-20991-3_1

debt and banking crises that mutually feed each other, and the result of this interaction is a gradual contagion to more countries and more asset classes.

As a result, after occurring in the USA, fears of insolvency caused a run on repo, which reduced interbank lending, also in Europe. The subsequent crisis reduced the pool of assets accepted as collateral, resulting in a liquidity shortage. This situation raised some doubts on the survival of the euro and the European Monetary Union (EMU).

Therefore, in this book, after having dealt with the Argentina's bankruptcy in 2002 (Chap. 2), we explore the very nature and the consequences of the recent Great Crisis, which appears as the most devastating one among modern financial crisis (Van Ours 2015).

As just mentioned above, in the book we distinguish two periods: the first includes the American crisis of 2007–2009, while the second consists of the European twin sovereign debt and banking crises, which began in 2010 and persist until 2015, at least with regard to the Greece's case. In this context, the 2002 Argentina's crisis complements, 5 years in advance, the blowup of the world financial system in most developed industrial countries. This is why in the book we speak of a Great Crisis.

This introductory chapter is organized as follows. Section 1.2 deals with the liquidity nature of financial crisis. Section 1.3 introduces the Greenspan put, also known as the too big to fail (TBTF) paradigm. Section 1.4 deals with the predictability of financial crises. Then, Sect. 1.5 compares two visions of the big financial crises: the first is known as a "Black Swan" case, which opposes to a historically regularity hypothesis of financial crises. Section 1.6 explores what modern financial crises tell us for economic theorizing, and Sect. 1.7 briefly deals with the extension of the Great Crisis to the European sovereign debt and banking sector. Finally, Sect. 1.8 concludes.

1.2 The Liquidity Nature of Financial Crises

The period since 1934, when deposit insurance was introduced in the USA, until the recent Great Crisis, has been a period of relative quiescence. But, from a historical perspective, banking panics are the norm. The banking system changed over the last decades and this transformation recreated the conditions for a panic. Understanding that the shadow banking system is, in fact, real banking and that recent events constituted a banking panic is a premise to understand the last Great Crisis.[1]

[1] The classical reference on financial crises is the famous and much cited essay by Kindleberger (1978), who notes that financial crises characterize the history of the capitalistic development all over the world. Recent review articles on the argument are Fratianni (2008), who shows that financial crises are far from being a rare phenomenon, and Reinhart and Rogoff (2008a, b, 2009a, b, 2013, 2014), who point out the regularities of financial crises along with eight centuries of economic history. Further articles on the subject include Shachmurove (2010), who agrees that

A banking panic means that the banking system is insolvent, that is, it cannot honor contractual obligations: there are no private agents who can buy the amount of assets necessary to recapitalize the banking system. When the banking system is insolvent, many markets stop functioning and this leads to significant effects on the real economy. Quoting Bagehot (1873, 122), "A financial crisis is any sudden event which creates a great demand for actual cash and may cause, and will tend to cause, a panic in a country where cash is much economized, and where debts payable on demand are large. In such a country an immense credit rests on a small cash reserve, and an unexpected and large diminution of that reserve may easily break up and shatter very much, if not the whole, of that credit".[2]

History is littered with bank runs, bank panics, debt crisis, security crashes, and financial tsunamis (Fratianni 2008).[3] Since its beginning, banking manifested its fragility, squeezed between its commitments to honor depositors on demand and extending hard-to-liquidate loans to business and sovereigns.[4] More than 140 years

financial crises are all similar, and Vives (2010), who reviews the state of the art of the academic theoretical and empirical literature on the potential trade-off between competition and stability in banking. Razin and Rosefielde (2011) survey three distinct types of financial crises which took place in the 1990s and 2000s, one of which is the 2007–2009 crisis. Claessens and Kose (2013) are focused on the main theoretical and empirical explanations of four types of financial crisis: currency crises, sudden stops, debt crises, and banking crises. Furthermore, a comprehensive investigation of the real effects of banking crises is reviewed by Carpinelli (2009), while Moro (2013) reviews the American turmoil of 2007–2009. Moro (2014) surveys the European twin sovereign debt and banking crises, while Moro (2012) deals with the theoretical debate on the recent Great Crisis. Finally, Brunnermeier and Oehmke (2012) survey the literature on bubbles, financial crisis, and systemic risk, and Goldstein and Razin (2013) review three branches of theoretical literature on financial crises: the first one deals with the banking crisis, the second with frictions in credit and interbank markets, and the third one deals with currency crises.

[2] Brunnermeier and Schnabel (2015) review some of the most prominent asset price bubbles from the past 400 years and document how central banks (or other institutions) reacted to those bubbles. According to them, the historical evidence suggests that the emergence of bubbles is often preceded or accompanied by an expansionary monetary policy, lending booms, capital inflows, and financial innovation or deregulation. They find that the severity of the economic crisis following the bursting of a bubble is less linked to the *type of asset* than to the *financing* of the bubble. Crises are most severe when they are accompanied by a lending boom, high leverage of market players, and when financial institutions themselves are participating in the buying frenzy.

[3] The first bank run documented in the history occurred in Paris in 1720 before the Banque Royale went bankruptcy. This bank was born in 1718 after the transformation of the previous Banque Générale created by John Law in 1716 (Cova 2009, 54). Banque Générale and then Banque Royale were the first banks to issue paper money according to Law's theory that it was possible to substitute paper money to gold and silver for transaction purposes (Law 1707). As long as, for the first 2 years, the Banque Royale maintained a leverage of 4 times in the quantity of paper money over gold and silver reserves, it had a great success and paper money was really accepted by everybody in exchange for goods. But in 1720 the bank issued 2 billion lire paper money with only 10 million lire of metal reserves, with a leverage of 200. It followed a run to the bank, which in a few weeks, between May and June 1720, the bank went bankruptcy. See Cova (2009, 45–78).

[4] Fratianni (2008, 170) adds the more recent crises to the Kindleberger's (1978) list of major financial crises from 1622 to 1978. The total of 68 is summarized as follows: 9 crises happened in the 1700s, 22 in the pre-gold standard 1800s, 7 during the international gold standard (1800–1913),

after Bagehot period, the nature of financial crises has not changed, and this is because the basic features of financial intermediation—asymmetric information and liquidity transformation—have not changed. In an intermediated financial system, one where institutions raise capital resources from investors, the asymmetric information between investors and intermediaries can cause withdrawals of capital even in the presence of good investments.

In the case where investments are relatively illiquid, as in the classic banking business, where banks finance long-term loans with short-term deposits, depositors not only worry about the way a bank uses the resources they lend to it, but they also worry about the possibility of not getting their money back in the case the withdrawal of deposits is widespread.

Consider the classic banking business model. When banks borrow short term and lend long term, they allow easier access to their funds by savers and at the same time they allow users of capital to take on long-term, more productive plans. In this way, liquidity transformation becomes a socially productive, hence desirable, function (Giovannini 2010). But the combination of asymmetric information and illiquidity gives rise to the possibility of a financial crisis, a situation whereby all depositors want their cash back. In this situation a financial contagion may occur, in which insolvency risk is transmitted from one bank to another. Iyer and Peydro (2011) document that deposit withdrawals from a distressed bank can trigger withdrawals at similar banks in the same region, especially if these banks have interbank exposures to the distressed bank. Therefore, financial contagion is seen as a key source of systemic risk in the financial sector.[5]

The 2007–2009 US financial crisis was not a classical banking crisis but a securities-based financial crisis. Nevertheless, it was similar to previous episodes

8 in the interwar period (1919–1939), 6 during Bretton Woods period, and 16 in the most recent period 1974–2008. For the USA, all the financial crises since 1854 are summarized by NBER (2010). To this calculus, we add the European banking and sovereign debt crisis that began in 2010 and it is not completely overcome 5 years later.

[5] A growing literature examines a wide range of channels through which contagion in the banking sector may occur, such as common asset exposure (Acharya 2009; Ibragimov et al. 2011; Wagner 2010), domino effects due to counterpart risk (Allen and Gale 2000; Dasgupta 2004; Freixas and Parigi 1998; Freixas et al. 2000), or price declines and resulting margin requirements (Brunnermeier and Pedersen 2009). Allen et al. (2011) identify five sources for systemic risk: the first is the common exposure to asset price bubbles; the second is the mispricing of assets; the third depends on fiscal deficits, excessive public debts, and the correlated possibility of sovereign default; the fourth depends on currency mismatches in the banking system; and, finally, the fifth depends on the maturity mismatches and liquidity provision of banks. Brown et al. (2014) use a laboratory experiment to explore under which information conditions a panic-based run at one bank may trigger a panic-based run at another bank and through which transmission channels this contagion occurs. Finally, according to Adalsoro et al. (2015), contagion occurs through liquidity hoarding, interbank interlinkages, and fire sale externalities. The resulting network configuration exhibits a core-periphery structure. Within this framework they analyze the effects of prudential policies on the stability/efficiency trade-off. Liquidity requirements unequivocally decrease systemic risk but at the cost of lower efficiency, while equity requirements tend to reduce risk (hence increase stability) without reducing significantly overall investment.

of banking crisis. In fact, a securities-based financial system has crises that are, fundamentally, identical to those of the traditional bank-based system, with some features that possibly exacerbate their disruptive impact (Gorton 2009; Wheelock 2010).

The most notable feature of the world financial system on the eve of the recent Great Crisis is the tremendous development of securities and derivatives. A securities-based financial system has some very attractive attributes. The non-proximity between issuers and investors is one. It broadens enormously the potential market for any issuer.

An additional attractive attribute of securities is that they typically have a secondary market, where their stock is frequently exchanged among investors. If one person is not compelled to keep a security in his investment portfolio until maturity, he may be more willing to buy it: the result is a wider potential set of investors with respect to the case in which a secondary market is absent.

Just like a bank aggregates diverse depositors with diversifiable short-term liquidity needs to commit long-term resources to higher-yielding and productive investments, the securities market aggregates diverse investors with diversifiable short-term liquidity needs to provide long-term resources (debt and equity capital in the form of bonds and stocks) for productive purposes. Therefore, liquid secondary markets represent a fundamentally productive resource in an economy, in that they allow greater access to financial resources for productive use (Giovannini 2010).

For securities markets to function properly, potential buyers and sellers need to obtain accurate information about the prices of the securities they are interested in, and actual buyers and sellers need to find willing counterparties and need to complete their transactions smoothly and with minimum risk. Therefore, a securities-based financial system necessitates intermediaries, whose functions are to service issuers on one side and investors on the other, but also to support the price-setting process as well as the settlement of transactions.

Another notable development of the financial system in the past 25 years has been the spreading of derivatives. Derivatives are a natural by-product of the boom in securities which has made available a plethora of prices in an equal number of markets, each representing different risks or combinations of risks. These prices provide references for derivative contracts, which themselves allow buyers and sellers to gain exposure to, or eliminate exposure from, those different risks. The development of derivative contracts has multiplied hedging and risk-taking opportunities to all actors (Giovannini 2010).

How does the standard "bank" crisis manifest itself in securities markets? Practically all financial intermediaries, banks, and nonbanks alike hold securities in their balance sheet. A number of them hold securities that are more vulnerable to the problems just described: securities which are normally called less liquid because they have markets with fewer willing counterparties than, say, Treasury securities. A liquidity mismatch between securities in the assets versus the liability side of the balance sheet has the same business justification as the traditional banking business. Providing liquidity in the loans and deposit markets is a risky activity, since liquidity demand fluctuates randomly, and as such it carries a risk premium or return.

Providing liquidity in securities markets by buying relatively illiquid securities and selling more liquid securities is the same risky activity and also carries a return (Gorton 2009). Just as in banking crises, and as in the 1873 description by Bagehot, a security crisis is associated with an increase in demand for liquidity or more liquid securities. This puts strain on the balance sheets of those intermediaries who provide liquidity in securities markets: their assets fall in value, and their liabilities increase in value. To restore their own financial equilibrium, those intermediaries have to sell their assets, in a situation where buyers are relatively fewer.[6]

In general, as the market for securities stops working, it stops providing the liquidity services described above. People become unwilling to trade and subsequently prices no longer convey information about the value of the securities. This happens either when market participants themselves become unable to value the securities traded or when participants lose confidence in other market participants' capability to settle their obligations in the market (Giovannini 2010). Both situations happened in the 2007–2009 US financial crisis.

1.3 The Greenspan Put or the TBTF Paradigm

Let us now concentrate in what really characterizes the central problem of financial crises, which is the "run", the "panic", the "flight to quality", or whatever you choose to call it. Short-term credit dries up, including the normally straightforward repurchase agreement ("the run on repo"), interbank lending, and commercial paper markets. This "panic" is usually followed by a very sharp recession.[7]

Why is there a financial panic? In the case of the US financial crisis, there were two obvious precipitating events: the Lehman Brothers failure and the chaotic week in Washington surrounding the TARP legislation.[8] Now, why would

[6] This unstable situation is well described by Brunnermeier and Pedersen (2009) and Geanakoplos (2009).

[7] An extension of the argument discussed in this section is exposed in Chap. 8, Sect. 8.6. According to Maffezzoli and Monacelli (2015), severe economic downturns, characterized by deleverage, are preceded by phenomena of debt overhang. Hence, large recessions may not result from large shocks, but, rather, from typical shocks interacting with the state of the economy. Maffezzoli and Monacelli study a stochastic economy with heterogeneous agents and occasionally binding collateral constraints, where private debt evolves endogenously. The effect of deleverage shocks on aggregate output is a nonlinear function of the accumulated level of debt, i.e., of the degree of financial fragility.

[8] The Troubled Asset Relief Program (TARP) was approved by the US government to purchase assets and equity from financial institutions to strengthen its financial sector. It is the largest component of the government's measures in 2008 to address the subprime mortgage crisis.

Lehman's failure cause a panic? After the Bear Stearns bailout, markets came to the conclusion that investment banks and bank holding companies were too big to fail (TBTF) and would be bailed out. This expectation is also known as the "Greenspan put".[9]

One highly disturbing consequence of the TBTF-bailout problem that has emerged since the September 2008 federal takeover of Fannie Mae and Freddie Mac is that market players are going to believe that every significant financial institution, should the occasion arise, would be subject to being bailed out with taxpayer funds. Businesses that are bailed out have competitive market and cost-of-capital advantages, but not efficiency advantages, over firms not thought to be systemically important (Greenspan 2010, 32).

Therefore, when the US government did not bail out Lehman and in fact said it lacked the legal authority to bailout Lehman, everyone reassessed that expectation. It was the repudiation of the "Greenspan put," the essential ingredient, that created panic: it was a panic induced by the moral hazard that comes from 30 years of "Greenspan put" or TBTF paradigm. It was this assumption, according to which there always existed in the market a lender of last resort, that had created a huge moral hazard problem that led to nonsense speculative behaviors. And the moral hazard extended from commercial banks to the entire financial sector.

Then, the government was stuck in an awful situation: once everyone expects a bailout, it has to bail out or chaos results. Now, the policy question is simply how to escape this horrible moral hazard trap.[10] To do this, we have to finally define what "systemic" means.[11] And then, we must define clearly what is not systemic and can

[9] Based on the premises that the financial market was taking too less, and not too much, risks, the "Greenspan put" was the market expectation that the central bank would have always assumed, in the case of a possible bankruptcy, the role of the lender of last resort. The put was actually followed in 1998 to contrast the failure of LTCM.

[10] According to Kindleberger (1978), having a lender of last resort exacerbates the problem. If one firm or institution thinks that in any extreme situation she cannot go bankruptcy, because there is someone that intervenes to bail out them, they partake in more risky practices. In fact, by simply bailing out these mismanaged firms or institutions, we are not giving them incentive to improve their operation. Thus, for Kindleberger, when the system runs from bubble to bubble and the subsequent panics and crashes are methodically cured with lender of last resort bailouts—as it seems to have happened over the last 15 years preceding the US financial crisis—those stabilization interventions turn out increasingly destabilizing.

[11] Dijkman (2010) sets out the main characteristics of a systemic risk assessment framework. The failure to spot emerging systemic risk and prevent the current global financial crisis warrants a reexamination of the approach taken so far to crisis prevention. In this regard, the paper by Kawai and Pomerleano (2010) argues that financial crises can be prevented, as they build up over time due to policy mistakes. While one cannot predict the precise timing of crises, one can avert them by identifying and dealing with sources of instability. For this purpose, policymakers need to strengthen top-down macro-prudential supervision, complemented by bottom-up micro-prudential supervision. The paper argues that national measures to promote financial stability are crucial and that once an effective national systemic regulator should be established, strong international cooperation is indispensable for financial stability. On the important distinction between micro-prudential and macro-prudential supervision approach, see Hanson et al. (2011).

really fail.[12] This limit must be written, in law or regulation. We cannot rely on the good intentions of powerful administrators.[13] The only way to limit expectations of a bailout is to not have the legal authority to do it. Lehman is actually a great example: it went to bankruptcy because the government could not save it (Cochrane 2009).

Risk limits are much more likely to work if they operate by clear and simple rules. For instance, you cannot have internal hedge funds or proprietary trading if you engage in overnight bank deposits. Institutions that offer "systemic" contracts must be as simple, small, and focused as possible.

The philosophy of Glass–Steagall Act is correct, and even if admitting this level of regulation is sometimes characterized as being anti-free market, that's not true. Bank deposits, because they are subject to runs, pose an externality. We all understand that markets can fail when there are externalities. If we need to allow bank deposits, we need a guarantee or priority in bankruptcy, which leads to moral hazard and puts the taxpayer at risk.

Some regulation and a forced separation of these "systemic" contracts from arbitrary risk taking are then necessary. This implies that the regulated banking system (commercial banks) with access to the lender of last resort must be clearly separated from the investment banks, hedge funds, and other institutions of the remaining shadow banking system.

1.4 Is a Financial Crisis Predictable?

A point much debated in the literature is that financial crises usually are not widely predicted by economists. In a 2006 IMF report on the global real estate boom, for instance, it was asserted that there was little evidence to suggest that the expected market corrections in the period ahead would have led to crises of systemic proportions. Then, in another report, it was confirmed by the IMF the conventional wisdom that there was little systematic evidence to support widely cited claims that financial globalization by itself could lead to deeper and more costly crises (IMF 2006).[14]

---

[12] According to Engle et al. (2014), systemic risk may be defined as the propensity of a financial institution to be undercapitalized when the financial system as a whole is undercapitalized. They investigate the case of non-US institutions, with several factors explaining the dynamics of financial firms returns and with a synchronicity of time zones. With reference to the 196 largest European financial firms, they estimate the systemic risk over the 2000–2012 period and find that, for certain countries, the cost for the taxpayer to rescue the riskiest domestic banks was so high that some banks might be considered too big to be saved.

[13] Systemically threatening institutions are among the major regulatory problems for which there are no good solutions. Early resolution of bank problems under the Federal Deposit Insurance Corporation Improvement Act of 1991 (FDICIA) appeared to have worked with smaller banks during periods of general prosperity. But the notion that risks can be identified in a sufficiently timely manner to enable the liquidation of a large failing bank with minimum loss has proved untenable during this crisis (Greenspan 2010).

[14] On this argument, see also Blanchard et al. (2010).

According to Greenspan (2005a), the increasingly complex financial instruments created by the financial market had contributed to the development of a far more flexible, efficient, and hence resilient financial system than the one that existed just a quarter-century before.

In line with these beliefs on increased resilience, Greenspan (2005b) also asserted he did not expect that "we will run into anything resembling a collapsing bubble, though it is conceivable that we will get some reduction in overall prices as we have had in the past, but that is not a particular problem". Three years later, in his testimony before the Committee of Government Oversight and Reform, Greenspan (2008) admitted to feel a "shocked disbelief while watching his whole intellectual edifice collapse in the summer of 2007".

Speaking at the Brookings Institution (2008) in Washington, former US Treasury Secretary Robert Rubin stated that "few, if any people anticipated the sort of meltdown that we are seeing in the credit markets at present", and Glenn Stevens, governor of the Reserve Bank of Australia, commenting on the international financial turmoil of 2007–2009, asserted he did not know anyone "who predicted this course of events. This should give us cause to reflect on how hard a job it is to make genuinely useful forecasts. What we have seen is truly a 'tail' outcome—the kind of outcome that the routine forecasting process never predicts. But it has occurred, it has implications, and so we must reflect on it" (RBA 2008).

Finally, Nout Wellink, chairman of the Basel Committee that formulates banking stability rules and president of the Dutch branch of the ECB, told that no one foresaw the volume of the current avalanche (Bezemer 2009).[15]

Popular articles published in the mass media have led the general public to believe that the majority of economists have failed in their obligation to predict the financial crisis.

One of few exceptions was Roubini (2007), who alerted of such crisis as early as September 2006, when he stood before an audience of economists at the IMF and announced that a crisis was brewing. In the coming months and years, he warned, the USA were likely to face a once-in-a-lifetime housing burst, an oil shock, sharply declining consumer confidence, and, ultimately, a deep recession. He laid out a bleak sequence of events: homeowners defaulting on mortgages, trillions of dollars of mortgage-backed securities unraveling worldwide, and the global financial system shuddering to a halt. These developments, he went on, could cripple or destroy hedge funds, investment banks, and other major financial institutions like Fannie Mae and Freddie Mac.[16]

According to the president of the ECB, Mario Draghi, the crisis could have been foreseen a few years before it happened, and in fact it was foreseen by some economists like Bob Shiller or Raghuram Rajan. The protagonists themselves

[15] A more extended analysis of this argument can be found in Chap. 3.

[16] Roubini concluded that the profession of economics is bad at predicting recessions, but he was ridiculed for predicting a collapse of the housing market and a worldwide recession, and for that reason he was nicknamed "Dr. Doom."

knew that things could not go on like they were. The financial sector overshot the mark. There was a reduction in the quality of loans, just think of subprime lending in the USA, in standards, checks, and oversight of lending. So, there were enough signs. Furthermore, in the early 2000s, several rules which certainly would have been helpful in mitigating the crisis were revoked. Anyway, he points out that since then a lot has been done to reinforce those rules and regulations (Draghi 2015).

Finally, according to a paper by Bezemer (2009), only some heterodox economists predicted the crisis, with varying arguments. Particularly, he credits 12 economists with supporting arguments and estimates of timing.[17] They are a mixed company of academics, government advisers, consultants, investors, stock market commentators, and one graduate student, often combining these roles. Already between 2000 and 2006, they warned specifically about a housing-led recession within years, going against the general mood and official assessment, and well before most observers turned critical from late 2007.

According to Bezemer, taken together these 12 economists belie the notion that "no one saw this crisis coming" or that those who did were either professional doomsayers or lucky guessers.

Within mainstream financial economics, most believed that financial crises were simply unpredictable (see Chaps. 8, 9, and 10). This conclusion followed from a strong interpretation of the Eugene Fama's efficient-market hypothesis and the related random walk hypothesis, which state, respectively, that markets contain all information about possible future movements and that the movement of financial prices are random and unpredictable (Fama 1965, 1998; Caballero 2010).

1.5 The Dispute on the "Black Swan" Versus the Regularity Hypothesis of Financial Crises

On another tone, a different but correlated problem was if a financial crisis is unavoidable, that is, a "Black Swan", in the sense that it is an unpredictable rare event. An event can be considered a Black Swan if (1) it is an outlier, as it lies outside the realm of regular expectations, because nothing in the past can convincingly point to its possibility, (2) it carries an extreme impact, and (3) in spite of its outlier status, human nature makes us concoct explanations for its occurrence after the fact, making it explainable and predictable (Taleb 2007).[18]

[17] These are Dean Baker (US), Wynne Godley (US), Fred Harrison (UK), Michael Hudson (US), Eric Janszen (US), Steve Keen (Australia), Jakob Brøchner Madsen and Jens Kjaer Sørensen (Denmark), Kurt Richebächer (US), Nouriel Roubini (US), Peter Schiff (US), and Robert Shiller (US).

[18] For Taleb, globalization creates devastating Black Swans: financial institutions have been merging into a smaller number of very large banks. Almost all banks are interrelated and the increased concentration among banks seems to have the effect of making financial crises less likely, but when they happen they are more global in scale and hit us very hard.

According to Taleb, a small number of Black Swans explain almost everything in our world, from the success of ideas and religions, to the dynamics of historical events, to elements of our own personal lives. This combination of low predictability and large impact makes the Black Swan a great puzzle. Add to this phenomenon the fact that we tend to act as if it does not exist because of our blindness with respect to randomness, particularly the large deviations or outliers. The inability to predict outliers implies the inability to predict the course of history, given the share of these events in the dynamics of events. Black Swans being unpredictable, Taleb suggests to adjust to their existence rather than try to predict them.

Another related human impediment comes from excessive focus on what we do know: we tend to learn the precise, the normal, not the extraordinary, which is uncertain: for Taleb, the rare event is synonymous of uncertainty. Therefore, there are two possible ways to approach these phenomena. The first is to rule out the "extraordinary" and focus on the "normal". The examiner leaves aside "outliers" and studies ordinary cases. The second approach is to consider that in order to understand a phenomenon, one needs to first consider the extremes, particularly if, like the Black Swans, they carry an extraordinary cumulative effect.[19]

The latter approach to the problem is assumed by Reinhart and Rogoff (2008b, 2009b, 2014), who argue that the economics profession has an unfortunate tendency to view recent experience in the narrow window provided by standard datasets. With a few notable exceptions, cross-country empirical studies on financial crises typically begin in 1980 and are limited in several other important respects.

Yet an event that is rare in a three-decade span may not be all that rare when placed in a broader context. Using a dataset covering 66 countries in Africa, Asia, Europe, Latin America, North America, and Oceania, Reinhart and Rogoff find that serial default is not a Black Swan, but a nearly universal phenomenon as countries struggle to transform themselves from emerging markets to advanced economies. Major default episodes are typically spaced some years (or decades) apart, creating an illusion that "this time is different" (which is another way to refer to Black Swans) among policymakers and investors. They also show how shocks emanating from the center countries can lead to financial crises worldwide.

In this respect, the American 2007–2009 financial crisis is hardly exceptional. Serial default remains the norm, with international waves of defaults typically separated by many years, if not decades, of lull.[20] To this respect, we can note

[19] Further arguments on Taleb's Black Swan theory can be found in Chap. 3, Sect. 3.6.

[20] After the Great Crisis, the claim that advanced countries do not need to resort to the standard toolkit of emerging markets, including debt restructurings and conversions, higher inflation, capital controls, and other forms of financial repression, is not correct. As Reinhart and Rogoff (2013) document, this claim is at odds with the historical track record of most advanced economies, where debt restructuring or conversions, financial repression, and a tolerance for higher inflation or a combination of these were an integral part of the resolution of significant past debt overhangs. The financial crisis has transformed the lives of many individuals and families, even in advanced countries, where millions of people fell, or are at risk of falling, into poverty and

that a lull followed the global financial crises during the 1990s (Mexico, 1994; East Asia, 1997; Russia, 1998; Brazil, 1999; Argentina and Turkey, 2001) and more in general after the "big five crises" (Spain, 1977; Norway, 1987; Finland, 1991; Sweden, 1991; and Japan, 1992).[21]

Using daily stock and bond returns on emerging and developed markets from 1998 to 2007, also Dungey et al. (2010) reach the conclusion that financial crises are indeed alike. Also for Claessens et al. (2010), the ongoing global financial crisis is rooted in a combination of factors common to previous financial crises, but some of them are new.

They point out that the 2007–2009 crisis has brought to light a number of deficiencies in financial regulation and architecture, particularly in the treatment of systemically important financial institutions, the assessments of systemic risks and vulnerabilities, and the resolution of financial institutions. They conclude that the global nature of the financial crisis has made clear that financially integrated markets, while offering many benefits, can also pose significant risks, with large real economic consequences.

An even stronger regularity found in the literature on modern financial crises is that countries experiencing sudden large capital inflows are at a high risk of having a debt crisis, with surges in capital inflows often preceding external debt crises (Kaminsky and Reinhart 1999; Reinhart and Rogoff 2008a).[22]

Also consonant with the modern theory of crises is the striking correlation between freer capital mobility and the incidence of banking crises. Periods of high international capital mobility have repeatedly produced international banking crises.[23]

exclusion. For most regions and income groups in developing countries, progress to meet the Millennium Development Goals by 2015 has slowed and income distribution has worsened for a number of countries. Countries hardest hit by the crisis lost more than a decade of economic time (Otker-Robe and Podpiera 2013).

[21] Reinhart and Rogoff (2008a, 2009a) find that the aftermath of severe financial crises shares three characteristics: first, asset market collapses are deep and prolonged, and real housing price declines with an average percent stretched out over 6 years, while equity price collapses with an average of 55 % over a downturn of about three and a half years; second, the aftermath of banking crises is associated with profound declines in output and employment. The unemployment rate rises with an average of 7 % points over the down phase of the cycle, which lasts on average over 4 years. Output falls an average of over 9 %, although the duration of the downturn, averaging roughly 2 years, is considerably shorter than for unemployment; third, the real value of government debt tends to explode, rising an average of 86 % in the major post-World War II episodes. Interestingly, the main cause of debt explosions is not the widely cited costs of bailing out and recapitalizing the banking system. In fact, the big drivers of debt increases are the inevitable collapse in tax revenues that governments suffer in the wake of deep and prolonged output contractions, as well as often ambitious countercyclical fiscal policies aimed at mitigating the downturn.

[22] This is the case of Ireland, whose very high growth at an annual average rate of 7–8 % in the 20 years 1990–2010 preceding the crisis was largely sustained by the injection of huge foreign direct investments (FDI). For that reason, Ireland has been one of the Eurozone countries most troubled by the European financial crisis.

[23] On the contrary, Stiglitz (2010a, b) explains how capital movement controls can be welfare enhancing, reducing the risk of adverse effects from contagion.

Another point of view is that the international financial system became increasingly inconsistent and instability prone because of the process of financial liberalization and the corresponding lack of regulation followed to the abandoning of the gold exchange standard (Eichengreen 2008, 2009a; Wolf 2008), whereas some authors identify a possible political-economy cycle of finance (D'Apice and Ferri 2010; Caprio et al. 2010).

Anyway, to mark the main point of this chapter, as Reinhart and Rogoff (2008a, 2009a, b) put it clear, the central question is: how relevant are historical benchmarks for assessing the trajectory of a global financial crisis? On the one hand, the authorities today have arguably more flexible monetary policy frameworks, thanks particularly to less rigid global exchange rate regimes.

Central banks have already shown an aggressiveness to act that was notably absent in the 1930s. On the other hand, one would be wise not to push too far the conceit that we are smarter than our predecessors. A few years back many people would have agreed with Greenspan (2005a, b) that improvements in financial engineering had done much to tame the business cycle and limit the risk of financial contagion.[24]

To conclude this point, what is important to stress is that the dispute on the different interpretations of the recent Great Crisis, that is, if the regularities of Reinhart and Rogoff's picture is more realistic than that of Taleb's Black Swan vision, does not solve the problem of early forecasting bad economic events. Therefore, once again, we must ask ourselves: was the devastating recent Great Crisis predictable with the usual economic tools? There is not a clear-cut answer to this question, so the problem deserves a further inquiry.

1.6 What Modern Financial Crises Tell Us for Economic Theorizing?

Though economists cannot be expected to have provided precise forecasts, it is legitimate to ask if they were aware that the financial system had set on an unsustainable path which could eventually lead to a crisis (see Chap. 10). In this regard, Spaventa (2009) recognizes that the profession as a whole fares poorly: the list of those who forewarned that risks to systemic stability were growing—a different category from the doomsayers—is embarrassingly short. We saw the

[24] With regard to policies created to address the financial crises, Willen (2014) distinguishes four cases: (1) the ability-to-repay requirement in mortgage underwriting, (2) reform of rating agency compensation, (3) risk retention in securitization, and (4) mandatory loan renegotiation. He shows that, according to standard models, policies (1)–(3) do not address the standard asymmetric information problems that afflict financial markets, and policy (4) could reduce the deadweight losses associated with asymmetric information, but requires that policymakers allocate gains and losses.

housing bubble, but not the consequences of its bursting. Nor was the literature on global macroeconomic imbalances (Bernanke 2005; Kaminsky and Reinhart 1999) much useful.

Spaventa agrees that a few saw some aspects of the danger and were aware of the deterioration of macro-financial conditions. One of them was Rajan (2005), who anticipated that banks' contingent commitments left them exposed to systemic risks, but the paper was criticized as largely misguiding by Larry Summers and others. Then it was the turn of Roubini (2007), who predicted gloom and doom since 2005, but he also passed unheeded. So were some researchers of the BIS (Borio 2006; White 2006a, b).

Most economists were unaware of, or unconcerned with, the tensions that were accumulating in the American financial system in the first 2000 years. Even after the crisis started in the early summer of 2007, it took many of them a long time to understand that what was going on was a serious matter (see Chap. 10). In this regard, Friedman (2009) and Akerlof and Shiller (2009) argue that what is missing in the worldview of today's economists is sufficient attention to "animal spirits", by which they mean the psychological and even irrational elements that figure importantly in so many other familiar aspects of personal choices and personal behavior and that, they believe, pervade economic behavior too.

A second question addressed by Spaventa is whether the problem was the state of economics or it was the economists that failed in using economic models. Quoting Eichengreen (2009b), a possible answer is that the problem was not economic theory. What Eichengreen has in mind are all those developments of microeconomic theory that provide obviously useful tools for an understanding of financial markets: agency theory, incentive theory, asymmetric information and its consequences, behavioral economics, models with heterogeneous agents and incomplete markets, and the recent literature on liquidity and leverage.

Anyway, in this regard Spaventa observes: "Does a general scheme or model exist that can accommodate financial assets, banks and financial intermediaries, heterogeneous agents and asymmetric information, agency problems and coordination failures and possibly institutions? Obviously it does not" (Spaventa 2009, 3). Therefore, the problem is not with economists reluctant to use the available theoretical tools, but with the fact that those tools (economic models) are unsuitable to deal with financial phenomena. In fact, the neglect of financial variables, far from being a specific feature of dynamic stochastic general equilibrium (DSGE) models, has characterized large part of modern macroeconomic modeling.

A final question is whether the costs of these failures are confined to a reputational damage for the profession (Caballero 2010) or were there social costs as well, as would be the case if the economists' doctrines and attitudes played a part in creating an environment congenial to the eruption of a crisis. In this regard, Spaventa's conclusion is that economists do indeed bear some responsibility for what has happened, as their doctrines, at least in their vulgate versions, often provided an intellectual justification to the unconstrained behavior of the private sector and to the negligence of regulators.[25] Also for this reason, he concludes, it is now the case to show greater humility, rather than an implausible defense of past rent positions, to provide new impetus to the discipline (Spaventa 2009, 6).

However, according to Boldrin (2010), the doctrines that provided intellectual justification to the unconstrained behavior of the private sector and to the negligence of regulators were those founded on the neo-Keynesian paradigm which dominated, and still dominate, in central banks (Fed, ECB, Bank of England, and Bank of Japan), Treasury departments, and main international institutions, like the IMF, the World Bank, and other places where the world monetary and banking policy was and still is decided.

This paradigm hold that deflation is the real problem to fight, and the only way to avoid it is pumping enormous quantities of fiat money that central banks offer at negative real interest rates. On the other side, Boldrin claims that since many years many liberal economists held that the rules of the financial market were sick, and the Fed monetary policy was based on the "Greenspan put", which was creating a huge moral hazard problem that would lead to dangerous speculative behaviors. Furthermore, because of the growing information asymmetries between lenders and borrowers, the banking sector was losing competitiveness and looking more like a monopolistic market where the regulators (Fed and SEC) were under the direct control of the big players of the monopolistic cartel.

Boldrin shares the conventional wisdom that the Greenspan monetary policy was inflating all US asset values, not only houses, and this inflationary bubble was the largest ever seen and was leading to an incorrect resources allocation. This misallocation was going to imply negative repercussions when all the liquidity artificially generated by the central bank would eventually disappear, and the long-lasting adjustment of asset prices would have happened all at once.

This, as expected, was what really happened in the American crisis and—according to Boldrin—it was predictable on the basis of elementary economic theory, together with the hypothesis that when you give people, either Wall Street bankers or sellers of housing loans, the opportunity to make money transferring risk to third parties, they take the chance without worrying about the systemic consequences of their behavior. And the more fiat money you give to these people at negative interest rates, the more they will indebt to exploit the opportunities that the policy of easy money was offering them.

Boldrin concludes that ignoring these facts in the analysis of the causes of modern financial crises and attributing this, as neo-Keynesians like Friedman

[25] According to Zingales (2014), the very same forces that induce economists to conclude that regulators are captured should lead us to conclude that the economic profession is captured as well. As evidence of this capture, he shows that papers whose conclusions are pro-management are more likely to be published in economic journals and more likely to be cited. He also shows that business school's faculty write papers that are more pro-management. To reduce the extent of this capture, Zingales suggests a reform of the publication process, which includes an enhanced data disclosure, from a stronger theoretical foundation to a mechanism of peer pressure.

(2009) and Akerlof and Shiller (2009) did, to "animal spirits", human irrationality, and market failure is a mistake.[26]

1.7 The Extension of the Great Crisis to the European Sovereign Debt and Banking Sector

One aspect of global contagion is the extension of American crisis to sovereign debts in Europe (Chaps. 5, 6, and 7). It began with Greece, but suddenly it spread over some other countries of the Eurozone. The risk of contagion is not confined to some euro countries, but it could extend to the world's biggest economies like Great Britain, Japan, and the USA. The problem is that the expansionary fiscal policies of deficit spending implemented by most states to tackle the crisis have created very large deficits, which are very difficult to adjust, as big, rich economies' budget deficits have risen more than fourfold to an average of 9 % of GDP. In many states, including the USA, the public debt largely exceeds GNP.

The European crisis is usually described as a sovereign debt crisis, but in fact it is really a sequence of interactions between sovereign problems and banking problems. With deteriorating public finances, sovereign risk has increased and worsened bank's balance sheets. In fact, as public debt approached sustainability limits in PIIGS countries (Portugal, Ireland, Italy, Greece, and Spain), a high bank exposure to sovereign risk gave rise to a fragile interdependence between fiscal and bank solvency and so the possibility of a self-fulfilling crisis.[27]

The interdependence between sovereign credit and banking systems has been a running theme of this sequence of events. Eurozone sovereign debt is held in large amounts by Eurozone banks, with a significant bias for the bonds of the country in which the bank is headquartered.

[26] A more comprehensive exposition of the theoretical aspects of the financial Great Crisis, also for the implications on the reputation of the economist's profession, is discussed in Chaps. 8, 9, and 10. Particularly, the theoretical debate on the Great Crisis between the neo-Keynesian and the neoclassical schools of thought will be extensively discussed in Chap. 8.

[27] Cukierman (2014) compares the behavior of euro area banks' credit and reserves with those of US banks following respective major crisis triggers (Lehman's collapse in the USA and the 2009 admission by Papandreou, that Greece's deficit was substantially higher than previously believed, in the euro area). He shows that, although the behavior of banks' credit following those widely observed crisis triggers is similar in the euro area and in the USA, the behavior of their reserves is quite different. In particular, while US banks' reserves have been on an uninterrupted upward trend since Lehman's collapse, those of euro area banks fluctuated markedly in both directions. The paper argues that, at the source, this is due to differences in the liquidity injections procedures between the Eurosystem and the Fed. Those different procedures are traced, in turn, to differences in the relative importance of banking credit within the total amount of credit intermediated through banks and bond issues in the euro area and the USA, as well as to the higher institutional aversion of the ECB to inflation relatively to that of the Fed.

This is partly due to policy choices before the crisis which in retrospect appear questionable, particularly the risk weighting at zero of Eurozone sovereign bonds in regulatory capital calculations, the long-standing acceptance of such bonds with no haircut by the ECB as collateral in its liquidity policies, and possible instances of moral suasion by home-country public authorities that resulted in large holdings of the home country's sovereign debt (Véron 2011).

In fact, a high level of public debt is not a problem per se, as long as the government is able to refinance itself and roll over its debt. This requires public debt and the interest burden to grow more slowly than the economy and the tax base. Unfortunately, this is not the case in the PIIGS countries.

The economic crisis in these countries is therefore not merely a debt crisis; it is first and foremost a competitiveness and growth crisis that has led to structural imbalances within the euro area (Holinski et al. 2012; Lane and Pels 2012; Bergsten and Kirkegaard 2012; Mayer 2011). According to this field of research, below the surface of the sovereign public debt and banking crises lies a balance-of-payment crisis, caused by a misalignment of internal real exchange rates (Sinn 2011, 2012; Sinn and Wollmershäeuser 2011; Neumann 2012; Lin and Treichel 2012).

In a fixed nominal exchange rate system, balance-of-payment imbalances can emerge when the real exchange rate is above or below its equilibrium value. In the first case, when the real exchange rate is overvalued, a country imports more than it exports so that the current account moves into deficit. At the same time, domestic asset prices in foreign currency are higher than foreign asset prices so that investors sell the first and buy the latter. This leads to net capital outflows and hence a deficit in the capital account. The combined deficits of the current and capital accounts then lead to a deficit of the balance of payments.[28]

In the second case, when the real exchange rate is undervalued, the current and capital accounts and hence the balance of payments are in surplus and the central bank accumulates international reserves. This process comes to an end only when reserve accumulation has increased the money supply to an extent that inflation rises to intolerable levels and the authorities upvalue the nominal exchange rate in an effort to regain price stability

Since the European Monetary Union (EMU) has been built as a union of sovereign states, each state has retained its own National Central Bank (NCB),

[28] A similar conclusion also applies to Argentina, as it is documented in Chap. 2. After the hyperinflationary processes of 1989 and 1990, drastic economic reforms took place in this country. The central piece of this program was the Convertibility Law, which established a fixed exchange rate of one peso to one dollar. The Central Bank could issue domestic currency only against foreign currency and could not make loans to the government except for a very tiny sum. It was taken for granted that this constraint was practically equivalent to excluding the possibility of running a fiscal deficit. However, soon this proved not to be true. In fact, thanks to the IMF support, from 1994, Argentina recovered access to international capital markets and since then increased its public debt at a very fast rate. As a result, for both 2002 and 2003, the repayment of principal exceeded 80 % of the exports. Adding interest payments of about $12 billion, Argentina's total debt servicing largely exceeded annual exports.

which has become a member of the so-called Eurosystem with the European Central Bank (ECB) at the top.

National interbank payment systems have been merged into a euro area interbank payment system (TARGET2),[29] where NCBs have assumed the role of the links between countries. So, TARGET2 plays a key role in ensuring the smooth conduct of monetary policy, the correct functioning of financial markets, and banking and financial stability in the euro area, by substantially reducing systemic risk (see Chap. 6).

The settlement of cross border payments between participants in TARGET2 results in intra-Eurosystem balances, that is, positions on the balance sheets of the respective NCBs that reflect claims/liabilities on/to the Eurosystem. According to Mayer (2011), a key consequence of this system is that each euro area country has a national balance of payments in the form of the net position of its central bank within TARGET2.

This net position can result in a claim (balance-of-payment surplus) or liability (balance-of-payment deficit) against the ECB, which sits in the center of the payment system. The consequence of this system is that a country with a balance-of-payment deficit automatically receives unlimited funding. Hence, Mayer's conclusion is that the ECB's funding operations become tilted toward the countries with overvalued real exchange rates (see Chap. 5, Sect. 5.4).

We will see in Chap. 6 that this conclusion is questionable, because TARGET2 flows also reflect a kind of lender of last resort intervention by the ECB through the free allotment program. They just reflect the funding necessity of banks in different regions, periphery banks being the most in need.

Anyway, we must recognize that, if the recent Great Crisis became particularly serious in the euro area, it is so also because of the design flaws in economic and monetary European Union (EU). The euro was built on an imperfect institutional framework, envisaged by the 1992 Maastricht Treaty and the 1997 Stability and Growth Pact (SGP).[30]

According to Benoît Cœuré (2015), the framework's principles may well have been appropriate in calm weather, but when the storm broke they proved inadequate. European authorities lacked the instruments for coordination, solidarity, and

---

[29] TARGET is the "Trans-European Automated Real-time Gross settlement Express Transfer" system. It was replaced by TARGET2 in November 2007, with a transition period lasting until May 2008, by which time all national platforms were replaced by a single platform. The processing and settlement of euro-denominated payments take place on an individual basis on the participants' accounts at NCBs connected to TARGET2. The transactions are settled in real time with immediate finality, thus enabling the beneficiary bank to reuse the liquidity to make other payments on that day.

[30] This institutional framework pushed the European crisis-hit countries to implement austerity programs to regain competitiveness with respect to non-euro countries, which revealed to be very costly in terms of lost output. In this case, Alesina et al. (2015) show that fiscal adjustments based upon cuts in spending appear to have been much less costly, in terms of output losses, than those based upon tax increases, and the difference between the two types of adjustment is very large.

responsibility which would have allowed them to handle the crisis and bounce back more quickly, as was the case in the USA.

This error has been progressively rectified since 2010 with the creation of the European Stability Mechanism (ESM) and the European banking union and the strengthening of economic governance and, in terms of monetary policy, with two very decisive policy instruments: the first was the OMT program approved on September 2012, which allowed the ECB to repurchase public debt if needed[31], and the second was the recent approval by the ECB, on January 22, 2015, of a nonconventional monetary policy of quantitative easing (Qe), which began in March 2015 (see Chap. 11, Sect. 11.4.5).

To conclude this section, the recent European Great Crisis shows once more that any fixed exchange rate arrangement (including the dollar peg in Argentina or the European Monetary Union) is prone to crisis if countries do not adjust their economies internally and imbalances are allowed to grow too large. If economic policies are not able to keep the domestic price level competitive vis-à-vis the rest of the integrating area, and the external adjustments via the nominal exchange rate are precluded, a real exchange rate appreciation will erode the countries' competitiveness. In most cases this will lead to both current account and capital account deficits that at some point will trigger a balance-of-payment crisis, then a currency crisis, and eventually a more traditional banking crisis (see Chap. 5).

However, we must not forget that most EU countries wanted the euro as a fundamental step of a process that in the long run should lead to greater and more significant political unity of Europe, and for that reason the euro was considered irreversible since its beginning. This was decided because of both political and economic reasons. Political reasons call back the impellent necessity for European countries not to repeat the tremendous disaster of two world wars combated in Europe in the last century.[32]

And, as long as the economic reasons are called for, let us say what would happen if the euro were to disappear, which was already a matter of speculation in the recent European Great Crisis. A clear answer to that question was recently given by the president of the ECB, Mario Draghi, who in a recent interview to *Die Zeit* answered as follows: "If all countries were to start devaluing, prices would no longer be stable. Would the countries where complaints about reforms and fiscal

---

[31] In January 2015, the OMT program has been validated as perfectly legal to EU Treaties by the Advocate General of the European Court of Justice.

[32] Europe's monetary union is part of a broader process of integration that started in the aftermath of World War II. Spolaore (2013) looks at the creation of the euro within the bigger picture of European integration. How and why were European institutions established? What are the goals and determinants of European integration? What is European integration really about? Spolaore addresses these questions from a political-economy perspective, building on ideas and results from the economic literature on the formation of states and political unions. Specifically, he looks at the motivations, assumptions, and limitations of the European strategy, initiated by Jean Monnet and his collaborators, of partially integrating policy functions in a few areas, with the expectation that more integration will follow in other areas, in a sort of chain reaction toward an ever-closer union. The euro with its current problems is a child of that strategy and its limits.

consolidation are the loudest be better off exiting the euro area? They would still have to continue with their reforms! You cannot simply keep on devaluing a currency forever. It would simply lead to higher prices" (Draghi 2015).

1.8 Conclusions

We conclude by summarizing the main questions raised in this chapter. First, was the Great Crisis predicted by standard economic models? The answer is no, if we mean that those models should have provided precise forecasts of timing. Second, is it a task of economic models to predict external events such as a systemic financial crisis? The answer is again no, because crises, like future asset prices, are simply unpredictable. This is the essence of rational expectations models.

Anyway, economic theory can show which regularities characterized other financial crises in the past, and in this way, we can better understand the ex post evolution of new crises. On the contrary, if we regard a new crisis as a standalone case, as it is implied in Taleb's "Black Swan" vision, we cannot see those regularities, which emerge only if we compare many crises along the history of financial crises.

Third, though economists cannot be expected to provide precise forecasts, are they aware when the financial system has set on an unsustainable path which can eventually lead to a crisis? In fact, most economists were unaware of, or unconcerned with, the tensions that were accumulating in the American financial system in the first 2000 years. From a Keynesian perspective, this failure depended on insufficient attention to "animal spirits", by which Akerlof and Shiller mean the psychological and even irrational elements that figure importantly in so many other familiar aspects of personal choices and personal behavior and that, they believe, pervade economic behavior too.

On the side of neoclassicals, Boldrin claims that since many years many liberal economists held that the rules of the financial market were sick, and the Fed monetary policy was based on the "Greenspan put", which was creating a huge moral hazard problem that would lead to dangerous speculative behaviors.

Furthermore, because of the growing information asymmetries between lenders and borrowers, the banking sector was losing competitiveness and looking more like a monopolistic market where the regulators (Fed and SEC) were under the direct control of the big players of the monopolistic cartel. In fact, the Greenspan monetary policy was inflating all US asset values, not only houses, and this inflationary bubble was the largest ever seen and was leading to an incorrect resources allocation.

This misallocation was going to imply negative repercussions when all the liquidity artificially generated by the central bank would eventually disappear, and the long-lasting adjustment of asset prices would have happened all at once.

Finally, as regards the extension of the Great Crisis to the European twin public debt and banking crises, the recent European experience shows that any fixed exchange rate arrangement is prone to crisis if countries do not adjust their economies internally and imbalances are allowed to grow too large. In most cases this will lead to both current account and capital account deficits that at some point will trigger a balance-of-payment crisis, then a currency crisis, and eventually a more traditional banking crisis.

References

Acharya V (2009) A theory of risk and design of prudent bank regulation. J Financ Stabil 5:224–255

Adalsoro I, Delli Gatti D, Faia E (2015) Bank networks: contagion, systemic risk and prudential policy. CEPR discussion paper no. DP10540, April. Available via http://papers.ssrn.com/sol3/papers.cfm?abstract_id=2593823

Akerlof GA, Shiller RJ (2009) Animal spirits: how human psychology drives the economy, and why it matters for global capitalism. Princeton University Press, Princeton

Alesina AF, Barbiero O, Favero CA, Giavazzi F, Paradisi M (2015) Austerity in 2009–2013. NBER working paper no. 20827, January. Available via http://www.nber.org/papers/w20827

Allen F, Gale D (2000) Financial contagion. J Polit Econ 108:1–33

Allen F, Beck T, Carletti E, Lane PR, Schoenmaker D, Wagner W (2011) Cross-border banking in Europe: implications for financial stability on macroeconomic policies. CEPR report, London. Available via http://www.voxeu.org/epubs/cepr-reports/cross-border-banking-europe-implications-financial-stability-and-macroeconomic-policies

Bagehot W (1873) Lombard street: a description of the money market. New York, Scribner. Available via http://books.google.it/books?id=MGYuAAAAYAAJ&dq=editions:v9KYeuq_PbgC&pg=PR3&hl=it#v=onepage&q&f=true

Bergsten F, Kirkegaard JF (2012) The coming resolution of the European crisis. Peterson institute for international economics. Policy brief, January. Available via http://www.iie.com/publications/pb/pb12-1.pdf

Bernanke BS (2005) The global saving Glut and the U.S. current account deficit. Remarks at the Sandridge lecture, Virginia association of economics, Richmond, VR, Mar 10. Available via http://www.federalreserve.gov/boarddocs/speeches/2005/200503102/

Bezemer D (2009) "No one saw this coming": understanding financial crisis through accounting models. MPRA working paper no. 15892, June 16. Available via http://mpra.ub.uni muenchen.de/15892/

Blanchard O, Dell'Ariccia G, Mauro P (2010) Rethinking macroeconomic policy. J Money Credit Banking 42(September):199–215

Boldrin M (2010) Due colpi al cerchio (I) .... NoiseFromAmerika, 3 marzo. Available via http://www.noisefromamerika.org/index.php/articoli/1732

Borio C (2006) Monetary and prudential policies at a crossroads? New challenges in the new century. BIS working papers no. 216, September. Available via https://ideas.repec.org/p/bis/biswps/216.html

Brookings Institution (2008) Addressing the foreclosure crisis: a Hamilton project policy discussion, Washington, DC, Mar 14. Available via http://www.brookings.edu/~/media/Files/events/2008/0314_mortgage/20080314_mortgage.pdf

Brown M, Trautmann ST, Vlahu R (2014) Understanding bank-run contagion. ECB working paper no. 1711, August

Brunnermeier MK, Oehmke M (2012) Bubbles, financial crisis, and systemic risk. In: Constantinides GM, Harris M, Stulz RM (eds) Handbook of the economics of finance, vol 2. North Holland, Amsterdam, pp 1221–1288

Brunnermeier MK, Pedersen LH (2009) Market liquidity and funding liquidity. Rev Financ Stud 22(6):2201–2238

Brunnermeier MK, Schnabel I (2015) Bubbles and central banks: historical perspectives. CPR discussion paper no. DP10528, Available via http://www.cepr.org/active/publications/discussion_papers/dp.php?dpno=10528

Caballero R (2010) Macroeconomics after the crisis: time to deal with the pretense-of-knowledge syndrome. J Econ Perspect 24:85–102

Caprio G, D'Apice V, Ferri G, Puopolo GW (2010) Macro financial determinants of the great financial crisis: implications for financial regulation. MPRA paper no. 26088. Available via http://www.astrid-online.it/Dossier--d1/Studi--ric/macro-financial-determinants-of-the-great-financial-crisis.pdf

Carpinelli L (2009) Effetti reali delle crisi bancarie: una rassegna della letteratura. Banca d'Italia, Questioni di Economia e Finanza, occasional paper no. 55, settembre

Claessens S, Kose MA (2013) Financial crises: explanations, types, and implications. CEPR discussion paper no. DP9329, February. Available via http://papers.ssrn.com/sol3/papers.cfm?abstract_id=2212005

Claessens S, Dell'Ariccia G, Igan D, Laeven L (2010) Lessons and policy implications from the global financial crisis. IMF working paper 10/44, February. Available via https://www.google.it/webhp?sourceid=chrome-instant&ion=1&espv=2&ie=UTF-8#nfpr=1&q=22.+Claessens+S.,+G.+Dell%27ariccia,+Igan,+and+L.+Laeven+(2010),+%E2%80%9CLessons+and+Policy+Implications+from+the+Global+Financial+Crisis%E2%80%9D,+IMF+Working+Paper+10/44.&spell=1

Cochrane JH (2009) The financial crisis and policy, talk at the Cato "policy perspectives". New York, Nov 5. Available via http://faculty.chicagobooth.edu/john.cochrane/research/Papers/cochrane_financial_crisis_and_policy.pdf

Cœuré B (2015) Interview with Libération. Jan 16. Available via http://www.ecb.europa.eu/press/inter/date/2015/html/sp150116_1.en.html

Cova A (2009) Banchieri e banche nell'Europa moderna e contemporanea: Giovanni Antonio Zerbi e John Law. Ciclo di conferenze e seminari "L'Uomo e il denaro", a cura dell'Associazione per lo Sviluppo degli Studi di Banca e Borsa e dell'Università Cattolica del Sacro Cuore, Milano, 9 febbraio. Available via http://www.assbb.it/CMI/quaderno_etica_34.pdf

Cukierman A (2014) Euro-area and US banks behavior, and ECB-fed monetary policies during the global financial crisis: a comparison. CEPR discussion paper no. DP10289, December. Available via http://www.cepr.org/active/publications/discussion_papers/dp.php?dpno=10289

D'Apice V, Ferri G (2010) Financial instability: toolkit and perspectives up to the current crisis. Palgrave/McMillan, London

Dasgupta A (2004) Financial contagion through capital connections: a model of the origin and spread of bank panics. J Eur Econ Assoc 2(6):1049–1084

Dijkman M (2010) A framework for assessing systemic risk. World bank, Policy research working paper no. 5282, April

Draghi M (2015) Interview with Die Zeit, Jan 15. Available via https://www.ecb.europa.eu/press/inter/date/2015/html/sp150115.en.html

Dungey M, Fry R, Gonzàles-Hermosillo B, Martin VL, Tang C (2010) Are financial crises alike? IMF working paper 10/14, January. Available via https://ideas.repec.org/p/imf/imfwpa/10-14.html

Eichengreen B (2008) Globalizing capital: a history of international monetary system. Princeton University Press, Princeton

Eichengreen B (2009a) Out of the box thoughts about the international financial architecture. IMF working paper 09/116, May. Available via https://www.imf.org/external/pubs/cat/longres.aspx?sk=22958.0

Eichengreen B (2009b) The last temptation of risk, Apr 30. Available via www.nationalinterest.org

Engle RF, Jondeau E, Rockinger M (2014) Systemic risk in Europe. Rev Financ. doi:10.1093/rof/rfu012. Available via http://rof.oxfordjournals.org/content/early/2014/03/29/rof.rfu012.short

Fama EF (1965) Random walks in stock market prices. Financ Anal J (September/October):55–59 (reprinted January-February 1995, 75–80)
Fama EF (1998) Market efficiency, long-term returns, and behavioral finance. J Financ Econ 49:283–306. Available via http://citeseerx.ist.psu.edu/viewdoc/download?rep=rep1&type=pdf&doi=10.1.1.10.4176
Fratianni M (2008) Financial crises, safety nets and regulation. J Ital Econ Assoc XIII(2):169–208
Freixas X, Parigi B (1998) Contagion and efficiency in gross and net interbank payment systems. J Financ Intermed 7(1):3–31
Freixas X, Parigi B, Rochet JC (2000) Systemic risk, interbank relations and liquidity provision by the central bank. J Money Credit Banking 32(2):611–638
Friedman BM (2009) The failure of the economy & the economists. The New York Review of Books, May 28
Geanakoplos J (2009) The leverage cycle. Cowles foundation discussion paper no. 1715, July. Available via https://www.google.it/webhp?sourceid=chrome-instant&ion=1&espv=2&ie=UTF-8#q=43.%20geanakoplos%20j.%20(2009)%2c%20%e2%80%9cthe%20leverage%20cycle%e2%80%9d%2c%20cowles%20foundation%20discussion%20paper%20n.%201715%2c%20july
Giovannini A (2010) Financial system reform proposals from first principles. CEPR policy insight, 45, January
Goldstein I, Razin A (2013) Review of theories of financial crises. NBER working paper no. w18670. Available via https://ideas.repec.org/p/red/sed012/214.html
Gorton G (2009) Slapped in the face by the invisible hand: banking and the panic of 2007. Prepared for the federal reserve bank of Atlanta's 2009 financial markets conference: financial innovation and crisis, May 11–13. Available via http://www.frbatlanta.org/news/CONFEREN/09fmc/gorton.pdf
Greenspan A (2005a) Economic flexibility, remarks before the National Italian American foundation, Washington, DC, Oct 12. Available via http://www.federalreserve.gov/boarddocs/speeches/2005/20051012/default.htm
Greenspan A (2005b) Federal reserve board's semi-annual monetary policy report to the congress. Testimony before the committee on banking, housing, and urban affairs, US Senate, Feb 16. Available via http://www.federalreserve.gov/boarddocs/hh/2005/february/testimony.htm
Greenspan A (2008) We will never have a perfect model of risk. Financial times, Mar 17, p 9. Available via http://blogs.ft.com/economistsforum/2008/03/we-will-never-have-a-perfect-model-of-risk/
Greenspan A (2010) The crisis, second draft, Mar 9. Available via http://www.brookings.edu/~/media/Files/Programs/ES/BPEA/2010_spring_bpea_papers/spring2010_greenspan.pdf
Hanson SG, Kashyap AK, Stein JC (2011) A macro-prudential approach to financial regulation. J Econ Perspect 25:3–28
Holinski N, Kool C, Muysken J (2012) Persistent macroeconomic imbalances in the euro area: causes and consequences. Fed Reserv Bank St Louis Rev 94(1):1–20
Ibragimov R, Jaffee D, Walden J (2011) Diversification disasters. J Financ Econ 99:333–348
IMF (2006) Financial globalization: a reappraisal, Washington, DC. Available via http://www.imf.org/external/pubs/ft/spn/2010/spn1003.pdf
Iyer R, Peydro JL (2011) Interbank contagion at work: evidence from a natural experiment. Rev Financ Stud 24:1337–1377
Kaminsky GL, Reinhart CM (1999) The twin crises: the causes of banking and balance of payments problems. Am Econ Rev 89:473–500
Kawai M, Pomerleano M (2010) Regulating systemic risk. ADBI working paper no. 189. Available via http://www.adbi.org/working-paper/2010/01/27/3447.regulating.systemic.risk
Kindleberger CP (1978) Manias, panics, and crashes: a history of financial crises. Wiley, New York
Lane PR, Pels B (2012) Current account imbalances in Europe. CEPR discussion paper no. 8958. Available via https://ideas.repec.org/p/cpr/ceprdp/8958.html

Law J (1707) Mémoire pour prouver qu'une nouvelle espèce de monnaie peut être meilleure que l'or et l'argent. Oeuvres completes de John Law, 1, Paris, Sirey, 1934
Lin JY, Treichel V (2012) The crisis in the euro zone: did the euro contribute to the evolution of the crisis? World bank policy research working paper no. 6127. Available via http://elibrary.worldbank.org/docserver/download/6127.pdf?expires=1349462386&id=id&accname=guest&checksum=76473E9201912E65FF539603A5F30DFC
Maffezzoli M, Monacelli T (2015) Deleverage and financial fragility. CEPR discussion paper no. DP10531, April. Available via http://www.cepr.org/active/publications/discussion_papers/dp.php?dpno=10531
Mayer T (2011) Euroland's hidden balance-of-payments crisis. EU monitor 88, Oct 26. Available via http://www.dbresearch.com/PROD/DBR_INTERNET_EN-PROD/PROD0000000000279906/Euroland%E2%80%99s+hidden+balance-of-payments+crisis.pdf
Moro B (2012) The theoretical debate on the recent great crisis. J Ital Econ Assoc XVII(1):3–42
Moro B (2013) The run on repo and the liquidity shortage problems of the current global financial crisis: Europe vs. US. Ekonomi-tek 2(1):41–77
Moro B (2014) Lessons from the European economic and financial great crisis: a survey. Eur J Polit Econ 34(Suppl):S9–S24
NBER (2010) Business cycle expansions and contractions: US business cycle expansions and contractions, Apr 8. Available via http://www.nber.org/cycles.html
Neumann MJM (2012) The refinancing of banks drives target debt. CESifo forum, 13, January, Special issue. Available via https://www.cesifo-group.de/ifoHome/publications/journals/CESifo-Forum/Archiv/CESifo-Forum-2012.html
Otker-Robe I, Podpiera AM (2013) The social impact of financial crises: evidence from the global financial crisis. World bank policy research working paper no. 6703, November. Available via http://econ.worldbank.org/external/default/main?pagePK=64210502&theSitePK=469372&piPK=64210520&menuPK=64166093&entityID=000158349_20131114113429
Rajan R (2005) Has financial development made the world riskier? NBER working paper no. 11728. Available via https://ideas.repec.org/p/nbr/nberwo/11728.html
Razin A, Rosefielde SS (2011) Currency and financial crisis of the 1990s and 2000s. CEPR discussion paper no. DP8264. Available via https://ideas.repec.org/a/oup/cesifo/v57y2011i3p499-530.html
RBA (2008) Interesting times. Speech by Glenn Stevens, Governor of the Reserve Bank of Australia, to the Australian Business Economists Annual Dinner, Sydney, 9 Dec 2008. Available via http://www.rba.gov.au/Speeches/2008/sp_gov_091208.html
Reinhart CM, Rogoff KS (2008a) Is the 2007 U.S. subprime crisis so different? An international historical comparison. Am Econ Rev 98:339–344
Reinhart CM, Rogoff S (2008b) This time is different: a panoramic view of eight centuries of financial crises. NBER working paper no. 13882. Available via http://www.nber.org/papers/w13882.pdf
Reinhart CM, Rogoff KS (2009a) The aftermath of financial crises. CEPR discussion paper no. 7209. Available via https://ideas.repec.org/p/nbr/nberwo/14656.html
Reinhart CM, Rogoff KS (2009b) This time is different: eight centuries of financial folly. Princeton University Press, Princeton
Reinhart CM, Rogoff KS (2013) Financial and sovereign debt crisis: some lessons learned and those forgotten. IMF working paper no. 13/266, December. Available via https://www.imf.org/external/pubs/cat/longres.aspx?sk=41173.0
Reinhart CM, Rogoff KS (2014) Recovery from financial crises: evidence from 100 episodes. Am Econ Rev 104(5):50–55
Roubini N (2007) Transcript of IMF seminar: the risk of a U.S. hard landing and implications for the global economy and financial markets, Washington, DC, Sept 13. Available via http://www.imf.org/external/np/tr/2007/tr070913.htm
Shachmurove Y (2010) Reoccurring financial crises in the United States. PIER working paper 11–006. Available via https://ideas.repec.org/p/pen/papers/11-006.html

Sinn HW (2011) The ECB stealth bailout. VoxEu, June 1. Available via https://www.cesifo-group.de/de/ifoHome/policy/Staff-Comments-in-the-Media/Press-articles-by-staff/Archive/Eigene-Artikel-2011/medienecho_16642402_ifostimme-voxeu-01-06-11.html

Sinn HW (2012) The European balance of payments crisis: an introduction. CESifo forum, January (Special Issue) 13:3–10

Sinn HW, Wollmershäeuser T (2011) Target loans, current account balances and capital flows: the ECB's rescue facility. CESifo working paper no. 3500, June. Available via https://ideas.repec.org/p/ces/ceswps/_3500.html

Spaventa L (2009) Economists and economics: what does the crisis tell us? CEPR policy insight, 38, August. Available via https://www.google.it/webhp?sourceid=chrome-instant&ion=1&espv=2&ie=UTF-8#q=spaventa%201.%20(2009)%2c%20%e2%80%9ceconomists%20and%20economics%3a%20what%20does%20the%20crisis%20tell%20us%3f%e2%80%9d%2c%20cepr%20policy%20insight%2c%2038%2c%20august

Spolaore E (2013) What is European integration really about? A political guide for economists. CESifo working paper series no. 4283, June. Available via http://papers.ssrn.com/sol3/papers.cfm?abstract_id=2284804

Stiglitz JE (2010a) Contagion, liberalization, and the optimal structure of globalization. J Glob Dev 1:1–45

Stiglitz JE (2010b) Interpreting the causes of the great recession of 2008. Eighth BIS annual conference, 25–26 June 2009. Financial system and macroeconomic resilience: revisited, BIS papers no. 53

Taleb NN (2007) The black Swan: the impact of the highly improbable. New York, Random House. Available via http://www.amazon.com/Black-Swan-Impact-Highly-Improbable/dp/1400063515

Van Ours JC (2015) The great recession was not so great. CEPER discussion paper no. DP103376, February. Available via http://www.cepr.org/active/publications/discussion_papers/dp.php?dpno=10376

Véron N (2011) The European debt and financial crisis: origins, options and implications for the US and global economy, draft, Sept 22. Available via http://banking.senate.gov/public/index.cfm?FuseAction=Files.View&FileStore_id=9bec6123-d58d-423d-bf17-4fdcb9b113c3

Vives X (2010) Competition and stability in banking. CESifo working paper no. 3050, May. Available via http://papers.ssrn.com/sol3/papers.cfm?abstract_id=1610086

Wagner W (2010) Diversification at financial institutions and systemic crises. J Financ Intermed 19:333–354

Wheelock DC (2010) Lessons learned? Comparing the federal reserve's responses to the crises of 1929–1933 and 2007-2009. Fed Reserv Bank St Louis Rev 92(2):89–107

White W (2006a) Procyclicality in the financial system: do we need a new macro-financial stabilisation framework? BIS working paper no. 193

White W (2006b) Is price stability enough? BIS working paper no. 205. Available via http://www.bis.org/publ/work205.htm

Willen P (2014) Evaluating policies to prevent another crisis: an economist's view. NBER working paper no. W20100, May. Available via http://www.nber.org/papers/w20100

Wolf M (2008) Fixing global finance. Johns Hopkins University Press, Baltimore

Zingales L (2014) Preventing economists' capture. CEPER discussion paper no. DP9867, March. Available via http://papers.ssrn.com/sol3/papers.cfm?abstract_id=2444888

Part II
The Case of Argentina

Chapter 2
Argentina's Debt Crisis

Victor A. Beker

2.1 Introduction

The story of Argentina's external debt can be summarized as follows. At the end of 1975, Argentina's external debt was $4 billion; at the end of 1982, $40 billion; and at the end of 2001, $140 billion. On December 2001, Argentina announced the default of its external debt. It was one of the largest defaults in present value terms since the Russian repudiation of 1918.

How was it that Argentina came to that shocking result? In August 1982, Mexico declared that it would no longer be able to service its debt. In the wake of Mexico's default, most commercial banks reduced significantly or halted new lending to Latin America. As much of Latin America's loans were short term, a crisis ensued when their refinancing was refused. Thereafter, Mexico, Brazil, and Argentina followed suit. Argentina's default lasted until 1992, when it reached an agreement with the creditor banks within the framework of the Brady Plan.

With this antecedent, nobody thought, in the early 1990s, that Argentina's public sector could easily recover access to capital markets. However, while at the end of 1991 Argentina's public debt amounted to $61 billion, by the end of 1999 it had soared to $145 billion (Fig. 2.1). How was it possible that such a serial defaulter[1] could more than double its external debt in such a short time? This seems to contradict the explanation given by Reinhart and Rogoff (2004, 13) related to the "paradox" of why so little capital flows to poor countries; they argue that countries that do not repay their debts have a relatively difficult time borrowing from the rest

[1] Although Argentina is known as a serial defaulter, its record is surpassed by many countries in the New World and by almost as many in the Old World including France and Germany (Reinhart and Rogoff 2004, 3).

V.A. Beker (✉)
University of Belgrano and University of Buenos Aires, Buenos Aires, Argentina
e-mail: victor.beker@ub.edu.ar

B. Moro, V.A. Beker, *Modern Financial Crises*, Financial and Monetary Policy Studies 42, DOI 10.1007/978-3-319-20991-3_2

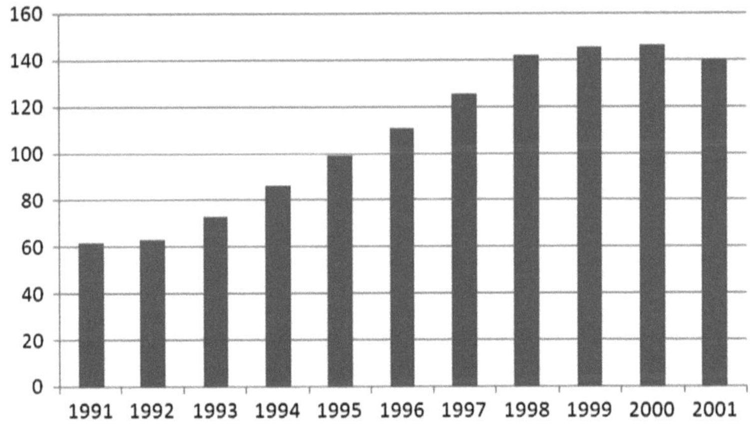

Fig. 2.1 Public indebtedness—national government—1991–2001 (billions of dollars at the end of each year) (*Source*: Ministry of Economy)

of the world. However, this does not seem to have been the case for Argentina, whose external debt largely increased in the 1990s despite just coming out from default.

Of course, lenders could argue that they lent money to a country that was at that time blessed by the IMF. The IMF's point of view was clearly reflected in its former First Deputy Managing Director Anne Krueger's words during the conference on "the Argentine crisis" in July 2002: "Between 1990 and 1997 its economy outperformed that of most other countries in Latin America, growing by more than 6 % a year. Contagion from the Tequila crisis in 1995 was severe, but short-lived with growth soon resuming. Argentina's performance was recognized internationally with President Menem's appearance alongside President Clinton at the 1999 annual meetings of the Fund and Bank" (Krueger 2002).

Of course, as Mrs. Krueger recognized on that occasion, there was mounting fiscal deficit but it was not then considered to be a problem; on the contrary, it was seen as an opportunity to lend money to the Argentine state, the same state that had been in default during most of the previous 10 years.

Figure 2.1 reflects the evolution of the national government public debt—external and domestic—from 1991 until 2001, when Argentina defaulted again. By that time, Argentina's total foreign currency debt was around five times the size of its annual foreign currency receipts from the exports of goods and services.

Mrs. Krueger prefers to play down the role of the IMF and to put the blame on investors and lenders for "providing an apparent vote of confidence by pouring capital in" (Krueger 2002). The fact is that in the 1990s, Argentina was the best pupil of the IMF, the World Bank, and the US government, as not only Mrs. Krueger but also the then Minister of Economy Domingo F. Cavallo recalls (Cavallo 2004, 1). For international organizations, it was a "star" country that had followed most of the policies recommended by the so-called Washington Consensus.

The IMF played a key role in restoring confidence in Argentina by capital markets. During the decade preceding the 2001 crisis, there were successive IMF financing arrangements for Argentina[2]; the IMF also provided extensive technical assistance during that period, dispatching some 50 missions between 1991 and 2002, mainly in the fiscal, monetary, and banking areas. It widely praised Argentina for its achievements in stabilization, economic growth, and market-oriented reforms under IMF-supported programs.

The misjudgment by the IMF of the sustainability of the Convertibility regime played a key role in reopening Argentina's access to capital markets. The successive bond issues that took place during the 1990s were carried out by a government whose economic policies were under the close scrutiny of the IMF, who had strongly praised them. Without its seal of approval to Argentina's economic policies, would investors and lenders have rushed to buy them? Therefore, in the case of Argentina, it seems to be clear that a primary responsibility in its 2001 public sector debt crisis was played by the IMF endorsement of an economic scheme that had been doomed to fail at least since 1995.[3]

The rest of the chapter is organized as follows. Section 2.2 is devoted to an analysis of Argentina's economic performance in the 1990s. Section 2.3 reviews the criteria for assessing the country's solvency and applies them to assess the Argentine case. Section 2.4 explains the reasons for Argentina's growing public sector debt. Section 2.5 is devoted to analyzing the role of the IMF in the Argentine debt crisis. Section 2.6 summarizes.

2.2 Argentina's Economic Performance in the 1990s

The economic performance of Latin American countries in the 1980s was unsatisfactory. In what has been called the "lost decade", the region's economy was disrupted by the debt crisis and raging inflation. This experience shocked the region; as a result, Latin America embraced structural economic reforms during the 1990s. All countries liberalized international trade and external capital flows and privatized public utilities. Argentina was no exception. Actually, it was one of the countries where more aggressive economic reforms were implemented.

After the hyperinflationary processes of 1989 and 1990, drastic economic reforms took place in Argentina. The key measures that shaped this economic program were the Convertibility Law, the liberalization of external trade and financial flows, and the privatization of public enterprises.

[2] During the 1990s, there were four IMF arrangements: that under the Extended Fund Facility (EFF) approved on March 31, 1992; the Stand-By Arrangement (SBA) approved on April 12, 1996; the arrangement under the EFF, approved on February 4, 1998; and the SBA approved on March 10, 2000.

[3] See Beker and Escudé (2008, 23–24).

The Convertibility Law established a fixed exchange rate of one peso to one dollar. The Central Bank was obliged to sell foreign currency at that rate as required by the market. In order to fulfill this obligation, it had to keep international reserves equivalent to at least 100 % of the monetary base (except for up to 10 % of the monetary base which could be backed by dollar-denominated government bonds). This meant, virtually, the transformation of the Central Bank into a Currency Board. As a result of this package, inflation was drastically abated from a level of 5 % per year in 1989 to just 0.16 % in 1996. Moreover, GDP grew by 40 % between 1990 and 1994.

Trade liberalization was reflected in a huge increase in foreign trade. Imports soared, from $4.1 billion to $21.6 billion in 1994, while exports rose from $3.7 billion to $20.1 billion in the same period. The participation of imports in aggregate supply expanded from 5.6 % in 1990 to 14.6 % in 1994. This increase in international trade was accompanied by substantial expansion in the deficit in the current account.

Convertibility together with trade liberalization assured the stability of tradable goods prices. Their domestic prices would not increase if international prices did not because imports could easily replace local production. However, this did not mean the stability of prices for non-tradable goods. The result was a change in relative prices in favor of non-tradables.

Excess demand—fueled by foreign capital inflow—resulted, on one hand, in an increase in the volume of imports and, on the other hand, in the price of non-tradable goods. This price behavior resulted in the continuous erosion of the competitiveness of tradable sectors. The current account deficit thus increased from $5.5 billion in 1992 to $12.1 billion in 1997—more than one-third of that year's exports.

Therefore, the current account deficit kept growing during the 1990s and more and more capital inflows were needed to make up for it. As can be seen in Table 2.1, Argentina needed a surplus of more than $10 billion per year in its capital and financial account not to lose foreign exchange reserves. When there was a sharp reduction in global capital flows to emerging market economies, as happened in 1995 due to the Tequila effect, real GDP fell 4.6 % and unemployment soared, reaching 17 %.

Contrary to the conclusion by the IMF and mainstream analysts that Argentina's economic behavior in the presence of the Tequila effect proved to be the strength of its economy, it showed its Achilles' heel: its high sensitivity to external flows. As later events proved, 1995 was a general rehearsal for the 2001 crisis. The lack of access to funds on international capital markets would strangle the Argentine economy under the Convertibility regime.

In the late 1990s, the Argentine economy suffered a series of external shocks: the East Asian crisis in 1997; the Russian one in 1998; the 1999 devaluation of the Brazilian real, which had a negative impact on the competitiveness of Argentina's significant exports to this country; and the appreciation of the US dollar against most other currencies, which increased Argentina's real effective exchange rate.

Table 2.1 Balance of payments—Argentina 1992–2002 (US dollars, millions)

Year	Current account	Capital and financial account	Net errors and omissions	Variation in international reserves
1992	−5548	9169	−347	3274
1993	−8206	14,196	−1740	4.250
1994	−10,979	13,781	−2120	682
1995	−5118	7701	−2685	−102
1996	−6769	12,249	−1598	3882
1997	−12,137	17,709	−2299	3273
1998	−14,482	18,354	−434	3438
1999	−11,944	13,772	−628	1201
2000	−8981	8737	−196	−439
2001	−3780	−5439	−3354	−12,083
2002	8668	−11,404	−1780	−4516

Source: Ministry of Economy

In the presence of all these adverse shocks, the Convertibility regime prevented a flexible domestic policy response.

The twin deficits required continuous access to external financing. However, far from being considered a drawback or a weakness of the economic program, they were considered by the government to be just a minor detail, assuming that foreign capital markets would always be available to finance both disequilibria. An increasing stock of external debt, rising country risk premiums, and sluggish growth caused the ratio of debt to GDP to rise uncontrollably until the default came in 2001.

Sovereign debt has usually been assumed to be almost risk-free because it is supposed that governments can always resort to an increase in taxes to service it. However, in the real world there is always a political limit for that.

2.3 Country's Solvency and the Argentine Case

Although no simple rule can help determine when foreign debt accumulation is sustainable or not, a number of criteria can be used in assessing the sustainability of the foreign debt of a country. The issue is summarized in Roubini (2001, 3–4).

The analytical literature on current account and foreign debt sustainability provides a theoretical criterion that is not particularly stringent. As long as the discounted value of trade balances is at least equal to its initial foreign debt, the country is solvent; this means only that the country cannot increase its foreign debt faster than the real interest rate on this debt.

Therefore, any path of the current account such that the infinite sum of all current accounts is equal to the initial foreign debt of the country is consistent with solvency. This means, for instance, that if the real interest rate is greater than the rate of the growth of an economy, solvency is consistent even with a foreign debt-to-GDP ratio that grows continuously over time.

A similar criterion applies in determining whether the public debt of a government is sustainable or not. Specifically, as long as the discounted value of primary balances is at least equal to the initial public debt, the public sector is solvent. However, the dynamics of the current account that lead to an increase without bounds of the foreign debt-to-GDP ratio can be seen as effectively unsustainable: financial markets will eventually become concerned about the country's ability and willingness to repay its debt and will limit its borrowing, leading to a foreign debt crisis. The same things apply for the case of domestic debt.

That is why a nonincreasing foreign debt-to-GDP ratio has been seen as a practical sufficient condition for sustainability: a country is likely to remain solvent as long as the ratio is not growing. Similarly, public debt can be viewed as sustainable as long as the public debt-to-GDP ratio is nonincreasing. The "resource balance gap" is thus the difference between the current trade balance and the trade surplus required to stabilize the debt-to-GDP ratio.

In the same way, the fiscal "primary gap" is the difference between the fiscal primary balance and the primary balance required to stabilize the debt-to-GDP ratio. This criterion provides a normative rule: how much a trade surplus or primary surplus is required to close the resource or primary gap. However, it does not directly provide a tool to assess whether a certain stock of debt is sustainable or not.

Several alternative indicators of fiscal and external debt sustainability can be used to assess insolvency. Three of the most commonly used are the debt-to-GDP ratio, the debt-to-export ratio, and the debt-to-government revenue ratio. The relevant denominator depends on the constraints that are most binding in an individual country, with GDP capturing overall resource constraints, exports those on foreign exchange, and revenues those on the government's ability to generate fiscal resources. In general, it is useful to monitor external debt in relation to GDP and export earnings and public debt in relation to GDP and fiscal revenues.

In this respect, the analysis by IMF staff for low-income countries yields a threshold value for the external debt-to-GDP ratio of around 43 %, for the external debt-to-export ratio of around 192 %, and 288 % for the debt-to-revenue ratio (IMF and IDA 2004, 57).

Based on the criterion of the external debt-to-GDP ratio, Argentina crossed the threshold in 1998 (Table 2.2). However, the GDP calculation was biased upward by the overvaluation of the peso, so entrance into the "danger area" might have happened a couple of years before.

Concerning the external debt-to-export ratio, Argentina had in 2001 a ratio of 561 %, well above the threshold value, although the same happened with all the values of this series in the 1990s (Table 2.3). Finally, the debt-to-government revenue ratio was 220 % in 2001, below the threshold value for this coefficient.

Therefore, the coefficients themselves do not explain why Argentina defaulted in 2001. If the relevant coefficient was the debt-to-export ratio, Argentina was already a potential defaulter in 1991. However, it managed to borrow almost $80 billion during the following 10 years, more than doubling its external debt.

Table 2.2 External debt-to-GDP ratio

Year	%
1991	32.35
1992	27.36
1993	30.53
1994	33.28
1995	38.20
1996	40.32
1997	42.61
1998	47.11
1999	51.54
2000	51.91
2001	51.95

Source: Ministry of Economy and IMF

Table 2.3 External debt-to-export ratio

Year	%
1991	503.54
1992	512.06
1993	511.53
1994	550.47
1995	540.78
1996	470.10
1997	460.95
1998	472.30
1999	532.97
2000	627.32
2001	560.60

Source: Ministry of Economy and IMF

Perhaps the most important issue at the time of default was the high share of short-term external debt. In fact, for both 2002 and 2003, the repayment of principal exceeded 80 % of the exports. Adding interest payments of about $12 billion, total debt servicing largely exceeded annual exports. Argentina depended on creditors' willingness to roll over its external debt. This became increasingly difficult since capital flows to Argentina quickly decelerated after the 1998 Russian crisis.

By mid-2001, the economic authorities initiated a process to improve the maturities by extending them. A $30 billion government debt swap took place in June. The government thought this transaction would offer financial relief in terms of the repayment of principal and interest payments of around $4.5 billion annually.

However, this was carried out at the price of accepting an implicit interest rate of 15 %,[4] which was interpreted by creditors as announcing a high probability of

[4] At that time, the one-year US Treasury interest rate fluctuated around 3.6 %.

default. After that, the failure of a Treasury bill auction confirmed that the Argentine government had lost access to credit. Default was then inevitable.

Argentina had been continuously issuing new bonds to cancel most of the principal and interests of the debt that were becoming due. Only when default was imminent did creditors refuse to go on playing this game. Even then—in September 2001—the IMF approved one last significant tranche of financing for Argentina.

In the analysis of its role in the Argentine crisis, the IMF (2003, 72) poses the dilemma its authorities faced at that time: even after realizing the high probabilities of failure, it went on supporting the Argentine economic program in light of the high and immediate costs of withdrawing support. This reflects the path dependency existing in decision-making: once you make a considerable wrong bet, you are doomed to increase it in order to try to save your initial investment.

In the context of political instability—the governing coalition was undergoing a political crisis since the resignation by the vice-president in October 2000—Argentina finally defaulted at the end of 2001 after the then president resigned from his job.

2.4 The Reasons for Argentina's Growing Public Sector Debt

When the Convertibility plan started in 1991, a restriction was placed on the Central Bank. It could not make loans to the government (except for short-term limited amounts). Given the reluctance by foreign lenders at that time to become involved in Argentina, it was taken for granted that the constraint was practically equivalent to excluding the possibility of running a fiscal deficit. During the transition, the government would resort to the proceedings from privatizations while leveling expenses with revenues.

In fact, in 1993—for the first time in decades—the nonfinancial public sector had no deficit. However, exactly at that time it was decided to reform the social security system. The main effect of this reform was to transfer most of the system revenues to the private sector while keeping most of the expenses within the public sector.

This meant that since 1994 the federal budget was again continuously in deficit, even in years of good economic growth. New debt was added to old debt year after year, and debt plus interest grew much faster than the economy.

At the end of 1994, the federal government's gross debt was \$75 billion, while GDP in 1994 was \$257 billion. By the end of 2001, debt was almost twice as large, \$140 billion, while GDP was only \$271 billion, just 5 % higher than in 1994.

Thus, what in 1991 was unthinkable did happen: since 1994, Argentina had recovered access to international capital markets. Therefore, the constraint placed on the Central Bank became nonbinding. Capital markets were willingly available to finance Argentina's public sector debt. How did this Copernican change happen?

First, since 1992 Argentina was under the umbrella of an IMF-supported program; second, it enthusiastically adhered to the Washington Consensus and its principles; third, the Currency Board was a guarantee of no devaluation; finally, high interest rates were a significant attraction. From 1994 on, what has been called a "bond festival" took place until the 2001 default put an abrupt end to it.[5]

How can we explain the increase in the nominal and real interest rates? Damill and Frenkel (2003, 8) give a clear explanation: the interest rate in local currency can be expressed as the sum of the international rate in dollars paid by the country plus the devaluation rate established in the exchange policy rules (zero in the case of fixed exchange rates), plus a residual that responds to the exchange risk and the local financial risk.

The sum of the exchange risk premium and the country risk premium—the aggregate price of the risk of devaluation and the risk of default—is the main variable whose increase causes the local interest rate to rise. A steady increase in the current account deficit and—after a certain point—the trend toward shrinking reserves undermines the credibility of the exchange regime on the one hand and, on the other, increases the probability that the debt will not be served in due time and form. Consequently, the risk premiums tend to rise.

The continuous support by the IMF to the Argentine program, even after the Tequila crisis showed its high sensitivity to external flows, allowed the government to pile up a huge debt, long after it was evident that the Currency Board was unsustainable. Therefore, it is worthwhile analyzing the role of the IMF in the Argentine crisis.

2.5 The Role of the IMF

After the 2001 crisis, the IMF produced two documents. One was aimed at examining the origins of the Argentine crisis and its evolution until early 2002 (IMF 2003). The second one was produced by the IMF's Independent Evaluation Office (IEO); this evaluated the role of the IMF in Argentina during 1991–2001 (IMF 2004).

In its report, the IEO recognizes that "the catastrophic collapse of the Argentine economy in 2001–2002 represents the failure of Argentine policymakers to take necessary corrective measures at a sufficiently early stage. The IMF on its part, supported by its major shareholders, also erred in failing to call an earlier halt to support for a strategy that, as implemented, was not sustainable" (IMF 2004, 64).

The IEO argues that favorable factors allowed the exchange rate regime to survive for a number of years without being severely tested but the situation changed in 1998–1999 when Argentina was hit by a series of adverse shocks.

[5] Those interested in Argentina's development after the 2001 devaluation and default may have a look at Frenkel (2012).

Table 2.4 Unemployment rates—May and October 1991–1995

Year	May	October
1991	6.9	6.0
1992	6.9	7.0
1993	9.9	9.3
1994	10.7	12.2
1995	18.4	16.6

Source: INDEC

However, it admits that "these shocks would have been difficult enough to handle at any time, given the rigidity of the fixed exchange rate and the lack of downward flexibility in domestic wages and prices" (Ibid.).

Therefore, it recognizes that the Convertibility regime, because of its rigidity, was incapable of dealing with any adverse shock of a certain volume. In fact, it did not pass the Tequila test: in order to keep a fixed exchange rate, the country's economy experienced a jump in its unemployment rate from 10.7 to 18.4 % between May 1994 and May 1995 (Table 2.4).

Therefore, if a test was needed, the Mexican crisis provided it. However, the IMF interpretation even in 2003 was that "the economy had successfully weathered the Tequila crisis of the mid-1990s" (IMF 2003, 3).

Calling a success the management of a crisis that meant an 80 % increase in the unemployment rate is evidence that the IMF underweights unemployment in its assessment scheme.

The IEO report goes onto admit that the IMF's "support gave credibility to Argentina's stabilization and structural reform efforts" (IMF 2004, 65), although the IMF was initially skeptical as to whether the Convertibility plan would work. This suggests that political considerations prevailed over the technical opinions of IMF staff.[6]

Although the report underlines that the IMF correctly identified the potential vulnerabilities inherent in the Convertibility regime, the fact is that in spite of that the IMF went on supporting that regime even after it was clear that this support allowed Argentine authorities to swiftly increase Argentine public debt to unsustainable levels. "Moreover, the IMF . . . began to endorse the exchange rate regime itself. Indeed, the IMF publicly lauded convertibility as an example of a Currency Board, the only type of fixed exchange rate regime that is fundamentally sustainable in a world of high capital mobility" (IMF 2004, 65).

In summary, the IMF's support was a necessary element without which it would have been difficult to increase Argentina's indebtedness as occurred during the 1990s.

[6]"... dissenting views were overruled by such considerations as the need to maintain influence with a member country or a desire to preserve the catalytic effect of the IMF's seal of approval" (IMF 2004, 66). Also see IMF and International Development Association (2004).

2.6 Summary

After the hyperinflationary processes of 1989 and 1990, drastic economic reforms took place in Argentina. The central piece of this program was the Convertibility Law, which established a fixed exchange rate of one peso to one dollar.

The Central Bank could issue domestic currency only against foreign currency and could not make loans to the government except for a very tiny sum. It was taken for granted that this constraint was practically equivalent to excluding the possibility of running a fiscal deficit.

However, soon this proved not to be true: from 1994, Argentina recovered access to international capital markets and since then increased its public debt at a very fast rate. How were lenders convinced to lend huge amounts of money to a serial defaulter such as Argentina? There is no explanation but endorsement by the IMF of Argentina's economic program. It is hard to believe that lenders would have rushed to buy Argentine bonds without the IMF's seal of approval.

The misjudgment by the IMF about the sustainability of the Convertibility regime played a key role in reopening Argentina's access to capital markets. Continuous support by the IMF to the Argentine program, even after the Tequila crisis showed its economy's high sensitivity to external flows, allowed the government to pile up a huge debt, long after it was evident that the Currency Board regime was unsustainable.

The IMF played in the Argentine case the same role as credit rating agencies played in the 2008 American crisis: to induce lenders to put their money into buying securities of doubtful collectability.

References

Boker VA, Escudé G (2008) Vida, pasión y muerte de la convertibilidad en Argentina. Estudios Económicos, 25(50):1–36. Available via http://bibliotecadigital.uns.edu.ar/scielo.php?script=sci_arttext&pid=S0425-368X2008000100001&lng=es&nrm=iso

Cavallo DF (2004) Clase N° 6. Argentina hasta la crisis brasileña. Harvard University, Cambridge. Available via http://www.cavallo.com.ar/wp-content/uploads/C6.pdf

Damill M, Frenkel R (2003) Argentina: Macroeconomic Performance and Crisis. CEDES. Available via http://policydialogue.org/files/publications/Argentina_MacroPerformance_Damill__Frenkel.pdf

Frenkel R (2012) Lessons from a comparative analysis of financial crises. INFER workshop on the euro: manage it or leave it! June:22–23. Available via http://www.unich.it/docenti/bagnai/euro/

IMF (2003) Lessons from the crisis in Argentina. Available via http://www.imf.org/external/np/pdr/lessons/100803.pdf

IMF (2004) Report on the evaluation of the role of the IMF in Argentina, 1991–2001. Available via http://www.imf.org/External/NP/ieo/2004/arg/eng/

IMF and International Development Association (2004) Debt sustainability in low-income countries-proposal for an operational framework and policy implications, mimeo. Available via http://siteresources.worldbank.org/INTDEBTDEPT/PublicationsAndReports/20261908/debtSust-complete%20paper.pdf

Krueger A (2002) Crisis prevention and resolution: lessons from Argentina. Paper presented at the conference "The Argentina Crisis". National Bureau of Economic Research, Cambridge. Available via http://www.imf.org/external/np/speeches/2002/071702.htm

Reinhart CM, Rogoff KS (2004) Serial default and the 'Paradox' of rich to poor capital flows. National Bureau of economic research working paper no. 10296. Available via http://www.nber.org/papers/w10296

Roubini N (2001) Debt sustainability: how to assess whether a country is insolvent. Stern School of Business, New York University. Available via http://people.stern.nyu.edu/nroubini/papers/debtsustainability.pdf

Part III
The American 2007–2009 Subprime Crisis

Chapter 3
The American Financial Crisis

Victor A. Beker

3.1 Introduction

The core of the 2007/2009 financial market crisis has been the discovery that many securities were actually far riskier than people originally thought they were. The process of securitization allowed trillions of dollars of risky assets—subprime mortgages in the first place—to be transformed into securities that were widely considered to be safe.

The American financial crisis is a typical case of professional malpractice, an extended malpractice by hundreds of professionals in banks and rating agencies who created and certified as almost risk-free securities assets that were actually highly risky as the events after 2007 overwhelmingly showed.

Subprime mortgage securitization models relied on assumptions and historical data that turned out to be incorrect and therefore made incorrect valuations. Substantial lending to subprime borrowers was a recent phenomenon and historical data on the defaults and delinquencies of this sector of the mortgage market was scarce (Coval et al. 2009, 15). Some models were not even based on historical data because they referred to transactions for which there was no active trading market. "The mathematical rigor, elegance and the numerical precision of the various risk-management and asset-pricing tools have a tendency to 'hide' the weaknesses of these models and their underlying assumptions, which are necessary to guarantee the models' values to those who have not developed them" (Schneider and Kirchgässner 2009, 6).

Securitization enabled mortgage lenders to sell off loans as they were made, thus creating moral hazard since this meant that lenders could pass along the risk of default to investors. Mortgage underwriting standards fell once lenders did not have to live with the credit consequences of their loans. Gorton (2008, 2009) disagrees

V.A. Beker (✉)
University of Belgrano and University of Buenos Aires, Buenos Aires, Argentina
e-mail: victor.beker@ub.edu.ar

B. Moro, V.A. Beker, *Modern Financial Crises*, Financial and Monetary Policy Studies 42, DOI 10.1007/978-3-319-20991-3_3

with this interpretation, arguing that many lenders went under after the crisis. However, one may use just the opposite argument: they went under precisely because the crisis burst out before they were able to distribute all the securitized debt they had created. On the other hand, lenders who did not sell all the loans they originated were able to buy relatively inexpensive protection against credit risks through credit default swaps, which was another way of transferring risk to a third party.

Securitization, which was supposedly aimed at reducing informational asymmetry,[1] became a tool to take advantage of that asymmetry. Because of the asymmetric information between the lender and the investor, rating agencies came on scene to provide the latter with accurate risk evaluation. However, the problem was that rating agencies are paid by the issuer not by the investor. This raised a conflict of interest, as it was clearly exposed by the high credit ratings given to actually highly risky assets.

Behind this extended malpractice was the pressure caused by a liquidity glut, which forced lenders to compete aggressively for business. That is why monetarists blame exclusively the money glut for the crisis. However, the existence of a money glut is a necessary but not sufficient condition for developing a bubble like the one that culminated in the crisis. It was the combination of this money glut with financial deregulation that was lethal for the American economy.

3.2 The Money Glut

Global current account imbalances have been singled out as a key factor contributing to the global financial crisis. Current account surpluses in several emerging market economies (China and other Asian countries plus oil-exporting countries) are said to have helped fuel the credit booms and risk taking in the major advanced deficit countries at the core of the crisis, by putting significant downward pressure on world interest rates and/or by simply financing the booms in those countries.

However, some authors—remarkably among them the former Federal Reserve Chairman Ben Bernanke—argued that a combination of diverse forces has created a significant increase in the global supply of saving—a global savings glut—which helps to explain both the increase in the US current account deficit and the relatively low level of long-term real interest rates in the world.

Bracke and Fidora (2012) test the global liquidity glut hypothesis versus the global savings glut one. They find that US monetary policy shocks explain the largest part of the variation in imbalances and financial market prices. Savings shocks and investment shocks explain less of the variation. Hence, according to them, a "liquidity glut" may have been a more important driver of the real and

[1] See, for example, Schwarcz (2011, 4).

financial imbalances in the USA and emerging Asia that ultimately triggered the 2007–2008 global financial crisis.

Borio and Disyatat (2011, 20) reject the dominant "excess saving" view, arguing that "the saving-investment framework describes the real side of the economy. The equality between ex ante saving and investment is an equilibrium condition for the goods market". For them, the focus of the analysis should be placed on monetary policy: "It is monetary policy that underpins the term structure of market interest rates" (Ibid., 24).

They argue that "the geographical breakdown of capital inflows into the US in the run-up to the crisis is hardly consistent with the excess savings view. By far the most important source of capital flows was Europe, not emerging markets. Of this, more than half came from the United Kingdom, a country running a current account deficit, and roughly one-third from the euro area, a region roughly in balance. This amount alone exceeded that from China and by an even larger margin that from Japan, two large surplus economies" (Ibid., 15).

They refer to Milesi-Ferretti (2009), according to whom on the eve of the crisis (June 2007) the holdings of privately issued mortgage-backed securities were concentrated in advanced economies and offshore centers. Contrary to the excess savings hypothesis, they maintain that "the focus on global current account imbalances misses the role of European banks in supporting the boom in US housing credit and the subsequent collapse of such financing" (Ibid., 20). They conclude that the main contributing factor to the financial crisis was the "excess elasticity" of the international monetary and financial system. They argue that "the financial system can endogenously generate financing means, regardless of the underlying real resources backing them. In other words, the system is highly elastic. And this elasticity can also result in the volume of financing expanding in ways that are disconnected from the underlying productive capacity of the economy" (Ibid., 28).

However, it does not seem that one approach necessarily excludes the other. The "excess saving" view may explain the huge increase in the official holdings of US Treasury securities by the countries that accumulated foreign exchange reserves during the past decade. This allowed the American economy to run twin deficits during these years and keep interest rates low. These low interest rates were validated by an expansionary monetary policy (the "liquidity glut").

The real issue is not the ultimate cause of cheap money, but why low interest rates did not stimulate investment in real productive capacity instead of feeding a colossal speculative bubble in the real estate market. The answer is that speculation promised greater benefits with almost no risk. Here comes the key role played by rating agencies. Trillions of dollars of risky assets were transformed into mostly AAA-rated securities. This was the key element in feeding the subprime mortgage bubble: "The three credit rating agencies were key enablers of the financial meltdown. The mortgage-related securities at the heart of the crisis could not have been marketed and sold without their seal of approval" (FCIC 2011, XXV).

3.3 The Role of Credit Rating Agencies

Credit rating agencies were an essential input into the process of manufacturing vast quantities of triple-rated securities with attractive yields. In a period of low interest rates, they were eagerly bought up by investors unaware of the real risks they entailed.

Risks were strongly mispriced. Investors thought they had bought a Mercedes Benz; it took a certain time for them to find out they were just "lemons". Coval et al. (2009) explain thoroughly the roots of rating agencies' errors and why they were unable to accurately assess securities risks, in particular systematic risks.

While house prices kept rising, risks stayed hidden. If an owner could not meet the monthly payments, the bank renegotiated the mortgage. The renegotiation would raise the principal to the new higher house value in exchange for lowering the monthly payment. Therefore, the delinquency rate was low.

The situation changed abruptly when house prices started falling. Most borrowers who could not afford the monthly payments had no alternative but to default their subprime mortgages, as many of them found themselves holding mortgages in excess of the market values of their homes. Subprime-related securities experienced large losses; investors learned the hard way how risky these assets were.

Few investors had been worried that the underlying assets might be overvalued. This is not surprising taking into consideration that credit rating agencies evaluated and deemed them to be safe. Therefore, there is no mystery why investors massively rushed to buy these "toxic" assets. The originating banks, which were presumably able to charge a higher interest rate to their subprime borrowers, and many US institutional investors, who needed high ratings to buy the securities at all, both had a vested interest in rating agencies awarding high ratings.

A theoretical argument advanced by Kartik et al. (2007) may help explain rating agencies' behavior. In the context of an analytical model of communication games, the authors assume a setting in which the sender of a message is interested in the average response of a population of receivers characterized by heterogeneous strategic sophistication. They demonstrate that in such cases there is a unique nondecreasing, differentiable separating equilibrium.

This equilibrium has the important property that in every state of the world, the sender induces a belief in naïve receivers such that the average population response is in fact his or her bliss point. That is, the sender can achieve his or her first-best outcome in such a setting, even though sophisticated receivers correctly infer the state of the world in equilibrium. In the equilibria they identify, the message sent by the sender has a literal meaning that is inflated, a literal meaning higher than the true state of the world.

Nevertheless, a sophisticated receiver correctly infers the true state by inverting the observed message according to the equilibrium language. A credulous receiver instead interprets the equilibrium messages with some nonequilibrium-based rule and is accordingly deceived, taking biased actions. If naïve receivers are on one side of the playing field and sophisticated ones are on the other one, we get something like the subprime meltdown.

3.4 The Role of Banks

Banks pursued an aggressive lending policy in order to get rid of the excess money in their vaults. As stated before, securitization created moral hazard since it meant that lenders could pass along the risk of default to investors or insurance companies. This encouraged excessive risk taking. The problem was magnified because the most aggressive institutions put pressure on the rest of them: safe institutions that desired to be more careful and scrutinize more deeply the repayment capacities of their potential customers would lose market share and make fewer loans. Just as bad money drives out good, bad financial institutions could drive out good ones.

The rapid increase in market share by unregulated brokers and originators put pressure on regulated banks to lower their underwriting standards. Securities backed by subprime mortgages lent to borrowers whose abilities to repay were doubtful became prominent in the banking business.

As documented in Fratianni and Marchionne (2009), large US banks were dominant in securitization. The ratio value of securitization activities—covering real estate loans, credit card receivables, automobile loans, other consumer loans, and commercial and industrial loans—of total bank assets for large US banks started at 14.5 % at the end of 2002 and reached a peak of 18.6 % in the first quarter of 2007. By contrast, the securitization/asset ratio for intermediate-sized banks was below 1 %, while small US banks were not materially involved in securitization. A similar pattern holds for derivatives.

Securitization gave birth to a complex shadow banking system to intermediate credit through a wide range of securitization and secured funding techniques such as asset-backed commercial papers, asset-backed securities, collateralized debt obligations (CDOs), and repurchase agreements (repos).

The shadow banking system—developed out of the regulated banking system—comprises securitization vehicles, asset-backed commercial paper vehicles, money market funds, investment banks, mortgage companies, and a variety of other entities. It provided sources of funding for credit by converting opaque, risky, long-term assets into money-like, short-term liabilities (Pozsar et al. 2012, 1). Therefore, credit intermediaries relied on short-term liabilities to fund illiquid long-term assets.

In the shadow banking system, loans, leases, and mortgages were securitized and thus they became tradable instruments (see Chap. 4). Funding was also in the form of tradable instruments, such as commercial papers and repos. However, the shadow banking system was presumed to be safe due to the liquidity and credit puts provided by the private sector. These puts underpinned the perceived risk-free, highly liquid nature of most AAA-rated assets that collateralized credit repos and shadow banks' liabilities more broadly (Ibid., p. 2).

The shadow banking system emerged from the transformation of the largest banks from low return-on-equity institutions that originate loans and hold and fund them until maturity with deposits to high return-on-equity entities that originate loans in order to warehouse and later securitize and distribute them or retain securitized loans through off-balance sheet asset management vehicles (Ibid., p. 15).

This allowed banks to conduct lending with less capital than if they had retained loans on their balance sheets. This process enhanced the return on equity of banks or, more precisely, of their holding companies. Moreover, it enabled them to bypass existing regulations regarding minimum capital ratios. The funding and maturity transformation of structured credit assets was not only conducted from the USA but also from Europe and offshore financial centers. The gross measure of shadow bank liabilities grew to nearly $22 trillion in June 2007, while traditional banking liabilities were around $14 trillion in 2007 (Ibid., p. 9).[2] At the beginning of the 1990s, both types of liabilities totaled practically the same.

When the housing bubble exploded in 2007, real estate markets went down together and mortgage defaults soared in Florida as well as in California. Mortgage-backed securities carried the dual risk of high rates of default due to the low credit quality of borrowers and the high level of default correlation as a result of pooling mortgages from similar geographical areas and vintages. When prices fell in the home market, subprime-related assets deteriorated. Repo depositors became concerned about the solvency of their counterparties.

In the summer of 2007, panic started in the repo market,[3] which suffered a run when depositors required increasing haircuts. In the repo market, depositors and borrowers are individually matched; each depositor gets his or her own collateral. Firms—often money market funds and corporations—deposit short-term cash; all types of securitized products are used as collateral.

The haircut is the percentage difference between the market value of the pledged collateral and the amount of funds lent. The size of the haircut reflects the credit risk of the borrower and the riskiness of the pledged collateral. Depositors can "withdraw" their funds by not rolling over their repo agreements and returning the collateral, or they can withdraw by increasing the haircut on the collateral. Haircuts were zero until August 2007. After that, haircuts rose and continued to rise; some asset classes became simply unacceptable in repo (Gorton 2009, 30–33).

There was a flight to quality. It was not known which counterparties were really at risk and consequently there was a run on all banks. Defaults and losses on other loan types also increased significantly as the crisis expanded from the housing market to other parts of the economy. The rest is a well-known story.

It is clear that the roots of the problem were the subprime mortgages recklessly provided to doubtful borrowers, including the so-called NINJA borrowers, those who had No Income, No Job, and no Assets. This behavior was stimulated by the

[2] This led Krugman (2009, 170) to call it "the nonbank banking crisis."

[3] On the repo market see also Chap. 4.

"originate-to-distribute" model implemented through the shadow banking system. As stated above, Gorton rejects this hypothesis; in support of his argument, he exemplifies that in 2006 and early 2007, some banks kept the most senior proportions of CDOs on their balance sheets.[4] In the same vein, he argues that when loans are sold in the secondary market, the mortgage servicing rights created are typically not sold. Although he admits that underwriting standards were lowered, he contends that it seems difficult to define a decline in lending standards.

Gorton (2008, 67) argues that the design of subprime mortgages and subprime securitizations are unique in that they are particularly sensitive to declines in house prices: "The key security design feature of subprime mortgages was the ability of borrowers to finance and refinance their homes based on the capital gains due to house price appreciation over short horizons and then turning this into collateral for a new mortgage" (Gorton 2008, 3). However, when house prices began to slow their growth and ultimately fell, the value of the chain of securities began to decrease. Gorton seems to argue that banks were not recklessly selling loans to doubtful debtors but that they were confident that house prices would never significantly decline. If so, they were justified in not taking care with underwriting standards and even keeping part of the risky assets in their portfolio without taking full advantage of the risk-minimizing originate-to-distribute system.

It is difficult to identify which of these hypotheses is right. Perhaps it was a combination of both. Anyway, it is clear that for one reason or the other—or both—banks had no incentives to carefully monitor the loans they were selling. Gorton (2008, 73) includes a table showing that mortgages with less than full documentation soared from 28.5 % in 2001 to 50.8 % in 2006.

On top of this, a gigantic interlinked structure of securities was created with the help of the mostly unregulated shadow banking system. This structure was ready to amplify and spread to the whole financial system following the failure of any mortgage loan. The conditions were right for a perfect storm. When house prices finally stopped rising, borrowers could not refinance their way out of financial difficulty, mortgage defaults soared, and the whole securitization building collapsed.

Every sector of the financial services industry was vulnerable to the effects of the toxic mortgage contagion. Then, the next question is why regulators did not foresee the likely storm or if they did why did they not act to prevent it.

[4] In fact, after manufacturing some security, some banks used to sell the highest-risk tranches and retain some of the super senior position. This only proves that they thought that only the junior tranches were highly risky.

3.5 The Role of Regulators

When asked how such huge mismanagement in the mortgage market could have happened, the first line of defense by regulators has been to argue that most of the problems originated in someone else's jurisdiction. In fact, financial activity regulation is deeply fragmented in the USA. There are at least 10 different types of institutions in charge of regulating the activities involved in the subprime meltdown. This is just an invitation to take advantage of the gaps such a partitioned system provides.

In spite of this plethora of regulating institutions, there was no statutory regulator for investment bank holding companies and the shadow financial system was mostly unregulated. A mortgage lent by a holding company affiliate was subject to very light regulation; a mortgage lender or a broker unaffiliated with a bank was virtually unregulated.

The 2000 Commodity Futures Modernization Act specifically prohibited swaps regulation. However, several subprime participants that performed poorly were in fact regulated by one of the banking agencies but the relevant banking agency failed to compel the institution to adequately comply with guidance (Robertson 2011, 17).

Obviously, with over 10 million mortgage applications for home purchases in 2006 and millions of mortgages making their way into mortgage-backed securities every year, it was not even remotely feasible to inspect every mortgage (Ibid., p. 20). However, in such a case, any auditor could have taken a test sample from any portfolio and, through the reverification of several loan items, estimate the credit quality of the portfolio relative to its advertised quality.[5] Even more, precisely the huge number of mortgages lent by each institution every month should have made regulators suspect that the loans were not subject to due assessment, unless they thought that due assessment was a waste of time because they believed that housing prices were going to rise forever.

The US Securities and Exchange Commission (SEC) was in charge of regulating or overseeing almost 35,000 financial firms and public companies. Each entity issuing an asset-backed security had to file a prospectus with the SEC, "a prospectus, which typically can be as long as 300 pages for a single security, contains an impressive amount of data regarding the asset pool. Regrettably, all of this prospectus information is unverified" (Ibid., p. 22).

Insurance companies such as AIG were subject to state insurance regulators. However, it seems that nobody noticed that AIG wrote $656 billion in credit insurance on structured finance products with only $54 billion in resources to pay those claims (Ibid., pp. 35–36).

National banks and their operating subsidiaries and the federal thrifts and their operating subsidiaries were subject to exclusive federal supervision by the Office of the Comptroller of the Currency (OCC) and the Office of Thrift Supervision, respectively.

---

[5] In fact, this is what Robertson (2011) proposes to do in the future.

State-chartered banks and thrifts and nonbank affiliates of bank and thrift holding companies were subject to both federal and state supervision, while mortgage lenders not affiliated with banks or thrifts were subject only to state supervision.

However, there is no substantial difference in the results achieved by these different regulators: 22 % of the non-prime loans originated by national banks and their subsidiaries subsequently entered the foreclosure process at some time after origination, while the market average was 25.7 % for those types of loans (Dugan 2010, 9). The slightly lower percentage of failures in the case of national banks does not include the defaulted subprime loans made through nonbank institutions. In fact, a number of large bank holding companies owning national banks often used nonbanks for their subprime lending (Ibid., 7).

In his testimony before the Financial Crisis Inquiry Commission (FCIC), the then Comptroller of the Currency argued that "most securitizations and structured credit activities have been conducted outside of banking subsidiaries in holding company affiliates registered as broker-dealers and regulated by the SEC and the Federal Reserve" (Ibid., 13).

Although the Federal Reserve's supervisory capital assessment program, popularly known as the "stress tests", demonstrated that many institutions' information systems could not provide timely, accurate information about bank exposures to counterparties nor complete information about the risks posed by different positions and portfolios, regulators did not press firms vigorously enough to fix them (Bernanke 2010). The Fed, in charge of regulating financial holding companies and state banks, did not identify and address abuses in subprime lending either.

None of this happened by chance. As Alan Greenspan, former chairman of the Fed, recognized, "those of us who have looked to the self-interest of lending institutions to protect shareholders' equity, myself included, are in a state of shocked disbelief" (*New York Times*, October 23, 2008). The blind confidence in self-regulation through market forces was the belief behind the huge deregulating process that took place in the 1980s and 1990s in the USA. The Gramm–Leach–Bliley Act removed barriers in the market among banking companies, securities companies, and insurance companies, expressly recognized national banks' authority to engage directly in asset-backed securitization activities, and repealed key provisions of the Glass–Steagall Act in order to allow banks to affiliate with full-service investment banks that engage extensively in, among other securities activities, asset securitizations. This allowed national banks and companies affiliated with such banks to be fully involved in securitization activities.

However, not only the regulatory framework was weakened; the regulators' power was too. The tenor of the times was to keep regulation as low as possible. The FCIC quotes Richard Spillenkothen, the Fed's director of banking supervision and regulation from 1991 to 2006, who discussed banking supervision in a memorandum submitted to the FCIC: "Supervisors understood that forceful and proactive supervision, especially early intervention before management weaknesses were reflected in poor financial performance, might be viewed as (1) overly-intrusive, burdensome, and heavy-handed, (2) an undesirable constraint on credit availability, or (3) inconsistent with the Fed's public posture" (FCIC 2011, 54).

The main concern was to create checks and balances and keep any agency from becoming arbitrary or inflexible, hence the opposition to any initiative to consolidate bank regulation. The FCIC report quotes Alan Greenspan's 1994 testimony on this matter: "The current structure provides banks with a method . . . of shifting their regulator, an effective test that provides a limit on the arbitrary position or excessively rigid posture of any one regulator. The pressure of a potential loss of institutions has inhibited excessive regulation and acted as a countervailing force to the bias of a regulatory agency to over regulate" (Ibid.).

Under the Gramm–Leach–Bliley Act, the Fed supervised financial holding companies as a whole, looking only for risks that cut across the various subsidiaries owned by the holding company. To avoid duplicating other regulators' work, the Fed was required to rely "to the fullest extent possible" on the examinations and reports of those agencies regarding subsidiaries of the holding company. According to the Fed's Chairman Ben Bernanke, this "made it difficult for any single regulator to reliably see the whole picture of activities and risks of large, complex banking institutions" (Ibid., p. 55).

Therefore, the financial regulatory system was deeply fragmented and weakened to avoid interference with the market-wise behavior. However, some people and institutions warned about the risks at stake. For example, in 2002 the state of Georgia passed a law by which investment banks that created mortgage-backed securities would be liable for financial damage if mortgages turned out to be fraudulent. However, the OCC ruled that the Georgia law did not apply to national banks or their subsidiaries. Finally, the law was amended in 2003: the liability provision was curtailed and other elements of the law were eliminated (*Newsweek*, October 20, 2008).

When in 2004 the state of Michigan tried to examine the books of the mortgage unit of Wachovia Bank that operated in that state, the OCC denied authority to the states to intervene in the operations of national banks. Michigan claimed that the constitution preserved the right of the states to protect their residents, but the Supreme Court ruled in April 2007 establishing that the OCC had exclusive powers over the bank. A year later, the Wachovia Bank had to be saved from bankruptcy through its acquisition by Wells Fargo.

Rajan's (2005) prescient analysis of how the developments observed in financial markets could degenerate into a crisis was not much listened to. No economic journal published his paper and on the SSRN site only collected 93 downloads, which made it rank 96,914th on the SSRN download ranking.

Nouriel Roubini, professor at New York University, in a presentation at the IMF in September 2006, predicted the outbreak of a crisis from a massive default in mortgages and the securities backed by them (Roubini 2010). Nobody paid too much attention to his words, especially when they included the prognosis of massive bankruptcies of hedge funds, investment banks, and other financial institutions such as Fannie Mae and Freddie Mac. A year and a half later, his predictions were fulfilled and Professor Roubini now travels the world giving talks explaining what happened and what is expected to happen.

However, these were isolated voices. A very typical argument in those Great Moderation days was the one reflected in the following quotation: "The passage of the Glass-Steagall Act was prompted by concerns about various kinds of abuses by commercial banks' investment banking affiliates, including overstating the quality of the underwritten securities issued by the commercial banks' clients, packaging bad commercial loans into securities, and misusing responsibility for trust accounts. *Recent research, however, suggests that those concerns were invalid*" (Kwan and Laderman 1999, 18; emphasis is ours). Unfortunately, the 2007–2008 events showed that the concerns that had prompted the 1933 Act were very well founded.

Even at the beginning of 2007, Wharton real estate Professor Todd Sinai argued that three things had to happen for the subprime market to tank: borrowers' incomes had to drop, interest rates had to rise, and housing prices had to fall. "It is extremely rare that all three things happen" he said (Wharton 2007).

The conclusion is that after the deregulation movement that took place during the 1980s and 1990s, the US financial regulatory system was unable to foresee, let alone prevent, the financial crisis.

3.6 A White or a Black Swan?

The finance professor and former Wall Street trader, Nassim Nicholas Taleb, coined the concept of Black Swan, to refer to an extremely rare and highly improbable event. He argued that although extreme events do happen and have a great effect, people are usually often caught off guard by them. Many people invoked Taleb's concept to label the 2008 financial crisis.

However, the NYU Professor Nouriel Roubini argues that it was not at all an improbable event; it was absolutely probable and predictable, it was just a White Swan. His explanation is a very simple one: American homeowners embraced the fiction that home prices could increase 20 % every year forever, and on the basis of that belief they borrowed more and more (Roubini and Mihm 2010, 18). People used their homes as ATMs. But at some point the bubble would stop growing. It happened when the home supply exceeded demand and home prices started falling. Borrowers were forced to sell off their homes at fire-sale prices. Some homeowners defaulted on their mortgages, the value of the securities derived from those loans collapsed, and the bust began (Ibid., 19).

The fact that the bubble could not go on forever made the crisis quite predictable. But one thing is to predict a crisis, another one is to forecast *when* it will happen. As long as cheap credit was available, "developers built innumerable tract homes, speculators snapped the up, and bankers packaged the resulting mortgages into fragile financial instruments" (Ibid., 269). Rating agencies handed out AAA ratings to these "fragile" instruments. But finally the day arrived at which prices stopped growing and then started declining. The positive feedback loop between home prices and borrowing started to work in reverse. Subprime borrowers sold off homes at fire-sale prices.

As prices fell down many properties were worth less than the outstanding balances on their mortgages. People that could no longer pay mortgages returned the keys to the bank or just walked away from their homes. As the delinquency rate for mortgage loans increased as well as foreclosures soared, the impressive pyramid of mortgage-backed securities blew up.[6] Investors fled toward safer assets like Treasury bills; this generated a run on shadow banks: their "depositors" demanded their money back or just refused to renew loans. Defaults and losses on other loan types also increased significantly as the crisis expanded from the housing market to other parts of the economy. Many financial institutions went bankrupt.

Roubini is right: the 2008 crisis was not substantially different from other crises starting with the 1630s tulip one. The catalyst may be the shortage of some commodity, the opening of a new market overseas, or a new way to package investments. As long as people believe that the bubble can grow forever, it will inflate for a long time before it blows up.

Let us now turn to the point of view of those who consider the crisis a Black Swan. For them the crisis was like the Black Swan, something which lies outside the realm of regular expectations. For this reason, it cannot be predicted. It is what in statistics is called an outlier. Taleb illustrates his point by imagining two provinces: Mediocristan and Extremistan. In the former, if you round up a thousand people randomly selected from the population and then you add the heaviest person you can find outside, he/she will represent a very small fraction of the weight of the entire population. No particular event is significant in comparison with the aggregate. By contrast, in Extremistan, inequalities among its members are such that if you add or subtract one observation, it will significantly impact the total. For example, if you compare the net worth of people, adding Bill Gates to the sample makes a substantial difference.

Height and weight are variables which belong to Mediocristan; wealth and income belong to Extremistan. If you live in Mediocristan, a sample lets you figure out what the average is. In Extremistan, one unit not included in the sample may affect the total in a disproportionate way. The Black Swan belongs to Extremistan.

You will never find 20-foot-tall people. If a Martian came to earth, a hundred human samples will be enough to get a good picture of the average human height. He can easily predict the height of any human being: most observations hover around the average. But after analyzing one hundred income tax returns submitted to the IRS, he will not be able to predict the next one if it belongs to Warren Buffett or Bill Gates. In Mediocristan you live comfortable with what you learn from the data. In Extremistan, you should always be suspicious of the knowledge you derive from data. The next observation can always be an outlier. Mediocristan is mostly Black Swan-free; the Black Swan belongs to Extremistan.

[6] See Chap. 9, Sect. 9.3.

Coming back to the 2007–2008 financial crisis, Taleb (2010, 50) believes that the crisis "happened because of an explosive combination of agency problems, moral hazard, and 'scientism'—the illusion that ostensibly scientific techniques would manage risks and predict rare events." In this respect he emphasizes that "ironically, while tail risks have increased, financial and economic theories that discount tail risks have been more vigorously promoted."

It is well known since the famous contribution by Mandelbrot (1963) that many economic and financial time series have fat tails, i.e., the probability of extreme events is higher than if the data-generating process were normal (the distribution of the probability of events is described by a bell curve). However, the usual practice among orthodox economists has been to assume—implicitly or explicitly—a normal distribution. This is the point that Taleb makes. The mistake is to assume that we live in Mediocristan where the Black Swan problem either does not exist or is of small consequence.

Anyway, complexity means a great degree of interdependence between elements which result in reinforcing feedback loops which cause fat tails. While thin tails belong to Mediocristan, fat tails belong to Extremistan. But fat tails lead to massive imprecision in the measurement of low-probability events, Taleb remarks. He adds that tail risks cannot be reliably priced, either mathematically or practically, as uncertainty about key aspects of tail risk has typically been on the order of, or greater than, understanding of the actuarial price of such risks. The subprime mortgage market development together with the securitization process based on it involved hidden risks associated with low-probability, large-consequence events as the crisis widely exposed.

For Taleb the crisis was an extreme event favored by "the fragility in systems built upon ignorance—and denial—of the notion of Black Swan events" (Taleb 2010, 321); as such it could not be predicted with the tools statistics provide us.

Roubini has a different point of view. For him, in modern capitalism, crises are the norm, not the exception. Any unsustainable boom is followed by a calamitous bust. Regardless of how the boom begins sooner or later, some asset becomes the focus of intense speculation interest. Its price rises far above its underlying fundamental value, giving way to a bubble. Rising prices encourage speculation and fuel further demand up, until when the bubble suddenly bursts and people rush to sell. Every bubble is condemned to burst, so its disastrous end is something quite predictable. What you cannot predict is *when* it will happen and, in connection with this, the magnitude of the crash. Due to its cumulative nature, the later the burst the greater the magnitude of the crash.

3.7 Conclusion

Credit rating agencies played a decisive role in the development of the subprime mortgage meltdown. They were an essential input into the process of manufacturing vast quantities of triple A-rated securities with attractive yields.

Banks pursued an aggressive lending policy in order to get rid of the excess money in their vaults. The rapid increase in market share by unregulated brokers and originators put pressure on regulated banks to lower their underwriting standards. Securities backed by subprime mortgages lent to borrowers whose abilities to repay were doubtful became prominent in banking businesses.

Safe institutions that desired to be more careful and scrutinize more deeply the repayment capacities of their potential customers were afraid of losing market share and making fewer loans. Just as bad money drives out good, bad financial institutions could drive out good ones.

On top of this, a gigantic interlinked structure of securities was created with the help of the mostly unregulated shadow banking system (see Chap. 4). This structure was ready to amplify and spread to the whole financial system following the failure of any mortgage loan. The conditions were right for a perfect storm.

When house prices finally stopped rising, borrowers could not refinance their way out of financial difficulty, mortgage defaults soared, and the whole securitization building collapsed.

References

Bernanke B (2010) Causes of the recent financial and economic crisis. Testimony before the financial crisis inquiry commission. Available via http://www.federalreserve.gov/newsevents/testimony/bernanke20100902a.htm

Borio C, Disyatat P (2011) Global imbalances and the financial crisis: link or no link? BIS working papers no. 346

Bracke T, Fidora M (2012) The macro-financial factors behind the crisis: global liquidity glut or global savings glut? North Am J Econ Finance 23(2):185–202

Coval J, Jurek J, Stafford E (2009) The economics of structured finance. J Econ Perspect 23 (1):3–25

Dugan JC (2010) Statement before the financial crisis inquiry commission, April. Available via http://fcic-static.law.stanford.edu/cdn_media/fcic-testimony/2010-0408-Dugan.pdf

FCIC (2011) Financial crisis inquiry commission report, Official Government Edition, Washington, DC. Available via http://fcic.law.stanford.edu/report

Fratianni M, Marchionne F (2009) The role of banks in the subprime financial crisis. Working papers 2009–02, Indiana University, Kelley School of Business, Department of Business Economics and Public Policy. Available via http://www.bus.indiana.edu/riharbau/RePEc/iuk/wpaper/bepp2009-02-fratianni-marchionne.pdf

Gorton GB (2008) The panic of 2007. Federal Reserve Bank of Kansas City, Jackson Hole Conference, August. Available via http://www.kc.frb.org/publicat/sympos/2008/gorton.08.04.08.pdf

Gorton GB (2009) Slapped by the invisible hand: the panic of 2007. Federal Reserve Bank of Atlanta's 2009 financial markets conference: financial innovation and crisis. Available via http://www.frbatlanta.org/news/CONFEREN/09fmc/gorton.pdf

Kartik N, Ottaviani M, Squintani F (2007) Credulity, lies, and costly talk. J Econ Theory 134 (1):93–116

Krugman PR (2009) The return of depression economics and the crisis of 2008. Norton, New York

Kwan SH, Laderman ES (1999) On the portfolio effects of financial convergence: a review of the literature. Fed Reserv Bank San Francisco Econ Rev 2:18–31

Mandelbrot B (1963) The variation of certain speculative prices. J Bus 36(4):394–419
Milesi-Ferretti G (2009) Notes on the financial crisis and global financial architecture. G-20 workshop on the global economy, causes of the crisis: key lessons, Mumbai, India, 24–26 May. Available via http://www.bancaditalia.it/studiricerche/convegni/atti/ocean_apart/sessione1/1_Milesi_Ferretti.pdf
Pozsar ZAT, Ashcraft A, Boesky H (2012) Shadow banking. Federal Reserve Bank of New York. Staff report no. 458. Available via http://www.ny.frb.org/research/staff_reports/sr458.pdf
Rajan R (2005) Has financial development made the world riskier? NBER working paper 11728. Available via http://papers.ssrn.com/sol3/papers.cfm?abstract_id=842464
Robertson D (2011) So that's operational risk! (How operational risk in mortgage-backed securities almost destroyed the world's financial markets and what we can do about it), OCC economics working paper 2011–1, March. Available via http://www.occ.gov/publications/publications-by-type/economics-working-papers/2011-2009/wp2011-1.pdf
Roubini N (2010) Roubini's IMF speech. Available via http://www.economonitor.com/nouriel/2010/09/02/economonitor-flashback-roubinis-imf-speech-september-7-2006/
Roubini N, Mihm S (2010) Crisis economics: a crash course in the future of finance. Penguin, New York
Schneider F, Kirchgässner G (2009) Financial and world economic crisis: what did economists contribute? Public Choice 140(3):319–327
Schwarcz S (2011) Securitization and structured finance, Duke Law & Economics Center. Available via http://www.masonlec.org/wp-content/uploads/2011/03/SCHWARCZ_Encyclopedia-of-Financial-Globalization-Elsevier.pdf?phpMyAdmin=9xTewdhiqRDcmliZ7d4fdRpssn1
Taleb NN (2010) The black swan. Random House, New York
Wharton (2007) Subprime meltdown: who's to blame and how should we fix it? Available via http://knowledge.wharton.upenn.edu/article/subprime-meltdown-whos-to-blame-and-how-should-we-fix-it/

Chapter 4
The Run on Repo and the Policy Interventions to Struggle the Great Crisis

Beniamino Moro

4.1 Introduction

As mentioned in Chaps. 1 and 3, a banking panic occurred in the USA in 2007 due to the shock to subprime mortgage values caused by house prices falling, which confirmed that uninsured bank debt is vulnerable to panic (Moro 2012, 2013).

The panic also caused a run on sale and repurchase (repo) market that was called a "run on repo". Understanding that the current Great Crisis is originated, as in the past, by a banking panic is essential to understand the dynamics of financial crises and to design regulation of the financial system.

After occurring in the USA, fears of insolvency caused a run on repo also in Europe, which reduced European interbank lending. The subsequent crisis reduced the pool of assets accepted as collateral, resulting in a liquidity shortage.

The core of the problem is the emergence in the last 35 years of the shadow banking system, which recreated the conditions for a panic. Shadow banking is, in fact, unregulated banking. Thus, it is riskier than conventional banking in that it recreates the kind of financial vulnerability that made the Great Depression possible.

In this chapter we deal with the run on repo followed by the American crisis of 2007–2009 and its successive extension to the repo market also in Europe. The chapter is organized as follows: Section 4.2 deals with the role of sale and repurchase market, while Sect. 4.3 analyzes the securitization process. Section 4.4 is dedicated to the demand for collateral and the rise of the repo market in the period preceding the explosion of the crisis. Section 4.5 deals with managerial compensation schemes and the pricing of risk, and finally Sect. 4.6 deals with fiscal

B. Moro (✉)
Department of Economics and Business, University of Cagliari, Viale San Ignazio 17, 09123 Cagliari, Italy
e-mail: moro@unica.it

B. Moro, V.A. Beker, *Modern Financial Crises*, Financial and Monetary Policy Studies 42, DOI 10.1007/978-3-319-20991-3_4

stimulus and monetary policy interventions employed to tackle the crisis. Finally, Sect. 4.7 concludes.

4.2 The Role of the Sale and Repurchase (Repo) Market

Usually, economists view the world as being the outcome of the "invisible hand", that is, a world where private decisions are unknowingly guided by prices to allocate resources efficiently. The current financial crisis raises the question of how it is that we could get slapped in the face by the invisible hand (Gorton 2009, 2010).

What happened? Although the answer is not easy, most economists agree that at the core of the problem, there is the shadow banking system. That system was vulnerable to a banking panic, which started in the USA in August 2007.

The period since 1934, when deposit insurance was introduced in the USA, until the recent Great Crisis has been a period of quiescence. But, from a historical perspective, banking panics are the norm. The banking system changed over the last decades and this transformation recreated the conditions for a panic.

A banking panic means that the banking system is insolvent, that is, it cannot honor contractual obligations: there are no private agents who can buy the amount of assets necessary to recapitalize the banking system. When the banking system is insolvent, many markets stop functioning, and this leads to significant effects on the real economy.

Gorton and Pennacchi (1990) argue that the essential function of banking is to create a special kind of debt that is immune to adverse selection by privately informed traders (Holmström 2008). The leading example of this is demand deposits. More generally, this kind of debt is very liquid because its value rarely changes, and so it can be traded without fear that some people have secret information about the value of the debt.

If speculators can learn information that is private (only they know it), then they can take advantage of the less informed in trade. This is not a problem if the value of the security is not sensitive to such information. This "informationally insensitive" debt originally was limited to demand deposits.

Anyway, demand deposits are of no use to large firms, banks, hedge funds, and corporate treasuries, which may need to deposit large amounts of money for a short period of time. These needs are satisfied by the sale and repurchase (repo) market where large amounts of money can be deposited with a bank and collateralized with bonds, which the depositor receives and that he can use elsewhere.

Further, repo is short term, like demand deposits, and it can be withdrawn at any time, like demand deposits. The bank backs the deposits with bonds as collateral, and often that collateral was securitized products, that is, bonds issued by special purpose vehicles (SPV) to finance portfolios of loans. The demand for collateral grew to include securitized products because of the growing need for collateral in the repo banking system, for collateralizing derivatives positions, and for use for settlement purposes (Gorton 2009).

Repo is essentially depository banking, built around informationally insensitive debt. In a repo transaction, one side of the transaction wants to borrow money and the other side wants to save money by depositing it somewhere safe.[1]

Think of the borrowers as a bank and the lender as a depositor that happens to be a corporation, a bank, insurance company, pension fund, institutional investor, or hedge fund. The depositor receives a bond as collateral for his deposit. When the depositor deposits money, the collateral may involve a "haircut" or margin. The haircut is the percentage difference between the market value of the pledged collateral and the amount of funds lent. For example, a haircut of 5 % means that a bank can borrow $95 for each $100 in pledged collateral.

The size of the haircut reflects the credit risk of the borrower and the riskiness of the pledged collateral. Another important feature of repo is that the collateral can be re-hypothecated. In other words, the collateral received by the depositor can be used or spent in another transaction, i.e., it can be used to collateralize a transaction with another party. Intuitively, re-hypothecation is tantamount to conducting transactions with the collateral received against the deposit.

Historically, only banks and the government could create informationally insensitive debt, but the demand for such debt has grown significantly. Now there is a range of securities with different information sensitivities. The notion of "informationally insensitive" debt corresponds to the institutions that surround debt, as distinct from equity.

Equity is very informationally sensitive. It is traded on centralized exchanges and individual stocks are followed by analysts. Because debt is senior and because securitized debt is backed by portfolios, senior tranches of securitizations are informationally insensitive, though not riskless like demand deposits.

Informationally insensitive debt does not need extensive institutional infrastructure, like equity. So, for example, the job of rating agencies need not be as in depth as equity analysts (Gorton and Pennacchi 1993; Gorton and Souleles 2006). Intuitively, informationally insensitive debt is debt that no one need devote a lot of time and resources to investigate. It is exactly designed to avoid that, just as consumers do not spend a lot of time doing due diligence on the bank that is holding the money of someone buying something from you.

[1] Does demand for safety create instability? Matta and Perotti (2015) answer to this question arguing that secured (repo) funding can be made so safe that it never runs but shifts risk to unsecured creditors. They show that this triggers more frequent runs by unsecured creditors, even in the absence of fundamental risk. This effect is separate from the liquidation externality caused by fire sales of seized collateral upon default. As more secured debt causes larger fire sales, it leads to higher haircuts which further increase the frequency of runs. While secured funding combined with high-yield unsecured debt may reduce instability, the private choice of repo funding always increases it. Regulators need to contain its reinforcing effect on liquidity risk, trading off its role in expanding funding by creating a safe asset.

A "systemic shock" to the financial system is an event that causes such debt to become *informationally sensitive*, that is, subject to adverse selection because the shock creates sufficient uncertainty as to make speculation profitable.

According to Gorton (2009), the current crisis has its roots in the transformation of the banking system, which involved two important changes. First, derivative securities have grown exponentially in the last 35 years, and this has created an enormous demand for collateral, i.e., informationally insensitive debt. Second, there has been the movement of massive amounts of loans originated by banks into the capital markets in the form of securitization and loan sales.

Securitization involves the issuance of bonds (tranches) that came to be used extensively as collateral in sale and repo transactions, freeing other categories of assets, mostly treasuries, for use as collateral for derivative transactions and for use in settlement systems.

Repo is a form of banking in that it involves the deposit of money on call (as repo is short term, e.g., mostly over night) backed by collateral. The current panic centered on the repo market, which suffered a run when depositors required increasing haircuts, due to concerns about the value and liquidity of the collateral should the counterparty bank fail. Therefore, in order to fully understand the present global financial crisis, it is important to agree that the shadow banking system is, in fact, banking.[2]

4.3 The Shadow Banking System and the Securitization Process

There is a widespread agreement that one of the key factors of the crisis was the lack of a regulatory framework regarding the shadow banking system, derivatives, and off-balance sheet financing.[3] Financial deregulation and liberalization have amplified the scope for speculation. In other cases, laws were changed or enforcement weakened in parts of the financial system.[4]

[2] This interpretation of the shadow banking system is extensively developed by Gorton (2009), Gorton and Metrick (2009b, 2012a), and Gorton and Ordonez (2012).

[3] The shadow banking system includes all financial institutions such as money market funds, investment banks, hedge funds, insurance companies, mortgage companies, government-sponsored enterprises, and other financial intermediaries involved in facilitating the creation of credit across the global financial system, but whose members are not subject to regulatory oversight. The shadow banking system also refers to unregulated activities by regulated institutions, such as over-the-counter (OTC) derivatives and particularly credit default swaps (CDS). The essence of this term is to differentiate between those parts of the financial system that are visible to regulators and under their direct control and those which are not.

[4] The process of banking deregulation that much contributed to the crisis began in October 1982, when President Ronald Reagan signed into Law the Garn-St. Germain Depository Institutions Act. In November 1999, President Bill Clinton signed into Law the Gramm–Leach–Bliley Act, which repealed part of the Glass–Steagall Act of 1933. This repeal has been criticized for reducing the

Financial institutions in the shadow banking system are not subject to the same regulations as depository banks, allowing them to assume additional debt obligations relative to their financial cushion or capital base. These entities were vulnerable because they borrowed short term in liquid markets to purchase long-term, illiquid, and risky assets. This meant that disruptions in credit markets would make them subject to rapid deleveraging, selling their long-term assets at depressed prices.

Paul Krugman described the run on the shadow banking system as the "core of what happened" to cause the crisis.

> As the shadow banking system expanded to rival or even surpass conventional banking in importance, politicians and government officials should have realized that they were re-creating the kind of financial vulnerability that made the Great Depression possible, and they should have responded by extending regulations and the financial safety net to cover these new institutions. Influential figures should have proclaimed a simple rule: anything that does what a bank does, anything that has to be rescued in crises the way banks are, should be regulated like a bank.

He referred to this lack of controls as "malign neglect" (Krugman 2009, 162–3).

Contrary to Krugman's advices, regulators and accounting standard setters allowed depository banks to move significant amounts of assets and liabilities off-balance sheet into complex legal entities called structured investment vehicles (SIV), masking the weakness of the capital base of the firm or degree of leverage or risk taken.

According to Greespan (2010, 20), inhibiting irrational behavior when it can be identified, through regulation, as recent history has demonstrated, could be stabilizing. But, there is an inevitable cost of regulation in terms of economic growth and standards of living when it imposes restraints beyond containing unproductive behavior. Regulation by its nature imposes restraints on competitive markets.

The elusive point of balance between growth and stability has always been a point of contention, especially when it comes to financial regulation. According to Strahan (2003, 111), deregulation was followed by better performance of the real economy. State economies grew faster and had higher rates of new business formation after this deregulation. At the same time macroeconomic stability improved.

The whole derivatives market was never regulated.[5] How was that possible? Following Gorton and Pennacchi (1990, 1993), we can say that banks created

---

separation between commercial banks, which traditionally had a conservative culture, and investment banks, which had a more risk-taking culture. Finally, in 2004, the Securities and Exchange Commission relaxed the net capital rule, which enabled investment banks to substantially increase the level of debt they were taking on. The role of institutions in explaining the recent financial crisis is analyzed by Shachmurove (2012).

[5] With the advice of the president's Working Group on Financial Markets, the Commodity Futures Modernization Act of 2000 allowed the self-regulation of the over-the-counter (OTC) derivatives market. Knight (2008) highlighted the key features of the turmoil as follows: the lack of transparency in the originate-to-distribute model (see the following footnote 6); the role played by credit rating agencies in the evaluation of structured products; and the covert reliance on special

liquidity by producing securities which were informationally insensitive. These bonds were not subject to adverse selection when traded because it was not profitable to produce private information to speculate on them. In the extreme, these securities were valued riskless, like insured demand deposits (Dang et al. 2009).

Shadow banking corresponds to the process of creating this type of debt. Clearly, if the debt is a claim on a diversified portfolio, like a portfolio of bank loans, this is made easier. But, this portfolio need not reside at a regulated commercial bank. A firm, however, may be financed by issuing securities that are claims on the general credit of the corporation, that is, they are backed by the assets of the company (bonds), or the firm can finance itself by segregating specified cash flows and selling claims specifically linked to these specified cash flows.

The latter strategy is accomplished by setting up another company, called a special purpose vehicle (SPV) or special purpose entity (SPE), and then selling the specified cash flows to this company. The SPV, in turn, issues securities into the capital market to finance the purchase of the cash flows from the company (called the "sponsor"). The sponsor services the cash flows, that is, makes sure that the cash flows are arriving. The SPV is not an operating company in the usual sense. It is more of a robot company in that it is a set of rules, without employees or physical location. This process is called securitization.

Securitization involves seniority and large portfolios. Figure 4.1 shows the general process of securitization, that is, how the cash flows from assets (loans) created by an originating firm are sold to a special purpose vehicle, which finances

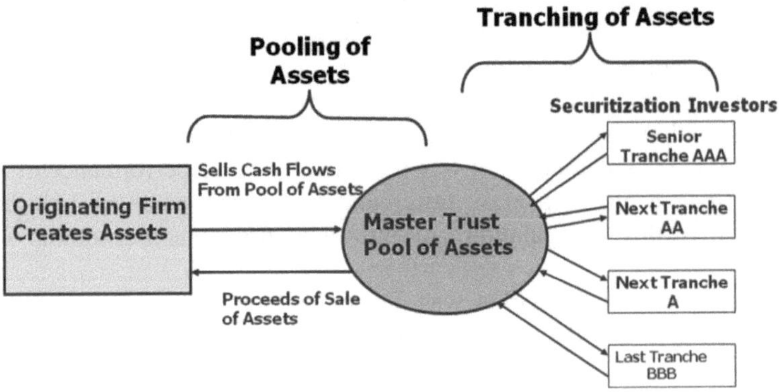

Fig. 4.1 The tranching mechanism (*Source* Gorton 2009)

purpose vehicles to conduct off-balance sheet financial transactions on a large scale. The effect of all these influences was that when the "Minsky moment" came, perceptions of risky exposures, both to credit losses and to liquidity shortages, rose sharply, as did uncertainty about where those exposures might materialize. The "Minsky moment" refers to Minsky's (1982) conviction that a new financial crisis was going to happen since the 1980s. On financial innovation, see Merton (1992), Tufano (2004), and Lerner (2006).

this by issuing securities in the capital markets. These securities are based on seniority and are called "tranches".

As shown in the figure, securitization involves two conceptual steps. First, underlying cash flows from assets are put into a pool. In other words, the specific assets that are generating the cash flows, usually loans of some sort, are identified and sold to the SPV (often its legal structure is a Master Trust).

The second conceptual step in securitization is that the pool of cash flows sold to the SPV is tranched, that is, securities with different seniorities are designed and issued against the pool. Another way to say this is that the SPV has to have a capital structure, so its liability side must be designed. This is called tranching (Gorton and Souleles 2006; Gorton 2009; Brunnermeier 2009).

According to Gorton (2009), securitized asset classes, e.g., mortgages, credit card receivables, and auto loans, may be examples of relatively informationally insensitive debt, created by the private sector without government insurance. Several features make securitization debt potentially immune from adverse selection. First, most of the debt is senior and investment grade. Second, with securitization, the debt is backed by portfolios. Third, a by-product of many structured products is that they are complex, as explained by Gorton (2008).

Complexity raises the cost of producing private information. Finally, securitization does not involve traded equity; this is important because there is no information leakage or externalities from the equity market, as with corporate bonds. In summary, senior tranches of securitizations are informationally insensitive, though not riskless like demand deposits. The most senior tranches of securitization transactions have never experienced defaults.

The banking model in which loans are pooled, tranched, and then resold via securitization is defined as the "originate-to-distribute" model, as opposed to the traditional banking model in which the issuing banks hold loans until their maturity, when they are repaid. This is known as the "originate-to-hold" model (Brunnermeier 2009; Hull 2009; Gorton and Metrick 2012b).[6]

[6] Gorton (2009, 2010) strongly disagrees with the "originate-to-distribute" explanation of the crisis, which places the blame on the misaligned incentives of the underwriters, who believed they had little exposure to risk, on the rating agencies, which did not properly represent risk to investors, and on a decline in lending standards which allowed increasingly poor loans to be made. Here Gorton becomes much less convincing, especially in light of later information, and he argues as if proponents of the originate-to-distribute explanation are directly attacking the general process of securitization itself. But there is little in Gorton's account to suggest that the originate-to-distribute explanation is excluded by the asymmetric information hypothesis. Simply because many lenders went under after the fact does not mean that their incentives were necessarily aligned correctly beforehand. However, there is some anecdotal evidence to suggest that a number of the most troubled financial institutions ran into difficulties in 2007–2008 precisely because they did not distribute all of the securitized debt they created, but kept a significant portion on their own balance sheets instead (Lo 2012, 10).

4.4 The Demand for Collateral and the Rise of Repo Market: The Explosion of the Crisis

Collateral is the currency for firms, that is, firms need to post collateral to mitigate default risk but also obtain collateral that can be reused. "Posting collateral" is a way to make good on a promise to pay, as long as the collateral does not lose value, while it is posted to the counterparty. Collateral is almost synonymous with informationally insensitive debt, although obviously there are degrees of sensitivity. The use of collateral has expanded rapidly in the last 20 years. This is due, in large part, to the use of bilateral collateral agreements to address counterparty risk.

There is a huge demand for collateral. Financial firms, e.g., dealer banks and commercial banks, have large needs for collateral, and this has grown to an enormous extent. First, collateral is needed in repo markets, where the transaction involves the deposit of cash in exchange for a bond as collateral. Second, collateral is also needed in derivatives markets, where it is used to offset counterparty credit risk. Finally, collateral is needed in payment and settlement systems (Bank for International Settlements 2001; Singh and Stella 2012).

Anyway, the largest demands for collateral come from the repo market. Creation of informationally insensitive debt is the function of the banking system. In the regulated bank sector, this corresponds to insured demand deposits. The characteristics of demand deposits are (1) they have no fixed maturity, that is, they can be exchanged for cash at par on demand; (2) they are senior claims; (3) they are claims on a portfolio; and (4) they can be used in transactions.

This form of debt is created by depository institutions and by money market mutual funds that offer checking. Shadow banking combines repo with securitization (or other forms of informationally insensitive debt) to accomplish the same function for firms. Senior tranches of securitized debt and commercial paper are also quite informationally insensitive. The shadow banking system, the combination of repo and securitized debt, is a kind of bank, as follows: (1) repo has a short maturity, it is typically overnight and can be withdrawn (not rolled over) on demand; (2) it is senior in that the collateral is senior but also senior in the sense that there may be a haircut (Gorton and Metrick 2009a) on the collateral; (3) repo collateral is backed by a portfolio if the collateral is securitization-based debt; and (4) the collateral can be used in other transactions, i.e., it can be re-hypothecated (Gorton 2009).

The shadow banking system is different than depository institutions in that the activity involves the repo market, where depositors and lenders are individually matched; each depositor gets his own collateral. So, the shadow banking system involves a market, the repo market. Securitization enters via the need for collateral.

If securitization debt is informationally insensitive, it can be an input into the repo system of creating a kind of transaction medium, i.e., collateral that can be re-hypothecated. Therefore, we can say that the shadow banking system is, in fact, an integral part of the banking system, although it is not regulated as commercial banks. The depositors (lenders) are firms seeking a place to save cash in the short term, often money market funds. The borrowers are financial firms seeking cash to finance themselves.

The deposits are designed to be informationally insensitive by backing them with informationally insensitive collateral. Often that collateral is securitization bond. The collateral can be spent or re-hypothecated. Depositors can withdraw their funds by not rolling over their repo agreements and returning the bond, or they can withdraw by increasing the haircut on the collateral. This is depository banking in a different form but banking nevertheless. Like demand deposits at regulated commercial banks, this system is vulnerable to panic (Gorton 2009).

The Great Crisis began in the USA with a shock in the subprime mortgage market, where subprime mortgages were used to create mortgage-backed securities (MBS), and those securities were used to create collateral debt obligations (CDO).[7] A CDO is a type of bond based on portfolios of other bonds such as mortgages, auto loans, student loans, or credit card receivables. These underlying assets serve as collateral for the CDOs.

In the event of default, the bondholders become owners of the collateral. As explained in Sect. 4.3, because CDOs have different classes of priority known as "tranches", their risk/reward characteristics can be very different from one tranche to the next, even if the collateral assets are relatively homogeneous.

The shock began with the popping of the housing bubble in 2006: house prices flattened and then began to decline.[8] Refinancing a mortgage became impossible, and mortgage delinquency rates rose. The products that were created by the securitization of mortgages lacked transparency, with the payoffs from one product depending on the performance of many other products. Market participants relied on the AAA ratings assigned to products without evaluating the models used by rating agencies (Hull 2009).

The opaqueness of the structures of the mortgage-backed securities delayed the unraveling of the bubble. No one knew what was going to happen—or rather, many people thought they knew, but no single view dominated the market. As a device for aggregating information, the market was very slow to come up with an answer in this case.

When the answer came to the market, structured investment vehicles and related conduits, which held a sixth of the highest-quality rating CDO tranches, simply stopped rolling over their short-term debt. This was not due to overexposure in the subprime market. Gorton (2009) estimates that only two percent of structured

[7] The term "subprime" refers to the credit quality of the mortgage borrower as determined by various consumer credit rating bureaus. The highest-quality borrowers are referred to as "prime"; hence the term "prime rate" refers to the interest rate charged on loans to such low-default-risk individuals. Accordingly, "subprime" borrowers have lower credit scores and are more likely to default than prime borrowers.

[8] Haavio et al. (2013) empirically study the linkages between financial variable downturns and economic recessions and present evidence that real asset prices tend to lead real cycles. They document that downturns in real asset prices, particularly real house prices, are useful leading indicators of economic recessions.

investment vehicle holdings were subprime. Rather, investors could not penetrate the portfolios far enough to make the determination, because there was asymmetric information.

At each step in the chain, one side knew significantly more than the other about the underlying structure of the securities involved (Hull 2009). At the top of the chain, an investor might know absolutely nothing about the hundreds of thousands of mortgages several layers below the derivative being traded, and in normal situations, this does not matter.

In a crisis, however, it clearly does. The rational investor will want to avoid risk, but, as Gorton analogizes, the riskier mortgages in mortgage-backed securities had been intermingled like salmonella-tainted frosting among a very small batch of cakes that have been randomly mixed with all the other cakes in the factory and then shipped to bakeries throughout the country. To continue the analogy, the collapse of the structured investment vehicle market, and the consequent stall in the repurchase market, represented the market recalling the contaminated cakes (Lo 2012, 9).[9]

Here the story becomes more familiar to the history of financial crises. Dislocation in the repo market was the first stage of a much broader liquidity crunch. Short-term lending rates between banks rose dramatically, almost overnight, in August 2007, as banks became more uncertain about which of their counterparties might be holding the cakes with tainted frosting and possibly shut down by food inspectors, i.e., which banks might be insolvent because of declines in the market value of their assets. Fears of insolvency will naturally reduce interbank lending, and this run on repo caused temporary disruptions in the pricing system of short-term debt markets, an important source of funding for many financial institutions (Gorton and Metrick 2009b, 2010, 2012c). The subsequent crisis has reduced the pool of assets considered acceptable as collateral, resulting in a liquidity shortage (Singh and Stella 2012). Concerns about the liquidity of markets for the bonds used as collateral led to increases in repo haircuts. With declining asset values and increasing haircuts, the US banking system was effectively insolvent for the first time since the Great Depression (Gorton and Metrick 2010).

In retrospect, the events in August 2007 were just a warm-up act for the main event that occurred in September 2008 when Lehman Brothers failed, triggering a much more severe run on repo in its aftermath. Gorton believes that the regulatory insistence of mark-to-market pricing, even in a market with little to no liquidity, exacerbated the crisis.[10] Certainly there was a substantial premium between mark-

[9] Gorton actually uses analogy of *E. coli*—tainted beef in millions of pounds of perfectly good hamburger.

[10] "Mark-to-market pricing" is the practice of updating the value of a financial asset to reflect the most recent market transaction price. For illiquid assets that do not trade actively, marking such assets to market can be quite challenging, particularly if the only transactions that have occurred are fire sales in which certain investors are desperate to rid themselves of such assets and sell them at substantial losses. This has the effect of causing all others who hold similar assets to recognize similar losses when they are forced to mark such assets to market, even if they have no intention of selling these assets (Lo 2012, 10).

to-market values and those calculated by actuarial methods. These lowered asset prices then had a feedback effect on further financing, since the assets now had much less value as collateral, creating a vicious circle.

4.5 Managerial Compensation Schemes and the Pricing of Risk

According to many commentators, a key role in the American crisis was also supposed to be played by managerial compensation schemes and the associated leaks in corporate governance. Compensation contracts—they say—were too focused on short-term trading profits rather than long-term incentives.

But, in a study of the executive compensation contracts at 95 banks, Fahlenbrach and Stulz (2011) conclude that CEOs aggregate stock and option holdings were more than eight times the value of their annual compensation, and the amount of their personal wealth at risk prior to the financial crisis makes it improbable that the rational CEO knew in advance of an impending financial crash or knowingly engaged in excessively risky behavior (Lo 2012).[11]

Furthermore, the rating agencies failed to signal the real risk associated to each financial product (Utzig 2010; Hull 2009). The central activity of financial industry is creating and trading assets of uncertain value, while the liabilities in the case of banks are guaranteed by the state. They are highly leveraged businesses: leverage of 30 to 1 was and still remains normal in most financial institutions, including banks, but higher leverage is not rare. Anyway, empirical data show that the leverage of investment banks was very high since the end of the 1990s, and in the cases of Goldman Sachs, Merrill Lynch, and Leman Brothers it was greater in 1998 than it was in 2007 at the brink of the financial crisis (Lo 2012).

The pricing of risk refers to the incremental compensation required by investors for taking on additional risk, which may be measured by interest rates or fees. For a

[11] Bebchuk and Spamann (2010) and Bhagat and Bolton (2013) seek to make some contributions to understand how banks' executive pay has produced incentives for excessive risk taking and how such pay should be reformed. In the case of Bear Stearns and Lehman Brothers, Bebchuk et al. (2009) argued that their CEOs cashed out hundreds of millions of dollars of company stock from 2000 to 2008; hence the remaining amount of equity they owned in their respective companies toward the end may not have been sufficiently large to have had an impact on their behavior. Nevertheless, in an extensive empirical study of major banks and broker–dealers before, during, and after the financial crisis, Murphy (2012) concludes that the Wall Street culture of low base salaries and outsized bonuses of cash, stock, and options actually reduces risk-taking incentives, not unlike the so-called fulcrum fee in which portfolio managers have to pay back a portion of their fees if they underperform (Lo 2012, 2). Finally, in a recent paper Edmans and Gabaix (2015) study traditional and modern theories of executive compensation, bringing them together under a unifying framework. They analyze assignment models of the level of pay, and static and dynamic moral hazard models of incentives, and compare their predictions to empirical findings.

variety of reasons, market participants did not accurately measure the risk inherent with financial innovation such as mortgage-backed securities (MBS) and collateral debt obligations (CDO) or understand its impact on the overall stability of the financial system (Hull 2009). These massive, practically unthinkable, losses have dramatically impacted the balance sheets of banks and insurance companies across the globe, leaving them with very little capital to continue operations.[12]

Another cause of the disaster was the large use of Li's formula, known as a Gaussian copula function, in pricing any kind of assets risk. This formula looked like an unambiguously positive breakthrough, a piece of financial technology that allowed hugely complex risks to be moderated with more ease and accuracy than ever before. Li made it possible for traders to sell vast quantities of new securities, expanding financial markets to unimaginable levels. This formula assumed that the price of credit default swaps (CDS) was correlated with and could predict the correct price of mortgage-backed securities. Because it was highly tractable, it rapidly came to be used by a huge percentage of CDO and CDS investors, issuers, and rating agencies.

Li's formula was adopted by everybody, from bond investors and Wall Street banks to rating agencies and regulators, and became so deeply intertwined that warnings about its limitations were largely ignored.[13] As financial assets became more and more complex and harder and harder to value, investors were reassured by the fact that both the international bond rating agencies and bank regulators, who came to rely on them, accepted as valid some complex mathematical models which theoretically showed that the risks were much smaller than they actually proved to be in practice (Hull 2009).

Similarly, the rating agencies relied on the information provided by the originators of synthetic products. It was a shocking abdication of responsibility. Li's Gaussian copula formula will go down in history as instrumental in causing the unfathomable losses that brought the world financial system to its knees. Anyway, what is important to stress here is that all these causes contributed to make systemic the level of risk in financial markets. In this regard, Brunnermeier et al. (2011) emphasize that systemic risk: first, cannot be detected based on measuring cash

[12] Farmer et al. (2012) demonstrate that financial markets, by their nature, cannot be Pareto efficient, except by chance. Although individuals are rational, they show that it is sufficient to assume heterogeneity in agent's subjective discount factor to conclude that markets are not Pareto efficient.

[13] For decades credit rating agencies were viewed as trusted arbiters of creditworthiness and their ratings as important tools for managing risk. The common narrative is that the value of ratings was compromised by the evolution of the industry to a form where issuers pay for ratings. Cole and Cooley (2014) show how credit ratings have value in equilibrium and how reputation insures that, in equilibrium, ratings will reflect sound assessments of credit worthiness. There will always be an information distortion because of the fact that purchasers of ratings need not reveal them. Cole and Cooley argue that regulatory reliance on ratings and the increasing importance of risk-weighted capital in prudential regulation have more likely contributed to distorted ratings than the matter of who pays for them. In this respect, they conclude that much of the regulatory obsession with the conflict created by issuers paying for ratings is a distraction.

instruments, e.g., balance sheet items or ratios such as leverage and income statement items; second, typically builds up in the background before materializing in a crisis; and, third, is determined by market participants' endogenous response to various shocks.

4.6 Fiscal Stimulus and Monetary Policy Interventions to Struggle the Crisis

The American crisis hit its peak in September and October 2008. Several major institutions either failed, were acquired under duress, or were subject to government takeover. The crisis rapidly developed and spread into a global economic shock, resulting in a number of European bank failures, declines in various stock indexes, and large reductions in the market value of equities and commodities. Both MBS and CDO were purchased by corporate and institutional investors globally. Derivatives such as CDS also increased the linkage between large financial institutions. Moreover, the deleveraging of financial institutions, as assets were sold to pay back obligations that could not be refinanced in frozen credit markets, further accelerated the liquidity crisis.

World political leaders, national ministers of finance, and central banks coordinated their efforts to reduce fears (Fraher and Kennedy 2008). At the end of October 2008, a currency crisis developed, with investors transferring vast capital resources into stronger currencies such as the euro, the yen, the dollar, and the Swiss franc, leading many emerging economies to seek aid from the IMF.[14] The US Federal Reserve and central banks around the world expanded money supplies to avoid the risk of a deflationary spiral. In addition, governments enacted large fiscal stimulus packages, by borrowing and spending to offset the reduction in private sector demand caused by the crisis.

The USA executed two stimulus packages, totaling nearly $1 trillion during 2008 and 2009. Governments have also bailed out a variety of firms as discussed above, incurring large financial obligations. Various US government agencies have

[14] Financial crises are often associated with significant movements in exchange rates, which reflect both increasing risk aversion and changes in the perceived risk of investing in certain currencies. Kohler (2010) explains why exchange rate movements during the global financial crisis of 2007–2009 were unusual. Unlike in two previous episodes—the Asian crisis of 1997–1998 and the crisis following the Russian debt default in 1998—in 2008 many countries that were not at the center of the crisis saw their currencies depreciate sharply. Such crisis-related movements reversed strongly for a number of countries. Two factors are likely to have contributed to these developments. First, during the latest crisis, safe haven effects went against the typical pattern of crisis-related flows. Second, interest rate differentials explain more of the crisis-related exchange rate movements in 2008–2009 than in the past. This probably reflects structural changes in the determinants of exchange rate dynamics such as the increased role of carry trade activity.

committed or spent trillions of dollars in loans, asset purchases, guarantees, and direct spending.[15]

The credit freeze brought the global financial system to the brink of collapse. The response of the US Federal Reserve, the European Central Bank, and other central banks was immediate and dramatic. During the last quarter of 2008, these central banks purchased $2.5 trillion of government debt and troubled private assets from banks. This was the largest liquidity injection into the credit market, and the largest monetary policy action, in world history. The governments of European nations and the USA also raised the capital of their national banking systems by $1.5 trillion, by purchasing newly issued preferred stock in their major banks (Altman 2009).

At the end of 2008, some analysts argued that the Fed was out of ammunition when overnight interest rates reached zero, but she continued to purchase assets and engaged in a quantitative easing policy.[16] From the beginning of 2009 until early December, the Fed, under the auspices of its Large-Scale Asset Purchase (LSAP) program, had bought approximately $300 billion in Treasury securities, $150 billion in debt securities of Fannie Mae and Freddie Mac, and $1.1 trillion of fixed rate mortgage-backed securities (MBS) guaranteed by Ginnie Mae, Fannie Mae, and Freddie Mac.

When completed, the Fed total assets will reach $2.6 trillion, and the Fed will own about one-fourth of the total outstanding amounts of Treasury and agency-guaranteed MBS.

The monetary base reached $2.4 trillion in 2010 and $3.1 trillion at the end of 2012. In December 2007, the monetary base was approximately $830 billion, with only 10–15 billion held by banks as deposits at the Fed (Bullard 2010). For a comparison, the Bank of England initiated quantitative easing in March 2009 and

[15] What happened in the USA during the 2007–2009 financial crisis is summerized by Carlson et al. (2015) as follows. There were severe reductions in the liquidity of financial markets, runs on the shadow banking system, and destabilizing defaults and near-defaults of major financial institutions. In response, the Federal Reserve, in its role as lender of last resort (LOLR), injected extraordinary amounts of liquidity. In the aftermath, lawmakers and regulators have taken steps to reduce the likelihood that such lending would be required in the future, including the introduction of liquidity regulations. These changes were motivated in part by the argument that central bank lending entails extremely high costs and should be made unnecessary by liquidity regulations. By contrast, some have argued that the loss of liquidity was the result of market failures, and that central banks could solve such failures by lending, making liquidity regulations unnecessary. They argue that LOLR lending and liquidity regulations are complementary tools. Liquidity shortfalls can arise for two very different reasons: first, sound institutions can face runs or a deterioration in the liquidity of markets they depend on for funding; second, solvency concerns can cause creditors to pull away from troubled institutions. Central bank lending is the best response in the former situation, while orderly resolution (by the institution as it gets through the problem on its own or via a controlled failure) is the best response in the second one.

[16] "Quantitative easing" is defined as a policy strategy by a Central Bank of seeking to reduce long-term interest rates by buying large quantities of financial assets when the overnight rate is near zero (Bullard 2010).

has purchased more than £175 billion in British Treasures; in 2010 it also holds more than one-quarter of all such securities outstanding (Bullard 2010).

4.7 Conclusions

The final effects of quantitative easing are not known. Economic theory has yet to develop macroeconomic models with financial sectors adequately detailed to explore channels through which quantitative easing might boost economic activity.

In fact, quantitative easing has a risk that the increased monetary base will fuel an undesirable large acceleration of credit expansion and, in turn, a large increase in inflation. Therefore, an important part of the monetary strategy must be the stabilization of inflation expectations.

All this leaves policymakers with an unenviable task: deciding when and how to withdraw from these extraordinarily stimulating fiscal and monetary policies. An "exit strategy" requires answers to three questions. First, timing: when should fiscal and monetary tightening begin? Second, tactics: is it more important to start by cutting budget deficits or by raising interest rates? Third, technique: how will central banks, with their balance sheets bloated by unconventional policies, respond to tightening monetary conditions?

References

Altman RC (2009) The great crash, 2008, Brooking Institution. Available via http://www.jmhinternational.com/news/news/selectednews/files/2009/01/20090201_20090101_Foreign%20Affairs_TheGreatCrash2008.pdf

Bank for International Settlements (2001) Collateral in wholesale financial markets: recent trends, risk management and market dynamics. Committee on the Global Financial System, March. Available via http://www.bis.org/publ/cgfs17.htm

Bebchuk L, Spamann H (2010) Regulating bankers' pay. Georgetown Law J 98:247–287

Bebchuk L, Cohen A, Spamann H (2009) The wages of failure: executive compensation at bear Stearns and Lehman 2000-2008. Harvard law and economics discussion paper no. 657, November. Available via http://papers.ssrn.com/sol3/papers.cfm?abstract_id=1513522

Bhagat S, Bolton B (2013) Bank executive compensation and capital requirements reform. Draft, May. Available via http://papers.ssrn.com/sol3/papers.cfm?abstract_id=1781318

Brunnermeier MK (2009) Deciphering the liquidity and credit crunch 2007-2008. J Econ Perspect 23(1):77–100

Brunnermeier MK, Gorton G, Krishnamurthy A (2011) Risk topography, draft, 31 May. Available via http://papers.ssrn.com/sol3/papers.cfm?abstract_id=1825124

Bullard J (2010) Quantitative easing: uncharted waters for monetary policy. Reg Econ 18(1)

Carlson MA, Duygan-Bump B, Nelson WR (2015) Why do we need both liquidity regulations and a lender of last resort? A perspective from federal reserve lending during the 2007–09 US financial crisis. BIS working paper no. 493, March. Available via http://papers.ssrn.com/sol3/papers.cfm?abstract_id=2575634

Cole HL, Cooley TF (2014) Rating agencies. NBER working paper no. 19972, March. Available via http://www.nber.org/papers/w19972
Dang TV, Gorton G, Holmström B (2009) Opacity and the optimality of debt for liquidity provision, draft, Nov 30. Available via https://www.google.it/webhp?sourceid=chrome-instant&ion=1&espv=2&ie=UTF-8#q=11.%20dang%20t.%20v.%2c%20g.%20gorton%20and%20b.%20holmstr%c3%b6m%20(2009)%2c%20%e2%80%9copacity%20and%20the%20optimality%20of%20debt%20for%20liquidity%20provision%e2%80%9d%2c%20draft%2c%20november%2030
Edmans A, Gabaix X (2015) Executive compensation: a modern primer. NBER working paper no. w21131, April. Available via http://papers.ssrn.com/sol3/papers.cfm?abstract_id=2602114
Fahlenbrach R, Stulz RM (2011) Bank CEO incentives and the credit crisis. J Financ Econ 99:11–26
Farmer REA, Nourry C, Venditti A (2012) The inefficient market hypothesis: why financial markets do not work well in the real world. NBER working paper no. 18647, December. Available via https://www.google.it/webhp?sourceid=chrome-instant&ion=1&espv=2&ie=UTF-8#q=Farmer+R.+E.+A.%2C+C.+Nourry+and+A.+Venditti+(2012)%2C+The+Inefficient+Market+Hypothesis:+Why+Financial+Markets+Do+Not+Work+Well+in+the+Real+World%2C+NBER+Working+Paper+No.+18647%2C+December
Fraher J, Kennedy S (2008) Central banks offer extra funds to calm money markets, Bloomberg.com, Sept 18. Available via http://www.bloomberg.com/apps/news?pid=20601087&refer=home&sid=ahBSRLQsJFzI#
Gorton G (2008) The panic of 2007. Maintaining stability in a changing financial system. In: Proceedings of the 2008 Jackson Hole conference, Federal Reserve Bank of Kansas City. Yale ICF working paper no. 08-24, August. Available via http://papers.ssrn.com/sol3/papers.cfm?abstract_id=1255362
Gorton G (2009) Slapped in the face by the invisible hand: banking and the panic of 2007. Prepared for the Federal Reserve Bank of Atlanta's 2009 financial markets conference: Financial innovation and crisis, May 11–13. Available via http://www.frbatlanta.org/news/CONFEREN/09fmc/gorton.pdf
Gorton G (2010) Slapped by the invisible hand: the panic of 2007. Oxford University Press, Oxford
Gorton G, Metrick A (2009a) Haircuts. NBER working paper no. 15273, August. Available via http://papers.ssrn.com/sol3/papers.cfm?abstract_id=1447438
Gorton G, Metrick A (2009b) The run on repo and the panic of 2007-2008. Yale working paper
Gorton G, Metrick A (2010) Securitized banking and the run on repo. Yale ICF working paper no. 09–14, November. Available via https://www.google.it/webhp?sourceid=chrome-instant&ion=1&espv=2&ie=UTF-8#q=Gorton+G.+and+A.+Metrick+(2009b)%2C+The+Run+on+Repo+and+the+Panic+of+2007-2008%2C+Yale+Working+Paper
Gorton G, Metrick A (2012a) Getting up to speed on the financial crisis: a one-weekend-reader's guide. NBER working paper no. 17778, January. Available via http://www.nber.org/papers/w17778.pdf?new_window=1
Gorton G, Metrick A (2012b) Securitization. NBER working paper no. W18611
Gorton G, Metrick A (2012c) Who ran on repo? NBER working paper no. w18455, October
Gorton G, Ordonez GL (2012) Collateral crises. NBER working paper no. 17771, January
Gorton G, Pennacchi G (1990) Financial intermediaries and liquidity creation. J Financ 45:49–72
Gorton G, Pennacchi G (1993) Security baskets and index-linked securities. J Bus 66(1):1–29
Gorton G, Souleles NS (2006) Special purpose vehicles and securitization. In: Stulz R, Carey M (eds) The risks of financial institutions. University of Chicago Press, Chicago
Greespan A (2010) The crisis, second draft, Mar 9. Available via http://www.brookings.edu/~/media/Files/Programs/ES/BPEA/2010_spring_bpea_papers/spring2010_greenspan.pdf
Haavio M, Mendicino C, Punzi MT (2013) Financial and economic downturns in OECD countries. Bank of Finland research discussion paper no. 35/2013, December. Available via http://www.suomenpankki.fi/en/julkaisut/tutkimukset/keskustelualoitteet/pages/dp2013_35.aspx

Holmström B (2008) Discussion of 'The Panic of 2007', by Gary Gorton. In: Proceedings of the 2008 Jackson Hole conference, maintaining stability in a changing financial system. Federal Reserve Bank of Kansas City

Hull JC (2009) The credit crunch of 2007: what went wrong? Why? What lessons can be learned? J Credit Risk 5(2):3–18

Knight MD (2008) Some reflections on the future of the originate-to-distribute model in the context of the current financial turmoil, speech at the Euro 50 group roundtable, London, Apr 21. Available via http://www.bis.org/speeches/sp080423.htm

Kohler M (2010) Exchange rates during financial crises. BIS Q Rev (March). Available via http://papers.ssrn.com/sol3/papers.cfm?abstract_id=1561579

Krugman P (2009) The return of depression economics and the crisis of 2008. Norton, New York

Lerner J (2006) The new new financial thing: the origins of financial innovations. J Financ Econ 79 (2):223–255

Lo AW (2012) Reading about the financial crisis: a 21-book review, draft, Jan 9. Available via http://papers.ssrn.com/sol3/papers.cfm?abstract_id=1949908

Matta R, Perotti EC (2015) Insecure debt. CEPR discussion paper no. DP10505, March. Available via http://papers.ssrn.com/sol3/papers.cfm?abstract_id=2584022

Merton R (1992) Financial innovation and economic performance. J Appl Corp Financ 4:12–22

Minsky H (1982) Can 'it' happen again? Sharpe, New York

Moro B (2012) The theoretical debate on the recent great crisis. J Italian Econ Assoc XVII(1):3–42

Moro B (2013) The run on repo and the liquidity shortage problems of the current global financial crisis: Europe vs. US. Ekonomi-tek 2(1):41–77

Murphy K (2012) Pay, politics and the financial crisis. In: Blinder A, Lo A, Solow R (eds) Economic lessons from the financial crisis. Russell Sage, New York

Shachmurove Y (2012) Falling institutions are at the core of the U.S. financial crisis. PIER working paper no. 12–040, Oct 17. Available via https://ideas.repec.org/p/pen/papers/12-041.html

Singh M, Stella P (2012) Money and collateral. IMF working paper no. 12/95, April. Available via https://books.google.it/books?hl=it&lr=&id=2C_udw17ebkC&oi=fnd&pg=PP2&dq=Singh+M.+and+P.+Stella+(2012),+%E2%80%9CMoney+and+Collateral%E2%80%9D,+IMF+Working+Paper+No.+12/95,+April.&ots=hJvKLXbu01&sig=bqhE4OMwwH62GdMcAjfNmYslMh8#v=onepage&q&f=false

Strahan P (2003) The real effects of bank deregulation. Fed Reserve Bank St Louis Econ Rev 85 (4):111–128

Tufano P (2004) Financial innovation. In: Constantinides G, Stulz R (eds) The handbook of the economics of finance. North Holland, Amsterdam

Utzig S (2010) The financial crisis and the regulation of credit rating agencies: a European banking perspective. ADBI working paper no. 188, January. Available via https://www.google.it/webhp?sourceid=chrome-instant&ion=1&espv=2&ie=UTF-8#q=47.%20utzig%20s.%20(2010)%2c%20%e2%80%9c%20the%20financial%20crisis%20and%20the%20regulation%20of%20credit%20rating%20agencies%3a%20a%20european%20banking%20perspective%e2%80%9d%2c%20adbi%20working%20paper%20no.%20188%2c%20january

Part IV
The European Public Debt Crisis

Chapter 5
From the American Financial Meltdown to the European Banking and Public Debt Crises

Beniamino Moro

5.1 Introduction

A relevant aspect of the global contagion is the extension of the Great Crisis to European countries' sovereign debts.[1] This extension represents the European counterpart to the American crisis. It began with Greece, but suddenly it spread over some other countries of the Eurozone, like Portugal, Ireland, Italy, and Spain (shortly indicated as the PIIGS countries). Lastly, on June 25, 2012, also Cyprus presented a formal request to euro area member states for external financial assistance.

The risk of contagion in sovereign debts is not confined to some euro countries, but it could extend to the world's biggest economies like the UK, Japan, and the USA. The problem is that the expansionary fiscal policies of deficit spending implemented by most states to tackle the crisis have created very large deficits, which are difficult to adjust in the next years. According to McKibbin et al. (2012), the emergence of substantial fiscal deficits and a large buildup of government debt in major advanced economies will inevitably lead to a period of fiscal consolidation in coming years.

---

[1] Forbes (2012) surveys and assesses the academic literature on defining, measuring, and identifying financial contagion and the various channels by which it can occur, highlighting contagion risks in the euro area. More in general, Das et al. (2012) discuss some salient features embedded in the current generation of sovereign asset and liability management approaches, including objectives, definitions of relevant assets and liabilities, and methodologies used in obtaining optimal outcomes. The European public debt problems are also analyzed by Driffill (2013) and reviewed from an empirical point of view by Tomz and Wright (2013).

B. Moro (✉)
Department of Economics and Business, University of Cagliari, Viale San Ignazio 17, 09123 Cagliari, Italy
e-mail: moro@unica.it

B. Moro, V.A. Beker, *Modern Financial Crises*, Financial and Monetary Policy Studies 42, DOI 10.1007/978-3-319-20991-3_5

Anyway, since 2010 until 2014, the new focus of turbulence was Europe, who faced a severe economic and financial crisis. It is often described as a sovereign debt crisis, but in fact it was really a sequence of interactions between sovereign problems and banking problems (Moro 2014).[2] Yet in 2015, we are not sure that the crisis is completely overcome.

This chapter analyzes the transition of the crisis from the American turmoil to the European counterpart. It is organized as follows. Section 5.2 deals with the shift of the Great Crisis into a European twin sovereign debt and banking crisis. Section 5.3 focuses on which country was responsible for triggering the European meltdown. Section 5.4 deals with the mispricing of sovereign risk by financial markets in the years before the triggering of the crisis. Section 5.5 illustrates the misalignment of internal real exchange rates among European countries and the ensuing balance-of-payment crisis. Section 5.6 clears the link between TARGET2 positions and EMU countries' balance of payments, while Sect. 5.7 demonstrates that large increases in TARGET2 liabilities are mostly related to capital flights. Finally, Sect. 5.8 concludes.

5.2 The Shift of the Great Crisis into a European Twin Sovereign Debt and Banking Crisis

The sovereign debt crisis has been directly linked to the global financial crisis and the ensuing problems of European countries' banking sector after the bankruptcy of Lehman Brothers. With deteriorating public finances, sovereign risk has increased and worsened bank's balance sheets.[3] In fact, as public debt approached sustainability limits in PIIGS countries, a high bank exposure to sovereign risk gave rise to a fragile interdependence between fiscal and bank solvency and so the possibility of a self-fulfilling crisis. Therefore, the European situation is best described as twin sovereign and banking crises that mutually feed each other, and the result of this interaction is a gradual contagion to more countries and more asset classes (Balteanu and Erce 2014; Adler 2012; Véron 2011; Correa and Sapriza 2014; Kollintzas and Tsoukalas 2015; Fratzscher and Rieth 2015).[4]

---

[2] Kollintzas and Tsoukalas (2015) study bank risk and sovereign risk interdependence in the euro area and find that an increase in capital investment risk shock results in a considerably deeper recession when sovereign risk is also present.

[3] In the euro area, the shadow banking system is less developed than in the USA (Bakk-Simon et al. 2011). This explains why European financial crisis follows some years later than in the USA.

[4] The mutation of the original financial crisis into a sovereign debt one in the euro area countries is investigated by Candelon and Palm (2010) and De Grauwe (2010). More in general, Sturm and Sauter (2010) analyze the impact of the crisis on Mediterranean countries, while Wyplosz (2010) compares the US and the European situations during the crisis and examines how much of the crisis has been imported by Europe from the USA. The paper argues that Europe never had a chance to avoid contagion from the USA. On the other side, a comparison between Japanese and

The origins of the European debt crisis can be directly traced back to the global financial crisis of 2008–2009, which spilled over into a sovereign debt crisis in several euro area countries in early 2010. To offset sharp falls in output, euro area governments (as governments in the rest of the world) responded with counter-cyclical fiscal policies that increased fiscal deficits.

Moreover, fiscal positions worsened as tax revenues declined and transfer payments grew larger due to rising unemployment during the crisis. In many countries, government bailouts of banking systems also contributed to an increase in public debt. Private debt became public debt, be it through banking crises or the burst of housing bubbles, leading to sovereign crisis.[5]

The debt crisis in several member states of the euro area has raised doubts about the viability of the European Economic and Monetary Union (EMU) and the future of the euro (Schmidt and Weigert 2013). The crisis has highlighted the problems and tensions that will inevitably arise within a monetary union when imbalances build up and become unsustainable (Volz 2012).

As far as banking crises are concerned, it had been understood that they could occur also within EMU. But what was not understood was that the combination of strong interdependence between banks and sovereigns and the absence of a lender of last resort for sovereigns made euro area countries particularly prone to such crises. The potential severity of what would become known as the "doom loop" was not foreseen. Furthermore, the EU relied on a rather loose framework of cooperation between national authorities and lacked a comprehensive template for dealing with cross border issues (Pisani-Ferri et al. 2013).

The generally prevailing view was that sovereign debt crises—also because of the prohibition of monetary financing—could occur. A substantial body of literature had emphasized that sovereign solvency would be a concern in a monetary union and that crises had to be prevented through fiscal surveillance. But no framework existed for such an eventuality and its potentially serious consequences (Eichengreen and Wyplosz 1998).[6]

European crises is made by Schnabl (2013), who argues that Europe may stand at the beginning of a persistent lingering crisis as it is observed in Japan since more than two decades. Finally, the strong relation existing between the soundness of the public budgets and the international financial stability for the Italian case is illustrated by Banca d'Italia (2010) and Albertazzi et al. (2012).

[5] Jordà et al. (2013) examine the coevolution of public and private sector debt in advanced countries since 1870 and find that in advanced economies, significant financial stability risks have mostly come from private sector credit booms rather than from the expansion of public debt. However, they find evidence that high levels of public debt have tended to exacerbate the effects of private sector deleveraging after crises, leading to more prolonged periods of economic depression. They uncover three key facts based on their analysis of around 150 recessions and recoveries since 1870: (1) in a normal recession and recovery, real GDP per capita falls by 1.5 % and takes only 2 years to regain its previous peak, but in a financial crisis recession, the drop is typically 5 % and it takes over 5 years to regain the previous peak; (2) the output drop is even worse and recovery even slower when the crisis is preceded by a credit boom; and (3) the path of recovery is worse still when a credit-fueled crisis coincides with elevated public debt levels.

[6] Aguiar and Amador (2013) use a benchmark limited-commitment model to explore key issues in the economics of sovereign debt like debt overhang, risk sharing, and capital flows in an

In setting up the EU policy framework, the focus was on crisis prevention mainly through the Stability and Growth Pact and other surveillance mechanisms. No thought was given to crisis management. In addition, until 2010, interpretations of the meaning of Article 125 of the EU Treaty (the no-bailout clause) differed in different countries and institutions, but these interpretations were not discussed let alone reconciled.

Finally, balance-of-payment (BOP) crises were deemed impossible since solvent agents within a country would always retain access to private funding. BOP crises were in fact ruled out by most authors.

5.3 Who Was Responsible for the European Crisis?

The Eurozone sovereign crisis started when the government of Greece, freshly elected in October 2009, revealed that its predecessor had misled its Eurozone neighbors and the public about the true state of the country's public finances. The budget deficit for 2009 was 14.7 % of GDP, more than double the previously published figure. This raised serious doubts about the country's ability to repay its debt (Katsimi and Moutos 2010).

On December 2009, rating agencies downgraded Greek debt below investment grade. Government bond yields rose to unsustainable levels and by the end of April 2010 Greece turned to the European Union (EU) and the International Monetary Fund (IMF) to activate a €45 billion bailout package. By early May 2010, the EU-IMF rescue package had to be increased to an amount of €110 billion over 3 years.

Soon after Greece's bailout, since 2010 EU decided to set up a European Financial Stabilisation Facility (EFSF) with €440 bn financial firepower to intervene in similar situations. Simultaneously, the ECB initiated a Securities Market Programme (SMP) under which it buys sovereign debt of troubled countries in secondary markets.[7] Subsequently, the EFSF and IMF jointly agreed to provide conditional assistance packages to Ireland (November 2010) and Portugal (April 2011).

In July 2011, further assistance to Greece was decided by the Eurozone heads of state and government. A relatively mild debt restructuring scheme, euphemistically known as "private sector involvement" (PSI), was made a condition for the new assistance package to Greece, whose outline was announced on July 2, 2011. Therefore, in March 2012 a new package of €130 billion to Greece was approved by the EU and IMF after Greece's creditors agreed to the PSI to restructure Greek government bonds, which implied losses of up to 75 %. More than 85 % of private

environment of limited enforcement. They also discuss recent progress on default and renegotiation, self-fulfilling debt crises, and incomplete markets and their quantitative implications.

[7] Kilponen et al. (2012) stress that the economically most significant effects on the bond yields have been due to the announcement of the ECB's Securities Market Programme.

bondholders agreed to the deal, but not doing the agreement could have meant that Greece would not qualify for more bailout money and could have faced default (Kirkegaard 2012).

The bailout, however, failed to restore market trust in the Greek economy. Moreover, it failed to halt contagion of the crisis to other countries of the euro area.[8] In particular, the Greek crisis and the hesitant political response from the other European countries raised concerns over the debt situation and the structural and competitiveness problems of the economically weaker periphery member countries of the euro area. As a consequence, the borrowing costs for the PIIGS countries increased significantly and the cost of insuring sovereign debt against default soared as trust in their ability to repay vanished.

The interdependence between sovereign credit and banking systems has been a running theme of this sequence of events. Eurozone sovereign debt is held in large amounts by Eurozone banks, with a significant bias for the bonds of the country in which the bank is headquartered, but also significant is cross border exposure to other Eurozone countries' sovereign debt. This is partly due to policy choices before the crisis which in retrospect appear questionable, particularly the risk weighting at zero of Eurozone sovereign bonds in regulatory capital calculations, the longstanding acceptance of such bonds with no haircut by the ECB as collateral in its liquidity policies, and possible instances of moral suasion by home-country public authorities that resulted in large holdings of the home country's sovereign debt (Véron 2011).[9]

Between 2007 and 2010, the debt-to-GDP ratio of the euro area increased from 66.3 to 85.4 %. Greece is a special case in the sense that the level of Greek debt had already been very high before the crisis, at 107.7 % of GDP in 2007. Greek debt, which has been on a continuous rise since 2003, reached a level of 144.9 % of GDP in 2010. Like Greece, Italy had a debt level above 100 % of GDP prior to the crisis, but unlike in the case of Greece the debt-to-GDP ratio fell between Italy's adoption of the euro in 1999 and 2007.[10]

---

[8] Forbes (2012) surveys and assesses the academic literature on defining, measuring, and identifying financial contagion and the various channels by which it can occur, highlighting contagion risks in the euro area. He shows that a country is more vulnerable to contagion if it has a more levered banking system, greater trade exposure, weaker macroeconomic fundamentals, and larger international portfolio investment liabilities.

[9] Uhlig (2014) argues that in a monetary union, regulators in risky countries have an incentive to allow their banks to hold home risky bonds and risk defaults, whereas regulators in other "safe" countries will impose tighter regulation. As a result, governments in risky countries get to borrow more cheaply, effectively shifting the risk of some of the potential sovereign default losses on the common central bank.

[10] In the case of Italy, Albertazzi et al. (2012) show that a rise in the 10-year yield spreads relative to Germany is followed by an increase in the cost of wholesale and of certain forms of retail funding for banks and in the cost of credit to firms and households; the impact tends to be larger during periods of financial turmoil. An increase in the spread also has a direct negative effect on lending growth, beyond that implied by the rise in lending rates. Finally, they document a negative impact of the spread on banks' profitability, stronger for larger intermediaries. More in general, Di

Among euro area countries, the most dramatic increase in public debt occurred in Ireland, where the country's debt problems can be clearly ascribed to the country's banking crisis. Ireland did not have a fiscal or debt problem until 2008. Indeed, between 1997 and 2007, Ireland had a fiscal surplus every year except for 2002, when the government recorded a tiny deficit of −0.4 % of GDP. Accordingly, the Irish debt-to-GDP ratio declined steadily over this period from 64.3 % in 1997 to 24.9 % in 2007, with Ireland being one of the EU countries with the lowest public debt burden.

The situation changed in the course of the Irish banking crisis in September 2008 when the Irish government, under pressure from European governments and institutions (including the ECB) but also from the US government, guaranteed most liabilities of Irish-owned banks (Regling and Watson 2010; McMahon 2010). The government guarantee was initially €400 billion but was later increased to €440 billion. As a consequence, the Irish deficit ballooned and the debt-to-GDP ratio shot up from 24.9 % in 2007 to 94.9 % in 2010. The ensuing deterioration of Ireland's access to capital markets in the autumn of 2010 led it to seek an international financial rescue package by the IMF and the EU over €90 billion in November 2010 to finance its borrowing and bank recapitalization needs.

Like Ireland, Spain did not have a fiscal or debt problem before 2008. In the period 1999–2007, Spain had an average annual budget surplus of 0.3 % of GDP. In 2007, Spain even recorded a fiscal surplus of 1.9 %. Until the outbreak of the global financial crisis, Spain did not violate a single time the EU's Stability and Growth Pact (SGP).[11]

Spain's fortunes changed when the global financial crisis put an abrupt end to a long cycle of high growth (which started around 1996) that had been accompanied by a construction and real estate boom (Suarez 2010; Moro and Nũno 2012). When output contracted in 2008, the Spanish housing bubble burst and destabilized the banking system. The Spanish fiscal position deteriorated, with Spain recording fiscal deficits of 4.5 % in 2008, 11.2 % in 2009, and 9.3 % in 2010. Spain's public debt rose from 36.5 % of GDP in 2007 to 61.0 % in 2010.

Even in Portugal, which was the first country to breach the SGP in 2002 and which had seen a steady increase of its debt-to-GDP ratio since joining the euro area in 1999 (when debt stood at 49.6 % of GDP), the by far largest increase of public debt occurred during and after the 2008–2009 crisis, with debt rising from 68.3 % in 2007 to 94.9 % in 2010 (Volz 2012).

Cesare et al. (2012) show that for several countries the spread has increased to levels that are well above those that could be justified on the basis of fiscal and macroeconomic fundamentals. Among the possible reasons for this gap, the analysis focuses on the perceived risk of a breakup of the euro area. Finally, the sustainability of Italian fiscal policy in the long run is analyzed by Bartoletto et al. (2011).

[11] The SGP requires EU member countries to have an annual budget deficit no higher than 3 % of GDP and a national debt lower than 60 % of GDP or approaching that value.

5.4 Mispricing of Sovereign Risk by Financial Markets

An important element that contributed to the European financial crisis was a mispricing of risk by capital markets and an ensuing misallocation of capital in the decade before the outbreak of the crisis. European monetary unification brought about a convergence of interest rates among euro area members. Countries with weaker positions that had joined the euro area could refinance themselves at roughly the same cost as the most solvent states.

Spreads of sovereign bonds of the PIIGS over Germany narrowed rapidly in the run-up to EMU membership and almost disappeared once they had become members of the euro area (Fig. 5.1).

By January 2001, the time of Greece's entry into the euro area, the yields on 10-year Greek bonds had fallen to 5 % from 25 % in 1992. The sovereign risk of virtually all euro area countries, including the PIIGS, was priced more or less the same as German sovereign debt.

Financial markets were too much optimistic, depending on the fact that the risk of euro area central government bonds was weighted at zero in regulatory capital calculations and because the ECB treated such debt with no haircut—basically as risk-free—when these were offered as collateral for repos and other collateral financing trades (Véron 2011). Buiter and Siebert (2005) early highlighted this

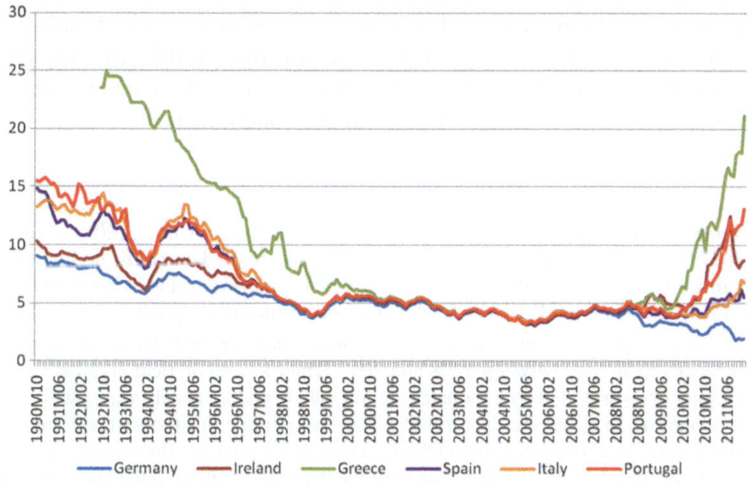

Fig. 5.1 Ten-year government bond yields (*% per annum*), October 1990–December 2011 (*Source*: Eurostat)

problem, maintaining that the ECB's open market operations created moral hazard by not discriminating sovereign risk within the euro area.[12]

On the contrary, soon after the explosion of European financial crisis, spreads of sovereign bonds of the PIIGS over Germany began to differentiate again (Fig. 5.1). De Santis (2012) found that three factors can explain the recorded developments in sovereign spreads: (1) an aggregate regional risk factor, (2) the country-specific credit risk, and (3) the spillover effect from Greece.[13]

Specifically, higher risk aversion has increased the demand for the Bund and this is behind the pricing of all euro area spreads, including those for Austria, Finland, and the Netherlands. Country-specific credit ratings have played a key role in the developments of the spreads for Greece, Ireland, Portugal, and Spain. Finally, the rating downgrade in Greece has contributed to developments in spreads of countries with weaker fiscal fundamentals: Ireland, Portugal, Italy, Spain, Belgium, and France.

On this argument, De Grauwe and Ji (2012) found two important pieces of evidence. First, since the start of the financial crisis, financial markets have started worrying about the high debt-to-GDP ratios in the Eurozone and have interpreted these high and increasing debt-to-GDP ratios as leading to default risk.[14] On the contrary, no such worries have developed in stand-alone countries despite the fact that debt-to-GDP ratios were equally high and increasing in these countries.

Second, they observe that in the Eurozone, the spreads can move away from underlying fundamentals (such as the debt-to-GDP ratio) in a "bubble-like" fashion. Once again, no such "bubbles" were observed in stand-alone countries.

A theoretical explanation of this fact was provided by De Grauwe (2011). Because members of a monetary union issue government debt in a currency they do not control, as a result the governments of these countries cannot guarantee that the cash will always be available to pay out the bondholders.

[12] Two empirical contributions on sovereign credit risk are Aspergis et al. (2011), who examine whether the efficiency market hypothesis for the Greek sovereign debt holds, finding that spreads and CDS are co-integrated, and Basse et al. (2012), who examine the relation between German and Italian government bond yields and its implication for insurance companies and regulators.

[13] Eijffinger et al. (2015) present a theory, which can account for the behavior of sovereign bond spreads in Southern Europe between 1998 and 2012. Their key theoretical argument is related to the bailout guarantee provided by a monetary union, which endogenously varies with the number of member countries in sovereign debt trouble. They incorporate this theoretical foundation in an otherwise standard small open-economy DSGE model and explain (1) the convergence of interest rates on sovereign bonds following the European monetary integration in the late 1990s and (2)—following the heightened default risk of Greece—the sudden surge in interest rates in countries with relatively sound economic and financial fundamentals. On the same topic, see also Bordon et al. (2014).

[14] Heinemann et al. (2013) study the determinants of sovereign risk premia in the EU countries between 1992 and 2008 and find that fiscal rules have the largest potential for countries with particularly poor fiscal stability culture in the past. For these countries, the effect of rules on risk premia is stronger than for high-stability countries. It seems that these countries could benefit from the establishment of external debt brakes which is intended by the Fiscal Compact.

This contrasts with stand-alone countries, which can always guarantee that their central bank will print the cash necessary to pay out bondholders. In a monetary union, instead, the absence of a guarantee that the cash will always be available creates a situation in which a liquidity crisis arises. And because such a crisis leads to large increases in the interest rate on government debt, it can drive governments of a monetary union into default.

The important ingredient in this dynamics is its self-fulfilling nature: when investors start fearing default, they will sell the bonds, creating a liquidity crisis that degenerates into a solvency crisis. The fear of insolvency creates conditions that make insolvency more likely.

When fear and panic takes over, sales of government bonds become massive, creating increases in the interest rates (and the spreads) on government bonds in the absence of observable changes in the fundamentals. When such movements of distrust are triggered, the government bond rates tend to be driven away from their fundamentals.

That is exactly what De Grauwe and Ji (2012, 2015) observed in the data of the Eurozone since 2010. They conclude that there is a widespread consensus that financial markets in the Eurozone have been systematically wrong when, during 2001–2008, they were charging the same risk premium on Greek and German government bonds, despite huge differences in debt-to-GDP ratios of these countries.

But why is it that if markets were systematically mispricing risks and failed to see any risk during 2001–2008, these same markets suddenly found the truth? De Grauwe and Ji argue that financial markets did not suddenly find the truth. Since the start of the sovereign debt crisis, they made errors in the other direction, i.e., they overestimated risks.

So, a large part of the surge in the spreads of the PIIGS countries during 2010–2011 was disconnected from underlying increases in the debt-to-GDP ratios and was the result of negative market sentiments that became very strong since the end of 2010. They also found evidence that after years of neglecting high debt-to-GDP ratios, investors became increasingly worried about the high debt-to-GDP ratios in the Eurozone and reacted by raising the spreads.[15]

Once again, no such worries developed in stand-alone countries, despite the fact that debt-to-GDP ratios were equally high and increasing in these countries. This is in line with De Grauwe's (2011) conclusion according to which government bond markets in a monetary union are more fragile and more susceptible to self-fulfilling liquidity crises, while the stand-alone countries have been immune from these liquidity crises. From this reasoning it derives the conclusion that one way to get out of the trouble in that situation is to attribute to the ECB the role of the lender of

[15] De Grauwe and Ji (2015) confirm the previous analysis, and in addition they find that the panic-induced austerity, as it occurs mainly in periods of recession, has the effect of reducing the power of the automatic stabilizers in the government budgets. As a result, the economic recessions are made more intense and can lead to social and political instability in the countries concerned.

last resort in the government bond market. In this way the ECB would become very similar to central banks of stand-alone countries, assuming the same behavior as the Fed or the Bank of England (see also Buiter and Rahbari 2012).

The systematic mispricing of sovereign debt observed in the Eurozone also had the effect of giving wrong incentives to policymakers. Greater financial integration between core and peripheral EMU members had an effect on both sets of countries.

Lower interest rates allowed peripheral countries to run bigger deficits, which inflated their economies by allowing credit booms. During the boom years, when financial markets were blind to the sovereign risks, no incentives were given to policymakers to reduce their debts, as the latter were priced so favorably. Since the start of the financial crisis, financial markets driven by panic overpriced risks and gave incentives to policymakers to introduce excessive austerity programs.[16]

This implies measures aimed at reducing the debt burden. If, however, there can be a disconnection between the spreads and the fundamentals, a policy geared exclusively toward affecting the fundamentals (i.e., reducing the debt burden) will not be sufficient. In that case policymakers should also try to stop countries from being driven into a bad equilibrium. This can be achieved by more active liquidity policies by the ECB that aim to prevent a liquidity crisis from leading to a self-fulfilling solvency crisis (Wyplosz 2011; De Grauwe 2011).

To this aim, between December 2011 and February 2012, the ECB first provided two unconventional longer-term refinancing operations (LTRO) for a total of more than €1.000 bn at a fixed rate of 1 %, maturing 3 years later. Then, on September 6, 2012, the ECB approved the Outright Monetary Transactions (OMT) program, under which the bank announced to be ready to purchase in secondary markets unlimited sovereign bonds of troubled countries having a maturity of between 1 and 3 years.

The purpose of this program was to reduce spreads in public bonds interest rates for the component not dependent on fundamentals, by contrasting fear and panic to take over. In fact, even if the OMT program had not been activated until now, both of these unconventional monetary policy decisions have greatly contributed to the maintenance of calm in the financial markets during the last years.

Anyway, it should be stressed that the policy aiming at improving the fundamentals through budgetary austerity and the policy of liquidity provision by the central bank are not substitutes but complements. When a member country of a monetary union is hit by a liquidity crisis that leads to a disconnection between the spreads and the fundamentals, both policies will in general be needed.

[16] Hale and Obstfeld (2014) analyze the geography of international debt flows using multiple data sources and provide evidence that after the euro's introduction, core euro area countries increased their borrowing from outside of EMU and their lending to the EMU periphery. Core EMU countries took on extra foreign leverage to expose themselves to the peripherals. The result has been asset-price bubbles and collapses in some of the peripheral countries, area-wide banking crisis, and sovereign debt problems.

5.5 The Misalignment of Internal Real Exchange Rates and the Ensuing Balance-of-Payment Crisis

Nowak and Shachmurove (2012) hold up that the European Union was created to promote economic, cultural, and regional prosperity. However, the global financial crisis demonstrates that its economic institutions are flawed. While each sovereign state in the Eurozone forfeits the control of its money supply, the lack of a common fiscal institution allows individual countries to pursue their own political and financial agendas.[17]

To avoid conflicts among countries, the no-bailout clause and the Stability and Growth Pact (SGP) were incorporated in the very core of the EMU Treaty. The first should have excluded free-rider incentives and the second should have aligned national fiscal policies to prevent negative spillover effects to the currency union as a whole.

The SGP was a compromise of quantifying fiscal soundness without interfering with the budgetary and fiscal policies of sovereign states. It aimed to maintain fiscal discipline within EMU. Member states adopting the euro had to meet the Maastricht convergence criteria, and the SGP should make sure that they continue to observe them. The compromise was also characterized by the strong belief that governments would be reactive to market discipline. The spirit of the SGP was also characterized by a strong belief in the power of free markets to discipline governments.[18]

But the global financial crisis has undoubtedly marked a turning point also in that context. With hindsight, it is now obvious that the availability of cheap credit led to an unsustainable accumulation of private (as in Ireland, Portugal, and Spain) and public (as in Greece, Italy, and Portugal) debt in crisis-hit countries. The drop in real interest rates in the periphery countries after their entry into the euro area and the inflowing capital fueled unsustainable developments, including excessive credit dynamics and real estate bubbles in Spain (Moro and Nũno 2012) and excessive fiscal spending in Greece.

It also reduced the pressure for economic reform to improve competitiveness within the monetary union as countries could easily finance their current account deficits through abundant inflowing capital. As stressed by Lin and Treichel (2012), the adoption of a single currency led to convergence of interest rates in periphery countries to the levels in core countries and, in combination with rising capital inflows owing to greater financial integration, set off a consumption and real estate boom in periphery countries, leading to higher growth and increases in government revenue and spending.

---

[17] Also Mersch (2011) points to flaws in the Maastricht Treaty as a factor that explains the deteriorating of the crisis.

[18] Farmer et al. (2012) present a model that invalidates the implication that competitive financial markets efficiently allocate risk. Their work demonstrates that financial markets, by their very nature, cannot be Pareto efficient, except by chance. Although individuals are rational, they conclude that markets are not.

The resulting appreciation of the real exchange rate decreased the competitiveness in these countries, which then caused rising current account imbalances (Fig. 5.2). These imbalances then sharply increased budget deficits and

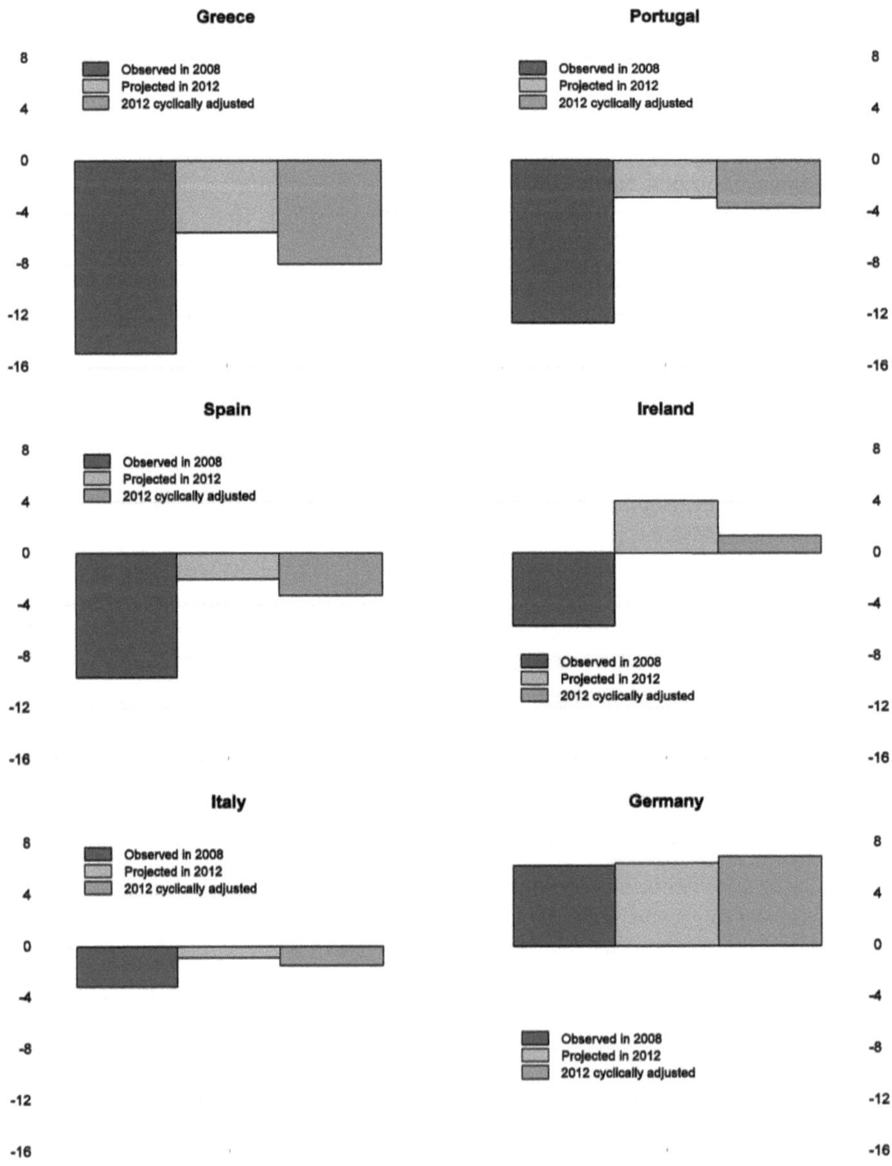

Fig. 5.2 Current account balances in euro area countries, in percent of GDP (*Source*: OECD Economic Outlook 92 database and OECD calculations)

worsened debt indicators, triggering the sovereign debt crisis (see Chap. 7, Sect. 7.6).[19]

In fact, a high level of public debt is not a problem per se, as long as the government is able to refinance itself and roll over its debt. This requires public debt and the interest burden to grow more slowly than the economy and the tax base. Unfortunately, this is not the case in the PIIGS countries. The economic crisis in these countries is therefore not merely a debt crisis; it is first and foremost a competitiveness and growth crisis that has led to structural imbalances within the euro area (Holinski et al. 2012; Lane and Pels 2012; Bergsten and Kirkegaard 2012; Mayer 2011).[20]

According to this field of research, below the surface of the sovereign public debt and banking crises lies a balance-of-payment crisis, caused by a misalignment of internal real exchange rates (Sinn 2012; Sinn and Wollmershäeuser 2011; Neumann 2012; Lin and Treichel 2012).

Until the beginning of the euro crisis in 2009, EU officials tended to ignore the current account imbalances among EMU member countries. Some of them, who failed to grasp the difference between a common currency area within a political union and a currency union of politically sovereign states, even insisted that these imbalances were irrelevant (Mayer 2011).

As long as financial markets were buoyant and credit is easily available at rock-bottom cost for borrowers of differing quality, the flaw in this argument was not laid bare.

This changed abruptly when risk appetite in credit markets plunged in the course of the financial crisis and EMU member countries with high government deficits or debt and a bleak economic outlook experienced a "sudden stop" of capital inflows and even net capital outflows.[21]

[19] Ma and McCauley (2013) analyze global and euro area imbalances by focusing on China and Germany as large surplus and creditor countries. In the 2000s, domestic reforms in both countries expanded the effective labour force, restrained wages, shifted income toward profits, and increased corporate saving. As a result, both economies' current account surpluses widened before the global financial crisis, and that of Germany has proven more persistent as domestic investment has remained subdued.

[20] According to Holinski et al. (2012), the growing current account imbalances in the euro area are a cause for serious concern, deserve monitoring, and ultimately require an appropriate policy response. Private agents' decisions with respect to savings and investment can lead to large external deficits without automatically generating sufficient domestic economic growth and productivity gains. The result can be unsustainable net foreign liability positions that can only be redressed at substantial macroeconomic costs. Once unsustainable imbalances emerge, adjustment mechanisms are scarce and costly. Without productivity gains, the burden of adjustment falls on prices and wages that need to fall and real interest rates that need to rise in southern relative to northern Europe. Such a process is accompanied by a painful period of economic contraction and will take a number of years to resolve.

[21] Lane and Pels (2012) show that the European crisis is partly attributable to the sharp increase in external imbalances across Europe during the pre-crisis period. They find that the discrete expansion in current account imbalances during the 2002–2007 period can be attributed to a strengthening in the link between growth forecasts and current account balances.

On the surface, the sudden stop has led to a government funding and banking crisis. In response, EU authorities began to extend financial support—associated with pressure for fiscal adjustment—to the affected countries, while the ECB supported the banks. Below the surface, however, lies a balance-of-payment crisis, which has so far received only scant attention.

Recall that the balance of payments is defined as the sum of the current and capital account.[22] In a floating exchange rate system, the balance of payments is always zero as the exchange rate adjusts so as to equilibrate the current with capital account balance. In a fixed nominal exchange rate system, however, balance-of-payment imbalances can emerge when the real exchange rate is above or below its equilibrium value.[23]

In the first case, when the real exchange rate is overvalued, a country imports more than it exports so that the current account moves into deficit. At the same time, domestic asset prices in foreign currency are higher than foreign asset prices, so that investors sell the first and buy the latter. This leads to net capital outflows and hence a deficit in the capital account. The combined deficits of the current and capital accounts then lead to a deficit of the balance of payments.

Traditionally, balance-of-payment deficits have been funded by the sale of international reserves of the central bank. When the stock of reserves is depleted and the central bank can no longer fund the balance-of-payment deficit, the nominal exchange rate depreciates so as to restore current and capital account balance. This happens because to a nominal exchange rate depreciation, in the short run, it also corresponds a real exchange rate drop.

In the second case, when the real exchange rate is undervalued, the current and capital accounts and hence the balance of payments are in surplus and the central bank accumulates international reserves. This process comes to an end only when reserve accumulation has increased the money supply to an extent that inflation grows to intolerable levels and the authorities upvalue the nominal exchange rate in an effort to regain price stability (Mayer 2011).

---

[22] The IMF balance-of-payment definition includes the current account, the capital account, and the financial account. In Mayer's (2011) reasoning, however, the financial account is mixed with the capital account.

[23] The connection between real exchange rates and growth remains an unsettled question in the academic literature. Bussière et al. (2014) try to fill this gap by providing an empirical assessment based on a broad sample of emerging and advanced economies. They assess the impact of appreciations, productivity booms, and capital inflow surges using a propensity score-matching approach to address causality issues. Appreciations associated with higher productivity have a larger impact on growth than those associated with capital inflows. Furthermore, appreciations per se tend to have a negative impact on growth. They provide a theoretical model that delivers a contrasted growth-appreciation pattern depending on the underlying shock. The model also implies adverse effects of shocks to international capital flows, so concerns about an appreciation are not inconsistent with concerns about a depreciation. While the presence of an externality through firms' destruction leads to inefficient allocations, addressing the inefficiency does not dampen exchange rate movements. Furthermore, Berka et al. (2014) investigate the link between real exchange rates and sectoral total factor productivity measures for countries in the Eurozone.

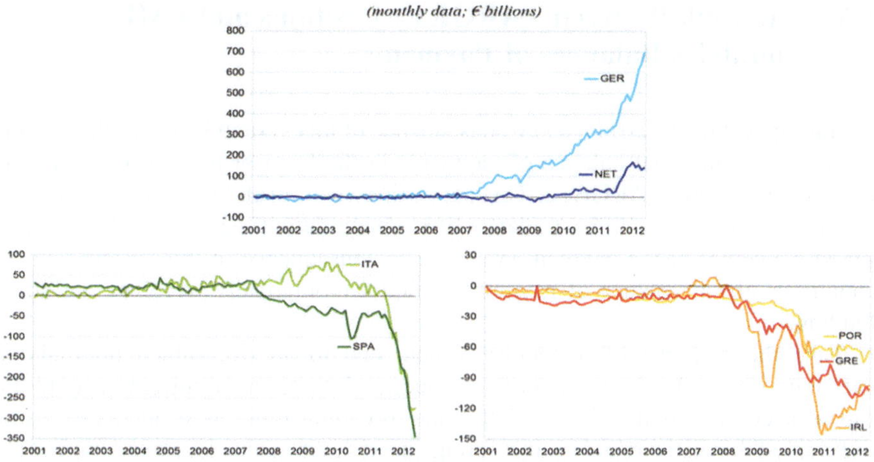

Fig. 5.3 TARGET2 cumulated net balances (*Source*: Cecioni and Ferrero 2012)

Because the EMU has been built as a union of sovereign states, each state has retained its own national central bank, which has become a member of the so-called Eurosystem with the ECB at the top.

National interbank payment systems have been merged into a euro area interbank payment system (TARGET2), where national central banks have assumed the role of the links between countries.[24]

So, TARGET2 plays a key role in ensuring the smooth conduct of monetary policy, the correct functioning of financial markets, and the banking and financial stability in the euro area, by substantially reducing systemic risk. The settlement of cross border payments between participants in TARGET2 results in intra-Eurosystem balances, that is, positions on the balance sheets of the respective central banks that reflect claims/liabilities on/to the Eurosystem.

They are reported on the NCBs' balance sheets as TARGET2 claims (if positive) or TARGET2 liabilities (if negative), vis-à-vis the ECB as the central counterpart (Fig. 5.3).

[24] TARGET is the "Trans-European Automated Real-Time Gross Settlement Express Transfer" system. It was replaced by TARGET2 in November 2007, with a transition period lasting until May 2008, by which time all national platforms were replaced by a single platform. The processing and settlement of euro-denominated payments takes place on an individual basis on the participants' accounts at NCBs connected to TARGET2. The transactions are settled in real time with immediate finality, thus enabling the beneficiary bank to reuse the liquidity to make other payments on that day.

5.6 The Link Between TARGET2 Positions and EMU Countries Balances of Payments

According to Mayer (2011), a key consequence of this system is that each euro area country has a national balance of payments in the form of the net position of its central bank within TARGET2. This net position can result in a claim (balance-of-payment surplus) or liability (balance-of-payment deficit) against the ECB, which sits in the center of the payment system. The consequence of this system is that a country with a balance-of-payment deficit automatically receives unlimited funding.

Take the example of a country which, due to an overvalued internal real exchange rate and a large government budget deficit, has a current account and capital account deficit (with the latter due to capital flight as residents exchange overvalued domestic assets against foreign assets). As the banks extend credit to an over-indebted government and an uncompetitive private sector, they are considered unsafe and are therefore cut off from private sources of funding. To ensure solvency, the banks in this country receive credit from their national central bank, which acts on behalf of the ECB. Thus, reserve money flows from the ECB to fund payment outflows induced by the current and capital account deficits.

Therefore, while banks in the country with the overvalued internal real exchange rate rely primarily on their national central banks and the ECB for funding of their balance sheets, banks in the country with the undervalued exchange rate that receive the payments have plenty of liquidity and therefore do not need ECB funds. Hence, Mayer's conclusion is that the ECB's funding operations become tilted toward the countries with overvalued real exchange rates.

Anyway, Mayer's idea that TARGET2 provides unlimited funding to the balance-of-payment deficits of peripheral EMU countries is questionable, as we will explain more extensively in the next chapter. TARGET2 flows reflect a type of lender of last resort intervention by the ECB through the free allotment program. They just reflect the funding necessity of banks in different regions, with periphery banks being the most in need, not because they lent to over-indebted governments—except in Greece—but because they were the ones in dire straits due to the large positions, for instance, in real estate markets as in Spain.

In fact, before the beginning of the financial crisis, up until July 2007, TARGET2 positions were balanced overall. Cross border payments were flowing in both directions and were netted out to zero at the close of business each day. The beginning of the financial crisis in August 2007 led to one-direction flows from "peripheral" countries (Greece, Ireland, and Portugal) to "core" countries (Germany and the Netherlands). The divergences widened with the outbreak of the sovereign debt crisis in May 2010. Since the summer of 2011, as the crisis has intensified and also affected Italy and Spain, divergences of TARGET2 positions have become even wider.

In mid-2012, the total value of TARGET2 claims (or equivalent liabilities) on the balance sheet of the euro NCBs reached €1 trillion. In particular, Germany and

Dutch net claims in TARGET2 increased from close to zero in the first half of 2007 to about €700 and €140 bn, respectively, by the end of May 2012. Conversely, in Greece, Ireland, and Portugal, net liabilities in TARGET2 increased from close to zero to €102, €97, and €63 bn, respectively. Finally, the NCBs of Italy and Spain, which had slightly positive TARGET2 net claims before the start of the crisis, registered net liabilities of €275 and €345 bn by the end of May 2012 (Fig. 5.3).

So far, the structural imbalances, reflected by high current account deficits of the periphery countries and matching surpluses in core countries (Fig. 5.2), apparently seem to be at the heart of the ongoing problems, since a lack of competitiveness reduces the periphery countries' chances of growing out of the crisis. To service their debt, deficit countries essentially need to become surplus countries. However, the fact that the PIIGS are members of a monetary union and hence cannot restore competitiveness by means of currency devaluation makes the adjustment much more painful. An internal devaluation requires harsh structural adjustments and real wage cuts to push down costs. This is politically much more difficult to administer than one-off currency devaluation.

Therefore, according to this field of research, the lackluster growth performance in the euro area periphery over the past years has been due to an erosion of competitiveness, both against other euro area countries and the rest of the world.[25] The domestic booms resulting from low real interest rates and capital inflows after accession to EMU led to large wage increases in excess of productivity growth and hence rising unit labor costs (Fig. 5.4) and higher price inflation than in Germany and other "core countries" of the euro area. The result was an erosion of competitiveness of peripheral members of the euro area vis-à-vis the core countries, particularly Germany, which has been able to improve its price competitiveness significantly since the launch of the euro through wage constraints and structural reforms.[26]

[25] While there are many methods to measure the competitiveness of an economy, most of these concepts ignore the fact that competitiveness can change because of market processes like wage negotiation but also because of political decision-making. Governments that compete with others for factors of production face the incentive to adjust key policy variables to improve their competitive position. Increasing country competitiveness is one of the key objectives currently discussed by policymakers in the context of creating an economic union in the euro area, to complement monetary union. Huemer et al. (2013) propose a new competitiveness index that captures the dimensions in which politics can influence competitiveness beyond factor price adjustments. Their index shows that the individual components of institutional competitiveness have developed heterogeneously among EMU member states. To explain these divergent developments, the uneven integration within the EU single market may play a role.

[26] Also interesting is the case of Italy. According to Tiffin (2014), in this country, price-based competitiveness measures are not always an accurate predictor of trade outcomes. Tiffin's paper offers a more comprehensive assessment of Italian competitiveness, focusing on the role of innovation and the evolution of Italy's export market share. Overall, Italy maintains a high-quality export mix, and the adaptability of small-scale specialized firms is still a source of strength. But, small firm size is becoming less of an asset, and even the most innovative sectors are weighed down by the structural barriers that have depressed productivity more broadly. Tiffin concludes that Italy's future competitiveness will depend on full implementation of a comprehensive structural-reform agenda.

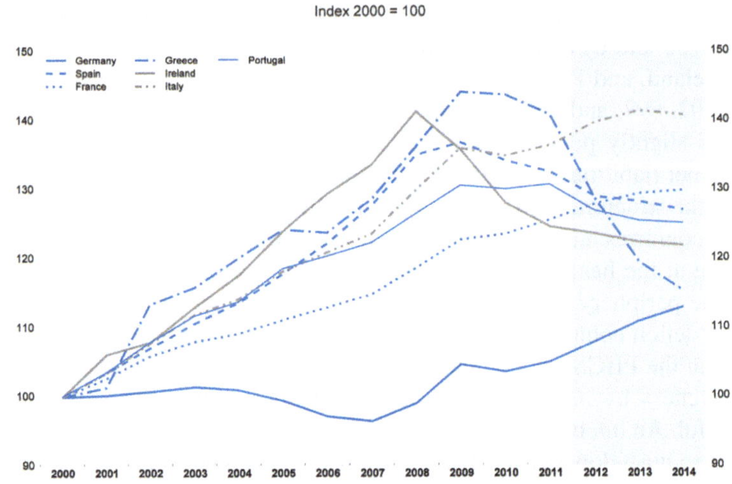

Note: The figures shown are for whole economy unit labour costs. If wage developments in the public sector diverge from those in the rest of the economy, changes in private sector costs may differ from those shown. This may mean that economy-wide labour costs are falling more sharply than private sector costs in the EU/IMF programme countries.

Source: OECD Economic Outlook 92 database.

Fig. 5.4 Unit labor costs

As emphasized by Véron (2011) and Weidmann (2011), besides fiscal adjustment and bank restructuring, structural reforms that enhance the crisis countries' growth potential are an indispensible dimension of any successful crisis resolution.

It is also the difficulties of economic adjustment, which require unpopular public policies that have caused markets to doubt the solvency of the periphery countries. Therefore, one key issue for defining and solving the Eurozone's difficulties also lies in readjusting the relationship between the center and the periphery (Fahrholz and Wójcik 2012).[27]

[27] Aizenman (2012) analyzes reforms and adjustments needed in the context of the euro and the global financial crisis, stressing the challenges associated with finding the proper balance between financial integration and financial regulations. As documented by Jakab et al. (2015), the euro area countries are more vulnerable to domestic and external demand shocks because adjustments in the real exchange rate between EMU countries occur more gradually through inflation differentials. Spillovers from tight credit conditions in each country are limited by direct trade channels.

5.7 Large Increases in TARGET2 Liabilities Are Mostly Related to Capital Flight

However, the view that European financial crisis was caused by external imbalances is not shared by all economists. According to Taylor (2012), for instance, there have been essentially two competing views of the global financial crisis, albeit there are some complementarities among them. One view mainly blames external imbalances, the large-scale mix of current account deficits and surpluses, which entailed massive and growing international financial flows in the last decade.

The alternative view finds more fault in the domestic arena of the afflicted countries, attributing the problems to financial systems where risks originated in excessive credit booms in local banks. Of the two, Taylor's view is that the credit boom explanation stands out as the most plausible predictor of financial crises. He concludes that, historically, global imbalances are not as important as a factor in financial crises as is often perceived, and they have much less correlation with subsequent episodes of financial distress compared to direct indicators like credit drawn from the financial system itself.

In addition, also the identification of the balance-of-payment imbalances with TARGET2 positions is questionable. In fact, Cecioni and Ferrero (2012) show that movements in the current account's deficits are significantly related to TARGET2 balances only for Greece, whereas intra-area trade balances are not related to TARGET2 in any other country. For all countries, the large increase in TARGET2 liabilities appears to be mostly related to capital flight, concerning both portfolio investments and cross border interbank activity.

As highlighted by ECB (2013), large TARGET2 imbalances emerged when the Governing Council of the European Central Bank, in order to maintain price stability over the medium term, decided to accommodate the liquidity needs of solvent banks. TARGET2 balances emerged as a result of imbalanced cross border payment flows between banks in the euro area and the Eurosystem's accommodation, in its operations, of the ensuing liquidity needs of solvent banks, against adequate collateral.

Furthermore, in analyzing the Eurosystem liquidity, it is also important to take account of the role played by the international financial assistance to crisis-hit countries. Figure 5.5 shows the role of international financial assistance and Eurosystem liquidity in the case of two program countries, Greece and Portugal, and in two countries, Spain and Italy, that suffered from capital-flow reversals but which did not apply for a program.

In Greece and Portugal, official financing has had to offset a complete reversal of private capital inflows accumulated since the beginning of the 2000s. This has been achieved through a combination of program financing and Eurosystem financing. Otherwise, no official financing was requested by Italy and Spain, except for the banking sector of the latter. Nevertheless, a nearly complete reversal of inflows in Spain and a sizeable outflow in Italy have been entirely offset by Eurosystem financing (Pisani-Ferri et al. 2013, p. 12).

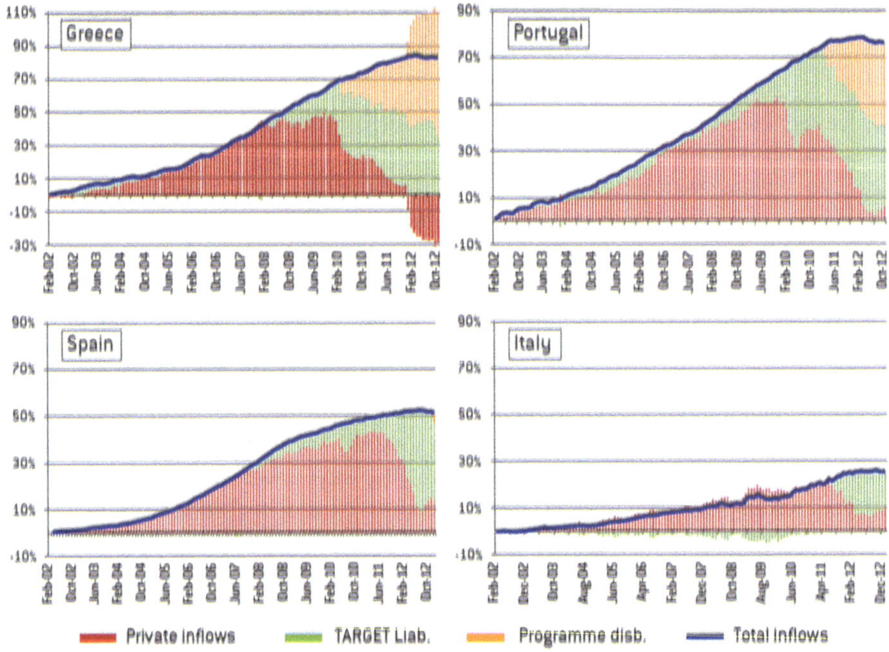

Fig. 5.5 Private capital flows, program financing, and Eurosystem financing, Greece, Portugal, Spain, and Italy, 2002–2012, in % of 2007 GDP (*Source*: Pisani-Ferri et al. (2013)

Figure 5.5 seems to suggest that euro area countries have not been confronted with any balance-of-payments constraint because the Eurosystem entirely offset the withdrawal of private capital. Anyway, this interpretation would not be correct: the Eurosystem does not provide unlimited financing of balance-of-payments deficits. ECB liquidity is being provided within the framework of its normal procedures such as the Main Refinancing Operations (MRO) and the Long-Term Refinancing Operations (LTRO).

In the case of general liquidity provision procedures, the quantity and quality of available collateral sets a limit on the amount of liquidity private banks can have access to. By reducing collateral standards for Greece, Portugal, and Ireland, the ECB made its liquidity more accessible. In spring 2011, the three program countries together made up more than 50 % of total liquidity provided through the MRO and the LTRO windows (Fig. 5.6).

Anyway, TARGET2 balances reflect funding stress in the banking systems of certain countries. Therefore, such imbalances must be interpreted with caution, as they also reflect transactions among multi-country banking groups. Further, any risk is attached to the Eurosystem operations themselves in the context of the monetary union, in particular not to the TARGET2 balances per se.

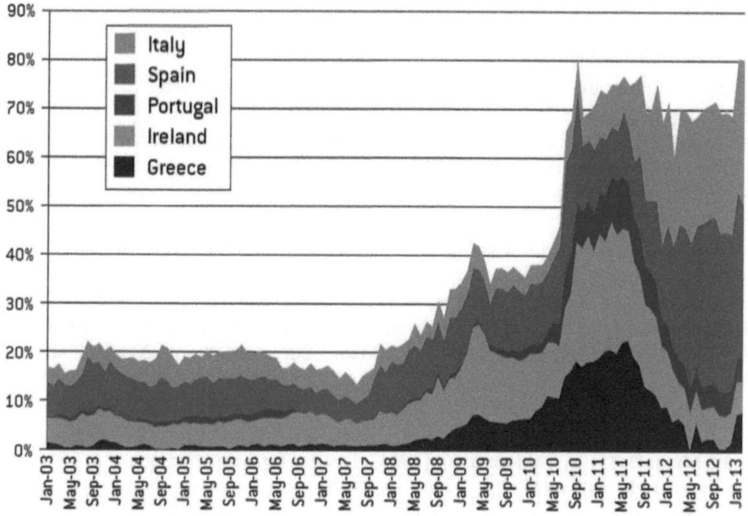

Fig. 5.6 Share of "periphery" countries in ECB main (MRO) and Longer-Term Refinancing Operations (LTRO), 2003–2012 (*Source*: Pisani-Ferri et al. 2013)

5.8 Conclusions

In conclusion, we can say that TARGET2 balances are a symptom of underlying tensions in the Economic and Monetary Union, highlighting the need for macroeconomic imbalances to be addressed, trust in banking systems to be reestablished, and the institutional foundations of EMU to be strengthened.

As will be more extensively explained in next chapter, interpretations of the role assumed by TARGET2 balances fall into two camps. The first is that these balances correspond to current account financing, which can be labeled the *flow* interpretation.

The second camp interprets TARGET2 balances as a "capital account reversal," that is, they see this as one symptom of a balance-of-payment crisis. Someone argues that the Eurosystem full-allotment refinancing operations should be seen as financing the reversal of an outstanding stock of cross border claims, while the TARGET2 payments system merely records the results. This corresponds to the *stock* interpretation of TARGET2 balances (see Chap. 6, Sect. 6.3).

To investigate on these more complex aspects of the problem, a deeper analysis on the accumulation of TARGET2 imbalances and the implied correlation of the external imbalances with them is needed at this point. The following Chap. 6 is therefore devoted to these arguments.

References

Adler G (2012) Intertwined sovereign and bank solvencies in a model of self-fulfilling crisis. IMF working paper no. 12/178

Aguiar M, Amador M (2013) Sovereign debt: a review. NBER working paper no. w19388, August. Available via http://papers.ssrn.com/sol3/papers.cfm?abstract_id=2318290

Aizenman J (2012) The euro and the global crisis: finding the balance between short term stabilization and forward looking reforms. NBER working paper no. w18138

Albertazzi U, Ropele T, Sene G, Signoretti FM (2012) The impact of the sovereign debt crisis on the activity of italian banks. Banca d'Italia, Questioni di Economia e Finanza, Occasional paper no. 133, 18 Sept. Available via https://www.google.it/webhp?sourceid=chrome-instant&ion=1&espv=2&ie=UTF-8#q=albertazzi%20u.%20et%20al%20(2012)%2c%20the%20impact%20of%20the%20sovereign%20debt%20crisis%20on%20the%20activity%20of%20italian%20banks%2c%20banca%20d%e2%80%99italia%2c%20questioni%20di%20economia%20e%20finanza%2c%20occasional%20paper%20n.%20133%2c%20september%2018.

Aspergis N, Mamatzakis E, Staikouras C (2011) Testing for regime changes in Greek sovereign debt crisis. Adv Econ Res 17:258–273

Bakk-Simon K, Borgioli S, Giron C, Hempell HS, Maddaloni A, Recine F, Rosati S (2011) Shadow banking in the Euro area: an overview. ECB occasional paper no. 133, September

Balteanu I, Erce A (2014) Bank crises and sovereign defaults in emerging markets: exploring the links. Working paper no. 184, June. Federal Reserve Bank of Dallas, Globalization and Monetary Policy Institute. Available via http://www.dallasfed.org/assets/documents/institute/wpapers/2014/0184.pdf

Banca d'Italia (2010) Rapporto sulla stabilità finanziaria, 1, dicembre

Bartoletto S, Chiarini B, Marzano E (2011) The sustainability of fiscal policy in Italy: a long-term perspective. CESifo working paper series no. 3812, 15 May

Basse T, Friedrich M, Kleffner A (2012) Italian government debt and sovereign credit risk: an empirical exploration and some thoughts about consequences for European insurers. Zeitschrift für die gesamte Versicherungswissenschaft 101(5):571–579

Bergsten F, Kirkegaard JF (2012) The coming resolution of the European crisis. Peterson Institute for international economics, policy brief, January. Available via http://www.iie.com/publications/pb/pb12-1.pdf

Berka M, Devereux MB, Engel C (2014) Real exchange rates and sectoral productivity in the eurozone. NBER working paper no. 20510, September. Available via http://www.nber.org/papers/w20510

Bordon IG, Schmid KD, Schmidt M (2014) Hypnosis before wake-up call? The revival of sovereign credit risk perception in the EMU-crisis. CESifo working paper series no. 4946, August. Available via http://www.cesifo-group.de/ifoHome/publications/working-papers/CESifoWP/CESifoWPdetails?wp_id=19121662

Buiter WH, Rahbari E (2012) The ECB as lender of last resort for sovereigns in the Euro area. CEPR discussion paper no. 8974. Available via http://willembuiter.com/lolr.pdf

Buiter WH, Siebert A (2005) How the Eurosystem's treatment of collateral in its open market operations weakens fiscal discipline in the eurozone (and what to do about it). CEPR discussion paper no. 5387, London

Bussière M, Lopez C, Tille C (2014) Do real exchange rate appreciations matter for growth? Econ Policy 30(81):5–45. Available via http://economicpolicy.oxfordjournals.org/content/30/81/5

Candelon B, Palm FC (2010) Banking and debt crises in Europe: the dangerous liaisons? CESIFO working paper no. 3001, March

Cecioni M, Ferrero G (2012) Determinants of TARGET2 imbalances. Banca d'Italia, Questioni di Economia e Finanza (occasional papers), 136, September

Correa R, Sapriza H (2014) Sovereign debt crises. Board of Governors of the Federal Reserve System, International finance discussion paper no. 1104, May. Available via https://www.

google.it/webhp?sourceid=chrome-instant&ion=1&espv=2&ie=UTF-8#q=twin+sovereign+and+banking+crises+in+Europe
Das U, Lu Y, Papaioannou MG, Petrova IK (2012) Sovereign risk and asset and liability management - conceptual issues. IMF working paper no. 12/241, October. Available via http://papers.ssrn.com/sol3/papers.cfm?abstract_id=2169782
De Grauwe P (2010) Crisis in the eurozone and how to deal with it. CEPS policy brief no. 204
De Grauwe P (2011) The European central bank: lender of last resort in the government bond markets? CESifo working paper no. 3569. Available via https://ideas.repec.org/p/ces/ceswps/_3569.html
De Grauwe P, Ji Y (2012) Mispricing of sovereign risk and macroeconomic stability in the eurozone. J Common Mark Stud 50(6):866–880
De Grauwe P, Ji Y (2015) Has the eurozone become less fragile? Some empirical tests. CESifo working paper series no. 5163, 26 Jan
De Santis RA (2012) The Euro area sovereign debt crisis: safe haven, credit rating agencies and the spread of the fever from Greece, Ireland and Portugal. ECB working paper no. 1419, February
Di Cesare A, Grande G, Manna M, Taboga M (2012) Recent estimates of sovereign risk premia for Euro-Area countries. Banca d'Italia, Questioni di Economia e Finanza, Occasional paper no. 128, September. Available via https://www.google.it/webhp?sourceid=chrome-instant&ion=1&espv=2&ie=UTF-8#q=di%20cesare%20a.%20et%20al%20(2012)%2c%20-recent%20estimates%20of%20sovereign%20risk%20premia%20for%20euro-area%20countries%2c%20banca%20d%e2%80%99italia%2c%20questioni%20di%20economia%20e%20finanza%2c%20occasional%20paper%20n.%20128%2c%20september.
Driffill J (2013) Financial shocks, unemployment, and public policy. CEPR discussion paper no. DP9321, January
ECB (2013) TARGET balances and monetary policy operations. Monthly Bulletin, May
Eichengreen B, Wyplosz CW (1998) The stability pact: more than a minor nuisance? Econ Policy 13(26):65–113
Eijffinger SCW, Kobielarz ML, Uras B (2015) Sovereign debt, bail-outs and contagion in a monetary union. CEPR discussion paper no. 10459. Available via http://papers.ssrn.com/sol3/papers.cfm?abstract_id=2572457
Fahrholz C, Wójcik C (2012) The eurozone needs exit rules. CESIFO working paper no. 3845, June
Farmer REA, Nourry C, Venditti A (2012) The inefficient market hypothesis: why financial markets do not work well in the real world. NBER working paper no. 18647, December
Forbes K (2012) The 'Big C': identifying contagion. NBER working paper no. 18465, October
Fratzscher M, Rieth MH (2015) Monetary policy, bank bailouts and the sovereign-bank risk nexus in the Euro area. CEPR discussion paper no. DP10370. Available via http://www.cepr.org/active/publications/discussion_papers/dp.php?dpno=10370#
Hale G, Obstfeld M (2014) The Euro and the geography of international debt flows. NBER working paper no. 20033, April. Available via http://www.nber.org/papers/w20033
Heinemann F, Osterloh S, Kalb A (2013) Sovereign risk premia: the link between fiscal rules and stability culture. ZEW discussion paper no. 13–016, Mar 1. Available via http://papers.ssrn.com/sol3/papers.cfm?abstract_id=2233388
Holinski N, Kool C, Muysken J (2012) Persistent macroeconomic imbalances in the Euro area: causes and consequences. FRB St Louis Rev 94(1):1–20
Huemer S, Scheubel BD, Walch F (2013) Measuring institutional competitiveness in Europe. ECB working paper no. 1556, May. Available via http://papers.ssrn.com/sol3/papers.cfm?abstract_id=2269640
Jakab Z, Lukyantsau P, Wang S (2015) A global projection model for Euro area large economies. IMF working paper no. 15/50, March. Available via https://www.imf.org/external/pubs/cat/longres.aspx?sk=42760.0

Jordà O, Schulatrick M, Taylor AM (2013) Sovereigns versus banks: credit, crises and consequences. Institute for new economic thinking working paper series no. 3. Available via http://ssrn.com/abstract=2585696

Katsimi M, Moutos T (2010) EMU and Greek crisis: the political-economy perspective. Eur J Polit Econ 26(4):568–576

Kilponen J, Laakkonen H, Vilmunen J (2012) Sovereign risk, European crisis resolution policies and bond yields. Research discussion papers no. 22, Bank of Finland. Available via http://www.suomenpankki.fi/en/julkaisut/tutkimukset/keskustelualoitteet/Documents/BoF_DP_1222.pdf

Kirkegaard JF (2012) Brinkmanship in Brussels, Sturm and Drachma for Greece and Europe. Vox, Mar 1

Kollintzas T, Tsoukalas K (2015) Bank and sovereign risk inter-dependence in the Euro area. CEPR discussion paper no. DP10485

Lane PR, Pels B (2012) Current account imbalances in Europe. CEPR discussion paper no. 8958

Lin JY, Treichel V (2012) The crisis in the Euro zone: did the Euro contribute to the evolution of the crisis? World bank policy research working paper no. 6127. Available via http://elibrary.worldbank.org/docserver/download/6127.pdf?expires=1349462386&id=id&accname=guest&checksum=76473E9201912E65FF 539603A5F30DFC

Ma G, McCauley RN (2013) Global and Euro imbalances: China and Germany. BIS working papers no. 424, September. Available via http://www.bis.org/publ/work424.htm

Mayer T (2011) Euroland's hidden balance-of-payments crisis. EU Monitor, 88, 26 Oct. Available via http://www.dbresearch.com/PROD/DBR_INTERNET_EN-PROD/PROD0000000000279906/Euroland%E2%80%99s+hidden+balance-of-payments+crisis.pdf

McKibbin WJ, Stoeckel A, Lu YY (2012) Global fiscal adjustment and trade rebalancing. World bank policy research working paper no. 6044, April

McMahon J (2010) The Irish banking crisis: lessons learned, future challenges, 26 May. Available via http://www.centralbank.ie/press-area/speeches/Documents/26%20May%202010%20-%20Address%20to%20Mazars%20Banking%20Conference,%202010%20by%20Jonathan%20McMahon.pdf

Mersch Y (2011) Optimal currency area revisited. European University Institute, Robert Schuman Center for Advanced Studies Distinguished Lecture, Florence, 26 Oct. Available via http://cadmus.eui.eu/bitstream/handle/1814/19495/RSCAS_DL_2011_01.pdf?sequence=1

Moro B (2014) Lessons from the European economic and financial great crisis: a survey. Eur J Polit Econ 34(Suppl):S9–S24

Moro A, Nũno G (2012) Does total-factor productivity drive housing prices? A growth-accounting exercise for four countries. Econ Lett 115:221–224

Neumann MJM (2012) The refinancing of banks drives target debt. CESifo Forum, 13 Jan (Special Issue)

Nowak AZ, Shachmurove Y (2012) Falling institutions are at the core of the Euro crisis. Penn institute for economic research working paper no. 12–041. Available via http://economics.sas.upenn.edu/sites/economics.sas.upenn.edu/files/12-041_0.pdf

Pisani-Ferri J, Sapir A, Wolff GB (2013) EU-IMF assistance to Euro-Area countries: an early assessment, Bruegel blueprint series, XIX

Regling K, Watson M (2010) A preliminary report on the sources of Ireland's banking crisis, Report commissioned by the Minister for Finance of Ireland, May. Available via http://www.bankinginquiry.gov.ie/Preliminary%20Report%20into%20Ireland%27s%20Banking%20Crisis%2031%20May%202010.pdf

Schmidt CM, Weigert B (2013) Weathering the crisis and beyond: perspectives for the Euro area. CEPR discussion paper no. DP9414, March. Available via http://papers.ssrn.com/sol3/papers.cfm?abstract_id=2244094

Schnabl G (2013) The macroeconomic policy challenges of balance sheet recession: lessons from Japan for the European crisis. CESifo working paper series no. 4249, 31 May. Available via http://papers.ssrn.com/sol3/papers.cfm?abstract_id=2274638

Sinn HW (2012) The European balance of payments crisis: an introduction. CESifo Forum, 13 Jan (Special Issue)
Sinn HW, Wollmershäeuser T (2011) Target loans, current account balances and capital flows: the ECB's rescue facility. NBER working paper no. 17626, November
Sturm M, Sauter N (2010) The impact of the global financial turmoil and recession on mediterranean countries' economies. ECB occasional paper series, no. 118, August
Suarez J (2010) The Spanish crisis: background and policy challenges. CEPR discussion paper no. 7909, London
Taylor AM (2012) External imbalances and financial crises. NBER working paper no. 18606, December
Tiffin A (2014) European productivity, innovation and competitiveness: the case of Italy. IMF working paper no. 14/79, May. Available via https://books.google.it/books?hl=it&lr=&id=Ofu1AwAAQBAJ&oi=fnd&pg=PP1&dq=european+productivity+innovation+and+competitiveness+the+case+of+italy&ots=D4s08kLneG&sig=L0eE1SA-9B8f1MqMYu1N34Jnkfw#v=onepage&q=european%20productivity%20innovation%20and%20competitiveness%20the%20case%20of%20italy&f=false
Tomz M, Wright MLJ (2013) Empirical research on sovereign debt and default. NBER working paper series no. 18855, February
Uhlig H (2014) Sovereign default risk and banks in monetary union. German Econ Rev 15 (1):23–41. doi:10.1111/geer.12039/abstract
Véron N (2011) The European debt and financial crisis: origins, options and implications for the US and global economy, draft, 22 Sept. Available via http://banking.senate.gov/public/index.cfm?FuseAction=Files.View&FileStore_id=9bec6123-d58d-423d-bf17-4fdcb9b113c3
Volz U (2012) Lessons of the European crisis for regional monetary and financial integration in East Asia. ADBI working paper no. 347, February. Available via http://www.scribd.com/doc/82534256/Lessons-of-the-European-Crisis-for-Regional-Monetary-and-Financial-Integration-in-East-Asia
Weidmann J (2011) Germany's role in the global economy. Speech by the president of the Deutsche Bundesbank at the American Council on Germany, Washington, DC, 26 Sept. Available via http://www.bis.org/review/r110930f.pdf?frames=0
Wyplosz C (2010) The eurozone in the current crisis. ADBI working paper no. 207, March
Wyplosz C (2011) A failsafe way to end the Euro area crisis. VoxEU, 26 Sept. Available via http://voxeu.org/index.php?q=node/7031

Chapter 6
The European Crisis and the Accumulation of TARGET2 Imbalances

Beniamino Moro

6.1 Introduction

How was it that Europe came to the recent Great Crisis? To answer the question, in this chapter some stylized facts are exposed and extensively discussed.

First, as illustrated in the previous chapter, an important element that much contributed to the crisis was the mispricing of risk by capital markets and an ensuing misallocation of capital in the decade before the outbreak of the crisis. This had the effect of giving wrong incentives to policymakers. In fact, during the boom years, when financial markets were blind to the sovereign risks, no incentives were given to policymakers to reduce their debts, as the latter were priced so favorably. Since the start of the financial crisis, financial markets driven by panic overpriced risks and gave incentives to policymakers to introduce excessive austerity programs.

Second, a high level of public debt is not a problem per se, as long as the government is able to refinance itself and roll over its debt. This requires public debt and the interest burden to grow more slowly than the economy and the tax base. This is not the case in many peripheral European countries. Therefore, today's debt crisis is not merely a debt crisis; as documented in the previous chapter, it is first and foremost a competitiveness and growth crisis that has led to structural imbalances within the euro area. In fact, below the surface of the sovereign public debt and banking crises lies a balance-of-payment crisis, caused by a misalignment of internal real exchange rates (Moro 2014).

Third, since the European Monetary Union (EMU) has been built as a union of sovereign states, each state has retained its own national central bank, which has become a member of the so-called Eurosystem with the European Central Bank

B. Moro (✉)
Department of Economics and Business, University of Cagliari, Viale San Ignazio 17, 09123 Cagliari, Italy
e-mail: moro@unica.it

B. Moro, V.A. Beker, *Modern Financial Crises*, Financial and Monetary Policy Studies 42, DOI 10.1007/978-3-319-20991-3_6

(ECB) at the top. National interbank payment systems have been merged into a euro area interbank payment system (TARGET2), where national central banks have assumed the role of the links between countries.[1] So, TARGET2 plays a key role in ensuring the smooth conduct of monetary policy, the correct functioning of financial markets, and banking and financial stability in the euro area, by substantially reducing systemic risk.

The settlement of cross border payments between participants in TARGET2 results in intra-Eurosystem balances—that is, positions on the balance sheets of the respective central banks that reflect claims/liabilities on/to the Eurosystem. They are reported on the National Central Banks' (NCB) balance sheets as TARGET2 claims, if positive, or TARGET2 liabilities, if negative, vis-à-vis the ECB as the central counterpart. TARGET2 balances reflect funding stress in the banking systems of crisis-hit countries, which must be interpreted with caution as they also reflect transactions among multi-country banking groups.

Fourth, interpretations of the role assumed by TARGET2 balances fall into two camps. The first is that these balances correspond to current account financing, which can be labeled the *flow* interpretation. The second camp interprets TARGET2 balances as a "capital account reversal", that, is they see this as one symptom of a balance-of-payment crisis. Someone argues that the Eurosystem full-allotment refinancing operations should be seen as financing the reversal of an outstanding stock of cross border claims, while the TARGET2 payment system merely records the results. This corresponds to the *stock* interpretation of TARGET2 balances.

Fifth, the tensions in sovereign debt markets and within the banking sector have fed each other, creating severe funding problems for many borrowers. These developments have also led to the fragmentation of the financial system along national borders, with a retrenchment of financial activities to national domestic markets. The resulting limited or costly access to funding for many businesses and households wishing to invest has been a major obstacle to recovery across Europe. At the same time, high levels of indebtedness mean that many economic actors need to reduce their financial exposure or increase their savings. Such "deleveraging" can also hamper recovery in the short term. The problems are particularly acute in the vulnerable euro area member states.

Sixth, the only possible way out to overcome the crisis is to launch a new phase of growth and promote a substantial increase in European employment. In the medium term, there is a widespread consent that a successful crisis resolution will need to include at least the following four components: (1) a fiscal union, i.e., a mechanism that ensures that fiscal policies in the Eurozone are partly centralized; (2) a banking union, i.e., a framework for banking policy and banking supervision at the European level; (3) an overhaul of EU/Eurozone institutions that

[1] Remember that TARGET is the "Trans-European Automated Real-time Gross settlement Express Transfer" system. It was replaced by TARGET2 in November 2007, with a transition period lasting until May 2008, by which time all national platforms were replaced by a single platform.

would enable fiscal and banking unions to be sustainable; and finally (4) short-term arrangements that chart a path toward the completion of the previous three points.

Finally, in the short run, we say that there exists a safe policy to promote growth in the European Union that can be implemented without interfering in the fiscal consolidation needs of the austerity-hit southern countries. This aim may be pursued if Germany does not maintain its public budget in balance for the next few years and commits itself to promote an expansionary fiscal policy. In fact, Germany is the only country in the EU that can expand its aggregate demand without paying a substantial increase in domestic inflation.

In order to expand European aggregate demand in the measure necessary to promote growth, Germany could also let domestic wages increase. The combined effects of the two policies (budget deficit plus wage increases) and the ensuing moderate increase in domestic inflation could be sufficient to appreciate the real exchange rate in Germany, permitting the austerity-hit EMU countries to regain their external competitiveness vis-à-vis surplus countries.

In order to extensively expose all these stylized facts, this chapter is organized as follows: Section 6.2 analyzes the accumulation of TARGET2 imbalances, Section 6.3 is devoted to the distinction between the "flow" and the "stock" interpretations of TARGET2 balances, and Sect. 6.4 deals with the insufficient responses and tensions among euro area governments. In Sect. 6.5 the fragmentation of the European financial system along national borders is analyzed, while Sect. 6.6 explains why the ECB has partly lost the control of interest rates in the crisis-hit countries. Section 6.7 is devoted to the credit channel paradox, and finally Sect. 6.8 concludes with an assessment of long- and short-run policies suggested to definitely overcome the European Great Crises.

6.2 The Accumulation of TARGET2 Imbalances

On the accumulation of TARGET2 imbalances, the debate was triggered by Sinn (2011, 2012a, b) and Sinn and Wollmershäeuser (2011, 2012), whose views can briefly be summarized as follows. By reducing the collateral requirements for the refinancing credits of Eurozone central banks, the ECB undercut market rates in the southern Eurozone countries and Ireland. This enabled a huge asymmetric expansion of refinancing credit and money creation, compensating for stalling capital imports and outright capital flight.

The monetary expansion in the southern countries in turn enabled a net outflow of central bank money to other Eurozone countries by way of international payment orders for the purpose of buying goods and assets and redeeming foreign debt. Sinn and Wollmershäeuser (2012) claim that this outflow is a classical balance-of-payment imbalance and that its accumulated value is measured by the TARGET2 balances.

In the surplus countries, commercial banks placed the funds they withdrew from the deficit countries with their own central banks, which implied a sterilization of the inflowing liquidity. Because of the sterilization, the policy has (thus far) not been inflationary, but for that same reason it is a pure fiscal credit transfer (a "stealth bailout") that resembles the official intergovernmental credit transfers (Sinn 2012b).

Sinn and Wollmershäeuser (2012) also argued that this policy was defensible at the time of the Lehman crisis but has meanwhile begun to undermine the allocative function of the capital market by offering credit at conditions that do not take idiosyncratic country risks into account and undercut the market rates. They also maintain that the TARGET2 debts impose risks on the rest of the Eurozone countries in proportion to their share in the ECB capital, should the deficit countries default and leave the Eurozone. In the case of a breakup of the Eurozone, the surplus countries' TARGET2 claims themselves would be at risk.

They note, moreover, that saying that the current account deficits were sustained with the extra refinancing credit behind the TARGET2 balances does not equate to claiming that current account deficits and TARGET2 deficits were positively correlated. On the contrary, to the extent that the ECB helped slow down the adjustment of precrisis current account deficits despite the reversal of private capital flows, the correlation should have been small if not zero, while the correlation between private capital imports and TARGET2 deficits should have been (and was) strongly negative (Sinn and Wollmershäeuser 2012).

This means that the ECB's extra refinancing credit, which resulted in TARGET2 debt, helped provide the funds needed to finance the current account deficits. This conclusion is confirmed by the definition of countries' budget constraint, according to which the sum of TARGET2 balances, private and intergovernmental international capital flows, and current account imbalances is zero.

The policy implication of this interpretation of TARGET2 balances is that, when exchange rate adjustments are impossible, the accumulation of credit and debit positions in TARGET2 needs to be limited and imbalances of cross border payment flows must be accommodated officially on an annual basis.

These arguments were rebutted by many authors, particularly by Whelan (2011, 2012), Buiter et al. (2011b), Buiter and Rahbari (2012), Bindseil and König (2011), Deutsche Bundesbank (2011), ECB (2011), and Banca d'Italia (2012). The main conclusions of these papers can be summarized as follows.

The fact that for some banking systems, such as Germany's, the refinancing obtained from the Eurosystem, net of the funds placed with the reserve account and the deposit facility, is negative in no way limits the ability of the Eurosystem to control the monetary base. What is important for the transmission of monetary policy is the net liquidity provided to euro area banks, not how it is distributed.

More generally, the increase of TARGET2 imbalances does not interfere with the conduct of monetary policy or the objective of price stability within the area. In particular, the existence of a large positive TARGET2 balance in some euro area countries does not entail a risk of inflation. The Eurosystem maintains its ability to mop up all the excess liquidity with appropriate instruments whenever changes in economic and financial conditions make this necessary.

Moreover, in the Eurosystem the increase of TARGET2 imbalances does not create any specific risk not already contained in monetary policy refinancing operations, which in any case for the NCBs is managed and mitigated by the threshold for the quality of collateral accepted in refinancing operations and the system of haircuts. Also, it is shared across the Eurosystem according to the ECB's capital key and thus independent of the credit or debit TARGET2 position of each single NCB.

Taking into account the mechanics of the transactions and the economic factors behind these imbalances and looking at balance-of-payment (BOP) identities, Cecioni and Ferrero (2012) argue that TARGET2 imbalances are correlated to the recourse to monetary policy refinancing operations, via NCBs' balance sheets, but they are not caused by them.

Adopting the fixed-rate full-allotment (FRFA) procedure in the refinancing operations and expanding the list of eligible collateral countered the pressures on banks' liquidity and on financial markets, which originated from the massive disruption of interbank and capital markets at the peak of the crisis and to the drying up of cross-country flows. These measures played a key role in preserving the functioning of the payment system and the financial stability of the euro area. The resulting increase in central bank's reserves was accompanied by the widening of the TARGET2 balances.

6.3 The *Flow* and the *Stock* Interpretation of TARGET2 Balances

The increase in TARGET2 balances has been closely linked to BOP imbalances. During the crisis, trade balance deficits were neither necessary nor sufficient conditions for the increase in TARGET2 imbalances. BOP financial account imbalances, instead, were a necessary condition. Before the crisis, both the BOP current account and the trade balance of the countries under stress were in deficit, with the exception of Italy where they were approximately balanced. These deficits were funded mostly from foreign investments in domestic securities and in the interbank market. The capital flowing in and out of the countries was almost completely netted out, leaving small average net balances for the individual items of the BOP financial account.

During the crisis, the absolute size of individual items in the BOP increased and its composition changed significantly. The main changes were in the financial accounts. The reversals of foreign investments in domestic securities and of liabilities issued by domestic monetary and financial institutions (MFIs) were not matched by a similar increase in disinvestments of domestic capital previously invested abroad. Net outflows in the financial accounts of the BOP were compensated by a considerable increase in the respective NCB's TARGET2 liabilities with the ECB (Cecioni and Ferrero 2012).

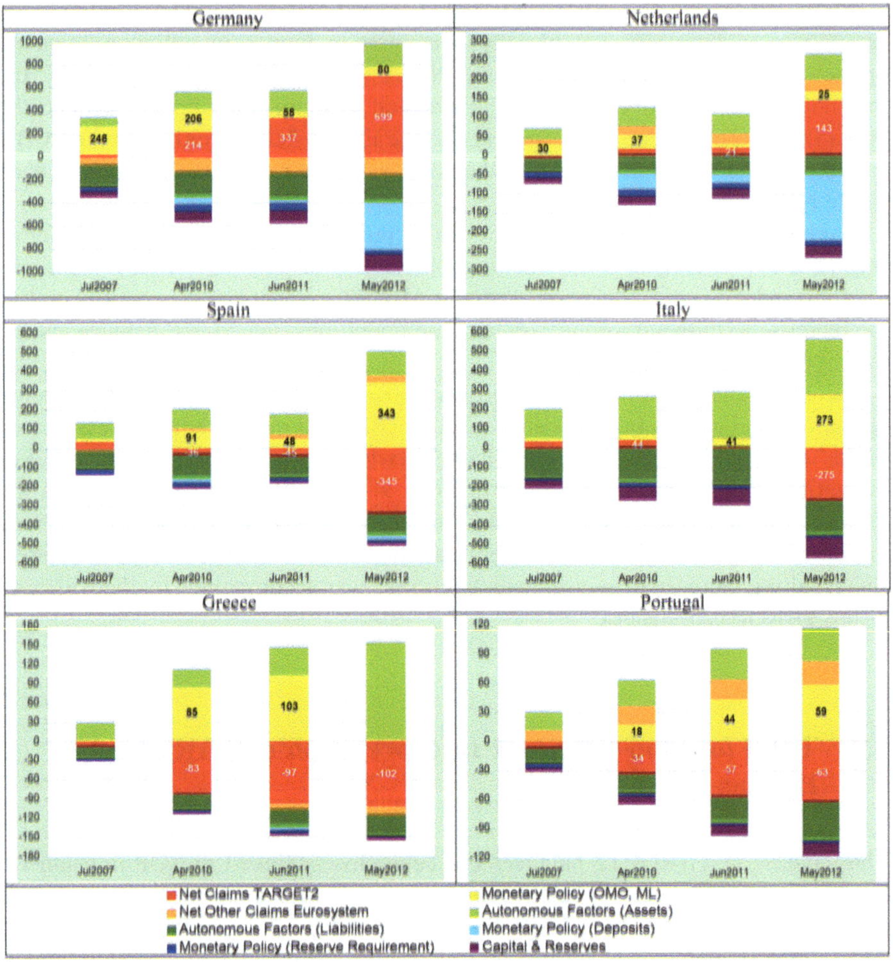

Fig. 6.1 NCB balance sheets (*billion €; outstanding amount at the end of the month*) (*Source:* Cecioni and Ferrero 2012)

The timing of these changes was uneven across countries. Referring to Fig. 6.1, during the global financial crisis (August 2007–April 2010) and in the first phase of the sovereign debt crisis (May 2010–June 2011), Italy's and Spain's financial accounts remained almost unchanged, while those of Greece and Portugal showed the largest adjustments. In the latter countries, foreigners disinvested from the interbank and the securities markets, and some signs of deposit flight from domestic banks by residents appeared.

In the second phase of the sovereign debt crisis (July 2011–May 2012), access to international financial markets by the Italian and Spanish governments and MFIs was also impaired. During this period, Italy and Spain recorded net outflows from the MFIs, respectively, of €118 and €182 bn and net outflows of portfolio investments of about €90 bn.

In Italy, in particular, net outflows of portfolio investments largely corresponded to a willingness in nonresidents not to roll over maturing sovereign debt securities and, to a lesser extent, to sales by nonresidents of sovereign debt securities on the secondary market.[2] In the same period, TARGET2 liabilities increased for Italy and Spain to approximately €280 and €300 bn, respectively.

As to the implications for the monetary policy transmission and the risks for the balance sheet of the Eurosystem, Cecioni and Ferrero's main conclusion is that the ECB's unconventional monetary policies contrast the risks of segmentation in the money markets along national lines with the aim of preserving the transmission of the unique monetary policy. Any institutional change that would limit the flow of payments through TARGET2 would have a pro-cyclical effect, by tightening further liquidity conditions in troubled countries, and it would increase asymmetries within the euro area, undermining the existence of the unique monetary policy.

Furthermore, when evaluating the cross-country risks, it should be taken into account that member states' net external positions have not changed because of the widening of TARGET2 balances. Rather, private credit (debit) positions have been substituted by NCBs' credit (debit) TARGET2 positions vis-à-vis the ECB. The risks that were previously entirely borne on the private sector of creditor countries are now shared across Eurosystem's NCBs.[3]

---

[2] In fact, what happened in the periphery countries was a twin crisis as described in Kaminsky and Reinhart (1999), as the financial crisis stopped the capital inflows ("sudden stop"), producing both a banking crisis (as banks could not be financed, here the causality is double, as the bad performance of banks is also responsible for the stop in inflows) and a current account crisis (as the capital inflows helped to finance the current account).

[3] Auer (2014) examines the extent to which changes in national TARGET2 balances can be statistically associated with cross border private capital flows and current account (CA) balances. In a quarterly panel spanning the years 1999 to 2012 and 12 countries, it is shown that while the CA and changes in TARGET2 balances were unrelated until the start of the 2007 financial crisis, since then the relation between these two variables has become statistically significant and economically sizeable. This reflects the "sudden stop" in private sector capital that had hitherto funded CA imbalances. Auer next examines how different types of private capital flows have evolved over the last few years and how this can be related to changes in TARGET2 balances, finding some deposit flight by private customers, a substantial retrenchment of cross border interbank lending, and also an increase in bank's holdings of high-quality sovereign debt. His first conclusion from this analysis is that since TARGET2 imbalances were caused by a sudden stop and are unlikely to grow without bounds as Eurozone CA imbalances are currently diminishing at a rapid pace, there is no evidence that the institutional setup of the European monetary union needs to be reformed fundamentally. A further conclusion relates to how the current system transfers risks across the currency union. Limiting or settling TARGET2 balances is not a viable option. Rather, policies must be geared to limiting the implicit risk transfer from the private to the public sector within TARGET2 creditor nations, which is facilitated by the current system as it may change the incidence of euro breakup risk.

Nevertheless, the banking system cannot permanently rely on central bank funds for its main source of funding. In the medium term, peripheral countries cannot continue to substitute inflows of foreign private sector liquidity with TARGET2 liabilities. Stressed countries must return to private markets and attract funds from the rest of the area. This requires the restoration of confidence in both the banking sector and in the sustainability of public finance.

Similar conclusions are reached by Whelan (2012), who first argues that the process by which TARGET2 liabilities are incurred does not change the net asset position of central banks because they either replace existing liabilities or are combined with the addition of new assets. Rather than an external bailout, in practice, the increase in TARGET2 balances reflects the ability of national central banks in the Eurosystem to create money to lend to banks experiencing funding problems and so, if anything, these balances reflect countries "bailing out themselves".

Whelan agrees that the large changes in intra-Eurosystem balances in recent years are the result of capital flight from the periphery rather than the accumulation of current account deficits. These balances have evolved due to the monetary policy strategy agreed by the ECB's Governing Council and because of the free movement of capital guaranteed by the EU rather than because of any special features of the TARGET2 payment system.

Indeed, he describes how large changes in intra-Eurosystem balances would have occurred due to capital flight even if electronic bank transfers via TARGET2 had been shut down and only cash payments allowed. The increasing risks for Germany associated with the Bundesbank's TARGET2 balance have been offset to a large extent by a significant decline in private German bank exposures to the periphery. Also in the extreme event of a full uncooperative euro breakup, Whelan argues that the underlying costs to German taxpayers would be far lower than the regularly cited full value of the TARGET2 balance.[4]

Finally, Whelan argues that the Eurosystem should consider proposals for annual settlement of TARGET2 balances with settlement taking place using assets acquired during monetary policy operations. Such a settlement procedure would see TARGET2 balances reset to zero each year.

While this proposal would imply a change in the Eurosystem's accounting procedures for dealing with balances owed between its members, it would not change the daily operations of the TARGET2 payment system nor would it change the nature of risk sharing on monetary policy operations currently in place for euro member states.

In contrast, Sinn's (2011) proposal to limit TARGET2 balances would imply an effective end to the euro as a common currency, while his proposal for annual settlement of balances using state-owned real estate or senior rights to future tax

[4] This is partly because the rest of the Eurosystem has a large claim of about €200 billion on Germany relating to banknote issuance and partly because the seigniorage powers of a post-breakup for the Bundesbank are likely to be considerably higher than at present. Whelan's conclusion is shared by De Grauwe and Ji (2012) who argue that, also in the extreme case of a euro breakup, the risk of losing TARGET2 claims for surplus countries does not exist.

revenue (Sinn 2012a) would represent a significant change to current risk-sharing arrangements in relation to monetary policy operations and would likely undermine the operation of a common monetary policy. Therefore, neither of these proposals is consistent with a continuation of the euro as a common currency.

To conclude on this point, according to Cecchetti et al. (2012), interpretations of TARGET2 balances fall into two camps. The first is that these balances correspond to current account financing, which can be labeled as the *flow* interpretation. Proponents of this view include most prominently Sinn and Wollmershäeuser (2011, 2012). The second camp, including Buiter et al. (2011a), Mody and Bornhorst (2012), Bindseil and König (2012), and Cecioni and Ferrero (2012), interprets TARGET2 balances as a "capital account reversal".[5] That is, they see this as one symptom of a balance-of-payment crisis.

Bindseil and König (2012) argue that the Eurosystem full-allotment refinancing operations should be seen as financing the reversal of an outstanding stock of cross border claims, while the TARGET2 payment system merely records the results. Cecchetti et al. (2012) label this the *stock* interpretation of TARGET2 balances.

Finally, it is worth mentioning that the members of the European Economic Advisory Group (2012) take an intermediate position. They read Sinn and Wollmershäeuser (2011, 2012) as arguing that Greece and Portugal financed their current account deficits since 2008–2010 through TARGET2, while Ireland's TARGET2 balance was associated with a capital outflow, and Spain's TARGET2 balance financed only a quarter of its cumulated current account. Italy is identified as a case of "capital flight" in late 2011.

6.4 Insufficient Responses and Tensions Among Euro Area Governments

The European crisis has highlighted that international financial integration will not automatically lead to an efficient allocation of capital, as predicted by neoclassical theory.

The Stability and Growth Pact (SGP) belief in the ability of free markets to efficiently allocate capital and discipline governments was certainly not warranted. What we have seen instead is that unrestricted financial integration in the euro area contributed to the development of unsustainable imbalances and bubbles. While financial markets underpriced sovereign risk in the euro's first decade, the pendulum has swung back and after 2010 gave way to excessive pessimism about the periphery countries' ability to repay their debt.

[5] This term was coined by Mody and Bornhorst (2012). Lane (2013) investigates the behavior of gross capital flows and net capital flows for euro area member countries; he highlights the extraordinary boom-bust cycles in both gross flows and net flows since 2003. He also shows that the "reversal" in net capital flows during the crisis has been very costly in terms of macroeconomic and financial outcomes for the high-deficit countries.

The European countries facing the crisis have experienced what a large number of developing and emerging countries went through over the past decades: a period of strong yet unsustainable output growth fueled by capital inflows comes to a halt at some point, leading to a "sudden stop" or reversal of capital flows (Kaminsky and Reinhart 1999; Reinhart and Reinhart 2009; Moro et al. 2015).

This pattern, which has often been repeated in the modern era of global finance, and now once more in Europe, should give pause to seriously reconsider the costs and benefits of international financial integration (Lama and Rabanal 2012). Fortunately, the Great Crisis has not only given impetus to fresh academic thinking on this matter but also led the IMF to reconsider its position on capital account management and regulation of international capital flows (IMF 2012; Ostry et al. 2010, 2011).

However, even the fund was unprepared for the possibility of balance-of-payment (BOP) crises in the euro area. In their surveillance work during the period 1999–2009, IMF staff never raised the possibility of major sovereign or BOP crises in the euro area despite their intimate knowledge of crises elsewhere and potential parallels with the euro area that should have drawn their attention, in particular consumption booms, real exchange rate appreciation, and large current account deficits, which are typical in countries before a BOP crisis (Pisani-Ferry et al. 2011).

We also must recognize that, if the Great Crisis became particularly serious in the euro area, it is also because of the design flaws in economic and monetary European Union (EU). The euro was built on an imperfect institutional framework, envisaged by the 1992 Maastricht Treaty and the 1997 Stability and Growth Pact (SGP).

The commission and the ECB were also unprepared. What was not well understood was that euro area countries could face BOP problems like emerging countries. A BOP crisis happens when private markets stop financing viable borrowers because of the country they belong to. Because it is within the confines of its jurisdiction, the state, as the ultimate insurer of private agents—notably banks—that risks incurred by households, companies, and banks tend to concentrate. Banks with assets that are not diversified internationally also concentrate risks resulting from the potential insolvency of private agents as well as of the sovereign (Pisani-Ferri et al. 2013, 9).

As they rely on the state as their backstop, they transfer the risk to it. Finally, because in the euro area the state issues debt in a currency over which it has no control (De Grauwe 2011), it is vulnerable to liquidity crises. This perspective in turn weakens private agents that hold large quantities of government paper. This web of interdependence between the state, banks, and nonfinancial agents may lead markets to price country risk and, in the extreme, to shun all agents located in a particular country, irrespective of their individual financial health.[6]

[6] Allen and Moessner (2012) examine the liquidity effects of the euro area sovereign debt crisis, including its effects on euro area banks as a group, on intra-euro area financial flows, on the supply of and demand for collateral, and on international liquidity.

After the Lehman Brothers' collapse, financial markets reassessed their exposure to euro area countries that had accumulated large current account deficits and net external investment positions before the financial crisis. They concluded that country risk existed in a monetary union and suddenly stopped the capital flows to those countries. The result was extreme pressure on the most vulnerable euro area countries (Pisani-Ferri et al. 2013).

But a classical currency crisis, which would have meant the partial disintegration of the monetary union, was avoided thanks to the provision of ample liquidity by the Eurosystem (reflected in TARGET2 balances). The private sector could and did lose access to private funding contrary to the predictions in the academic literature. Yet, this did not lead to a lack in funding because the Eurosystem through its liquidity operations replaced outflowing liquidity (see Chap. 5, Sects. 5.6 and 5.7).

The private capital flow reversals led to acute liquidity shortages in the banking systems of the countries concerned. The ECB provided liquidity to the banks. It did so in the framework of its Long-Term Refinancing Operations (LTRO) as well as the Main Refinancing Operation (MRO) (Pisani-Ferry and Wolff 2012). This is in contrast to typical currency crises, in which national central banks cannot replace the withdrawal of foreign currency financing, which then leads to a crisis.

Nonetheless, sovereigns in affected countries did face a payment crisis. Because they had lost access to private markets or at least because they were facing escalating borrowing costs, governments in Greece, Ireland, and Portugal had no choice but to seek foreign assistance to fill their financing gap.

Anyway, the crisis was not merely an economic and financial crisis. It was also a political crisis, stemming from erratic responses and tensions among euro area governments, quarreling over the right crisis diagnosis and response. European leaders were caught wrong-footed in 2010, as they believed that a balance-of-payment crisis was impossible within a monetary union. Since such a crisis was not considered a priori, no crisis resolution mechanism had been put in place.

European policymakers hence faced the challenge of crafting a crisis response from scratch in the midst of crisis, first agreeing on bilateral lending to Greece and, when this appeared insufficient, on the creation of the European Financial Stability Facility (EFSF) and the European Financial Stability Mechanism (EFSM). This task has been complicated not only because the negotiations involve a large number of parties but also because the chosen crisis resolution measures have serious ramifications for the long-term institutional framework and functioning of the monetary union. As Bergsten and Kirkegaard (2012) note, achieving the dual policy goals of solving a current crisis while trying also to prevent the next one—and using the same policy tools to do both—is rarely easy.

Collignon (2012) agrees that the crisis is due partly to fundamental economic developments, such as growth and competitiveness, and partly to uncooperative behavior between the main policymakers in Europe. Also Orphanides (2014) explores the dominant role of politics in decisions made by euro area governments during the crisis and discusses decisions that appear to have been driven by local political considerations to the detriment of the euro area as a whole.

The domination of politics over economics has led to crisis mismanagement. The underlying cause of tension is identified by Orphanides as a misalignment of political incentives. Member state governments tended to defend their own interests in a noncooperative manner. This has magnified the costs of the crisis and has resulted in an unbalanced and divisive incidence of the costs across the euro area. In the absence of a federal government, no institution but the ECB can adequately defend the interests of the euro area as a whole. European political institutions instead appear weak and incapable of defending European principles and the proper functioning of the euro. Political reform is needed to sustain the euro, but this is unlikely to pass the political feasibility test with the current governments of Europe.

The fears of the surplus countries, led by Germany, that an easy bailout of Greece would set a negative precedent and create moral hazard problems with other deficit countries—especially the larger euro area members, Spain and Italy, both of which are considered "too big to save"—prevented a quick resolution of the Greek crisis and led to piecemeal solutions, which were never comprehensive enough to end the crisis, and eventually caused contagion to other weak euro countries.

Worries of moral hazard and the risk to build up a "transfer union", where deficit countries would have to be financed permanently through direct or indirect transfers and subsidies, made surplus countries also reluctant to endorse proposals such as those for eurobonds (Delpla and Von Weizsäcker 2010, 2011) or a partial guarantee of all euro area sovereign bonds by the ECB (Wyplosz 2011).

6.5 The Fragmentation of the European Financial System Along National Borders

The crisis has not only had a strong impact on the financial situation of many European countries, but has also affected investors' and lenders' confidence and the effectiveness of the financial sector. The tensions in sovereign debt markets and within the banking sector have fed each other, creating severe funding problems for many borrowers.

These developments have also led to the fragmentation of the financial system along national borders, with a retrenchment of financial activities to national domestic markets. The resulting limited or costly access to funding for many businesses and households wishing to invest has been a major obstacle to recovery across Europe.

At the same time, high levels of indebtedness mean that many economic actors must reduce their financial exposure or increase their savings. Such "deleveraging" can also hamper recovery in the short term. The problems are particularly acute in the vulnerable euro area member states (Van Rixtel and Gasperini 2013; Al-Eyd and Berkmen 2013; De Sola Perea and van Nieuwenhuyze 2014; European Commission 2013).

To overcome these problems and tensions, in July 2012 President Mario Draghi announced at an investors' conference in London that the ECB would do "whatever it takes" to preserve the euro and fight the crisis. Soon after this commitment, on September 6, the ECB approved the Outright Monetary Transactions (OMT) program. Under this program, the bank promised to buy unlimited sovereign bonds of troubled countries in secondary markets, with a maturity of between 1 and 3 years.

The program could be activated by the ECB only after an explicit request of the troubled country in which the latter agreed to accept the ECB's direct control and supervision of its financial and budgetary public policies.

The purpose of this program, first, was to reduce the spreads in the interest rates for public bonds of troubled countries with respect to German bonds and, second, to safeguard the monetary policy transmission mechanism in all countries of the euro area, preserving the uniqueness of Eurozone monetary policy and ensuring the proper transmission of the policy stance to the real economy throughout the area.

As shown in Fig. 6.2, soon after Draghi's London speech, TARGET2 net positions stopped to increase and began to decrease toward lower levels. On December 31, 2014, TARGET2 balances had fallen by half since July 2012 (Draghi 2015), and this means that confidence was again growing in the Eurosystem. Private money is now coming into circulation again, and it is being invested in other countries. This is clearly the evidence of the strong power that the ECB has in influencing the expectations of financial flows among euro area countries.

In fact, also the spreads in public bond interest rates have considerably fallen, in line with interest rates reductions among European crisis-hit countries (Fig. 6.3). After Draghi's London speech, Spanish and Italian bond yields have also greatly fallen, according to the decrease of their spreads with respect to German public bonds.

As shown in Fig. 6.4, the level of Italian and Spanish spreads on March 12, 2015, were, respectively, 89 and 90 basis points, very close to the levels they had at the end of 2009 before the outburst of the sovereign debt crisis.[7]

This means that soon after the first months in 2015, those spreads incorporate only the country risk due to fundamentals, without any risk premium due to the potential breakup of the whole monetary union. The ECB has bought time for governments to overhaul their economies and banks, but it happened that politicians have taken advantage of the financial-market calm to slow their recovery efforts.[8]

Eurozone leaders agreed during the June 29, 2012, summit to build a banking union that would include a single banking supervisor housed within the ECB, a common deposit insurance for households, and a common bank resolution rule. However, the lack of progress on the banking union and doubts about the financial

---

[7] Altavilla et al. (2014) evaluate the macroeconomic effects of OMT announcements by the ECB. They find that Italian and Spanish 2-year government bond yields decreased by about 2 % points while leaving unchanged the bond yields of the same maturity in Germany and France.

[8] Aizenman et al. (2013) investigate the impact of credit rating changes on the sovereign spreads in the EU. They find that the association between credit rating changes and spreads shifted markedly between the precrisis and crisis periods. European countries had quite similar CDS responses to credit rating changes during the precrisis period, but large differences emerged during the crisis period between the now highly sensitive PIIGS group and other European country groupings (EU and euro area excluding PIIGS and the non-EU area). They also find a complicated nonlinear pattern dependent on the level of the credit rating. In addition, contagion from rating downgrades in PIIGS to other euro countries is not evident once own-country credit rating changes are taken into account.

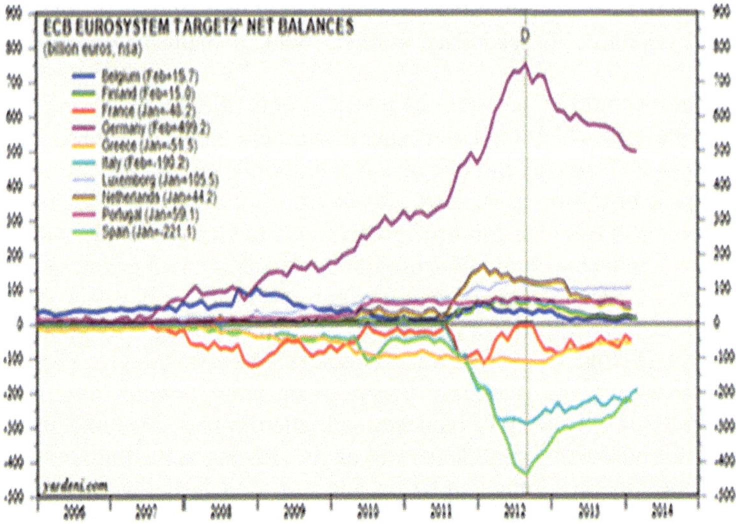

Fig. 6.2 European TARGET2 balances from 2006 to May 2014 (*billion €*) (*Source:* Il Sole-24Ore)

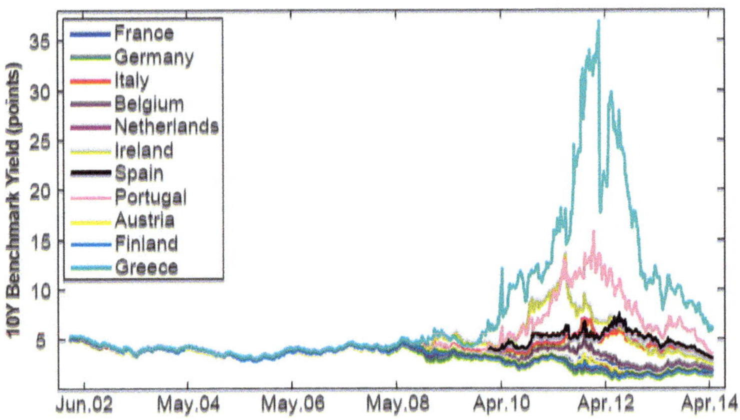

Fig. 6.3 EMU sovereign 10-year public bond yields, from March 2002 to May 2014 (*Source:* Sensoy et al. 2015)

strength of the banks in crisis-hit countries are hindering cross border lending. So, the fragmentation of the financial system along national borders and the retrenchment of financial activities to national domestic markets persist.[9]

[9] The financial crisis also led to a systematic divergence in credit spreads for financial firms across national boundaries. This divergence in cross-country credit risk increased further as the European debt crisis has unfolded since 2010. Since that time, credit spreads for both nonfinancial and financial firms increasingly reflected national rather than euro area financial conditions (Gilchrist and Mojon 2014).

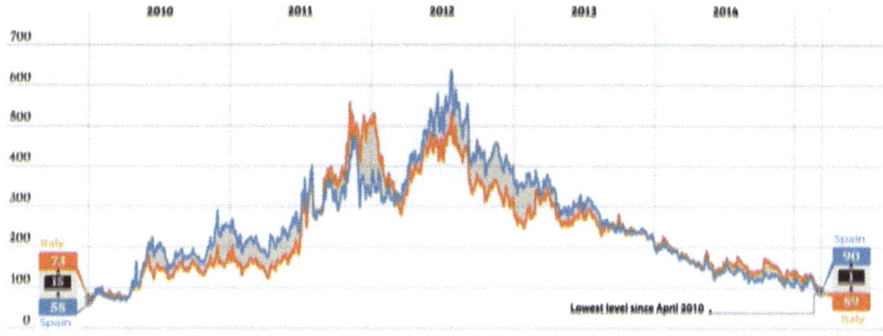

Fig. 6.4 Italy's and Spain's spreads on 10-year public bond yields with respect to the German Bund. Final data are on March 12, 2015 (*Source:* Il Sole-24Ore)

The crisis has caused significant disruptions to the functioning of the banking system and the financial markets within the euro area. The process of financial integration and convergence toward a single financial market that had been under way for a number of years was abruptly halted by the crisis, triggering a reversal of the integration process, which was then reinforced by the reemergence of country risks within the euro area and by the related and perverse bank-sovereign feedback loop.[10]

6.6 The ECB's Loss of Control over Interest Rates in the Crisis-Hit Countries

Bologna and Caccavaio (2014) show that the determinants of cross border banking change substantially over time: first, in the precrisis period of financial integration, the physical and the financial distances between countries were the main drivers; second, during the global financial crisis, banks reduced the concentration in their foreign claims portfolio and retrenched from the more externally vulnerable countries but kept on investing in the still-profitable countries with a sound fiscal position; and third, during the euro area sovereign tensions, while portfolio diversification and the pullback from externally vulnerable countries continued, foreign

[10] Reichlin (2013) shows that while in the two recent episodes of euro area recession and financial stress the ECB acted aggressively providing liquidity to banks, the second recession, unlike the first, has been characterized by an abnormal decline of loans with respect to both real economic activity and the monetary aggregates. This shows that euro area banks, over the 2008–2012 period, did not change neither the capital to asset ratio nor the size of their balance sheet relative to GDP, keeping them at the precrisis level.

claims were also driven by the deteriorating sovereign conditions, the bank-sovereign link, and opportunities for flight to quality.[11]

Another problem was the transmission mechanism of the monetary policy to the economies of various countries. Since the early part of 2010, tensions in the sovereign debt markets of some euro area countries have progressively distorted monetary and credit conditions, hindering the ECB monetary policy transmission mechanism and raising the cost of loans to nonfinancial corporations and households.[12]

In fact, the precise transmission mechanism of the ECB monetary policy is not so clear. The problem of troubled EMU countries, especially Italy and Spain, but also the UK, is that the interest rates that small- and medium-sized enterprises (SMEs) must pay to borrow money are far above those set by the ECB and those paid to depositors. Therefore, the link between the ECB's policy rate and borrowing in the real economy is broken (Van Rixtel and Gasperini 2013; Neri 2013).[13]

As documented by Illes et al. (2015), the global financial crisis pushed central banks in many countries to cut short-term policy rates to near zero. Based on the precrisis relationship between bank-lending rates on mortgages or loans to businesses with policy rates, it would have been reasonable to expect lending rates to have fallen by similar amounts.

But examination of the lending rates reveals they did not fall that much (Illes and Lombardi 2013; Gambacorta et al. 2014). In fact, the margins over policy rates have widened as policy rates have fallen (Fig. 6.5). Comparing the average margins on short-term and long-term loans to small business for nine euro area countries, Denmark and the UK in the precrisis (January 2003–August 2008) and post-crisis period (September 2008–April 2014) show that they rose by 19.5 %, while margins on short-term and long-term mortgage loans rose by 41.8 and 37.5 %, respectively.

---

[11] Quoting BIS (2012) data, Bologna and Caccavaio (2014) provide a clear and reliable picture of cross border banking at aggregate level by country of residence, which allows to identify a number of stylized features. Total gross consolidated foreign claims on an immediate risk basis of banks headquartered in euro area countries decreased by 35 % from the peak in March 2008 (€11,696 bn) to June 2012 (€7,579 bn), returning to levels previously seen at the end of 2005. The decline was more pronounced for claims on euro area countries (−40 %) than for those vis-à-vis non-euro area countries (−32 %).

[12] Neri (2013) makes an empirical assessment of the impact of the tensions on bank-lending rates in the main euro area countries, concluding that they have had a significant impact on the cost of credit in the peripheral countries. A counterfactual exercise indicates that if the spreads had remained constant at the average levels recorded in April 2010, the interest rates on new loans to nonfinancial corporations and on residential mortgage loans to households in the peripheral countries would have been, on average, lower by 130 and 60 basis points, respectively, at the end of 2011.

[13] The literature on the pass-through of monetary policy to lending rates is vast. From an empirical point of view, a recent paper by Gambacorta et al. (2014) investigates the pass-through of monetary policy to lending rates applied to nonfinancial firms in major advanced economies, prior and after the global Great Crisis. They find evidence of a structural break after Lehman Brothers' default, due to a strong increase in the markup between the lending rate and the policy rate of central banks, both in the USA and in Europe.

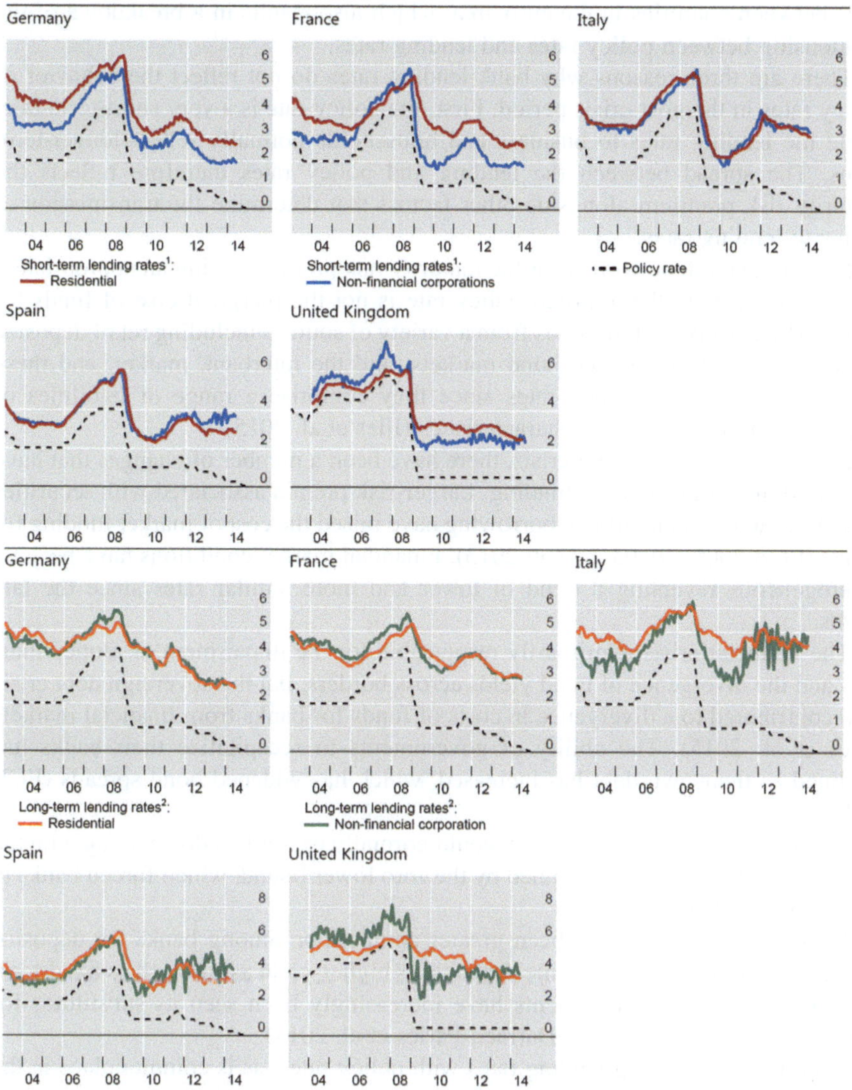

[1] The short-term concerns rates less than 1-year maturity. [2] The long-term concerns rates above 1-year maturity. The average maturity assumed for the long-term securities is 5-years.

Fig. 6.5 MFIs lending rates: short and long term (*Source:* European Central Bank, national data)

This reflects opportunistic behavior by banks, which have taken advantage of the reduction in official interest rates without transferring these benefits to borrowers. Inevitably this has raised the question of whether banks were taking advantage of the low interest rate environment by failing to pass on lower rates to loans (Arestei and Gallo 2014). Also the ECB (2013) gives a reason for divergence of lending rates between countries in the euro area, which also results in a breakdown of the relationship between policy rates and lending rates.

There are three reasons why bank-lending rates do not reflect the behavior of policy rates in the post-crisis period. First, the policy rate is a very short-term rate, while the lending rates to business and households normally reflect longer-term loans. The spread between the lending and policy rates therefore reflects the maturity risk premium alongside other factors that determine the transmission of policy to lending rates.

Second, even if we correct for the maturity risk premium using an appropriately adjusted swap rate, the adjusted policy rate is not the marginal cost of funds for banks. Third, banks obtain funds from a variety of sources including retail deposits, senior unsecured or covered bond markets, and the interbank market, and these differ in nature from policy rates since they comprise a range of liabilities of differing maturities and risk characteristics (Illes et al. 2015).

Since the global financial crisis, there have been a number of changes that have increased the cost of market funding. Larger-risk premia associated with securities issued by banks and interbank borrowing have raised the cost of market funding for banks (ECB 2009, 2010a, b; Zoli 2013). Financial market conditions have become heterogeneous reversing a trend of lower and more similar rates since the late 1990s.

The financial crisis is primarily responsible for the impairment of money markets and the divergence of bond yields across borders; but the sovereign debt crisis also contributed to a divergence in costs of funds for banks from financial markets (Illes et al. 2015). The ability of governments to recapitalize their banks has declined as their own debt has increased, which has widened bond spreads (ECB 2012).

In addition, deposit rates, which would normally be marked down along with the policy rates, have been constrained by the zero lower bound, which forced banks to reduce the markdowns.

On top of that, there has been greater competition among banks for deposits, which further raised rates on time deposits, as higher-yield assets such as fixed-term securities issued by governments have increasingly been seen as substitutes for low-yield deposits by savers (Darracq-Paries et al. 2014).

Therefore, comparing lending rates with policy rates, as is commonplace in the empirical pass-through literature, is highly misleading, since the latter do not reflect the effective cost of funding of banks. Greater focus should be placed on the whole range of liabilities that banks use to acquire funds (Adrian et al. 2013; Turner 2013). The focus should shift to the spread between lending rates versus a measure of effective bank funding costs, i.e., the weighted-average cost of liabilities (Illes et al. 2015).

To overcome all these problems, on March 2015, the ECB for the first time inaugurated a European quantitative easing (Qe) monetary policy. The ECB had lowered its main lending rate in September 2014 to just 0.05 % while charging banks on deposits they leave with it through a negative rate of 0.2 %. She had hoped to reverse the shrinking of its balance sheet, after commercial banks reimbursed their 2011–2012 LTROs, through another more extended round of long-term funding operations, providing liquidity until 2018 at a fixed rate of just 0.15 % a year.

But the first two of eight ECB's planned lenders have been a disappointment: in September and December 2014, banks borrowed only €212 bn, little more than half the €400 bn available. So, the only way for the ECB to expand the size of its own balance sheet, which she intends returning at least to the high of €3.000 bn that it reached in early 2012, after the successful two extraordinary LTROs of December 2011 and February 2012, was to proceed without further delay with Qe (see Chap. 11, Sect. 11.4.5).[14]

6.7 The Credit Channel Paradox

An alternative explanation for the fact that the link between the ECB's policy rate and the market borrowing rates in the real economy was broken is given by Bernanke and Gertler's (1995) "black-box" analysis. According to this view, when interest rates rise, credit supply might fall. This is known as the "credit channel paradox", which works as follows. Because of the capital rules of lending, banks can loan to SMEs only if they have a corresponding amount of capital or deposits on hand, while the rule does not apply when banks buy public bonds.

High interest rates on public bonds, therefore, crowd out the bank-lending channel to SMEs. Furthermore, banks lose deposits as customers prefer to use them to buy public bonds with higher rates of return. To plug the gap, banks offer long-term deposits that also pay higher interest rates. So, the entire cost of funding for the banks increases. As their own costs rise, banks' loans become scarcer and dearer. This then slows the economy by increasing costs for bank-dependent borrowers, which is the case for SMEs.

For the bank-lending channel to hold, it is necessary that: first, banks' costs rise and this depends on the shortfall of customers' deposits, plus the deterioration of insolvencies by firms and households, and, second, it will be important only in countries where firms are dependent on bank borrowing. This is the case where

[14] Crowley (2015) presents an overview of exposures in the balance sheets of central banks, banks, and other depository institutions during the past decade, with emphasis on asset growth and currency composition. He exploits the IMF's standardized report form-based monetary data to show (1) there was a widely observed buildup of assets prior to the global financial crisis, but there has been no significant reduction in its wake; (2) the foreign currency composition of the balance sheets of banks and other depository institutions remained remarkably constant in spite of the crisis, significant changes in the composition of balance sheets, and globalization and does not seem to have been significantly influenced by the behavior of exchange rates; and (3) exposure to households increased prior to the crisis, but this increased risk was offset by increased capitalization.

SMEs prevail, as in Italy, Spain, and the UK, where the loans that banks make exceed the cash they collect as deposits.

In 2008, as the Eurozone started to contract, the ECB slashed its main rate from 4.25 % to 1 %, but because investors were worried about the state of the banks, the returns that banks had to offer on their own bonds rose. This offset the ECB's easing, so that firms' borrowing rates fell by less than normal. When the euro crisis intensified in 2010, the ECB's influence on interest rates in Spain and Italy waned even further. Banks' bond yields rose in line with their governments' cost of borrowing. The supply of loans contracted as predicted by the bank-lending channel but now as a result of a change that the ECB did not control.

The amount of borrowing in Italy and Spain has started to fall again. Some of this may be due to weak demand, but Cappiello et al. (2010) provided empirical evidence for the existence of a bank-lending channel of monetary policy transmission in the euro area. Furthermore, they found that changes in the supply of credit, both in terms of volumes and in terms of credit standards applied on loans to enterprises, had significant effects on real economic activity.

To support the smooth transmission of its interest rate decisions to the wider economy, the ECB decided to accommodate the liquidity needs of banks that could not be satisfied in the financial market. Thus, since October 2008 the Eurosystem has been conducting most of its liquidity-providing tenders with a fixed-rate, full-allotment procedure. This means that all bids received from counterparties are fully satisfied, against adequate collateral. In the context of a dysfunctional interbank market, banks could thus turn to the Eurosystem for liquidity. This enabled them to build up buffers to meet future liquidity needs while access to interbank funding was uncertain. Consequently, the Eurosystem provided more liquidity than needed on aggregate by the banking sector, at the same time taking on an intermediation function. This prevented a disorderly deleveraging process and the ensuing adverse consequences for the euro area economy and price stability.

As the sovereign debt crisis emerged in some euro area countries, starting in spring 2010, the segmentation in funding markets for banks became more marked along national borders. The central bank intermediation allowed the banking systems in those countries to withstand the withdrawal of private capital and the reversal of cross border capital flows. The recourse to central bank funding is therefore closely linked to the emergence of significant TARGET2 liabilities for countries most affected by the crisis and, on aggregate, at the euro area level.

The sovereign debt crisis and resulting bank funding market segmentation also led to a flow of capital into the more resilient countries, resulting in significant amounts being directed toward the central banks' liquidity absorbing facilities, for example, via use of the deposit facility or via counterparties accruing amounts in excess of their reserve requirements in their current accounts at the central bank. In particular, the repatriation of previous investments and the lack of renewed lending to banks in crisis-hit countries led to significant net payment inflows, a concurrent increase in the TARGET2 claims of the NCBs in the more resilient countries and an increase in liquidity in the banking systems of those countries.

In the second half of 2011 and the first half of 2012, the sharp increase in TARGET2 liabilities and claims was also due to concerns about the integrity of the monetary union. A number of banks from resilient countries had decided to replace head office funding for subsidiaries in financially stressed jurisdictions with local funding. This meant that borrowing from the Eurosystem replaced intergroup funding from resilient countries. This behavior was in some cases encouraged by national banking regulators aiming to safeguard their domestic banking system (ECB 2013).

6.8 Concluding Remarks: The Role of Germany in Promoting European Recovery

The European financial crisis has demonstrated once more that any fixed exchange rate arrangement (including the monetary union) is prone to crisis if countries do not adjust their economies internally and imbalances are allowed to grow too large. If economic policies are not able to keep the domestic price level competitive vis-à-vis the rest of the integrating area, and external adjustments via the nominal exchange rate are precluded, real exchange rate appreciation will erode the countries' competitiveness. In most cases this will lead to current account deficits that at some point will trigger a balance-of-payment crisis.[15]

Therefore, structural reforms are unavoidable in indebted countries to improve productivity and increase competitiveness. Unfortunately, they will produce positive results only in the long run.

In the medium term, there is a widespread consent that a successful crisis resolution needs to include at least the following four components: (1) a fiscal union, i.e., a mechanism that ensures that fiscal policies in the Eurozone are partly centralized with shared backing across countries so as to meet the requirements of a monetary union; (2) a banking union, i.e., a framework for banking policy and banking supervision at the European level that credibly supports the vision of a single European market for financial services; (3) an overhaul of EU/Eurozone institutions that would enable fiscal and banking unions to be sustainable, by allowing centralized executive decision-making to the extent necessary and by guaranteeing democratic accountability; and finally (4) short-term arrangements

[15] According to Bordo and James (2013), there are some striking similarities between the pre-1914 gold standard and EMU today. Both arrangements are based on fixed exchange rates and monetary and fiscal orthodoxy. Each regime gave easy access by financially underdeveloped peripheral countries to capital from the core countries. But the gold standard was a contingent rule, because in the case of an emergency like a major war or a serious financial crisis, a country could temporarily devalue its currency. The EMU has no such safety valve. Capital flows in both regimes fueled asset price booms via the banking system ending in major crises in the peripheral countries. But not having the escape clause has meant that present-day peripheral European countries have suffered much greater economic harm than did Argentina in the Baring Crisis of 1890.

that chart a path toward the completion of the previous three points, which is bound to take some time.

In the European summit held in Brussels on June 28 and 29, 2012, Europe's political leaders committed themselves to the creation of a banking union and a unified banking supervision.[16] They also decided to move toward a fiscal union and more political integration and that troubled countries and their banking systems could directly access to Eurozone rescue funds (EFSF, EFSM, and ESM).[17]

Over the following months, many steps forward have been taken toward an effective governance of the Eurozone in order to guarantee financial stability, through the signature of the Treaty on Stability, Coordination and Governance (the Fiscal Compact), and the Six Pack and the Two Pack Agreements.[18]

The Fiscal Compact entered into force on January 1, 2013, and in March 2014, Eurozone leaders agreed to build a banking union that would include a single banking supervisor housed within the ECB, a common deposit insurance for households, and a common bank resolution rule. These decisions have enforced the process of convergence of TARGET2 balances depicted in Fig. 6.2.

Furthermore, there is now a general consensus that every country is obliged to pay off its own debt accumulated in the past. Therefore, the way is open to ensuring that financial stability will be pursued by each member state within the Eurozone, under strict European control.

However, fiscal consolidation will be difficult to achieve without a strong recovery of the European economy. There is no national way out of the crisis. Expansionary measures are impossible at the level of member states, which are obliged to choose fiscal consolidation as a priority; and in any case they would be domestically ineffective since most of the effects resulting from national measures would be lost through increased imports from other European countries. Therefore,

---

[16] Steps toward the creation of European supervisory authorities to help oversee Europe's financial sector from a pan-European perspective were taken in late 2008, when the president of the European Commission mandated a high-level expert group on financial supervision in the EU. The expert group, led by Jacques de Larosière, proposed three new supervisory authorities, which were established in November 2010 and started operation in January 2011: the European Banking Authority (EBA) based in London, the European Securities and Markets Authority (ESMA) based in Paris, and the European Insurance and Occupational Pensions Authority (EIOPA) based in Frankfurt. These three supervisory authorities were complemented by the creation of the European Systemic Risk Board (ESRB), which is responsible for the macro-prudential oversight of the financial system within the EU and which has a secretariat hosted by the ECB.

[17] Honkapoja (2013)) discusses on institutional improvements that can help in resolving the European crisis and avoiding a future one. These include the banking union and the strengthened Stability and Growth Pact and related institutional rules.

[18] Kilponen et al. (2012) find that European crisis resolution policies succeeded in reducing stress in the financial market. However, the impact of the same policy decision might have been positive for some countries while negative for others, suggesting that contagion effects may be important. Anyway, they stress that the economically most significant effects on the bond yields have been due to the announcement of the ECB's Securities Market Programme, whose further evolution was the Outright Monetary Transactions program.

in the short run, the only possible way to overcome the crisis is to launch a new phase of growth at European level and promote a substantial increase in European employment.

In this regard, there is a deep division between the economies of the prosperous North (Germany, Austria, the Netherlands, and Finland) and those of the austerity-hit South (France, Italy, Spain, Greece, and Portugal). As the unemployment rates in Spain and Greece (both 27 %), in Portugal (18.2 %), and even in France (11.2 %) and Italy (12 %) have become unsustainable, a long simmering growth-versus-austerity debate has boiled over with increasing calls from outside Germany to rethink crisis-fighting measures.

Up to now, Germany has been a staunch advocate of austerity, outlining plans to balance its own budget a year ahead of schedule, while France, Italy, and Spain, as well as the European Commission, have all indicated their strong concerns to promote growth without delaying fiscal consolidation. There is only one way to promote growth in the European Union without interfering in the fiscal consolidation needs of the austerity-hit southern countries. It is possible if Germany does not maintain a balanced public budget for the next few years and commits itself to promote an expansionary fiscal policy with deficits ranging from 1 % to 3 % of GDP. This can be achieved by expanding public expenditures or cutting the tax rate, or both. In fact, Germany is the only country in the EU that can expand its aggregate demand without paying a substantial increase in domestic inflation.

To expand European aggregate demand to the extent necessary to promote growth, Germany could also let domestic wages increase. The combined effects of the two policies (budget deficit plus wage increases) and the ensuing moderate increase in domestic inflation could be sufficient to appreciate the real exchange rate in Germany, permitting the austerity-hit Southern EMU countries to regain their external competitiveness. In this way, German surplus of the current account (7 % of GDP in 2014) will decrease, while exports of deficit EMU countries will increase, fueling again the economic growth of the entire union.[19]

[19] The same conclusion is reached by Holinski et al. (2012), who agree that changes in competitiveness and fiscal stance are a joint responsibility of and will affect both surplus and deficit countries. Recognizing this joint responsibility will greatly increase the economic and political stability of the euro area and hasten adjustment. In a recent paper, Kollmann et al. (2015) analyze the determinants of Germany's current account surplus after the launch of the euro. The most important factors driving the German surplus were positive shocks to the German saving rate and to the rest of the world demand for German exports, as well as German labor market reforms and other positive German aggregate supply shocks. The convergence of the rest of the euro area interest rates to German rates due to the creation of the euro only had a modest effect on the German current account and on German real activity. The key shocks that drove the rise in the German current account tended to worsen the rest of the euro area trade balance but had a weak effect on real activity. These driving factors are likely to be slowly eroded, leading to a very gradual reduction of the German current account surplus. An expansion in German government consumption and investment would raise German GDP and reduce the current account surplus, but the effects on the surplus are likely to be weak.

The final effect of this policy will be a further reduction of net claims and liabilities in the TARGET2 payment system.

References

Adrian T, Colla P, Shin HS (2013) Which financial frictions? Parsing the evidence from the financial crisis of 2007 to 2009. NBER macroeconomics annual 2012, 27, pp 159–214. Available via http://papers.nber.org/books/acem12-2

Aizenman J, Binici M, Hutchison MM (2013) Credit ratings and the pricing of sovereign debt during the euro crisis. NBER working paper series no. w19125, June. Available via http://papers.ssrn.com/sol3/papers.cfm?abstract_id=2280977

Al-Eyd A, Berkmen P (2013) Fragmentation and monetary policy in the euro area. IMF working paper no. 13/208, October. Available via http://papers.ssrn.com/sol3/papers.cfm?abstract_id=2346258

Allen WA, Moessner R (2012) The liquidity consequences of the euro area sovereign debt crisis. BIS working papers no. 390, November

Altavilla C, Giannone D, Lenza M (2014) The financial and macroeconomic effects of OMT announcements. CSEF working paper no. 352, January. Available via http://www.csef.it/WP/wp352.pdf

Arestei D, Gallo M (2014) Interest rate pass-through in the euro area during the financial crisis: a multivariate regime switching approach. J Policy Model 36:273–295

Auer R (2014) What drives target2 balances? Evidence from a panel analysis. Econ Policy 29 (77):139–197

Banca d'Italia (2012) Recent evolution of the balances of the TARGET2 payment system. Econ Bull 63(January)

Bergsten F, Kirkegaard JF (2012) The coming resolution of the European crisis. Peterson Institute for International Economics, Policy brief, January. Available via http://www.iie.com/publications/pb/pb12-1.pdf

Bernanke B, Gertler M (1995) Inside the black box: the credit channel of monetary policy transmission. J Econ Perspect 9(4):27–48

Bindseil U, König P (2011) The economics of TARGET2 balance. SFB 649 working paper no. 35. Available via http://sfb649.wiwi.hu-berlin.de/papers/pdf/SFB649DP2011-035.pdf

Bindseil U, König P (2012) TARGET2 and the European sovereign debt crisis. Kredit und Kapital 45(2):135–174

BIS (2012) Detailed tables on preliminary locational and consolidated banking statistics at end-June 2012, October. Available via http://www.bis.org/statistics/consstats.htm

Bologna P, Caccavaio M (2014) Euro area (cross-border?) banking. Bank of Italy occasional paper no. 228. Available via http://papers.ssrn.com/sol3/papers.cfm?abstract_id=2564111

Bordo MD, James H (2013) The European crisis in the context of the history of previous financial crisis. NBER working paper no. w19112, June. Available via http://papers.ssrn.com/sol3/papers.cfm?abstract_id=2276374

Buiter WH, Rahbari E (2012) Target2 redux: the simple accountancy and slightly more complex economics of Bundesbank loss exposure through the eurosystem. CEPR discussion paper no. 9211. Available via http://www.willembuiter.com/target2redux.pdf

Buiter WH, Rahbari E, Michels J (2011a) TARGETing the wrong Villain: intra-eurosystem imbalances in credit flows. Citi global economics view, June 9

Buiter WH, Rahbari E, Michels J (2011b) The implications of intra-euro area imbalances in credit flows. CEPR policy insight no. 57, August

Cappiello L, Kadareja A, Sørensen CK, Protopapa M (2010) Do bank loans and credit standards have an effect on output? A panel approach for the euro area. ECB working paper no. 1150,

January. Available via https://www.google.it/webhp?sourceid=chrome-instant&ion=1&espv=2&ie=UTF-8#q=19.%20cappiello%20l.%20et%20al%20(2010)%2c%20%e2%80%9cdo%20bank%20loans%20and%20credit%20standards%20have%20an%20effect%20on%20output%3f%20a%20panel%20approach%20for%20the%20euro%20area%e2%80%9d%2c%20ecb%20working%20paper%20n.%201150%2c%20january

Cecchetti SG, McCauley RN, McGuire P (2012) Interpreting TARGET2 balances. BIS working paper no. 393, December

Cecioni M, Ferrero G (2012) Determinants of TARGET2 imbalances. Banca d'Italia, Questioni di Economia e Finanza (Occasional papers), 136, September

Collignon S (2012) Europe's debt crisis, coordination failure, and international effects. ADBI working paper no. 370, July

Crowley J (2015) Central and commercial bank balance sheet risk before, during, and after the global financial crisis. IMF working paper no. 15/47, February. Available via http://www.imf.org/external/pubs/cat/longres.aspx?sk=42749.0

Darracq-Paries M, Moccero DN, Krylova E, Marchini C (2014) The retail bank interest rate pass-through: the case of the euro area during the financial and sovereign debt crisis. ECB occasional paper series no. 155, August

De Grauwe P (2011) The European central bank: lender of last resort in the government bond markets? CESifo working paper no. 3569, September. Available via https://ideas.repec.org/p/ces/ceswps/_3569.html

De Grauwe P, Ji Y (2012) What Germany should fear most is its own fear. Vox, Sept 18

De Sola Perea M, van Nieuwenhuyze C (2014) Financial integration and fragmentation in the euro area. NBB Economic Review, June, pp 99–125

Delpla J, Von Weizsäcker J (2010) The blue bond proposal. Bruguel policy brief, 3, May

Delpla J, Von Weizsäcker J (2011) Eurobonds: the blue bond concept and its implications. Bruguel policy contribution, 2, March

Deutsche Bundesbank (2011) The dynamics of the Bundesbank's TARGET2 balances. Monthly report, March

Draghi M (2015) Interview with Die Zeit, Jan 15. Available via https://www.ecb.europa.eu/press/inter/date/2015/html/sp150115.en.html

ECB (2009) Recent development in the retail bank interest rate pass-through in the euro area. Monthly Bull (August):93–105

ECB (2010a) The ECB's response to the financial crisis. Monthly Bull (October):59–74

ECB (2010b) Euro money market study, December. Available via http://www.ecb.europa.eu/pub/pdf/other/euromoneymarketstudy201012en.pdf

ECB (2011) TARGET2 balances of national central banks in the euro area. Monthly Bull, October

ECB (2012) Heterogeneity in euro area financial conditions and policy implications. Monthly Bull (August):63–75

ECB (2013) Assessing the retail bank interest rate pass-through in the euro area at times of financial fragmentation. Monthly Bull (August):75–91

European Commission (2013) Annual growth survey, Brussels, 28 Nov 2012

European Economic Advisory Group (2012) The EEAG report on the European economy, Chapter 2. In: The European balance-of-payments problem, CESifo, Munich, pp 57–81

Gambacorta L, Illes A, Lombardi MJ (2014) Has the transmission of policy rates to lending rates been impaired by the global financial crisis? Bis working paper no. 477, December. Available via http://papers.ssrn.com/sol3/papers.cfm?abstract_id=2542221

Gilchrist S, Mojon B (2014) Credit risk in the euro area. NBER working paper no. 20041, April. Available via http://www.nber.org/papers/w20041

Holinski N, Kool C, Muysken J (2012) Persistent macroeconomic imbalances in the euro area: causes and consequences. FRB St Louis Rev 94(1):1–20

Honkapoja S (2013) The euro crisis: a view from the north. Bank of Finland research discussion paper no. 12 June 2013. Available via http://papers.ssrn.com/sol3/papers.cfm?abstract_id=2291933

Illes A. and M. Lombardi (2013) "Interest Rate Pass Through Since the Financial Crisis", *BIS Quarterly Review*, September, 57–66. Available via http://www.bis.org/publ/qtrpdf/r_qt1309g.pdf

Illes A, Lombardi M, Mizen P (2015) Why did bank lending rates diverge from policy rates after the financial crisis? BIS working paper no. 486, February. Available via https://www.bis.org/publ/work486.htm

IMF (2012) The liberalization and management of capital flows: an institutional view. IMF report, Nov 14. Available via http://www.imf.org/external/np/pp/eng/2012/111412.pdf

Kaminsky GL, Reinhart CM (1999) The twin crises: the causes of banking and balance-of-payments problems. Am Econ Rev 89(3):473–500

Kilponen J, Laakkonen H, Vilmunen J (2012) Sovereign risk, European Crisis resolution policies and bond yields. Bank of Finland, Research discussion papers, no. 22. Available via http://www.suomenpankki.fi/en/julkaisut/tutkimukset/keskustelualoitteet/Documents/BoF_DP_1222.pdf

Kollmann R, Ratto M, Roeger W, in't Veld J, Vogel L (2015) What drives the German current account? And how does it affect other EU member states? European commission economic papers, directorate-general for economic and financial affairs unit communication. Available via http://ec.europa.eu/economy_finance/publications/economic_paper/2014/ecp516_en.htm

Lama R, Rabanal P (2012) Deciding to enter a monetary union: the role of trade and financial linkages. IMF working paper no. 12/240, October

Lane PR (2013) Capital flows in the euro area. CEPR discussion paper no. DP9493, May. Available via http://papers.ssrn.com/sol3/papers.cfm?abstract_id=2271944

Mody A, Bornhorst F (2012) TARGET imbalances: financing the capital-account reversal in Europe. VoxEU, Mar 7

Moro B (2014) Lessons from the European economic and financial great crisis: a survey. Eur J Polit Econ 34(Supplement):S9–S24, June

Moro A, Nuño G, Tedde P (2015) A twin crisis with multiple banks of issue: Spain in the 1860s. Eur Rev Econ Hist 19(2):171–194

Neri S (2013) The impact of the sovereign debt crisis on bank lending rates in the euro area. Bank of Italy occasional paper no. 170, June. Available via http://papers.ssrn.com/sol3/papers.cfm?abstract_id=2284804

Orphanides A (2014) The euro area crisis: politics over economics. CEPR discussion paper no. DP 10033, June. Available via http://papers.ssrn.com/sol3/papers.cfm?abstract_id=2448197

Ostry JD, Ghosh AR, Habermeier K, Chamon M, Qureshi MS, Reinhardt DBS (2010) Capital inflows: the role of controls. IMF staff position note no. 10/04. International Monetary Fund, Washington, DC

Ostry JD, Ghosh AR, Habermeier K, Chamon M, Qureshi MS, Laeven L, Kokenyne A (2011) Managing capital inflows: what tools to use? IMF staff discussion note no. 11/06. International Monetary Fund, Washington, DC

Pisani-Ferri J, Sapir A, Wolff GB (2013) EU-IMF assistance to euro-area countries: an early assessment. Bruegel blueprint series, XIX

Pisani-Ferry J, Wolff GB (2012) Propping up Europe? Policy contribution, 7, Bruegel

Pisani-Ferry J, Sapir A, Wolff GB (2011) An evaluation of IMF surveillance of the euro area. Blueprint 14, Bruegel

Reichlin L (2013) The ECB and the banks: the tale of two crises. CEPR discussion paper no. DP9647, September. Available via http://papers.ssrn.com/sol3/papers.cfm?abstract_id=2326511

Reinhart CM, Reinhart V (2009) Capital flow bonanzas: an encompassing view of the past and present. In: Frankel J, Pissarides C (eds) NBER international seminar on macroeconomics 2008. University of Chicago Press, Chicago

Sensoy A, Hacihasanoglu E, Rostom AM (2015) European economic and monetary union sovereign debt markets. World bank policy research working paper no. 7149, Jan 1. Available via http://papers.ssrn.com/sol3/papers.cfm?abstract_id=2546123

Sinn HW (2011) The ECB stealth bailout. VoxEu, June 1
Sinn HW (2012a) Fed versus ECB: how target debt can be repaid. Vox, Mar 10. Available via http://www.voxeu.org/article/fed-versus-ecb-how-target-debts-can-be-repaid
Sinn HW (2012b) TARGET losses in case of a euro breakup. Vox, Oct 22
Sinn HW, Wollmershäeuser T (2011) Target loans, current account balances and capital flows: the ECB's rescue facility. NBER working paper no. 17626, November
Sinn HW, Wollmershäeuser T (2012) Target balances and the German financial account in light of the European balance-of-payments crisis. CESifo working paper no. 4051. Available via http://www.cesifo-group.de/portal/pls/portal/docs/1/1218218.PDF
Turner P (2013) Benign neglect of the long term interest rate. BIS working paper no. 403, February. Available via http://www.bis.org/publ/work403.pdf
Van Rixtel AARJM, Gasperini G (2013) Financial crisis and bank funding: recent experience in the euro. BIS working paper no. 405, March
Whelan K (2011) Professor Sinn misses the target. VoxEu, June 9. Available via http://www.voxeu.org/article/there-hidden-eurozone-bailout
Whelan K (2012) TARGET2 and central bank balance sheets. University College Dublin, School of Economics, working paper no. 12/29, November. Available via http://www.ucd.ie/t4cms/WP12_29.pdf
Wyplosz C (2011) A failsafe way to end the euro area crisis. VoxEU, 26 September. Available via http://voxeu.org/index.php?q=node/7031
Zoli E (2013) Italian sovereign spreads: their determinants and pass-through to bank funding costs and lending conditions. IMF working paper no. 13/84, April. Available via https://www.imf.org/external/pubs/ft/wp/2013/wp1384.pdf

Chapter 7
The European Debt Crisis

Victor A. Beker

7.1 Introduction

In late 2009, the then recently appointed Greek Prime Minister George Papandreou announced that previous governments had failed to reveal the true size of the nation's deficits. Greece's debts were larger than what had been reported.[1] After that, the Portuguese, Spanish, and Italian public debts also became a matter of concern because their government debt-to-GDP ratios were near to the Greek one. The European sovereign debt crisis had started.

Between 2010 and 2012, Greece, Ireland, and Portugal entered into European Union and International Monetary Fund financial assistance programs, involving deep economic policy adjustments, including those pertaining to structural reforms. Spain entered into an EU financial assistance program for the recapitalization of its financial institutions, and other vulnerable countries such as Italy implemented a series of fiscal consolidation measures and some structural reforms.

The financial crisis has calmed down somewhat after the announcement by the president of the ECB, in mid-2012, that he would have done "whatever it takes" to preserve the euro and to struggle the crisis (Chap. 6, Sect. 6.5), allowing European authorities to buy time to figure out how they could get the area out of the debt crisis.

As Reinhart and Rogoff (2008) exhaustively show, financial crises and sovereign debt defaults are far from being strange events in economic history, in both less developed as well as developed countries. These authors conclude that "serial

[1] In fact, in 2004, Eurostat had already revealed that the statistics for the budget deficit had been underreported at the time Greece was accepted into the European Monetary Union in 2000. According to Eurostat, the 1999 deficit was 3.4 % of GDP instead of the originally reported 1.8 %.

V.A. Beker (✉)
University of Belgrano and University of Buenos Aires, Buenos Aires, Argentina
e-mail: victor.beker@ub.edu.ar

B. Moro, V.A. Beker, *Modern Financial Crises*, Financial and Monetary Policy Studies 42, DOI 10.1007/978-3-319-20991-3_7

default on external debt—that is, repeated sovereign default—is the norm throughout every region in the world, even including Asia and Europe".

However, economists have paid little attention to the subject particularly during the optimistic years of the so-called Great Moderation. The current European crisis challenges economists to analyze its causes and find ways out of it as well as means to avoid future crises.

This chapter is organized as follows. Section 7.2 analyzes the origin of the crisis in these European countries. In Sect. 7.3, the specifics of euro debt are discussed. Section 7.4 analyzes the cases of Ireland and Iceland, whose debt crises preceded the Greek one. Section 7.5 is devoted to the latter. The role of a single currency on regional imbalances is underlined in Sect. 7.6. Section 7.7 is devoted to discuss what Greek can learn from the Argentine crisis. The cases of Portugal and Spain are analyzed in Sects. 7.8 and 7.9. Section 7.10 is devoted to the analysis of the Italian case. Section 7.11 discusses if the euro rate of exchange can play some role in solving the debt crisis. Section 7.12 summarizes the findings of the chapter.

7.2 Evolution of Countries' Indebtedness

A first issue has to do with the origin of the European debt crisis.[2] Some people have pointed their fingers at the American financial crisis. "This crisis was not originated in Europe," claimed the EU Commission President Jose M. Barroso, who added: "This crisis originated in North America and much of our financial sector was contaminated by ... unorthodox practices from some sectors of the financial market".[3]

However, as we shall see, Greece and Italy were already heavily indebted as early as 1996, long before the US financial crisis blew up. However, this does not exclude the possibility of some connection between both crises, which is explored below by comparing the debt situation before and after 2007.[4]

A second question is how the debtor country governments as the Greek one became so highly indebted. A common explanation for this has been the following.[5] Banks in Germany, France, and elsewhere had bought and exposed themselves massively to Greek debt because they assumed that Greek debt, like other euro area public debt, was essentially risk-free.

---

[2] Moro (2014) characterizes the European crisis as a sequence of interactions between sovereign problems and banking problems. Véron (2012) adds that the situation is best described as twin sovereign and banking crises that mutually feed each other.

[3] *The Week*. June 20, 2012. http://theweek.com/article/index/229570/did-the-us-cause-the-european-debt-crisis

[4] According to Moro (2014), "the current European crisis can be directly traced back to the global financial crisis of 2007–2009, which spilled over into a sovereign debt crisis in several euro area countries in early 2010".

[5] See, for example, Feldstein (2012).

Fig. 7.1 General government gross debt (percentage of GDP)—2010 (*Source*: Eurostat)

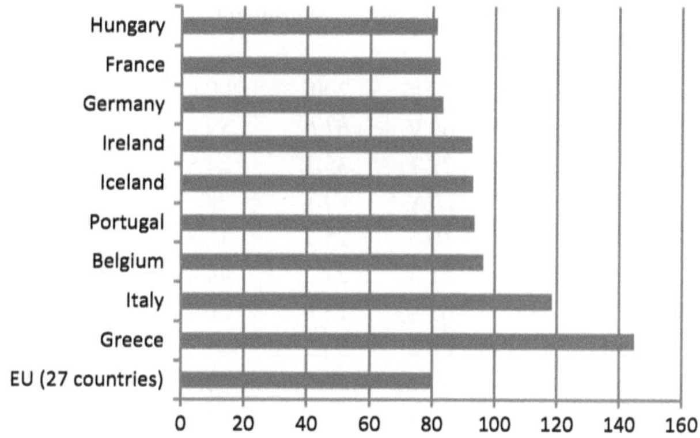

Because the European Monetary Union (EMU) made the commitment to low inflation more credible, the introduction of the euro in 2001 caused interest rates to fall in those countries where expectations of high inflation previously kept interest rates high.

Bond buyers assumed that a bond issued by any government in the European Monetary Union was equally safe. As a result, the interest rates on Greek and Italian government bonds were not significantly different from the interest rate on German government bonds.[6] Governments responded to these low interest rates by increasing their borrowing.

However, the data do not fully endorse the former explanation. Figure 7.1 shows the general government gross debt-to-GDP ratio in 2010 for those countries whose public debt ratio exceeded the average for the 27 EU countries as a whole. France and Germany are among the more-than-average indebted countries, which show that high indebtedness is not solely a southern Europe country phenomenon.

Table 7.1 shows the evolution of government debt-to-GDP ratio between 1996 and 2010 for a selected group of countries; the last column shows the increase in that percentage between 2007 and 2010. It can be noted that some of the now highly indebted countries did not exceed the Maastricht limit of 60 % of GDP until as recently as 2007.

Second, the public debt-to-GDP ratios of Greece, Ireland, Belgium, Spain, and Italy were almost the same in 2007 as they were in 2001 (in some cases, they were even lower). This contradicts the idea that it was the introduction of the euro and the consequent fall in interest rates that stimulated governments to substantially increase their borrowing.

On the other hand, Greece, Italy, Portugal, Belgium, and Hungary had already exceeded the 60 % Maastricht limit in 2007,[7] when the American subprime crisis started. However, they shared the slowest increasing government debt-to-GDP

[6] Moro (2014) stresses the role that mispricing of risk by financial markets played in the European financial crisis.

[7] As Hungary is not a member of the Eurozone, the Maastricht criteria were not mandatory for it.

Table 7.1 Evolution of general government gross debt (percentage of GDP)—1996/2010 and 2007/2010

Country	1996	2001	2007	2008	2009	2010	2010/2007
EU (27 countries)	*69.9*	*61.0*	*59.0*	*62.5*	*74.7*	*80.1*	*35.76*
Ireland	71.7	35.1	24.8	44.2	65.2	92.5	272.98
Iceland	N/A	N/A	28.5	70.3	87.9	92.9	225.96
Romania	10.6	25.7	12.8	13.4	23.6	31.0	142.19
UK	51.3	37.7	44.4	54.8	69.6	79.9	79.95
Spain	67.4	55.6	36.2	40.1	53.8	61.0	68.51
Portugal	58.2	53.5	68.3	71.6	83.0	93.3	36.60
Greece	99.4	103.7	107.4	113.0	129.3	144.9	34.92
Hungary	72.4	52.7	67.0	72.9	79.7	81.3	21.34
Italy	120.2	108.2	103.1	105.8	115.5	118.4	14.84
Belgium	127.2	106.5	84.1	89.3	95.9	96.2	14.39

Source: Eurostat

ratios between 2007 and 2010. Even more, by 1996—before the introduction of the euro—Italy, Greece, and Belgium were already highly indebted countries.

Therefore, we can distinguish a first group of countries whose debt problems have roots before 2007 and did not worsen significantly after that year: Greece, Italy, Portugal, Belgium, and Hungary. Moreover, by 2001 Greece's public debt-to-GDP ratio was already 103.7, compared with 108.2 for Italy and 106.5 for Belgium. This last country is a special case because it is the only one in the group that reduced its debt between 2001 and 2007.

A second group is formed by those "new" highly indebted countries: Ireland and Iceland. They showed the highest rates of increase in their public debt-to-GDP ratios between 2007 and 2010 and their 2010 ratios were above the average for the EU. Romania also had a fast-growing ratio but the level of public debt attained in 2010 as a percentage of GDP was still far below the average for the EU.

The UK comes immediately below these countries with a debt-to-GDP ratio practically equivalent to the EU average. Finally, we have Spain, whose government debt-to-GDP ratio was in 2010 only a bit above the Maastricht limit and had increased at a lower rate than the UK's ratio between 2007 and 2010. However, while the UK's debt was considered to be safe, Spain's debt was no better rated than those of Portugal or Italy.

Thus, there are different cases to consider rather than a single story for European countries' indebtedness process. The idea that we may have a unique explanation for the debt crisis is also presented in Perez-Caldentey and Vernengo (2012, 3), who argue that "the crisis in Europe is the result of an imbalance between core and noncore countries that is inherent in the euro economic model". They also maintain that it was the euro, and its effects on external competitiveness, that triggered mounting disequilibria and debt accumulation in noncore countries or peripheries.

As we will see, this argument seems to be valid to a certain extent just in the cases of Greece and Portugal, but not for the rest of the countries involved in the crisis where other factors seem to have played a major role.

In what follows, we concentrate our analysis on the five euro area countries in the eye of the debt crisis storm with a casual reference to the case of Iceland.[8]

7.3 Specifics of the Euro Area Public Debt

A first peculiarity of the euro area public debt is that, strictly speaking, it is neither purely domestic nor purely external. Most of the public debt issued by euro area countries is denominated in euro and is mostly held by euro area residents. Yet, it is different from the domestic debt of countries owning their own currencies because more of it is held outside the issuing country and because the issuing country does not have full control over the currency in which the debt is denominated. Therefore, debt in the euro area can be considered to be both "foreign" and "domestic" (Gianviti et al 2010, 18).

This means that euro area public debt is not subject to the currency mismatch associated with external debt: governments have to pay their debts in the same currency they collect their revenues. However, it also means that a national government cannot revert to high inflation to rid itself of an excessive debt burden, as might be the case if the debt were strictly domestic.

The EMU seems to assume that sovereign debt crises cannot happen. At least, it has no provision for them. Moreover, the common reading of Article 125 of the Lisbon Treaty has been that it rules out the possibility of a bailout of an EU member state by other member states or by the EU.

Therefore, without these inflation and bailout channels, a country with a situation of excessive debt has only two ways out of it: severe and harmful fiscal retrenchment or default.

7.4 The New Highly Indebted Countries: The Cases of Ireland and Iceland

7.4.1 The Case of Ireland

Ireland's economy had by 2007 already become dangerously dependent on construction and housing as a source of economic growth and tax revenue. The total stock of dwellings—which had stood at 1.2 million homes in 1991 and had gradually increased to 1.4 million homes in 2000—exploded to 1.9 million homes in 2008. House completions went from 19,000 in 1990 to 50,000 in 2000 to a whopping 93,000 in 2006 (Whelan 2013, p. 6).

[8] The Cyprus banking crisis is a special case, mainly the result of the Greek sovereign debt haircut, although it has something in common with Iceland's case.

A lightly regulated financial system fed on this process. In fact, the growing construction boom was fueled by the increasing reliance of Irish banks on wholesale external borrowing at a time when international financial markets were awash with cheap investable funds. The fact that Ireland was a founder member of the euro zone brought a dramatic and sustained fall in nominal and real interest rates that stimulated the protracted building boom. Specific tax incentives boosted the overheated construction sector. From late 2003 onward, banks stimulated demand with financial innovations such as 100 % loan-to-value mortgages.

When the global economic environment changed at the beginning of 2007, Irish residential property prices started falling and kept falling during the rest of 2007 and 2008. Heavy loan losses on the development property portfolios acquired at the peak of the market became inevitable. The decline in property prices and the collapse in construction activity resulted in severe losses in the Irish banking system.

The story is not very different from the one that led to the US subprime crisis. "In their anxiety to protect market share against the competitive inroads of Anglo Irish Bank and UK-based retail lenders, their (Irish) banks' management tolerated a gradual lowering of lending standards, including decisions to authorize numerous exceptions to stated policies" (Governor of the Central Bank of Ireland 2010, 8). This was tolerated by an unduly deferential approach to the banking industry by regulators. Outside bodies such as the IMF and OECD never drew attention to the threats that lay ahead.

Although banks carried out a quantification of risks in the context of the stress test exercises reported annually to the regulatory authority, "the capacity of the banks to undertake the exercise differed greatly; indeed none of them had reliable models, tested and calibrated on Irish data, which could credibly predict loan losses under varying scenarios" (Ibid., 11).

While at the end of 2003, the net indebtedness of Irish banks to the rest of the world was just 10 % of GDP, by early 2008 borrowing, mainly for property, had jumped to over 60 % of GDP. By early 2008, Irish banks found it more difficult to maintain funding in the international wholesale markets and, at the same time, there was a more rapid pullback by domestic investors from the property market.

The severe exposure of the Irish banks to any downturn in the property market was plain to see for anyone who read their annual reports. However, as discussed in Honohan (2010), the supervisory culture at the Central Bank during this period meant there was very little supervisory interference in bank operations (Whelan 2013, p. 12).

Two weeks after Lehman Brothers announced it would file for bankruptcy protection (Chap. 11), the provision of a blanket system-wide state guarantee for Irish banks was announced. This measure was taken because of the drain of liquidity that had been affecting all Irish banks and that had brought one important bank to the point of failure.

Government spending doubled in real terms between 1995 and 2007, rising at an annual average rate of 6 %. With the economy growing at an even faster rate, this implied a generally falling or stable expenditure ratio of expenditure to GDP until

2003. However, thereafter the ratio rose, especially after output growth began to slow in 2007 and the collapse in tax revenues in 2008–2009.

Much of the reason for the revenue collapse lies in the systematic shift over the previous two decades away from stable and reliable sources such as personal income tax, VAT, and excises toward cyclically sensitive taxes as corporation tax, stamp duties, and capital gains tax. The collapse in construction activity, and the corresponding jump in unemployment, resulted in a huge loss in tax revenues as well as a big increase in social welfare payments.

In April 2009, the Irish government established the National Asset Management Agency (NAMA), with the mandate to purchase the universe of development-related loans (above a certain value) from banks. This category of loans was the main source of uncertainty concerning total loan losses. During 2009–2010, NAMA purchased most of these loans at a steep average discount, but this meant that banks required substantial upfront recapitalization programs, which could only be provided by the state. These higher capitalization costs led to a sharp increase in gross government debt. Extra capital requirements by the banking system in 2009 and 2010 contributed to increased market concerns about the sustainability of the fiscal position.

In fact, the deficit, as measured by the general government balance, widened from balance in 2007 to 7.3 % of GDP in 2008 and to 14.1 % in 2009, before it increased to 31.2 % of GDP in 2010 due to the substantial government support to Irish banks. Excluding support to the banking system, the deficit was 11.5 % of GDP in 2009 and 10.9 % of GDP in 2010. The public funds aimed at rescuing the Irish banking sector represented 12.5 % of Ireland's GDP. As shown in Table 1, Irish public debt soared from 24.8 % of GDP in 2007 to 92.5 % in 2010. Finally, the Irish government had to request assistance from the EU and IMF in November 2010 to avoid default on its public debt.

The Irish government agreed a multiyear funding deal with the EU and the IMF. The program provided funding commitments of €67.5 billion. Ireland made steady progress in reducing its fiscal deficit and meeting the program's fiscal targets. In spite of fiscal contraction, economic growth was resumed thanks to a reorientation of the economy away from domestic demand and toward exports.

However, economic growth did not generate increases in employment and the relative success of Ireland in regaining competitiveness partly reflects the depressed state of its labor market. At the end of 2013, the rate of unemployment was still 12.1 %, while it had been only 4.5 % in July 2007.

7.4.2 The Case of Iceland

Although it has many features in common with the Irish one, Iceland's case has some particularities. The first one is that Iceland does not belong to the Eurozone. Property lending was neither as central to the Icelandic case. Access to international financial markets was, for banks, the principal premise for their large growth.

Because of their—at that time—good credit rating, they had access to European markets; when funding in European debt securities markets became more difficult, the debt securities market in the USA opened up.

That opening was largely due to CDOs. Icelandic bank securities were packaged into these CDOs because of the high credit rating of the Icelandic financial undertakings, according to rating agencies. Further, Icelandic banks paid high interest rates considering that credit rating.

Thanks to the injection of foreign funds, the Icelandic financial system became far too large relative to the size of the Icelandic economy. On the other hand, the largest owners of all the large banks had abnormally easy access to credit at the banks they owned. The examination conducted by the Icelandic Special Investigation Commission showed that in the three largest banks, their principal owners were among the largest borrowers. The money market funds under the aegis of the management companies of these banks invested a great deal in securities connected to the owners of the banks.

Bank risk was highly concentrated. This applied both to lending to certain groups within each bank as well as to how the same groups also constituted high-risk exposures in more than one bank. Moreover, the banks had invested funds equivalent to more than 25 % of their capital bases in their own shares. In addition, each of them invested in other banks' shares. It seems that the financing of owners' equity in the Icelandic banking system had been based, to such a great extent, on borrowing from the system itself. The shares owned by the largest shareholders of the banks were especially leveraged.

The onset of the international financial crisis in 2007 found Icelandic banks increasingly dependent on funding through international financial markets. Total deposits in the banks kept shrinking from the autumn of 2007 until their collapse. Collateralized loans, mostly from the Central Bank of Ireland and the European Central Bank (ECB), increased substantially in all three banks as the liquidity crisis became more widespread.

When the prices of shares started dropping, all banks purchased their own shares on a large scale. As stated before, the banks held a lot of their own shares as collateral for their lending. With share prices declining, the quality of their loan portfolios would decline. Finally, the Financial Supervisory Authority of Iceland took over the domestic operations of the three largest banks in October 2008.

Outside Iceland, more than half a million depositors (far more than the entire population of Iceland) found their bank accounts frozen when the banks finally collapsed. In August 2009, a bill was passed to pay the UK and the Netherlands more than $5 billion lost in Icelandic deposit accounts. The Icelandic government debt increased from 28.5 % of GDP in 2007 to 70.3 % in 2008 after the takeover of the three largest Icelandic banks.

7.5 The "Old" Indebted Countries: The Case of Greece

As stated before, Greece did not comply with the Maastricht criterion with respect to the budget deficit at the time it joined the Eurozone in 2001. "Creative" statistics allowed it to be admitted into what has been conceived as a very exclusive club. Its debt-to-GDP ratio was already 103.7 in 2001, far above the 60 % Maastricht criterion.[9]

However, it declined to 97.4 in 2003. From then on, it kept increasing until reaching 144.9 in 2010. This reflected the increasing budget deficit Greece's public accounts had shown since 2000. Figure 7.2 shows the expenditure/GDP, revenue/GDP, and deficit/GDP ratios for the period 2000/2011.

Entrance into the Eurozone meant that Greece—as the other members of the Eurozone—gave up one of the tools a country has to reduce its budget deficit: devaluation. In fact, in equilibrium:

$$(I_d - S) + (G - T) = M - X$$

where I_d is domestic investment, S is national saving, G is government expenditure, T is government revenue, and $(M-X)$ stands for current account balance (M are imports and X are exports). A devaluation will reduce the deficit value of $(M-X)$; if the domestic private balance does not change, the government balance will be reduced.[10] The most direct way to do this is by taxing exports, as Argentina did in 2002, where export taxes absorbed a good part of the devaluation effect on exportable domestic prices.

As a matter of fact, Georgantopoulos and Tsamis (2011, 161) find for Greece, during the period 1980–2009, a significant unidirectional causal relationship between exchange rates and budget deficit running from the nominal effective

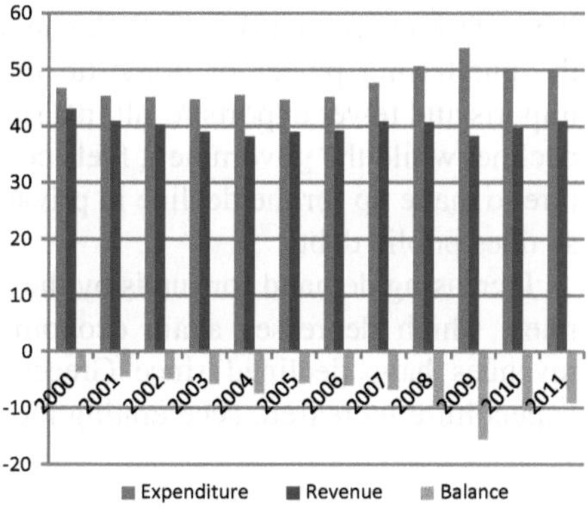

Fig. 7.2 General government expenditure, revenue and deficit 2000/2011 (Percentage of GDP) (*Source*: Eurostat)

[9] Notwithstanding its noncompliance with the Maastricht debt standard, Greece was admitted with the argument that it was expected to be making progress over time toward that goal.

[10] The opposite happens, of course, in the case of a revaluation of the local currency.

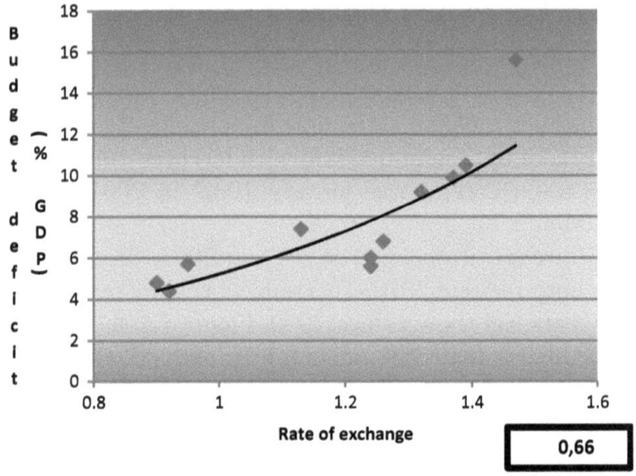

Fig. 7.3 Budget deficit and euro rate of exchange 2000–2011

exchange rate to the budget deficit. Moreover, they concluded that "a significant part of budget deficits' variance is caused by exchange rates since with a seven period lag 61.89 % of [the budget deficit] is explained by [the nominal effective exchange rate] and by the end of the 10-year lag 83.97 % of budget deficits' variance is caused by nominal effective exchange rates".

The continuous revaluation of the euro worsened Greece's budget imbalance after 2000. Figure 7.3 illustrates the relationship between the euro/dollar rate of exchange and the 1-year lagged budget deficit/GDP ratio between 2000 and 2011. This runs in the same direction as the relationship found by Georgantopoulos and Tsamis.

What is the explanation for this positive association between the rate of exchange and budget imbalance? The appreciation of the euro[11] resulted in a loss of external competitiveness in the Greek economy, which led to a persistent deficit in the current account (Fig. 7.4). An appreciation of the real exchange rate increases the purchasing power of domestic incomes in terms of imported goods. More imports and fewer exports result in a slowdown in economic activity. Tax revenues decline, while the government feels compelled to keep or increase public expenditure to make up for the decline in private demand. The budget deficit increases and so does public debt.

Increasing demand for funds by the public sector leads to an increase in interest rates, which depresses again economic activity. According to Fig. 7.2, public revenues have declined since Greece joined the Eurozone; since 2007, public expenditure increased, accelerating the rise in the budget deficit.

[11] The exchange rate between dollar and euro was, in October 2000, 0.85 $/€ and reached in April 2008 1.60 $/€, an appreciation of 88 %.

Fig. 7.4 Current account deficit and the euro rate of exchange 2001/2011

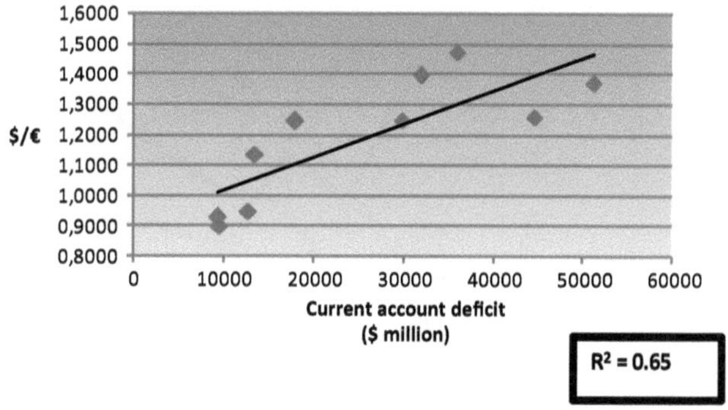

However, in the literature related to the "twin deficits hypothesis," it has usually been argued that causality runs from the government budget deficit to the current account, not the other way around.

However, empirical studies are far from conclusive: in some cases, they support the conventional hypothesis;[12] others support the reverse causality running from the current account deficit to the fiscal deficit;[13] some support the Ricardian equivalence that budget and trade deficits are not correlated.[14] And, finally, some find both types of evidence or a bilateral relationship.[15]

In the case of Greece, it is clear that since the introduction of the euro, causality cannot run from the budget deficit to the nominal rate of exchange moreover when the budget deficit variable is introduced with a 1-year lag. The increasing Greek debt was primarily the result of growing budget deficits triggered by the appreciation of the euro and the consequent loss of competitiveness experienced by the Greek economy. This brings us to the issue of regional imbalances raised by Pérez-Caldentey and Vernengo (2012).

7.6 Exchange Rate and Regional Imbalances

The euro area aggregate trade and current account position have always been close to balance, but this only means that the euro rate of exchange is in line with the competitiveness of the core countries of the Eurozone. Many industries in Greece and other peripheral countries are not competitive at that rate of exchange; that is why these countries run increasing current account deficits (see Figs. 7.5 and 7.6).

---

[12] Abell (1990), Bachman (1992), Piersanti (2000), Leachman and Francis (2002), Cavallo (2005), and Erceg and Guerrieri (2005).

[13] Anoruo and Ramchander (1998), Khalid and Teo (1999), and Alkswani (2000).

[14] Miller and Russek (1989), Dewald and Ulan (1990), Enders and Lee (1990), and Kim (1995).

[15] Mukhtar et al. (2007) and Islam (1998).

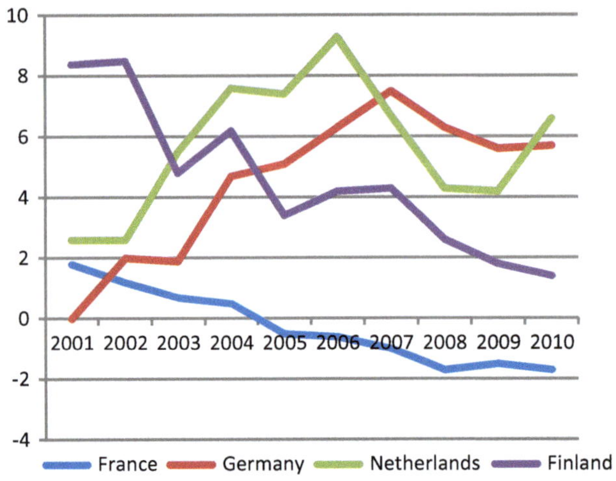

Fig. 7.5 Current account balance in selected EMU countries, 2001–2010 (percentage of GDP): Finland, France, Germany, and the Netherlands (*Source*: Eurostat)

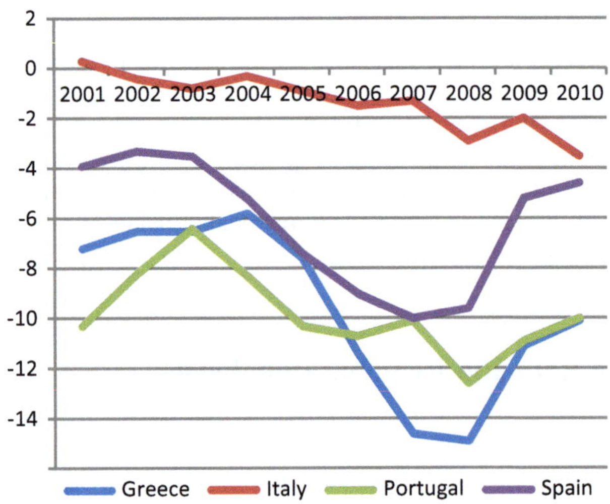

Fig. 7.6 Current account balance in selected EMU countries, 2001–2010 (percentage of GDP): Greece, Italy, Portugal, and Spain (*Source*: Eurostat)

In fact, external imbalances diverge sharply in the euro area: while Germany, the Netherlands, and Finland run significant surpluses, countries in southern Europe run huge deficits (see also Chap. 5, Sect. 5.5).

Coudert et al (2012) compare currency misalignment before and after the launch of euro. They find that the three countries that have been adversely affected by the sovereign debt crisis in 2010–2011, Greece, Ireland, and Portugal, are exhibiting the largest overvaluation of their real exchange rates. On the other hand, it is worthwhile noting that Germany had run persistent current account deficits during the 1990s which turned into surpluses only after 2000.

The Eurozone reproduces the sort of regional problems that exist within many countries. There is a highly competitive core and a relatively backward periphery.[16]

Therefore, a long-run strategy for regional convergence is needed and, at the same time, a short-run one to smooth the transition process. Although EU regional policy aims at promoting the "harmonious, balanced and sustainable development of the European Union", it has proven up to now to be insufficient to face the specific consequences of the monetary union.

Therefore, the Greek government had to face the outcome of joining the Eurozone and had to take decisions that resulted in a worsening of the heavy indebtedness preexisting at the time of joining the Eurozone.

Katsimi and Moutos (2010) emphasize the role of current account imbalances due to the loss in Greek international competitiveness. However, productivity gaps and external deficits exist within each country. Do all American states have the same productivity? What about East and West Germany? Who cares what their external balances are? A region within a country can run a current account deficit indefinitely as long as there is a transfer of resources from the richer to the poorer regions.

Therefore, this should not be a problem for the Eurozone provided those who, thanks to the Eurozone, benefit of external surpluses are ready to transfer resources to the backward periphery. This is the real issue at stake as far as the productivity gap is concerned. The problem is that the Eurozone is officially a currency union of politically sovereign states and not a common currency area within a political union. This is the original sin in the design of the Eurozone.

Germany's unification process could have been an interesting antecedent to take into consideration. The major economic implication of German economic and monetary union was precisely that East Germany would run a current account deficit with the rest of the country that was financed by transfers from the West. In the case of Germany, the New Länder began with an enormous competitive disadvantage and West Germans were supposed to transfer between 3 and 4 % of GDP per annum to the East (Carlin 1998, 16).

However, no provision was taken in the Eurozone to make up for the short-run negative consequences that peripheral economies could suffer from joining the euro.[17] In fact, when the monetary union was implemented in 1999, the functioning of the single currency was seen as a sort of panacea, making additional policy targeting seem superfluous. However, the result has been an increasing current account deficit for Greece and other peripheral countries. What has not been done before in the form of resource transfers from the richer to the poorer countries of the

[16] The role of structural imbalances in the European crisis, reflected by high current account deficits of the periphery countries and matching surpluses in core countries, is extensively discussed in Moro (2014). See also Chap. 5.

[17] I refer here to the specific consequences of joining the euro, which are independent of those following the EU integration to make up for which there were significant resource transfers, particularly through structural funds.

Eurozone has to be done in the way of helping these countries restructure their debts.

Somebody may argue that internal devaluation is the way through which Greek could become competitive.[18] Downward price and wage inflexibility make this a very painful and unbearably long process.

Sinn (2013) reminds us that Keynes and Friedman alike coincided on the phenomenon of downward price stickiness. Internal devaluation did not work in Argentina, which, after 3 years of an ever-deepening recession/depression, had no alternative but to default and devalue its currency. It does not seem to be a valid alternative for Greece either.

The often mentioned as successful internal devaluation cases—Ireland and the Baltic countries—suffered an output loss of between 15 and 25 %, while unemployment jumped to something between 10 and 20 % (EEAG 2013, p. 66). Given the large economic costs associated with these strategies, it is far from clear whether these experiences should qualify as success stories and could be extended to bigger and more complex economies.

In spite of the relative success of 2012 Greek debt restructuring, which implied that private sector bondholders reduced their nominal claims by 75 %, at the end of 2013 the debt-to-GDP coefficient has reached a peak of 175 %. Through the successive rescue packages, Greece received huge amount of funds borrowed from official institutions. The result was that 70 % of the debts were owed to "official" creditors (Eurozone states, ECB, and the IMF).

7.7 Is Argentina a Valid Example for Greece?

Some analysts have argued that the only way out of the crisis for Greece is to do what Argentina did in 2002. Then Argentina applied the 3D formula: default, devaluation, and de-dollarization. In the case of Argentina, devaluation was a necessary component of the crisis solution because most of its public debt was denominated in foreign currency.

This is not the case of Greece where most of the government debt is denominated in euro that is the same currency in which government revenues are denominated. So, the issue is just to adjust revenues and expenditures. Essentially, it means to reduce the debt burden to an amount compatible with a reasonable fiscal primary surplus target. Restructuring the debt in a way that allows the Greek economy to resume growth is the only sound solution. Devaluation, which in the case of Greece and other euro countries means to leave the Eurozone, does not seem to be a necessary step to solve the debt problems. On the contrary, it may only aggravate the country's economic situation.

[18] Sinn (2013) mentions that, according to a Goldman Sachs study, relative prices in Greece have to come down between 25 and 35 % to achieve external debt sustainability.

In Argentina, devaluation—that was accompanied by a necessary internal debt de-dollarization—resulted in a 50 % of the population falling below the poverty line, while unemployment soared to 22 % of the labor force. Of course, depressed real wages allowed the country to recover competitiveness. Increased exports and depressed imports allowed the country to earn the foreign currency it badly needed to meet the service obligations of its foreign debt.

In fact, it was not enough for Argentina to have a fiscal surplus; it was also necessary to have a current account surplus so the local currency-denominated fiscal surplus could be transformed into world money to service the foreign debt. But once again, this is not the case of Greece whose debt problem is due to a fiscal gap not to a foreign currency gap. Definitely, Argentina is a valid example for Greece only as far as debt relief is concerned.

7.8 The Case of Portugal

In the second half of the 1990s, Portugal showed impressive economic results. Its GDP per capita grew faster than the EU average and Portugal fulfilled the Maastricht criteria for the monetary union. However, by 2000 Portugal had already become the first country to be subjected to the EU's Excessive Deficit Procedure specified in the Stability and Growth Pact legislation and again in 2005 when its deficit reached more than 6 % of GDP.[19]

As in the case of Greece, the continuous revaluation of the euro worsened Portugal's budget imbalance after 2000. Figure 7.7 illustrates the positive relationship between the euro/dollar rate of exchange and the 1-year lagged budget deficit/GDP ratio between 2001 and 2011.

However, the financial crisis worsened Portugal's economic situation. Its impact was first felt in Portugal at the beginning of 2008, with a severe credit squeeze, a reduction in banks' abilities to access capital markets, and the collapse of two banks: BPN, which was nationalized in November 2008, and BPP, which was intervened in by the state and finally went bankrupt in 2010.

The Portuguese government reacted by implementing an "Initiative to Strengthen Financial Stability", which focused on improving the information and transparency obligations of financial institutions, increasing deposit guarantees, granting state guarantees to banks, and strengthening their financial soundness.

These measures—particularly the nationalization of BPN and the intervention in BPP—implied an increase in public deficit and public debt. The international financial crisis, shrinking exports, declining investment (including in construction), and dampening consumer spending, all contributed to the contraction of Portugal's economy.

[19] Indeed, throughout the entire democratic period following the 1974 revolution, Portugal never had a surplus in the state budget.

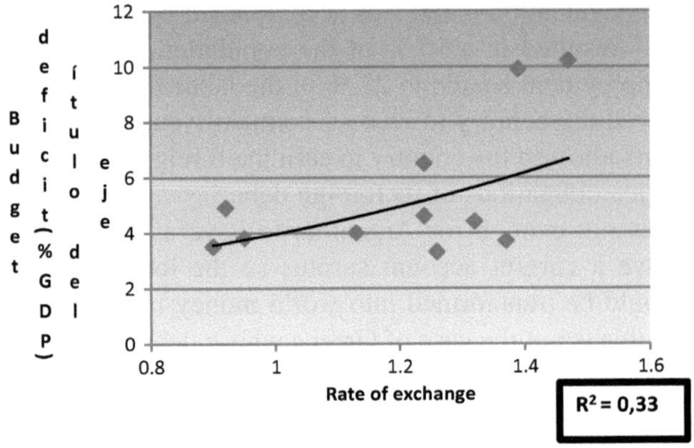

Fig. 7.7 Portugal's budget deficit and the euro/dollar rate of exchange, 2001/2011

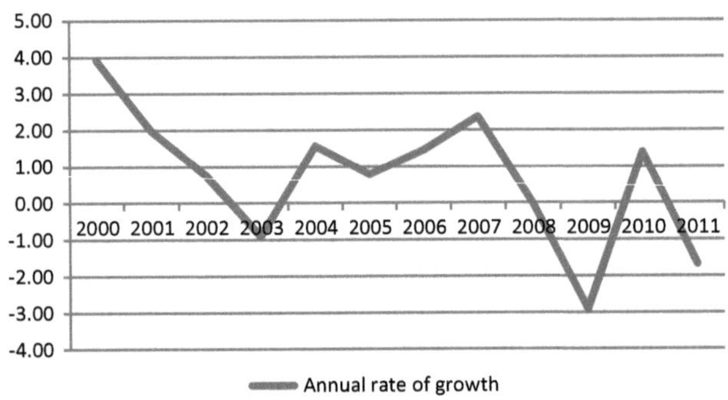

Fig. 7.8 Portugal: annual rates of growth. 2000–2011 (*Source*: Eurostat)

Portugal's already low rate of growth became negative in 2008 and 2009 (Fig. 7.8). The first reaction to the crisis was to stimulate demand. This increase in public expenditure on top of the measures taken to preserve the Portuguese financial system meant that the public deficit soared to 10.2 % in 2009 (Fig. 7.9) and Portugal's public debt-to-GDP ratio jumped from 68.3 % in 2007 to 93.3 % in 2010. However, public accounts improved in 2011 after a series of tax hikes and salary cuts for public servants took place.

These measures allowed Portugal, in the first half of 2011, to receive a €78 billion IMF/EU bailout package in a bid to stabilize its public finances, as Greece and Ireland had done before. In 2012, the Portuguese government used €3 billion from the bailout package to rescue Portugal's largest listed bank by assets, Millennium BCP.

By the end of 2012, Portugal had regained access to financial markets when the state managed to renew one-third of the outstanding bonds at a reasonable yield level (5.12 %). The bailout funding program was supposed to run until June 2014, but at the same time it requires Portugal to regain complete bond market access by September 2013. While the budget deficit for 2012 was forecasted to end at 5 %, the

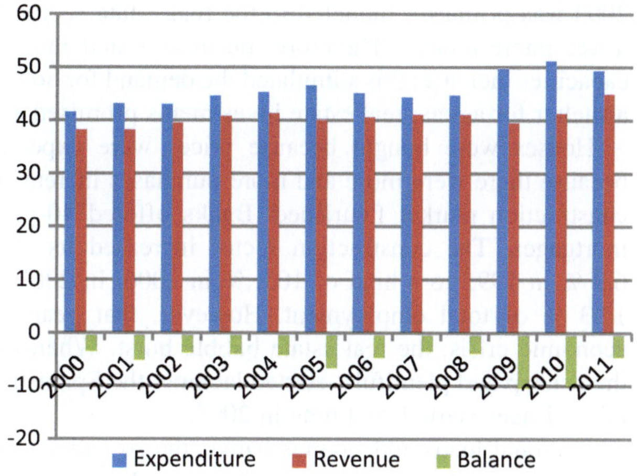

Fig. 7.9 Portugal: general government expenditure, revenue, and balance, 2000–2011 (percentage of GDP) (*Source*: Eurostat)

country is expected to reduce the budget deficit to a level below 3 % of GDP in 2014.

7.9 Spain: A Special Case

The weight of Spain's public debt as of 2011 was substantially lower than the weight of the debt of the UK and of Germany. Spain's government debt ratio was just 68.5 of GDP against 85.7 in the UK and 81.2 in Germany, not to mention 165.3 in Greece and 120.1 in Italy. Why was, then, Spain involved in the European financial crisis? There is just one single reason: because it evoked the Irish case. In 2007, the public debt-to-GDP ratio in Ireland was only 24.8. However, it soared to 65.2 in 2009.

As in Ireland, construction had been a fast-growing industry in Spain. It expanded at a rate of 5 % per year between 1996 and 2007. Between 1998 and 2007, the number of housing units grew 30 % (Arellano and Bentolila 2009, 28). House prices increased dramatically and people expected the process to go on without an end. Real house prices—adjusted for the change in the consumer price index—increased by 127 % between 1996 and 2007 (André 2010, 9).

Therefore, real estate became the preferred destination for savings. Tax benefits stimulated even greater demand for real estate, biasing household investment to housing in place of other types of assets.[20] This process was reinforced after 1999.

After becoming a member of the Eurozone, Spain benefited—as in the case of Greece and other southern Europe countries—from a drastic reduction in interest rates. The flight of capital from the equity markets that occurred between 2000 and

[20] Altogether, 15 % of mortgage payments are deductible from personal income taxes in Spain.

2003 was primarily funneled to the real estate sector. Loans became available at lower interest rates. Therefore, businesses and individuals saw their borrowing capacities increase; this stimulated the demand for house building. Housing became a shelter for assets: real estate investments promised attractive capital gains.

Houses were bought because prices were expected to rise and prices rose because there were more and more purchases increasingly financed by loans. The construction market flourished. Banks offered 40-year and, later, even 50-year mortgages. The construction sector increased its share of Spanish GDP from 6.9 % in 1995 to a high of 10.8 % in 2006. In 2007, construction accounted for 13.3 % of total employment. However, that year, coinciding with the global economic crisis, the real estate bubble burst. When international liquidity—until then cheap and plentiful—started lacking, the Spanish real estate market entered a crisis. Prices started declining in 2008.

Regional loans and savings banks, the so-called *cajas*, were very active in the real estate market. They owned 56 % of the country's mortgages in 2009. They were the first victims when the market crashed that year: debtors fell into bankruptcy and bad loans dramatically increased. In March 2009, the Spanish government announced its first bailout of a *caja*.

After that, more bank bailouts were announced by the Spanish government. While these government bailouts kept these banks from going bankrupt, investor confidence in the Spanish economy sunk even lower. Many real estate developers avoided bankruptcy only because banks kept permitting them to refinance their loans. In this way, loans were reported as performing. In May 2012, Bankia, a bank that resulted from the merger of several *cajas*, had to be bailed out by the government. At that time, it was the fourth bank by size in the Spanish ranking of banking institutions.

Figure 7.10 shows the evolution of general government expenditure, revenue and deficit between 2000 and 2011. It shows that Spain had a small deficit between 2000 and 2004, far below the ceiling of 3 % of GDP that the European Stability and Growth Pact established for member states after the introduction of the euro on January 1, 1999. From 2005 to 2007, the increase in revenues allowed the government to run a surplus. The situation abruptly reversed in 2008 precipitated by a significant decrease in revenues, a decline that deepened in the following years, as a reflection of the international financial crisis.

As can be seen in Fig. 7.11, the rate of growth plummeted in 2008 and became negative in 2009 and 2010. The contraction in international liquidity supply was followed by a restriction on credit and subsequently by a sharp decline in construction and employment. The increase in unemployment meant a rise in spending on unemployment and other social benefits. The bailout of several *cajas* was another source of increase in public expenditure. On the other hand, the decline in GDP was followed by a weakening of public revenues, especially those linked with the real estate sector.

Therefore, the swift deterioration of Spain's public finance flashed warning lights on the capacity of its government to face the services of its increasing public

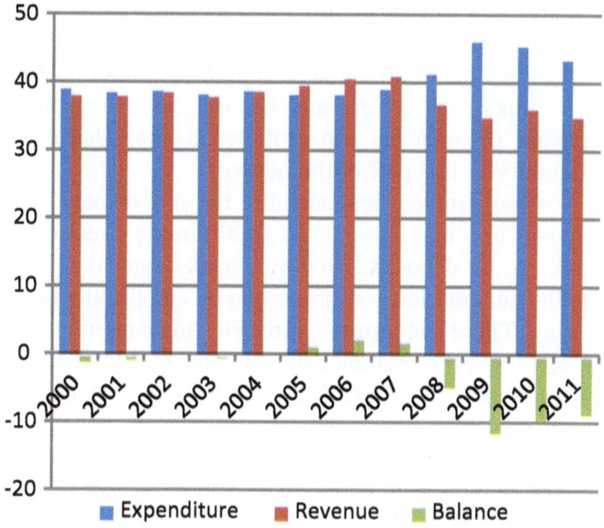

Fig. 7.10 Spain: general government expenditure, revenue, and balance, 2000–2011 (percentage of GDP) (*Source*: Eurostat)

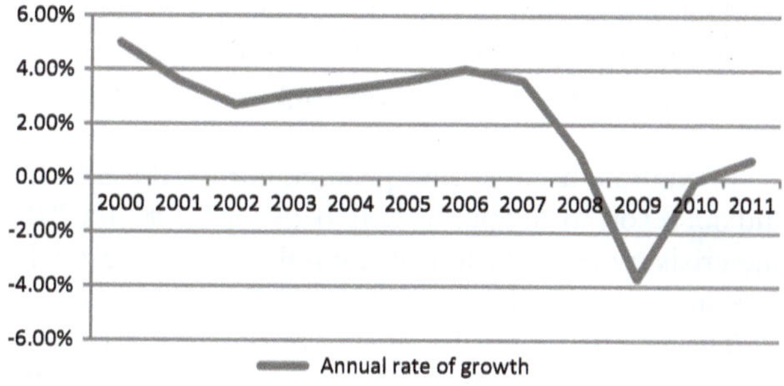

Fig. 7.11 Spain: annual rates of growth 2000–2011 (*Source*: INE)

debt, which had exceptionally short maturity structures. Spain was following Ireland's steps with a 3-year delay.

7.10 Italy: A Different "Old" Debtor

The Italian government was highly indebted long before the crisis outburst. In 2007, the general government debt-to-GDP ratio was already 103.1, second only to Greece, and well above the 60 % Maastricht criterion. However, nobody worried at that time for the Italian public debt and the Italian government had no problem refinancing it. Between 2007 and 2010, it only increased 15 %.

However, the American financial crisis deeply affected the Italian economy. The transmission mechanism was the contraction in the interbank loan market that was the immediate consequence of the crisis. Banks refused to lend money to each other because of a lack of liquidity and the uncertainty about the financial soundness of borrowers (see Chap. 6, Sects. 6.5, 6.6, and 6.7).

Besides the contraction in liquidity, Italian banks were also affected by their close links with central and eastern European countries where they had built a network of branches and affiliated banks. There was a risk of the collapse or illiquidity of this part of the network.

The government responded to the risk of banking crisis by guaranteeing bank deposits to a maximum of €103,000 in the event of a bankruptcy. This avoided a bank run on deposits. However, banks reacted to the liquidity crisis by reducing credit to clients and consumers and raising the amount of collateral required for new loans. These measures affected investment and consumption. Bugamelli et al (2009, 11) estimate that in the period from January 2008 to June 2009, production fell by more than 35 % in sectors such as electrical machinery, metallurgy, and cars. The GDP rate of growth became negative in 2008 and 2009 (Fig. 7.12). Growth resumed in 2010, but was snuffed out in 2011.

The reduction in economic activity cut the amount of tax collected and anti-cyclical policies increased public expenditure. As a result, there was a significant increase in the public deficit (Fig. 7.13).

After Berlusconi stepped down, the new Prime Minister Mario Monti launched a deep austerity plan including measures such as increasing the retirement age, raising property taxes, simplifying the operation of government agencies, and going after tax evaders.

In contrast to most European countries, the banking system in Italy practically did not resort to any public help between 2008 and 2011. Italian banks mainly faced the crisis by raising funds in capital markets. Italy's banking system required very low support from the ECB (Table 7.2).

The results of the EU-wide stress test carried out by the European Banking Association in 2010 and 2011 show that the included Italian banks successfully passed the test. Moreover, the Italian banking system seems to have low exposure to government debt; it holds less than 10 % of domestic public debt—against more than 40 % in the case of Spanish banks—as well as low exposure to foreign sovereign risk, which represents only 23 % of the total government debt Italian banks hold (Bolton and Jeanne 2011).

Therefore, in contrast to Spain, Italy's problem seems to be essentially located in its public debt, whose ratio to GDP, although high, is no worse than it was 20 years ago, when nobody worried about it. In fact, the country's debt first hit 120 % of GDP in 1993, after the public deficit reached 10.37 % of GDP in 1992.

After the exchange rate turmoil that hit the European monetary system in 1992, Italy devalued the lira. Italian trade performance improved as import growth slowed, while export growth remained relatively constant. Therefore, Italy went into the Eurozone with a large surplus on its trade accounts. The high levels of Italian public debt only became a problem when, in the context of the 2011–2012 European economic climate, the private sector began to lose confidence in the ability of the Italian state to service its debt.

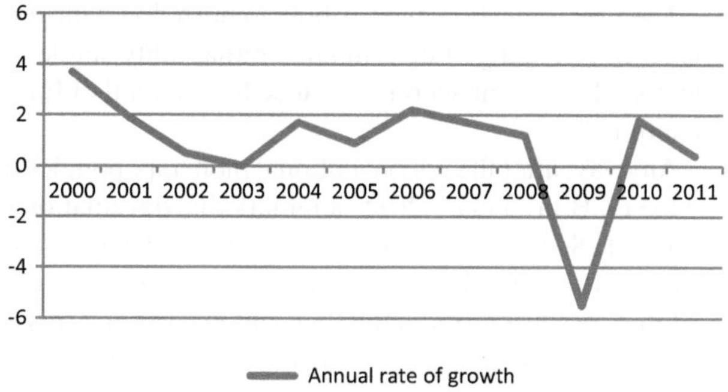

Fig. 7.12 Italy: annual rates of growth 2000–2011 (*Source*: Eurostat)

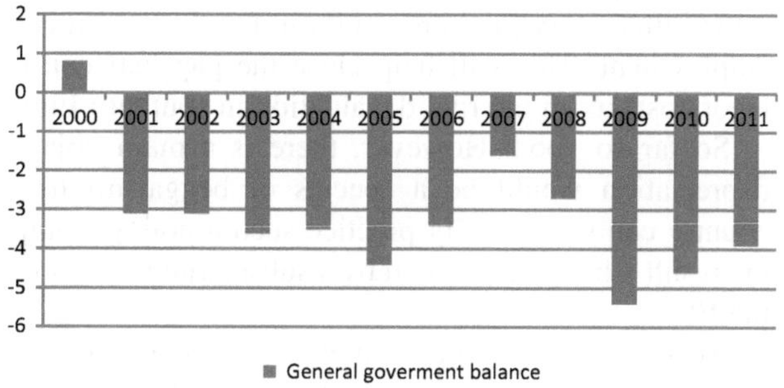

Fig. 7.13 Italy: general government balance 2000–2011 (percentage of GDP) (*Source*: Eurostat)

Table 7.2 Funds provided by the ECB to national banking systems as of December 2011: percentage of GDP

Country	%
Ireland	87.79
Greece	61.46
Portugal	27.65
Netherlands	26.9
Spain	16.83
Italy	12.65
France	10.89
Belgium	9.54
Austria	4.5
Germany	2.16

Source: OECD

7.11 Is There Any Role the Euro Rate of Exchange Can Play in the Adjustment Process?

Some scholars have argued that a way to alleviate the debt crisis might be euro devaluation. This would improve external competitiveness for Europe as a whole and for the indebted countries in particular. A weaker euro would foster an export-led growth process.

The first issue, however, is how to push down the euro. In spite of the debt crisis, the euro's exchange rate remained remarkably stable. This may be attributed to the fact that the current account balance for the total of Eurozone countries as a whole is in surplus.

Anyway, after the unconventional monetary policies of quantitative easing decided by the ECB in January 2015, a remarkable devaluation of the euro has followed (see Chap. 11, Sects. 11.4.4 and 11.4.5). After a devaluation, the depressed economies of southern Europe will improve their exports and contract their imports. Export-related and import-substitution industries will expand and this expansion will be transmitted to the rest of the economy. Growing activity will provide higher revenues to governments to pay for the debt.

Euro depreciation would push the German trade surplus even higher and cause some inflationary pressures in those few European countries that are still near full employment. This will help close the gap between German and other European labor costs as an internal devaluation in southern Europe countries would do.

So far so good. However, there is a main objection to this reasoning. Euro depreciation would be a species of beggar-my-neighbor policy. Whereas one country can successfully practice such a policy, competitive devaluations may be the result when it is pursued by a substantial number of countries as it is the case of the EU.

Nevertheless, the impact of euro devaluation on the global market may be rather limited. Most of the international trade of European countries is with European partners. The northern euro members' historically large current account surpluses and southern Europe's sizable current account deficits are two sides of the same coin. Therefore, euro devaluation may be part of the solution although by no means is the solution to the sovereign debt crisis.

7.12 Summary and Conclusions

The European indebtedness process does not accept a unique explanation. Of course, it may be argued that the European and the American crises are just chapters in a *global* credit bubble (McKinsey Global Institute 2011) or the consequences of a global money or savings glut. However, this explains little except that Europeans and Americans have had access to cheap money during the past 15 years.

This chapter shows that among the most indebted European countries, there are at least two different groups. One is made up of "old" debtors, whose debt-to-GDP ratios slightly grew between 2001 and 2007. This means that in these countries the debt problem antecedes the introduction of the euro. A second group of "new" debtors comprises those countries whose debt suddenly increased as a result of the 2007–2009 financial crisis. These are the cases of Ireland and Iceland.

Spain is a special case whose debt-to-GDP ratio was substantially lower than the weight of the debt of the UK and Germany, not to mention Greece or Italy. However, its public debt was severely punished by the market because of the doubts about its banking system's health, which raised suspicion that it might require governmental support, as in the cases of Ireland and Iceland.

Therefore, although it is true that the US financial crisis triggered the European debt crisis, it did it through different channels. In the cases of Ireland and Iceland, through a severe credit squeeze and a reduction in banks' abilities to access the capital markets. The drain of liquidity experienced by the banking system precipitated governmental intervention with the consequential jump in public debt.

However, in the cases of Greece, Italy, and Portugal, the American financial crisis mainly brought attention upon the fiscal situation of countries already heavily indebted, who could face growing difficulties to roll over their debts in an increasing climate of fear and distrust.

Far from helping to reverse their preexisting fiscal imbalances, entrance into the Eurozone had aggravated them for Greece and Portugal. In fact, the continuous revaluation of the euro worsened their budget imbalances after 2000, increasing their public debt. A positive association between the rate of exchange and budget imbalance was found for both countries. After the debt crisis burst, both countries found themselves without access to capital markets and had to resort to IMF/EU bailout packages in an attempt to stabilize their public finances.

In 2007, Italy's general government debt-to-GDP ratio was 103.1, second only to Greece, and well above the 60 % Maastricht criterion. However, nobody worried at that time for the Italian public debt and the Italian government had no problem in refinancing it. Moreover, it only increased 15 % between 2007 and 2010. Therefore, the Italian debt crisis is a clear example of the change in humor in financial markets after the American financial crisis.

The announcement by the President of the ECB, in mid-2012, that the ECB would have done "whatever it takes" to preserve the euro and to struggle the crisis (see Chap. 6, Sect. 6.5) and the following purchase of sovereign bonds of the area's stricken economies with a quantitative easing monetary policy (see Chap. 11, Sect. 11.4.5) calmed the waters, allowing European authorities to buy time to figure out how they could get the area out of the debt crisis.

As Lane (2011, 60) points out, a country with a high level of sovereign debt is vulnerable to increases in the interest rate. "This risk can give rise to self-fulfilling speculative attacks: an increase in perceptions of default risk induces investors to demand higher yields, which in turn makes default more likely". The opposite happens if default risk is perceived to be low. So, we are in the presence of a multiple equilibrium problem. The announcement by the ECB acted as a signal to push the system to the "good" equilibrium.

On top of this, a new European Stability Mechanism was created to replace the European Financial Stability Facility and the European Financial Stabilization Mechanism. This offered bank recapitalization packages directly to the financial sector, rather than doing so via national treasuries as in the past with existing EU funding programs. In parallel, a Single Supervisory Mechanism was established for the oversight of credit institutions.

Although the financial crisis has temporarily calmed down, it has not been solved. As stated above, what has not been done before in the form of resource transfers from the richer to the poorer countries of the Eurozone will have to be done now in the way of helping these countries reduce the burden of their debts if the monetary union is to be saved. This is nothing else but the application of the principle of solidarity which requires the stronger member countries to support the weaker ones in times of severe crisis.

One way of doing this may be by implementing the mechanism of the European redemption pact proposed in the 2011 annual report of the German Council of Economic Experts (GCEE).[21] According to it, debt amounts above the Maastricht reference value of 60 % of GDP would be transferred to a common redemption fund subject to joint liability. Each country would be obliged to autonomously redeem the transferred debt over a period of 20–25 years. This will extend debt maturity and lower interest rates for highly indebted countries. A simulation exercise of the redemption plan for Italy[22] shows this proposal is feasible at least for this highly indebted country: assuming an average real rate of growth of 1 % per year, the debt transferred to the redemption fund is fully redeemed after 23 years.

Countries like Germany, the Netherlands, and Finland will presumably have to pay higher interest rates than at present as a consequence of the liability risk they will face. In fact, they would have to meet more obligations if eventually some European borrower defaults and cannot service its debt.

In this respect it is worthwhile remembering the 1953 London Debt Agreement that relieved the young federal republic of its pre- and postwar external debts. This debt relief represented about 50 % out of its total external debt at that time, roughly 10 % of West Germany's GDP in 1953, and 80 % of its export earnings that year. This debt restructuring marked the transition from critical indebtedness to a situation where debt was no longer an obstacle to economic and social development.[23]

In 2001 the European Union created the EU Solidarity Fund to respond to major natural disasters; the European redemption fund may be the response to a major economic disaster—the debt crisis—and would allow keeping the monetary union alive. In exchange, it should be ensured that the structural budget deficit for each country which has transferred debts to the redemption fund does not exceed the threshold of 0.5 % of GDP, as the GCEE proposed. If a member country fails to honor its commitments, the transfer of the debt to the fund would immediately be stopped and the collateral lost, as also was proposed by the GCEE.

A scheme of mutualization of financial risk may create moral hazard. Mechanisms to contain moral hazard need to be introduced in order to avoid that some governments take more risk than they would otherwise. Different alternatives are broadly discussed in the report by the Expert Group on Debt Redemption Fund and Eurobills (2014). It is clear that most of the solutions to the crisis would be much easier to implement if Europe were a single country with a single government. This

[21] GCEE (2011, third chapter, 107).

[22] Parello and Visco (2012, 5–8).

[23] See Kaiser (2013) for a discussion of the arguments on the comparability of the London agreement with current debt relief operations.

shows that institutional reforms are badly needed in order to develop a governance structure that can handle the complex challenges posed by the monetary union.

References

Abell JD (1990) Twin deficits during the 1980's: an empirical investigation. J Macroecon 12:81–96

Alkswani M (2000) The twin deficits phenomenon in petroleum economy: evidence from Saudi Arabia. Paper presented at the seventh annual conference, economic research forum (ERF). Available via http://www.erf.org.eg/CMS/uploads/pdf/1185358196_finance1.pdf

André C (2010) A bird's eye view of OECD housing markets. OECD economics department working paper no. 746. Available via http://www.cchpr.landecon.cam.ac.uk/Conference2010/Downloads/Papers/Plenary/Andre%20C%20Paper.pdf

Anoruo E, Ramchander S (1998) Current account and fiscal deficits: evidence from five developing economies of Asia. J Asian Econ 9:487–501

Arellano M, Bentolila S (2009) La burbuja inmobiliaria: causas y responsables. La Crisis de la Economía Española: Lecciones y Propuestas, FEDEA, pp 28–31. Available via http://www.crisis09.es/PDF/la-crisis-de-la-economia-espanola.pdf

Bachman DD (1992) Why is the US current account deficit so large: evidence from vector autoregressions. South Econ J 59:232–240

Bolton P, Jeanne O (2011) Sovereign default risk and bank fragility in financially integrated economies. IMF Econ Rev 59:162–194. http://www.palgrave-journals.com/imfer/journal/v59/n2/abs/imfer20115a.html

Bugamelli M, Cristadoro R, Zevi G (2009) La crisi internazionale e il sistema produttivo italiano: un'analisi su dati a livello di impresa. Occasional Papers 58, Banca d'Italia, Rome. Available via http://www.bancaditalia.it/pubblicazioni/econo/quest_ecofin_2/QF_58

Carlin W (1998) The new east German economy: problems of transition, unification and institutional mismatch, University College London. Available via http://www.ucl.ac.uk/~uctpa36/East%20Germany%203%20problems.pdf

Cavallo M (2005) Government consumption expenditures and the current account. Federal reserve bank of san francisco working paper 2005–03. Available via http://www.frbsf.org/publications/economics/papers/2005/wp05-03bk.pdf

Coudert V, Couharde C, Mignon V (2012) On currency misalignments within the euro area. Center d'études projectives et d'informations internationales, CEPII, No. 2012–07. Available via http://www.cepii.com/PDF_PUB/wp/2012/wp2012-07.pdf

Dewald WG, Ulan M (1990) The twin deficit illusion. Cato J 10:689–707

EEAG (2013) The EEAG report on the European economy 2013. CESifo, Munich

Enders W, Lee BS (1990) Current account and budget deficits: twins or distant cousins? Rev Econ Stat 72:373–381

Erceg C, Guerrieri L (2005) Expansionary fiscal shocks and the trade deficit. Computing in economics and finance, Society for Computational Economics

Expert Group on Debt Redemption Fund and Eurobill (2014) Final report. Available via http://ec.europa.eu/economy_finance/articles/governance/pdf/20140331_report_en.pdf

Feldstein M (2012) The failure of the euro. Foreign affairs, January–February. Available via http://www.foreignaffairs.com/articles/136752/martin-feldstein/the-failure-of-the-euro

Georgantopoulos AG, Tsamis A (2011) The macroeconomic effects of budget deficits in Greece: a VAR-VECM approach. Int Res J Financ Econ 79:156–166

German Council of Economic Experts (2011) Annual report 2011/12. Assume responsibility for Europe, Wiesbaden

Gianviti F, Krueger A, Pisani-Ferry J, Sapir A, von Hagen J (2010) A European mechanism for sovereign debt crisis resolution: a proposal, Bruegel. Available via http://aei.pitt.edu/15123/1/101109_BP_Debt_resolution_BP_clean_01.pdf

Governor of the Central Bank of Ireland (2010) The Irish banking crisis regulatory and financial stability policy 2003–2008. Available via http://www.financialregulator.ie/press-area/pressreleases/Pages/TheIrishBankingCrisis,RegulatoryandFinancialStabilityPolicy2003%E2%80%932008.aspx

Honohan P (2010) The Irish banking crisis regulatory and financial stability policy 2003–2008. Report to the Irish minister for finance by the governor of the central bank. Available via http://www.karlwhelan.com/Papers/Whelan-IrelandPaper-June2013.pdf

Islam MF (1998) Brazil's twin deficits: an empirical examination. Atl Econ J 2:121–128

Kaiser J (2013) One made it out of the debt trap. Lessons from the London debt agreement of 1953 for current debt crises, Friedriech Ebert Stiftung. Available via http://library.fes.de/pdf-files/iez/10137.pdf

Katsimi M, Moutos T (2010) EMU and the Greek crisis. Eur J Polit Econ 26(4):568–576

Khalid AM, Teo WG (1999) Causality tests of budget and current account deficits: cross-country comparisons. Empir Econ 24:389–402

Kim KH (1995) On the long-run determinants of the US trade balance: a comment. J Post Keynesian Econ 17:447–455

Lane PR (2011) The Irish crisis, IIIS discussion paper no. 356. Available via http://www.tcd.ie/iiis/documents/discussion/pdfs/iiisdp356.pdf

Leachman LL, Francis B (2002) Twin deficits: apparition or reality? Appl Econ 34:1121–1132

McKinsey Global Institute (2011) Debt and deleveraging: the global credit bubble and its economic consequences (Updated Analysis). Available via http://www.mckinsey.com/insights/mgi/research/financial_markets/debt_and_deleveraging_the_global_credit_bubble_update

Miller SM, Russek FS (1989) Are the twin deficits really related? Contemp Policy Iss 7:91–115

Moro B (2014) Lessons from the European economic and financial great crisis: a survey. Eur J Polit Econ 34(Supplement):S9–S24, June

Mukhtar T, Zakaria M, Ahmed M (2007) An empirical investigation for the twin deficits in Pakistan. J Econ Coop 28(4):63–80

Parello CP, Visco V (2012) The European redemption fund: a comparison of two proposals. MPRA 42874:5–8

Pérez-Caldentey E, Vernengo M (2012) The euro imbalances and financial deregulation: a post-Keynesian interpretation of the European debt crisis. Levy economics institute of bard college working paper no. 702. Available via http://www.levyinstitute.org/pubs/wp_702.pdf

Piersanti G (2000) Current account dynamics and expected future budget deficits: some international evidence. J Int Money Financ 19(2):255–271

Reinhart CM, Rogoff KS (2008) This time is different: a panoramic view of eight centuries of financial crises. NBER working paper no. 13882. Available via http://www.nber.org/papers/w13882.pdf

Sinn HW (2013) Austerity, growth and inflation. Remarks on the Eurozone's unresolved competitiveness problem. CESifo working paper no. 4086

Véron N (2012) Financial reform after the crisis. In: Eichengreen B, Park B (eds) The world economy after the global crisis. A new economic order for the 21st century. World Scientific Studies in International Economics, Singapore, Chapter 2

Whelan K (2013) Ireland's economic crisis. University College, Dublin

Part V
The Impact of the Great Crisis on Economic Thought

Chapter 8
The Theoretical Debate on the Great Crisis

Beniamino Moro

8.1 Introduction

On the recent Great Crisis, it has grown an animated debate between the Keynesian and the neoclassical schools of thought, which was extended from the predictive capabilities of the respective theoretical models to the political interventions to fight the crisis and to the suggested regulation needed to prevent a new catastrophic meltdown. This chapter is dedicated to illustrate this debate (Moro 2012).

The chapter is organized as follows. Section 8.2 summarizes Paul Krugman's view on saltwater versus freshwater economists, while Sect. 8.3 exposes the Keynesian tradition from the Great Moderation to the Great Crisis. Section 8.4 deals with the neoclassical view of financial crises and discusses the meaning of the efficient-market hypothesis. Section 8.5 summarizes the Leijonhufvud's position on stabilization policies and the trade-off between stagnation and high inflation. Section 8.6 deals with panic, systemic risk, and the need for a new financial regulation. Finally, in Sect. 8.7 some concluding remarks are summarized.

The main conclusion of the chapter is that commercial banks, who are allowed to manage systemic contracts like bank deposits, and for that reason they have access to the lender of last resort, should be kept strictly separated from investment banks, hedge funds, and other financial speculative institutions, none of which should be considered too big to fail.

B. Moro (✉)
Department of Economics and Business, University of Cagliari, Viale San Ignazio 17, 09123 Cagliari, Italy
e-mail: moro@unica.it

B. Moro, V.A. Beker, *Modern Financial Crises*, Financial and Monetary Policy Studies 42, DOI 10.1007/978-3-319-20991-3_8

8.2 Paul Krugman on Saltwater Versus Freshwater Economists

Following the Keynesian tradition of the animal spirits and the irrationality of the human behavior, in a much debated article, Krugman (2009) holds that few economists saw the crisis coming, but for him this predictive failure was the least of the field's problems, as long as more important was the profession's blindness to the very possibility of catastrophic failures in a market economy. He asserts that, during the golden years of the Great Moderation,[1] financial economists believed that markets were inherently stable and that stocks and other assets were always priced just right.

There was nothing in the prevailing models suggesting the possibility of the kind of collapse that happened in 2008. Meanwhile, macroeconomists were divided in their views. But—according to Krugman—the main division was between those who insisted that free-market economies never go astray and those who believed that economies may stray now and then but that any major deviations from the path of prosperity could and would be corrected by the all-powerful Fed. Neither side was prepared to cope with an economy that went off the rails despite the Fed's best efforts.

According to Krugman, the economics profession went astray because economists, as a group, mistook "beauty," which was clad in impressive-looking mathematics, for "truth," that is to say for the essence of economic inquiry. Economists fell back in love with the old, idealized vision of an economy in which rational individuals interact in perfect markets. In fact, the central cause of the profession's failure was the desire for an all-encompassing, intellectually elegant approach that also gave economists a chance to show off their mathematical prowess.

This vision of the economy led most economists to ignore all the things that can go wrong. Like Akerlof and Shiller (2009),[2] also Krugman agrees that they turned a blind eye to the limitations of human rationality that often lead to bubbles and busts, to the problems of institutions that run amok, to the imperfections of markets, especially financial markets, that can cause the economy's operating system to undergo sudden, unpredictable crashes, and to the dangers created when regulators do not believe in regulation.

In other words, the central cause of the profession's failure for Krugman was the same as Akerlof and Shiller's, that is, the abandoning of Keynesian theory to explain crises and depressions and the prevailing of monetarism and neoclassical vision that whatever happens in a market economy must be right.[3]

---

[1] The Great Moderation is a term sometimes used to describe the perceived end to economic volatility created by twentieth century banking systems. In 2004, Bernanke (2004) celebrated the Great Moderation in economic performance over the previous two decades, which he attributed in part to improved economic policymaking. The term was coined by Stock and Watson (2002).

[2] See Chap. 1, Sect. 1.6.

[3] For a more detailed analysis of this view, see Chap. 10.

Krugman regrets that Keynes's disparaging vision of financial markets as a "casino" was replaced among financial economists by "efficient-market" theory, which asserted that financial markets always get asset prices right given the available information.

Of course, he recognizes that there were exceptions to these trends: a few economists challenged the assumption of rational behavior, questioned the belief that financial markets can be trusted, and pointed to the long history of financial crises that had devastating economic consequences. But for Krugman they were swimming against the tide, and when the capital development of a country becomes a by-product of the financial activities viewed as a "casino," the job is likely to be ill-done. He also notes that discussion of investor irrationality, of bubbles, and of destructive speculation had virtually disappeared from academic debates, and the field was mainly dominated by the "efficient-market hypothesis".

The theoretical model that finance economists developed by assuming that every investor rationally balances risk against reward (the so-called capital asset pricing model, or CAPM), according to Krugman, is wonderfully elegant and, if one accepts its premises, it is also extremely useful. The CAPM does not only tell us how to choose our portfolio, but, even more important from the financial industry's point of view, it tells how to put a price on financial derivatives, claims on claims.[4]

Anyway, finance theorists did not accept the efficient-market hypothesis merely because it was elegant, convenient, and lucrative. They also produced a great deal of statistical evidence, which at first seemed strongly supportive. But this evidence—Krugman notes—was of an oddly limited form. Finance economists rarely asked the seemingly obvious question of whether asset prices made sense given real-world fundamentals like earnings. Instead, they asked only whether asset prices made sense given other asset prices.[5]

Among these economists was Alan Greenspan, who is considered as a long-time supporter of financial deregulation. By October 2008, however, Greenspan admitted that he felt a "shocked disbelief" because his whole intellectual edifice had collapsed (see Chap. 1, Sect. 1.3). But for Krugman, since this was also a collapse of real-world markets, the result was a severe recession, the worst, by many measures, since the Great Depression.

According to Krugman, 40 years ago most economists would have agreed with a Keynesian interpretation of the crisis, but since then macroeconomics has divided

[4] Presumably, here Krugman refers to the *empirical* CAPM, as opposed to the *theoretical* CAPM which, being consumption based, determines asset prices in absolute terms. The theoretical wealth portfolio return is in fact tightly linked to the intertemporal marginal rate of substitution between consumption levels in two successive periods, whereas its empirical counterpart is generally represented by a benchmark portfolio of financial assets. See Cochrane (2001, Chap. 9).

[5] Larry Summers once mocked finance professors with a parable about "ketchup economists" who "have shown that two-quart bottles of ketchup invariably sell for exactly twice as much as one-quart bottles of ketchup" and conclude from this that the ketchup market is perfectly efficient. This reasoning is labeled "ketchup economics." See http://marginalfoodie.blogspot.com/2007/09/ketchup-economics-explained.html.

into two great factions: "saltwater economists" (mainly in coastal US universities), who have a more or less Keynesian vision of what recessions are all about, and "freshwater economists" (mainly at inland schools), who consider that vision nonsense. Freshwater economists are, essentially, neoclassical purists. They believe that all worthwhile economic analysis starts from the premise that people are rational and markets work. As they see it, a general lack of aggregate demand is not possible, because prices always move to match supply with demand.

As long as freshwater economists remained purists, saltwater economists became pragmatists. While economists like Gregory Mankiw, Olivier Blanchard, and David Romer acknowledged that it was hard to reconcile a Keynesian demand-side view of recessions with neoclassical theory, they also found that the demand-driven explanation of recessions was, in fact, too compelling to reject. So they were willing to deviate from the assumption of perfect markets or perfect rationality, or both, adding enough imperfections to accommodate a more or less Keynesian view of recessions.

And—what is very important for Krugman—in the saltwater view, active policy to fight recessions remained desirable. But these "self-described New Keynesian economists" were not immune to the charms of rational individuals and perfect markets. They tried to keep their deviations from neoclassical orthodoxy as limited as possible.

This meant that there was no room, also in the prevailing New Keynesian models, for such things as bubbles and banking system collapse. Therefore, the fact that such things continued to happen in the real world, according to Krugman, was not reflected in the mainstream of New Keynesian thinking.

Even so, it was reasonable to think that the differing worldviews of freshwater and saltwater economists would have put them constantly at loggerheads over economic policy. Somewhat surprisingly, however, between around 1985 and 2007 the disputes between freshwater and saltwater economists were mainly about theory, not action.

According to Krugman, the reason is that New Keynesians, unlike the original Keynesians like himself, did not think fiscal policy was needed to fight recessions. They believed that monetary policy, administered by the technocrats at the Fed, could provide whatever remedies the economy needed.

At the 90th birthday celebration for Milton Friedman, Ben Bernanke declared about the Great Depression that, thanks to the Fed, "it will not happen again".[6] The clear message was that all you need to avoid depressions is a smarter Fed. And as long as macroeconomic policy was left in the hands of the "maestro" Greenspan, without Keynesian-type stimulus programs, freshwater economists found little to complain about, as they did not believe that monetary policy did any good, but they also did not believe it did any harm, either.

[6] The implicit allusion of this sentence is to the book, much debated during the 1980s, written by the post-Keynesian economist Hyman Minsky (1982). See Chap. 10, Sect. 10.6.

Anyway, Krugman advises that there was something else going on: a general belief that bubbles just do not happen. What is striking in Greenspan's assurances is that they were not based on evidence, but on the a priori assertion that there simply could not be a bubble in housing. And the finance theorists were even more adamant on this point.

8.3 The Keynesian Tradition from the Great Moderation to the Great Crisis

Between 1985 and 2007, a false peace settled over the field of macroeconomics. These were the years of the Great Moderation, an extended period during which inflation was subdued and recessions were relatively mild. Saltwater economists believed that the Federal Reserve had everything under control. Freshwater economists did not think the Fed's actions were actually beneficial, but they were willing to let matters lie.

Anyway, the crisis ended the phony peace, and suddenly the narrow, technocratic policies both sides were willing to accept were no longer sufficient. The need for a broader policy response brought the old conflicts out into the open, fiercer than ever. This happened when conventional monetary policy stopped to be effective in a situation of liquidity trap, and the Fed engaged in quantitative easing policies.

In fact, by late 2008, with interest rates basically at the "zero lower bound" even as the recession continued to deepen, conventional monetary policy had lost all traction, which meant that, for the second time after the Great Depression, the US economic system was fallen in a liquidity trap situation. It is the same situation that in the1930s led Keynes to advocate higher government spending: when monetary policy is ineffective and the private sector cannot be persuaded to spend more, the public sector must take its place in supporting the economy. Fiscal stimulus should have been the Keynesian answer to the kind of depression-type economic situation triggered by the Great Crisis.

Yet, according to Krugman, if the crisis had crowded out freshwater economists, it had also created a lot of soul-searching among saltwater economists. Their framework, unlike that of the neoclassicals, allowed for the possibility of involuntary unemployment, but the New Keynesian models also assumed that people are perfectly rational and financial markets are perfectly efficient.

For Krugman, these two hypotheses are incoherent each other. Therefore, to get the Great Crisis into their models, New Keynesians were forced to introduce some kind of fudge factor that for unspecified reasons temporarily depresses private spending. And if the analysis depends on this fudge factor, how much confidence can we have in the models' predictions about where we are going?

Krugman concludes with the following three observations. First, economists must consider the inconvenient reality that financial markets fall far short of perfection, that they are subject to extraordinary delusions, and that it does exist the madness of crowds (herd behavior). Therefore, when we consider the problem of recessions and depressions, economists need to abandon the neat but wrong solution of assuming that everyone is rational and markets work perfectly. Second, they have to admit that Keynesian economics remains the best framework we have for making sense of recessions and depressions, and third, they will have to do their best to incorporate the realities of finance into macroeconomics.[7]

The role of externalities and the herd behavior of people are also analyzed by Kirman (2009a, b), who notes that individuals who are close to each other, as they are in a market, do not take independent decisions, but they watch each other and "herd". Therefore, we cannot ignore the direct interaction between individuals and its influence on preferences. And if we take account of externalities, that is, the influence of one person's action on another, then we have to specify the structure of that interaction at the center of action than regarding them as "imperfections" in our equilibrium model. This means that we have to study the structure and fragility of the networks that govern the interaction between individuals and make this central in our analysis.

One of the major points much debated from a Keynesian perspective, as it has been highlighted by Krugman, is the need for a fiscal stimulus to overcome the crisis. Advocates of the stimulus usually make reference to some papers by the IMF (2008, 2009a, b, c) and OECD (2009a, b) which contain detailed information about fiscal policies followed in many countries all over the world. Particularly, the first IMF (2008) paper was an influential early guide to fiscal policy in the crisis, which suggested the criteria (timely, temporary, and targeted) to be respected by the fiscal stimulus in order to be efficient.[8]

Some view the financial crisis as a heart attack to the economic system. In this regard, Caballero (2009a) explains why the financial sector can be seen as the heart and the arteries of the world economy, while Corden (2009, 2010) speaks of the "ambulance economics" to advocate an immediate, urgent, and temporary rescue process made by an appropriate fiscal stimulus. As the ambulance has been called upon all over the world, from China and Japan to the USA and Germany, this means, according to Corden, that Keynesian economics has won and the policies that Keynesians have inevitably favored have, to a great extent, been implemented. Thanks to the ambulance—he concludes—a new Great Depression has been avoided.

[7] This conclusion was shared by Caballero (2010), who questioned that the core of the theoretical dispute on the recent Great Crisis was a matter of freshwater versus saltwater economics. Rather, it was a problem of distinction between core and periphery macroeconomics. For the core he meant the essence of the so-called dynamic stochastic general equilibrium approach, to which he attributed the confusion between the precision it had achieved about its own structure with the precision that it has about the real world, while for periphery macroeconomics he meant all those works at the intersection of macroeconomics and corporate finance that played a central role during the crisis, including liquidity evaporation, collateral shortages, bubbles, panics, fire sales, risk shifting, contagion, and the like. According to Caballero, the risk of economic theorizing was that the periphery descriptive analysis prevailed against the sound, but not always correct, core theoretical models.

[8] The paper by Coenen et al. (2010) assesses, using seven structural models used heavily by policymaking institutions, the effectiveness of temporary fiscal stimulus.

Anyway, one can observe that, in this regard, there is some confusion between the stimulus that is suggested by the IMF and also Corden advocates, which consists of public expenditures in infrastructures, and the relevant public expenses undertaken to bail out banks and many other financial institutions from failing.[9]

Inside the Keynesian tradition, also Leijonhufvud (2009b) rejects what he calls the "new neoclassical synthesis" (NNS) summarized in dynamic stochastic general equilibrium (DSGE) models, namely, that the economy can be truly represented as a stable self-regulating system in which effective market forces will always tend to bring it into a state of general equilibrium, except in so far as frictions of one sort or another put the break on the equilibrating process. He points out that a modern economy is not globally stable. Theories that assume that the economy is a stable general equilibrium system, albeit beset with some frictions and imperfections, do not hold true in general. The instabilities that such theories ignore are precisely those problems that should be the particular responsibility of macroeconomists.

Furthermore, as frictions also characterize the more recent neo-Keynesian models,[10] as pointed out by Krugman's vision, and although freshwater and saltwater economists disagree on many things in more or less disagreeable ways, anyway both groups, according to Leijonhufvud, undeniably remain in the "mainstream." Outside the mainstream, we must recognize that it would take a prolonged period of rather massive unemployment for the economy to end up being trapped in a Keynesian unemployment state. This is not how the economy functions in normal times, but it is an important aspect of how one would expect it to function in the wake of a financial crisis.

Considerations of this sort led Leijonhufvud to re-propose his old "corridor hypothesis", which suggests that the capabilities of an economic system for self-regulation are bound.[11] Within some "corridor" around an equilibrium time path, the usual adaptive market mechanisms would operate to coordinate activities. But further away from equilibrium, effective demand failures would impair the system's ability to restore itself to a coordinated state and beyond the bounds of the corridor it would languish in far-from equilibrium states indefinitely, unless salvaged by effective policy interventions.

As Leijonhufvud recognizes, this corridor hypothesis was heartily disliked by both Keynesian and neoclassical economists. This may be the reason why Leijonhufvud groups them together in the "mainstream economics." Anyway, Leijonhufvud's representation fits so well with the contribution on financial crises given by another leading Keynesian economist, Hyman Minsky (1982), who explained that the endogenous instability of a financially unregulated capitalist economy extends beyond the deposit-taking banking system.

[9] Among Keynesians, it is worth noting that Fitoussi and Saraceno (2010) sustain that the roots of the crisis are real and can be traced to the deepening income inequality of the last three decades, which led to a chronic deficiency of aggregate demand.

[10] The term is used by Leijonhufvud in the same meaning as New Keynesian models.

[11] The "corridor hypothesis" was put forward for the first time in Leijonhufvud (1973).

Minsky argued that prolonged periods of stability, during which anticipated risks do not materialize, will lead agents to revise their estimates of risk downward. As the financial system adapts to the changed perception of risk, it becomes increasingly fragile. According to Leijonhufvud, the late lamented era of the Great Moderation illustrates this aspect of Minsky's theory perfectly.[12]

8.4 The Neoclassical Views and the Efficient-Market Hypothesis

Opposite to Keynesians', particularly to Krugman's view, was the neoclassical interpretation of the Great Crisis. Among others, this was illustrated by two prominent freshwater economists like David Levine and John Cochrane. Levine (2009) questions Krugman's assertion that few economists saw the recent crisis coming.

For Levine, as we have just seen for Greenspan (2010) and Caballero (2010), this is not a problem of the field; it is a problem for those who are under the impression that we should be able to predict crises. In fact, neoclassical models do not just fail to predict the timing of financial crises, they say that we cannot. This common sense is the heart of rational expectations models. So the correct conclusion should be that our inability to predict the crisis confirms neoclassical theories.

As regards the efficient-market hypothesis, Levine asserts that modern theory of how financial markets incorporate information is that they do so imperfectly. The technical device is that of noise traders as in Admati (1985) and Admati and Pfleiderer (1985). Furthermore, we really do not need some sort of behavioral model, as asserted by Krugman, to understand why asset prices fall abruptly. If opinions about asset values change, prices must fall abruptly: it is not irrational to run for the exits when the theater is on fire.

There is a large literature on bank runs and contagion, not to speak of credit and collateral cycles. If there was some sort of irrationality involved in a panic, prices ought to bounce right back the next day when everyone wakes up and sheepishly realizes that they were wrong. In fact asset prices seem to be tracking news of fundamentals pretty well, gradually recovering as we get better news about fundamentals.

Finally, Levine asks whether behavioral economics offered anything that would help to solve the market failures that occurred in the Great Crisis. These failures characterized risks that were not being priced. Serious behavioral economists should try to analyze how liquidity risks created systemic problems and think about how to incorporate them into our understanding of how to prevent future breakdowns.

---

[12] For a recent exposition of Minsky's financial theory, see Ertürk and Özgür (2009) and Roncaglia (2010), while for a brief summary of his theory, see Chap. 10, Sect. 10.6.

Crises have been ubiquitous throughout history: while we cannot forecast them, we do know how to learn from them, as the papers and the book by Reinhart and Rogoff (2008a, b; 2009a, b; 2013; 2014) show. And we certainly have a good idea what to do in response: do what Chile did successfully (let bad banks fail and recycle them) or not do what Japan did unsuccessfully (keep the zombie banks limping feebly around). Levine concludes asserting that Krugman, like him, saw the bank bailout plan for what it really was: not a necessary step to save the credit sector from collapse, but a giveaway of taxpayers' money to investment bankers.

Let us now turn to Cochrane (2009a), who asserts that Krugman's attack has two goals. First, Krugman thinks financial markets are inefficient fundamentally due to irrational investors and thus prey to excessive volatility which needs government control. Second, as we have just seen for many other Keynesians like Caballero and Corden, he likes the huge fiscal stimulus provided by multi-trillion dollar deficits.

In regard to market inefficiency, Cochrane notes that it is funny to say "we did not see the crisis coming," because the central empirical prediction of the efficient-market hypothesis is precisely that nobody can tell where markets are going, neither benevolent government bureaucrats nor crafty hedge-fund managers nor ivory-tower academics. This is probably the best-tested proposition in all the social sciences.

Krugman knows this, so all he can do is "huff and puff" about his dislike for a theory whose central prediction is that nobody can be a reliable soothsayer. And of course it makes no sense whatsoever to try to discredit efficient-market finance because its followers did not see the crash coming. Krugman writes as if the volatility of stock prices alone disproves market efficiency, and efficient marketers just ignored it all these years. There is nothing about "efficiency" that promises "stability". Stable growth would in fact be a major violation of efficiency. In fact, the great "equity premium puzzle" is that, if efficient, stock markets do not seem risky enough to deter more people from investing.

It is true and very well documented that asset prices move more than reasonable expectations of future cash flows. This might be because people are prey to bursts of irrational optimism and pessimism. It might also be because people's willingness to take on risk varies over time and is lower in bad economic times. These are observationally equivalent explanations.

Unless you are willing to elaborate your theory to the point that it can quantitatively describe how much and when risk premiums, or waves of "optimism" and "pessimism," can vary, you know nothing. No theory is particularly good at that right now. This difficulty is not surprising. It is the central prediction of free-market economics that no academic, bureaucrat, or regulator will ever be able to fully explain market price movements.

The case for free markets never was that markets are perfect. The case for free markets is that government control of markets, especially asset markets, has always been much worse. Krugman at bottom is arguing that the government should massively intervene in financial markets and take charge of the allocation of capital. He cannot quite come out and say this, but he does say "Keynes considered it a very bad idea to let such markets . . . dictate important business decisions, . . . and finance economists believed that we should put the capital development of the nation in the hands of what Keynes had called a casino" (Krugman 2009).

Well, if markets cannot be trusted to allocate capital, we do not have to connect too many dots to imagine who Krugman has in mind. In fact, as Wessel (2009) makes perfectly clear, government regulators failed just as abysmally as private investors and economists to see the storm coming. And contrary to Krugman's assertions, good serious behavioral economists know this, and they are circumspect in their explanatory claims.

The behavioral view gives us a new and stronger argument against regulation and control. Regulators are just as human and irrational as market participants. If bankers are, in Krugman's words, "idiots", then so must be the typical Treasury secretary, Fed chairman, and regulatory staff. They act alone or in committees, where behavioral biases are much better documented than in market settings. They are still easily captured by industries and face politically distorted incentives.[13]

Coming to the second question, Cochrane stresses that Krugman likes fiscal stimulus. In this quest, he accuses freshwater economists and the rest of the economics profession of "mistaking beauty for truth." However, according to Cochrane, the first siren of beauty is simple logical consistency. On the contrary, Krugman's Keynesian economics requires that people make logically inconsistent plans to consume more, invest more, and pay more taxes with the same income.

The second siren is plausible assumptions about how people behave. Keynesian economics requires that the government is able to systematically fool people again and again. It presumes that people do not think about the future in making decisions today. Logical consistency and plausible foundations are indeed "beautiful," but they are also basic preconditions for "truth."

Recently, the focus of the dispute is changed. The hard and central policy debate over the last years was how to manage this financial crisis. Now it is how to set up the incentives of banks and other financial institutions so this mess does not happen again.

In fact, leaving aside the string of bailouts, the Fed and more recently also the ECB started term lending to security dealers and engaged in a quantitative easing monetary policy, which also includes the purchase of massive quantities of mortgage-backed securities and long-term Treasury debt.

Then, rather than buy treasuries in exchange for reserves, the Fed essentially sold treasuries in exchange for private debt. Though the fund rate was near zero, it noticed huge commercial paper and securitized debt spreads and intervened in those

[13] According to Zingales (2014), the very same forces that induce economists to conclude that regulators are captured should lead us to conclude that the economic profession is captured as well. As evidence of this capture, he shows that papers whose conclusions are pro-management are more likely to be published in economic journals and more likely to be cited. He also shows that business school's faculty write papers that are more pro-management. To reduce the extent of this capture, Zingales suggests a reform of the publication process, which includes an enhanced data disclosure, from a stronger theoretical foundation to a mechanism of peer pressure. See Chap. 1, Sect. 1.6.

markets. There is not "the" interest rate anymore, rather the Fed and recently also the ECB are attempting to manage the entire term structure of interest rates.

Therefore, monetary policy now has little to do with "money versus bonds," with all the latter lumped together. Monetary policy has become wide-ranging financial policy. Does any of this work? What are the dangers? Can the two central banks stay independent in this new role? These are the questions of our time.[14]

8.5 Stabilization Policies and the Trade-Off Between Stagnation and High Inflation

According to Leijonhufvud (2009b), there are three major issues that demand action if we are to have a reasonable prospect of a return to "Moderation". They are as follows: first, the instability of leverage in the economy; second, the increased connectivity of the global financial network; and third, the potential instability of the price level.

Considering the first point, high leverage is the easy way to high rates of return, as long as the business is good. When, in a system of endogenous base money, there is no quantitative limit to the liquidity being fed into the system, the situation can stay good for quite some time. Underestimation of risk leads institutions to increase their leverage (Minsky 1982).

But also those who do not underestimate risk find that competitive pressures make it difficult to step off the gravy train. Those who do not participate lose out. When most financial institutions play this game, the margin of return between the assets they invest in and the liabilities they issue will shrink. The players can adapt to this threat by increasing leverage still further or by turning to riskier asset classes promising higher returns or eventually by issuing shorter-term liabilities on which they pay less.

Thus, the recent boom ended up with historically high leverage ratios, low risk premia, high volumes of assets soon to be revealed as toxic, and some billion dollar positions financed in the overnight repo market (Leijonhufvud, 2009a). High leverage means that small losses can spell insolvency. Widespread losses on subprime mortgages, for example, will cause interbank markets to freeze and create intense pressure to scramble back onto terra firma by deleveraging.

Banks can deleverage by selling assets or by using loan service revenues to draw down debt instead of relending the funds. When the financial sector as a whole strives to deleverage in this way, falling asset prices will erode the balance sheets of banks further, while the contraction of credit drives the real sector into recession.

[14] This alternative approach to "unconventional" monetary policy has generated much discussion and a heated and at times confusing debate. The debate has been complicated by the use of different definitions and conflicting views of the mechanisms at work. Borio and Disyatat (2009) set out a framework for classifying and thinking about such policies, highlighting how they can be viewed within the overall context of monetary policy implementation. As regards the ECB's quantitative easing policy, see Chap. 11, Sect. 11.4.5.

The recession, in turn, erodes the quality of bank assets. It is a profoundly destabilizing process from which the only way out will be government bailouts ultimately funded by the tax payer.

As regards the second point, Leijonhufvud observes that much blame has been showered on regulators for failing to enforce more transparency in various markets for new instruments and for not putting checks on the growth of the shadow banking system, the over-the-counter (OTC) markets, the credit default swaps, etc. But the most fundamental change brought about by deregulation has been the greatly increased connectivity of the global financial network.

The old Glass–Steagall system in the USA compartmentalized the financial sector into a number of distinct industries, each characterized by the assets in which it was allowed to invest and the liabilities it could issue. There was no direct competition across compartment boundaries and very little diversification of risk within each compartment.[15]

Today, a financial institution can compete in virtually any market it wants and the big global banks have a presence in almost all markets. It is this structural change that has created a financial system so interconnected that a disturbance in one part of it can be felt everywhere else all around the globe.

Whether a shock to some part of it will propagate in a destructive way or peter out harmlessly depends on the general level of leverage, on the presence of highly interconnected banks that are too big to fail (TBTF), and on the volume and distribution of toxic assets in the system.

Finally, as regards the third point, Leijonhufvud finds that it is the most insidious of the three, because the satisfaction is so widespread that we have it under control. Inflation-targeting policy misled the Fed into thinking that its interest rate policy from 2002 onward was right because the inflation rate stayed low and basically constant.

But interest rate policy is more complicated than we thought, and there is a deeper problem. The Wicksellian recipe for stabilizing the price level in a pure inside money system instructs the central banker that he will know whether the interest rate is too high or too low because the price level will be, respectively, falling or rising. How fast it does not say. This does not matter at all if you happen to be living through a Great Moderation, but if we ever were to end up in an inflationary period with volatile inflation expectations, it will not work anymore. The same reasoning applies if we are living in a strong deflationary period as we do after 2015.

Therefore, Leijonhufvud's conclusion is that the USA and Europe are poised between the dangers of Japanese stagnation and Latin American high inflation. At this time, all the signs point to stagnation as the more immediate prospect. But with the longer-term soundness of the public finances in doubt, the navigable channel

[15] The same rule as the 1933 Glass–Steagall Act was passed in Europe with the 1934 German Banking Act and the 1936 Italian Banking Act, both of which compartmentalized the financial sector also in Europe.

between Scylla and Charybdis has become quite narrow. Making sure that we avoid stagnation means risking a hard-to-control inflation.

One overwhelmingly important fact must guide stabilization policy and financial reform efforts at this time. It is that we cannot afford to have another bubble burst. The recent stimulus packages and bailouts have not only been added to preexisting high deficits and large public debts but to large, unfunded liabilities. We do not have the resources required to handle another emergency like the Great Crisis. We need to go as far as possible in the direction of fail-safe strategies from now on. And to reduce the risk of another crash, it is imperative that leverage be curbed. At present, however, we face a dilemma from which there is no easy escape.

Governments have as far as possible avoided taking controlling stakes in the big banks. Having made that choice, they do not want the financial sector to deleverage because the falling asset prices and curtailed credit that this would entail could only make the recession much more severe. The surviving big banks themselves seem happy to return to their old high-stakes game, secure in their TBTF status. They cannot very well attract private capital with the promise that it will be used to reduce leverage since this would reduce the rate of return on capital.

The central banks assure us that they are planning their exit strategies which are supposed to restore their balance sheets to something resembling normalcy while keeping inflation under control. But even if they succeed, they remain in the situation where the boundaries of their lender-of-last resort responsibilities have lost all definition. Should another crisis arrive, the monetary authorities would again find themselves bailing out insurance companies and extending credit in "frozen markets" to all sorts of nonbank enterprises.

To get back to a structure where the responsibilities of central banks are limited and clearly defined will not be at all easy. One would like to see a system with at least two "compartments." One would be the regulated banking system with access to the lender of last resort and the other a more lightly regulated "swim-or-sink" sector.

The regulated sector would have to be in some degree insulated from the riskier sector. But the TBTF banks already straddle any such dividing line, so they would have to be forced to divest themselves of certain lines of business.

Compartmentalization would, however, give rise to a "boundary problem." Rates of return would differ between the sectors which would make the boundary exceedingly difficult to maintain (Brunnermeier et al 2009). This is a problem for which we do not have a clear solution as yet.

Finally, the problem of the potential instability of the price level requires the reintroduction of a nominal anchor in some form. Leijonhufvud's preference would be to reintroduce reserve requirements on all liquid liabilities of commercial banks and to impose them also on all other financial institutions that issue the same type of liabilities.

8.6 Panic, Systemic Risks, and the Need of a New Financial Regulation

Let us now concentrate in what really was the central problem of the Great Crisis and ask ourselves what are the most important policy changes needed to avoid a repetition.[16] In this regard, Cochrane (2009b) asserts that the usual suspects are not that important: global imbalances of saving or imports, the Fed's low policy rates, a housing bubble, subprime mortgages, or fancy derivatives.

Once we put all that aside, we can focus much more quickly on the real basic problem which was the "run," the "panic," the "flight to quality," or whatever you choose to call it that started late September 2008 and receded over the winter. Short-term credit dried up, including the normally straightforward repurchase agreement, interbank lending, and commercial paper markets. Without this panic, it is unlikely that anything really terrible or much worse than the dot-com bust and mild 2001 recession would have followed. This "panic" was followed by a very sharp recession (Caballero 2009b).

Why was there a financial panic? There were two obvious precipitating events: the Lehman Brothers failure, in the context of Fannie Mae and Freddie Mac, AIG, and Wamu, and the chaotic week in Washington surrounding the TARP legislation.[17] Now, why would Lehman's failure cause a panic? After the Bear Stearns bailout, markets came to the conclusion that investment banks and bank holding companies were too big to fail (TBTF) and in case of need they would be bailed out.[18] When the government did not bail out Lehman and in fact said it lacked the legal authority to bail out Lehman, everyone reassessed that expectation.

It was the repudiation of the TBTF paradigm, also known as the "Greenspan put" (see Chap. 1, Sect. 1.3), the essential ingredient that created panic: it was a panic induced by the moral hazard that comes from 30 years of "Greenspan put" or TBTF paradigm. It was this assumption, according to which there always existed in the market a lender of last resort, that had created a huge moral hazard problem that led to nonsense speculative behaviors. And the moral hazard extended from commercial banks to the entire financial sector. Then, the government was stuck in an awful situation: once everyone expects a bailout, it has to bail out or chaos results.

[16] This section is an extension of Sect. 1.3 of Chap. 1.

[17] The Troubled Asset Relief Program (TARP) was the instrument used by the US government to purchase assets and equity from financial institutions to strengthen its financial sector. It was the largest component of the government's measures in 2008 to address the subprime mortgage crisis.

[18] One highly disturbing consequence of the TBTF-bailout problem that has emerged since the September 2008 federal takeover of Fannie Mae and Freddie Mac is that market players are going to believe that every significant financial institution, should the occasion arise, would be subject to being bailed out with taxpayer funds. Businesses that are bailed out have competitive market and cost-of-capital advantages, but not efficiency advantages, over firms not thought to be systemically important (Greenspan 2010, p. 32).

Therefore, the policy question simply becomes how to escape this horrible moral hazard trap.[19]

Also for Levine (2010), the collapse of the global financial system reflects a systemic failure of the governance of financial regulation, the system associated with designing, enacting, implementing, and reforming financial policies. Senior policymakers repeatedly designed, implemented, and most importantly maintained policies that destabilized the global financial system. They maintained these policies even as the regulatory authorities acquired information that their policies were increasing financial system fragility.

Moreover, the authorities acquired this information during the decade before the crisis, when they had ample time to adjust their policies under relatively calm conditions. Yet, financial policymakers did not adjust, advertising weaknesses in the underlying governance of financial regulation.

It is often accused that free deregulated markets failed.[20] That is not fully true, because the free, relatively deregulated equity market absorbed massive losses with relatively little turmoil. In fact, it was the regulated, supervised part of the market that also failed. Nothing in this fragility is specific to mortgages or mortgage-backed securities. If we try to hold equity or corporate debt in highly leveraged entities funded by short-term debt, we have the same problems.

Therefore, the central policy problem is how to escape the bailout expectation trap. To do this, we have to finally define what "systemic" means.[21] And then, we must define clearly what is not systemic and can really fail. This limit must be written, in law or regulation. We cannot rely on the good intentions of powerful

[19] According to Kindleberger (1978), having a lender of last resort exacerbates the problem. If one firm or institution thinks that in any extreme situation she cannot go bankruptcy, because there is someone that intervenes to bail out them, they partake in more risky practices. In fact, by simply bailing out these mismanaged firms or institutions, we are not giving them incentive to improve their operation. Thus, for Kindleberger, when the system runs from bubble to bubble and the subsequent panics and crashes are methodically cured with lender of last resort bailouts—as it seems to have happened over the last 15 years before the Great Crisis in the USA—those stabilization interventions turn out increasingly destabilizing.

[20] Among others, this was the opinion expressed by Paul Krugman and US Treasury Secretary Timothy Geithner, who attributed the credit crisis to the implosion of the shadow banking system.

[21] Dijkman (2010) sets out the main characteristics of a systemic risk assessment framework. The failure to spot emerging systemic risk and prevent the current global financial crisis warrants a reexamination of the approach taken so far to crisis prevention. In this regard, the paper by Kawai and Pomerleano (2010) argues that financial crises can be prevented, as they build up over time due to policy mistake. While one cannot predict the precise timing of crises, one can avert them by identifying and dealing with sources of instability (Chap. 1, Sect. 1.6). For this purpose, policymakers need to strengthen top-down macro-prudential supervision, complemented by bottom-up micro-prudential supervision. The paper argues that national measures to promote financial stability are crucial and that once an effective national systemic regulator should be established, strong international cooperation is indispensable for financial stability. On the important distinction between micro-prudential and macro-prudential supervision approach, see Hanson et al (2011).

administrators.[22] The only way to limit expectations of a bailout is to not have the legal authority to do it. Lehman is actually a great example: it went to bankruptcy because the government could not save it (Cochrane 2009b).

In Cochrane's view, there really are no genuinely systemic institutions, but there are systemically dangerous contracts. Bank deposits are a good and familiar example. If you fund mortgages with bank deposits, there is a problem. Deposits promise face value and they are redeemed in first-come-first-serve order. Thus, there is an incentive to run at the first rumor of trouble. Furthermore, if a bank can arbitrarily issue guaranteed deposits to fund the internal hedge funds or proprietary trading, we are obviously in deep trouble. Short-term debt, including collateralized or repurchase agreements, brokerage accounts, and some other financial products, are susceptible to similar runs.

Risk limits are much more likely to work if they operate by clear and simple rules. For instance, you cannot have internal hedge funds or proprietary trading if you engage in overnight bank deposits. Institutions that offer "systemic" contracts must be as simple, small, and focused as possible. The philosophy of the Glass–Steagall Act is correct, and even if admitting this level of regulation is sometimes characterized as being anti-free market, that's not true. Bank deposits, because they are subject to runs, pose an externality. We all understand that markets can fail when there are externalities. If we need to allow bank deposits, we need a guarantee or priority in bankruptcy, which leads to moral hazard and puts the taxpayer at risk.

Some regulation and a forced separation of these "systemic" contracts from arbitrary risk taking are then necessary. This implies that the regulated banking system (commercial banks) with access to the lender of last resort must be clearly separated from the investment banks, hedge funds, and other institutions of the remaining shadow banking system, which represent, in Leijonhufvud's words reported in Sect. 8.5, the "swim-or-sink" sector.

With this minimal but very important conclusion agree both Keynesians (Krugman 2009; Leijonhufvud 2009b) and neoclassicals (Cochrane 2009b), and this is one of the few convergences still shared among them. Anyway, this is a very minimal level of regulation compared to the TBTF guarantee and extensive discretionary supervision and regulation now being applied to the entire financial system.

Therefore, in the end of the Great Crisis, we are in an ever-increasing cycle of risk taking and TBTF bailouts. We know that bank holding companies and investment banks are too big to fail, and their activities are not going to be fundamentally restricted in size and scope.

This crisis strained the fiscal limits of the USA and European countries to make good on bailout expectations. So the old Minsky's (1982) warning that the crisis can

[22] Systemically threatening institutions is among the major regulatory problems for which there are no good solutions. Early resolution of bank problems under the Federal Deposit Insurance Corporation Improvement Act of 1991 (FDICIA) appeared to have worked with smaller banks during periods of general prosperity. But the notion that risks can be identified in a sufficiently timely manner to enable the liquidation of a large failing bank with minimum loss has proved untenable during the crisis (Greenspan 2010, p. 33).

really happen again may now be updated. But, as Cochrane (2009b) warns, the next one could be bigger. Where will it come from? State and local government defaults? Defined benefit pension funds? Commercial real estate? A new Asian bubble? Default by Greece or another European country? Who knows?

Excessive debts justify reasonable doubts about solvency and monetary stability, not only for European countries but also for the USA (Bohn 2010). The big, still now unsolved, problem is that when the governments no longer have the fiscal resources to bail out their financial institutions, the crisis could be much, much worse than the recent Great Crisis. Governments and international institutions are actually deep involved in order to avoid a new catastrophic occurrence for the future.

8.7 Conclusions

We conclude by summarizing the main questions raised in this chapter. First, is there a difference in predicting capabilities among models belonging to different schools of thought? The answer is no. Both Keynesians and neoclassicals failed to predict the exact timing of the Great Crisis. The difference between them is that neoclassicals think that it is not the job of economic theory to predict the right timing of a crisis (random walk hypothesis), while Keynesians claim that crises can be predicted if we abandon the assumptions that people are rational and markets always clear (efficient-market hypothesis).

The latter turn back their eyes to the original Keynesian theory to claim that Keynes' vision of financial markets as a "casino" is sufficient to explain the recent Great Crisis (see Chap. 10 for a more extensive exposition of the Keynesian paradigm). There is clearly an ideological bias in the implications from the economic policy point of view: Keynesians suggest that deficit spending is the right policy to put the economic system in a full employment equilibrium path, while neoclassicals think that fiscal stimulus is only a bad way to transfer money from taxpayers to inefficient bureaucrats, policymakers, and zombie firms. Therefore, on this issue the old contrast between the two schools of thought still prevails, and we are far from any agreement on the effectiveness of fiscal policy.

Second, is there a difference between the two schools of thought in the suggested monetary policy and/or in the proposals of financial reform and the need of more regulation? Once again the answer is no in regard to the conventional monetary policy, while the nonconventional one is a field not sufficiently explored at the theoretical level. In fact, both the Fed and more recently also the ECB have engaged in quantitative easing monetary policies, whose final long-term effects are not known at the moment.

Finally, the two schools of thought agree as regards financial reform and the need of a more tightening regulation. This is the most important convergence that now exists between the two schools of thought. In fact, both agree on the need that systemic contracts like bank deposits should be kept strictly separated from riskier activities and speculation. In some way, this is a return to the past of the Glass–Steagall Act in the USA and to the banking legislation of the 1930s in European countries (especially in Germany and Italy).

This means that in the new financial reform suggested by international organizations (G-20, IMF, Financial Stability Board, Basel agreements), commercial banks, who are allowed to manage systemic contracts like bank deposits, and for that reason they have access to the lender of last resort, should be kept strictly separated from investment banks, hedge funds, and other financial speculative institutions, none of which should be considered too big to fail.

References

Admati A (1985) A noisy rational expectations equilibrium for multi-asset securities markets. Econometrica 53(3):629–658

Admati A, Pfleiderer P (1985) Interpreting the factor risk premia in the arbitrage pricing theory. J Econ Theory 35(1):191–195

Akerlof GA, Shiller RJ (2009) Animal spirits: how human psychology drives the economy, and why it matters for global capitalism. Princeton University Press, Princeton

Bernanke BS (2004) The great moderation. Remarks at the meetings of the Eastern Economic Association, Washington, DC, Feb 20. Available via http://www.federalreserve.gov/BOARDDOCS/SPEECHES/2004/20040220/default.htm

Bohn H (2010) The economic consequences of rising U.S. Government debt: privileges at risk. CESIFO working paper no. 3079. Available via https://www.google.it/webhp?sourceid=chrome-instant&ion=1&espv=2&ie=UTF-8#q=Bohn+H.+(2010)%2C+The+Economic+Consequences+of+Rising+U.S.+Government+Debt%3A+Privileges+at+Risk%2C+CESIFO+Working+Paper+$32#No.+3079

Borio C, Disyatat P (2009) Unconventional monetary policies: an appraisal. BIS working paper no. 292, November. Available via https://www.google.it/webhp?sourceid=chrome-instant&ion=1&espv=2&ie=UTF-8#q=6.+Borio+C.+and+P.+Disyatat+(2009)%2C+%E2%80%9CUnconventional+Monetary+Policies%3A+An+Appraisal%E2%80%9D%2C+BIS+Working+Paper+No.+292%2C+November

Brunnermeier MK, Crocket A, Goodhart C, Hellwig M, Persaud AD, Shin H (2009) The fundamental principles of financial regulation. Geneva report on the world economy 11, Geneva, International Center for Monetary and Banking. Studies/CEPR, June

Caballero RJ (2009a) Sudden financial arrest. VoxEU.org, Nov 17. Available via http://www.voxeu.org/index.php?q=node/4216

Caballero RJ (2009b) The 'other' imbalance and the financial crisis. In: Banca d'Italia (ed) Lezioni Paolo Baffi di Economia e Finanza, dicembre

Caballero RJ (2010) Macroeconomics after the crisis: time to deal with the pretense-of-knowledge syndrome. J Econ Perspect 24:85–102

Cochrane JH (2001) Asset pricing. Princeton, University Press. Available via http://sylvainletoulousain.chez-alice.fr/download/finbook.pdf

Cochrane JH (2009a) How did Paul Krugman get it so wrong? Sept 16. Available via http://faculty.chicagobooth.edu/john.cochrane/research/Papers/krugman_response.htm

Cochrane JH (2009b) The financial crisis and policy. Talk given at the Cato "Policy Perspectives" in New York, Nov 5. Available via http://faculty.chicagobooth.edu/john.cochrane/research/Papers/cochrane_financial_crisis_and_policy.pdf

Coenen et al (2010) Effects of fiscal stimulus in structural models. IMF working paper no. 10/73, March. Available via https://www.google.it/webhp?sourceid=chrome-instant&ion=1&espv=2&

ie=UTF-8#q=14.+Coenen+et+al+(2010)%2C+%E2%80%9CEffects+of+Fiscal+Stimulus+in+Structural+Models%E2%80%9D%2C+IMF+Working+Paper+n.+10%2F73
Corden WM (2009) The theory of fiscal stimulus: how will a debt-financed stimulus affect the future. CEPR policy insight, 34, May
Corden WM (2010) Ambulance economics: the pros and cons of fiscal stimuli. CEPR policy insight, 43, January
Dijkman M (2010) A framework for assessing systemic risk. World bank, Policy research working paper no. 5282, April. Available via https://www.google.it/webhp?sourceid=chrome-instant&ion=1&espv=2&ie=UTF-8#q=17.+Dijkman+M.+(2010)%2C+%E2%80%9CA+Framework+for+Assessing+Systemic+Risk%E2%80%9D%2C+World+Bank%2C+Policy+Research+Working+Paper+n.+5282%2C+April
Ertürk K, Özgür G (2009) What is Minsky all about, anyway. Real-world economic review, 50. Available via https://www.google.it/webhp?sourceid=chrome-instant&ion=1&espv=2&ie=UTF-8#q=18.+Ert%C3%BCrk+K.+and+G.+%C3%96zg%C3%BCr+(2009)%2C+%E2%80%9CWhat+Is+Minsky+All+About%2C+Anyway%E2%80%9D%2C+Real-World+Economic+Review%2C+50
Fitoussi JP, Saraceno F (2010) Europe: how deep is a crisis? Policy responses and structural factors behind diverging performances. J Glob Dev 1:1–16
Greenspan A (2010) The crisis, Second draft, Mar 9. Available via http://www.brookings.edu/~/media/Files/Programs/ES/BPEA/2010_spring_bpea_papers/spring2010_greenspan.pdf
Hanson SG, Kashyap AK, Stein JC (2011) A macro-prudential approach to financial regulation. J Econ Perspect 25:3–28
IMF (2008) Fiscal policy for the crisis, prepared by Spilimbergo A, Symansky S, Blanchard O, Cottarelli C, December. Available via https://www.google.it/webhp?sourceid=chrome-instant&ion=1&espv=2&ie=UTF-8#q=22.+IMF+(2008),+Fiscal+Policy+for+the+Crisis,+prepared+by+A.+Spilimbergo,+Symansky,+O.+Blanchard+and+C.+Cottarelli,+December.&spell=1
IMF (2009a) A strategy for renormalizing fiscal and monetary policies in advanced economies, prepared by Cottarelli C, Viñals J, Sept 22. Available via http://www.imf.org/external/pubs/ft/spn/2009/spn0922.pdf
IMF (2009b) Fiscal implications of the global economic and financial crisis, June 9. Available via https://www.google.it/webhp?sourceid=chrome-instant&ion=1&espv=2&ie=UTF-8#q=24.+IMF+(2009b)%2C+Fiscal+Implications+of+the+Global+Economic+and+Financial+Crisis%2C+June+9
IMF (2009c) The state of public finances: outlook and medium-term policies after the 2008 crisis, Mar 6. Available via https://www.google.it/webhp?sourceid=chrome-instant&ion=1&espv=2&ie=UTF-8#q=25.+IMF+(2009c)%2C+The+State+of+Public+Finances%3A+Outlook+and+Medium-Term+Policies+after+the+2008+Crisis%2C+March
Kawai M, Pomerleano M (2010) Regulating systemic risk. ADBI working paper 189. Available via http://www.adbi.org/working-paper/2010/01/27/3447.regulating.systemic.risk
Kindleberger CP (1978) Manias, panics, and crashes: a history of financial crises. Wiley, New York
Kirman A (2009a) Complex economics: individual and collective rationality. Routledge, Abingdon
Kirman A (2009b) Economic theory and the crisis. Vox, Nov 14. Available via http://www.voxeu.org/index.php?q=node/4208
Krugman P (2009) How did economists get it so wrong? The New York Times Magazine, Sept 2. Available via http://www.nytimes.com/2009/09/06/magazine/06Economic-t.html
Leijonhufvud A (1973) Effective demand failures. Swed Econ J 75(1):27–48
Leijonhufvud A (2009a) Curbing instability: policy and regulation. CEPR Policy Insight 36:1–8
Leijonhufvud A (2009b) Macroeconomics and the crisis: a personal appraisal. CEPR Policy Insight 41:2–8

Levine DK (2009) An open letter to Paul Krugman, Sept 18. Available via http://www.huffingtonpost.com/david-k-levine/an-open-letter-to-paul-kr_b_289768.html

Levine DK (2010) The governance of financial regulation: reform lessons from the recent crisis. BIS working paper no. 329, November. Available via https://ideas.repec.org/p/bis/biswps/329.html

Minsky H (1982) Can 'it' happen again? Sharpe, New York

Moro B (2012) The theoretical debate on the recent great crisis. J Ital Econ Assoc XVII(1):3–42

OECD (2009a) Fiscal packages across OECD countries: overview and country details, Mar 31. Available via http://www.nens.it/_public-file/OECD%20Fiscal%20packages%20across%20OECD%20countries.pdf

OECD (2009b) The effectiveness and scope of fiscal stimulus. The interim report of OECD economic outlook (Chapter 3). Available via http://www.oecd.org/eco/outlook/42421337.pdf

Reinhart CM, Rogoff KS (2008a) Is the 2007 U.S. subprime crisis so different? An international historical comparison. Am Econ Rev 98:339–344

Reinhart CM, Rogoff KS (2008b) This time is different: a panoramic view of eight centuries of financial crises, mimeo. Available via http://www.google.it/search?aq=f&sourceid=chrome&ie=UTF-8&q=Reinhart,+Rogoff,+This+time+is+different

Reinhart CM, Rogoff KS (2009a) The aftermath of financial crises. Am Econ Rev 99(2):466–472

Reinhart CM, Rogoff KS (2009b) This time is different: eight centuries of financial folly. Princeton University Press, Princeton

Reinhart CM, Rogoff KS (2013) Financial and sovereign debt crisis: some lessons learned and those forgotten. IMF working paper no. 13/266, December. Available via https://www.imf.org/external/pubs/cat/longres.aspx?sk=41173.0

Reinhart CM, Rogoff KS (2014) Recovery from financial crises: evidence from 100 episodes. NBER working paper no. W19823, January. Available via http://www.nber.org/papers/w19823

Roncaglia A (2010) Economisti che sbagliano. Le radici culturali della crisi, Bari, Laterza

Stock J, Watson M (2002) Has the business cycle changed and why? NBER Macroecon Annu 17:159–218

Wessel D (2009) In FED we trust. Ben Bernanke's war on the great panic. Crown Business, New York

Zingales L (2014) Preventing economists' capture. CEPER discussion paper no. DP9867, March. Available via http://papers.ssrn.com/sol3/papers.cfm?abstract_id=2444888

Chapter 9
From the Economic Crisis to the Crisis of Economics

Victor A. Beker

> *So in summary, Your Majesty, the failure to foresee the timing, extent and severity of the crisis and to head it off, while it had many causes, was principally a failure of the collective imagination of many bright people, both in this country and internationally, to understand the risks to the system as a whole.*
>
> (Letter to the Queen of England by the British Academy, July 2009)

9.1 Introduction

After having analyzed several recent examples of economic and financial crises, we will focus on what implications these events have in the field of economic theory. In particular, the global economic crisis that started in 2008 seriously damaged the reputation of economics. As Heymann and Stiglitz (2014, 1) note, "Crises put into doubt the relevance of models that assume that self-equilibrating mechanisms work automatically in the economy and that economic decisions are based always and everywhere on a correct perception of the properties of the environment".

Neoclassical economic theory has been blamed for not having even considered the possibility of the type of collapse that the subprime mortgage meltdown unleashed.[1] Before the crisis, there was a widespread belief in the self-correcting power of markets; in Alan Greenspan's words, "those of us who have looked to the self-interest of lending institutions to protect shareholders' equity, myself included, are in a state of shocked disbelief".[2] If we follow Joan Robinson (1972), this was

[1] For a distinction between the concepts of neoclassical, orthodox, heterodox, and mainstream economics, see Colander et al. (2004).

[2] New York Times, October, 23,2008.

V.A. Beker (✉)
University of Belgrano and University of Buenos Aires, Buenos Aires, Argentina
e-mail: victor.beker@ub.edu.ar

B. Moro, V.A. Beker, *Modern Financial Crises*, Financial and Monetary Policy Studies 42, DOI 10.1007/978-3-319-20991-3_9

the third main crisis economic theory has faced. She associated the first one with the great slump of the 1930s and the second one with the 1971 dollar crisis.

The purpose of this chapter is threefold. First, to make clear what economics is guilty of; second, to spell out what sort of science economics is, what is legitimate to expect from it, and what is not; and, third, to discuss the flaws economics suffers and how to correct them. In Sect. 9.2, I start with a survey of some of the criticisms that are being made of mainstream economics. In Sect. 9.3 an analysis is made of the responsibility of economics and economists in the recent financial crisis. In Sect. 9.4, the main features of economics as a social science are recalled. Section 9.5 is devoted to the analysis of the arguments on the use of mathematics in economic theory. In Sect. 9.6, I discuss the economics research agenda and argue that priorities are misplaced in it. Section 9.7 has to do with the relationship between orthodox and heterodox economic theories. The primary conclusions are presented in Sect. 9.8.

9.2 The Criticisms of the Economics Profession

Conspicuous among the critics, Nobel Prize-winning Paul Krugman (2009) blamed the profession for its "blindness to the very possibility of catastrophic failures in a market economy." In his view, "the economics profession went astray because economists, as a group, mistook beauty, clad in impressive-looking mathematics, for truth". This led to turn "a blind eye to the limitations of human rationality that often lead to bubbles and busts; to the problems of institutions that run amok; to the imperfections of markets—especially financial markets—that can cause the economy's operating system to undergo sudden, unpredictable crashes; and to the dangers created when regulators don't believe in regulation" (Krugman 2009).

Most economists not only failed to foresee the depth of the current crisis, they did not even consider it possible. One can agree with Caballero (2010, 85) that "it is almost tautological that severe crises are essentially unpredictable, for otherwise they would not cause such a high degree of distress." Not being able to predict the timing of a crisis is one thing; not even considering the possibility of the type of collapse that the subprime mortgage meltdown unleashed is quite another.

Mainstream macroeconomics failed to envisage even the possibility of a financial crisis similar to the one that took place in 2008. Even after the crisis started in the early summer of 2007, it took a long time for orthodox economists to admit that what was going on was a serious matter. Even worse, the institutional changes that made the crisis possible were inspired by neoclassical thought based on the holy trinity of utter competition, rationality, and efficiency. These were also the foundations of the analytical models used to build the subprime mortgage securitization pyramid that nearly blew up the financial system in the USA.

Sachs (2009, 1) argued that "sustained and widespread future prosperity will require basic reforms in global macroeconomic governance and in macroeconomic science". He concluded that "a new science of macroeconomics must supersede the stale debates of Keynesian and rational expectations theories" (Sachs 2009, 3).

Behavioral macroeconomists such as the Nobel Prize George Akerlof and Robert Shiller (2009) blamed the rationality assumption of mainstream neoclassical economics. Only "if we thought that people were totally rational, and that they acted almost entirely out of economic motives, we too would believe that government should play little role in the regulation of financial markets, and perhaps even in determining the level of aggregate demand".[3]

Gintis (2009) goes further. Although he coincides with Akerlof and Shiller in their criticism of orthodox economic theory, he argues that "there is nothing in economic theory that says that rational individuals interacting on markets will produce either stable or socially efficient outcomes" (Gintis 2009, 4). He concludes that there are "slim grounds for Akerlof and Shiller to attribute macroeconomic fluctuations wholly to 'animal spirits' that would not exist were economic actors rational".[4] Gintis vindicates then, as an alternative perspective, the modeling of the market economy as a complex nonlinear system.

Direct from the battle front, Willem Buiter, the chief economist of Citigroup and former member of the Monetary Policy Committee of the Bank of England, said that in his opinion, macroeconomic research programs tend to be motivated by the internal logic, intellectual sunk capital, and aesthetic puzzles of established research programs rather than by a powerful desire to understand how the economy works—let alone how the economy works during times of stress and financial instability. Therefore, the economics profession was caught unprepared when the crisis struck (Buiter 2009).

The political scientist Jon Elster (2009) offers what he calls "outsider criticism" of economic theory. He argues that the problem with economics and other social sciences is "excessive ambitions". Economists look for a level of precision and robustness that cannot be warranted in the social sciences.

Two conditions are crucial for mainstream neoclassical economics: determinate prediction and rational behavior. If the theory is indeterminate or the agents are irrational, no explanation will be forthcoming. Elster argues why more often than not these conditions do not hold. Indeterminacy stems from the difficulty agents face in assessing the numerical probabilities of the possible outcome of actions. Rationality faces the restriction of agents' capacities. Economic agents are supposed to make calculations that occupy many pages of mathematical appendixes in leading journals.

Elster discards the "as if" rationality argument, arguing that it is based on the assumption that the economic agent is able to spend absurdly large amounts of time searching for a good rule. He observes that economists make assumptions for the sake of simplicity without telling the reader how many of the conclusions can be expected to hold in non-simplistic cases. His conclusion is that a considerable amount of work in economics and political science is devoid of empirical, aesthetic,

[3] Akerlof and Shiller (2009, 173).

[4] Ibid., 5.

or mathematical interest. Many articles published by eminent economists, he says, are nothing more than works of science fiction. Therefore, according to Elster, many students of economics waste their time studying useless theories.

Some of these criticisms have a long standing in economics, such as the lack of realism of the assumptions[5] or the argument that people do not behave as theory says they will or should behave. Although he vindicates behavioral economics as an alternative to neoclassical thought, Elster admits that its drawback is that there are relatively few applications of behavioral economics outside the laboratory. He maintains that a flaw from which economics suffers is the belief that social science can only become a science on the model of the natural sciences.

However, he remarks that despite this belief none of the many mainstream economists who have won the Nobel Prize received it for confirmed empirical predictions. The opposite happens in physics, he adds. For example, string theory is the dominant paradigm today in most physics departments at major research universities. However, it has not been awarded a single Nobel Prize mainly because it has yet to generate confirmed predictions that are not also consequences of rival theories. Elster's observation coincides with what Hausman (1992, 222) has called *methodological schizophrenia*, referring to the fact that in economics methodological pronouncements and practice often do not coincide.

Elster proposes to replace the aim of prediction with that of retrodiction, explaining the past, which he considers a perfectly respectable intellectual enterprise. He maintains that the past can be falsified no less than predictions about the future. Elster's conclusion is that instead of excessive ambitions economists should have humble but attainable aspirations.

9.3 What Is Economics Guilty of?

Having outlined the main accusations against economics, let us have a look at the facts. As we saw in Chap. 3, the core of the 2008 financial market crisis has been the discovery that many securities were actually far riskier than what people originally thought to be the case.

The process of securitization allowed trillions of dollars of risky assets—subprime mortgages in the first place—to be transformed into securities that were widely considered to be safe. Subprime mortgages are mortgages that are considered to be significantly riskier than average. The 1990s saw the development of "private-label securities" issued by commercial banks and other entities generally free of the regulations governing ordinary banks. These were similar to the mortgage-backed securities sold to investors by government-authorized entities, such as Fannie Mae and Freddie Mac, but they did not carry the same implicit

[5] I have already dealt with this argument in Beker (2005, 17). We will come back on this later on.

government guarantee that investors would be protected against unexpectedly high default rates.

Initially, private-label securities involved only "prime" mortgages issued to low-risk borrowers, but at the end of the decade, lenders started using them to back subprime loans to borrowers with poor credit histories. The higher mortgage rates charged to riskier borrowers meant higher yields on the mortgage-backed securities. On the other hand, securitization meant that lenders could pass along the risk of default to investors.

The essence of structured finance is the pooling of economic assets, such as loans, bonds, and mortgages, and the subsequent issuance of a prioritized capital structure of claims against these collateral pools. Although it was argued that this was a way of diversifying risks, the truth is that the resulting securities were subject to highly correlated risks. Coval et al. (2009) show how modest imprecision in the parameter estimates can lead to variation in the default risk of the structured finance securities, which is sufficient to cause a security rated AAA to default with reasonable likelihood.

A key factor in determining if an asset is relatively safe is the extent to which defaults are correlated across the underlying assets. The lower the default correlation, the more improbable it is that all assets default simultaneously. However, the securities backed by large asset pools are strongly affected by the performance of the economy as a whole, so they have far less chance of surviving a severe economic downturn than, for instance, traditional corporate securities of equal rating. This was precisely what happened; when the housing bubble finally exploded, real estate markets declined together and mortgage defaults soared in Florida and California. Many of the subprime borrowers found themselves holding mortgages in excess of the market value of their homes.

Mortgage-backed securities "carried the dual risk of high rates of default due to the low credit quality of the borrowers and high level of default correlation as a result of pooling mortgages from similar geographical areas and vintages. In turn, many subprime-backed bonds were themselves re-securitized into what are called collateralized mortgage obligations" (Coval et al. 2009, 16). These second-generation securities were highly sensitive to even slight changes in default probabilities and correlations among the underlying assets, as Coval et al. show. Moreover, the share of collateralized debt obligations, which had other structured assets as their collateral, increased from 2.6 % in 1998 to 55 % in 2006 as a fraction of the total notional value of all securitizations. Many of all these first- and second-generation securities were rated as investment grade, which made them eligible to become a portfolio component for pension funds, hedge funds, and investment banks. Therefore, the conditions for a perfect storm had been created.

So far so good, but what does economics have to do with all of this? First, there was a reckless use of economic models to evaluate risks. The nature of structured finance means that even minute errors at the level of the underlying securities that would be insufficient to alter the security's rating can dramatically alter the ratings of the structured finance securities (Ibid., 9). On the other hand, substantial lending to subprime borrowers was a recent phenomenon, and historical data on defaults and delinquencies in this sector of the mortgage market were scarce. Therefore, the possibility for errors in the assessment of the default correlations, the default probabilities, and the ensuing recovery rates for these securities was significant. Such errors were magnified by the process of re-securitization, leading to the devastating losses that the securities market experienced (Ibid., 15).

However, no special warning accompanied evaluations made on such weak and fragile basis. "The mathematical rigor, elegance and the numerical precision of the various risk-management and asset-pricing tools have a tendency to hide the weaknesses of these models and their underlying assumptions, which are necessary to guarantee the models' values to those who have not developed them" (Schneider and Kirchgässner 2009). As Colander et al. (2009) put it: "economists, as all other social scientists, have an ethical responsibility to communicate the limitations of the models and the potential misuse of their research". Unfortunately, this was not done at all.

As we can see, this has more to do with economists than with economics. It seems to be a typical case of professional malpractice. Of course, extended malpractice was committed by hundreds of professionals in banks and rating agencies who created and certified as almost risk-free securities assets that were actually highly risky, as the events after 2007 overwhelmingly demonstrated. Such a massive case of malpractice exposes deep failures in the regulatory system. Many economic tools were misused or used without having been duly subject to previous testing. This was similar to widespread use of a new vaccine without having tested it according to FDA regulations.

Some isolated voices tried to alert to the perils of the huge changes that took place in the financial industry. Perhaps the most striking was that of Rajan (2005), whose prescient analysis of how the developments observed in financial markets could degenerate into a crisis. Unfortunately, his voice was almost unique and received very little attention. No economic journal published his paper, and at the SSRN site it collected only 93 downloads, giving it a rank of 96,914th in the SSRN download ranking.[6]

On the other hand, the financial market is clearly characterized by information asymmetry and externalities, both of which require regulatory measures. Investors do not have access to the amount and quality of information that issuers of securities have, which is why rating agencies provide them with accurate risk evaluation. The problem is that rating agencies are paid by issuers rather than by investors. This raises a conflict of interest, as was exposed by the high credit ratings given to assets that were highly risky in reality. To set up a public credit ratings agency may be a step toward correcting the perverse incentive system presently facing private agencies.

A second argument in favor of regulating the financial system is externalities. The huge effects the banking system has on the rest of the economy are self-evident. The impact of a bank's bankruptcy goes far beyond the losses its shareholders may suffer.

---

[6] Accessed April 2010.

However, the 1980 Depository Institutions Deregulation and Monetary Control Act deeply deregulated financial activities in the USA. Additionally, the final repeal of Glass–Steagall by the Financial Services Modernization Act of 1999 lifted restrictions on the sort of investments that banks can make.

While the 1933 Act limited banks to buying and selling securities as agents and prohibited all banks from underwriting and dealing in most securities, the 1999 Act eliminated those restrictions. It also allowed commercial banks, investment banks, securities firms, and insurance companies to consolidate. This opened the door to the development of many unregulated instruments of "creative" financing. Through them, the repackaging of risks to create supposedly "safe" assets took place. It also made possible the vast involvement of banks in the subprime mortgage market.

Finally, in 2000 the Commodity Futures Modernization Act removed from regulation the now famous credit default swaps (CDS) meant to protect investors from defaults on the bonds they own. The CDS market grew from next to nothing to over $60 trillion by 2008. AIG was the main actor in this market.

In 1996, the Office of the Comptroller of the Currency (OCC) reinterpreted certain "incidental" powers that it was granted under the National Banking Act of 1864 to permit operating subsidiaries ("op subs") of national banks to engage in activities beyond those permitted to the bank. Op subs have been allowed to underwrite bonds and even equity securities. Furthermore, the OCC decided that certain financial products, such as annuities, were not insurance products but instead banking products, which meant that banks could sell them. The OCC also continued to allow national banks to engage in a wider range of securities and insurance activities (Barth et al. 2000, 9).

As mentioned in Chap. 3, the state of Georgia passed a law in 2002 by which investment banks that created mortgage-backed securities would be liable for financial damage if mortgages turned out to be fraudulent. However, the OCC ruled that the Georgia law did not apply to national banks or their subsidiaries. Finally, the law was amended in 2003: the liability provision was curtailed and other elements of the law were eliminated.

The replacement of Basel I by Basel II was a step toward self-regulation of financial institutions. The deregulation movement that took place during the 1980s and 1990s was inspired by an almost religious belief in the power of market forces to solve any economic problem. Mainstream neoclassical economics nourished that belief. In this respect, neoclassical economics can be blamed for creating the ideological climate that stimulated the deregulation movement in the USA during the 1980s and 1990s. The belief that market forces would solve potential problems was behind the financial deregulation, which proved to be a fatal flaw of the financial system in the USA.

On the contrary, a highly regulated financial system, such as the Indian one, generally avoided the crisis. Very strict rules hampered the creation of toxic assets of the sort that proliferated in the USA. Stringent rules governing leverage and capital ratios in Canada have been recognized as contributing to Canada's impressive performance during the crisis.

In this respect, Paul Krugman seems to be right when he blames the profession—dominated by the neoclassical school in the 1980s and the 1990s—for its blindness to the very possibility of catastrophic failures in a market economy. Although Caballero is right when he argues that severe crises are essentially unpredictable, the real issue is that the very possibility of a crisis was practically unthinkable for the orthodoxy. The real issue is not whether economists are capable of predicting a singular crisis but whether the prevalent economic theory makes room for the possibility of the development of crises.

9.3.1 Is Neoclassical Economics Innocent?

Of course, it is always possible to argue that the ideas that are criticized are not the true ideas of mainstream economics, as Levine did in his response to Krugman (Levine 2009). In this respect, we have to take into consideration the fact that the scholars who have had great influence on policymakers around the world are those from the neoclassical school of thought. Their ideas have dominated economic policy since 1980.

Levine argues that Krugman is shooting at a nonexistent target, with his clock 30 years late. In this respect, he advises considering, for example, the book by Timothy Kehoe and Ed Prescott (2007) called Great Depressions of the twentieth century. Kehoe and Prescott begin their book stating: "The general equilibrium growth model is the workhorse of modern economics. It is the accepted paradigm for studying most macroeconomic phenomena, including business cycles, tax policy, monetary policy, and growth".

The authors' point of departure is to assume flexible prices and perfect foresight. However, if prices are completely flexible and people have perfect foresight, the main reasons for a downward adjustment in quantities are a priori excluded. Then, not surprisingly, the conclusion is that the main reason for a depression should be found in exogenous TFP shocks. The answer is implicit in the assumptions. These are the usual assumptions of neoclassical economics.

Moreover, as Michael Woodford states in his blurb for the volume, it shows "how neoclassical theory can be applied. . .." It is therefore a typical neoclassical contribution with new analytical instruments, but the ideas are the same ones we could find 30 or 50 years ago—not unlike old wine in new bottles. In this respect, it seems that it is the clock of neoclassical economics which is late, late although still alive.

9.3.2 What Economists Do Know

However, the answer to the last economic crisis has proven that economists are better prepared than in 1930 to face this sort of challenge. Of course, the measures taken by policymakers were far from what orthodoxy recommends. A massive bailout of banks and corporations saved them from collapse and saved many jobs in the American economy. Countercyclical fiscal policy played a key role in fighting recession. The level of state intervention in the economy has reached unparalleled levels in American history.

In the 1930s, we learned that we could not wait for the market to solve the gigantic disequilibria in the financial markets. As the crisis unfolded, it quickly became apparent that another Great Depression would only be averted by rapid and concerted policy action around the world. Fortunately, policymakers pulled together to respond to this profound economic calamity. A range of bold actions was taken to ease monetary conditions, adopt fiscal stimulus, and cooperate on cross border financial problems. International lending reached unprecedented levels.

As stated before, this whole package was far from the orthodox thinking. Moreover, something that was completely unthinkable some years ago did happen: the IMF managing director paid an enthusiastic tribute to ... John M. Keynes's ideas! (Strauss-Kan 2010).

9.4 What Sort of Science Is Economics?

Before proceeding, let us make clear the main characteristics of economics as a social science to illuminate what we can expect from it and what we cannot. Economics is not an exact science. However, many economists act as if it were and try to convince society that it is. I have dealt elsewhere with some methodological issues in economics (Beker 2005). Let me make a summary of the main conclusions I arrived at there.

As Blaug (1992, 243) notes, "mainstream neoclassical economists ... preach the importance of submitting theories to empirical tests, but they rarely live up to their declared methodological canons. Analytical elegance, economy of theoretical means, and the widest possible scope obtained by ever more heroic simplification have been too often prized above predictability and significance for policy questions".

In fact, in economics there is, broadly speaking, nothing like a crucial experiment. No matter how sophisticated the economic tools are and how detailed the set of data one uses, very few robust relationships can be obtained. Although potentially falsifiable, most statements in economics are only imperfectly testable. Precisely, the main characteristic that distinguishes it from, for instance, natural sciences, is that theories, in most cases, cannot be falsified in practice. This is why, as Hausman (1992) states, economists trust more in the implications deduced from the theory's axioms than in the negative results that may emerge from empirical testing. It is very rare to see a theory disregarded because of an apparent disconfirmation.

Because economists are typically concerned with complex phenomena in which many simplifications are required and in which many interferences may appear, it does not seem rational to surrender a credible hypothesis because of predictive failure. What role does empirical research play, then? As a matter of fact, most empirical results in economics are more useful to illustrate theories than to test their validity.[7]

This is the attitude that the whole profession implicitly has toward empirical results; they are mainly viewed as a way of illustrating that a theory *may* be true (Mayer 1993, 148). For example, no journal—be it orthodox or heterodox—induces the authors of an empirical paper, or its critics, to test the hypotheses included in it by using new data some time after publication.

Of course, as Colander et al. (2009, 11) propose, "the goal should be to put theoretical models to scientific test (as the naïve believer in positive science would expect)". If this were always possible, economists would have to face far fewer difficulties. However, the problem is precisely that in economics there is nothing like a crucial experiment. Colander (2009) himself gives an example that shows a lack of robustness of empirical results. He mentions the DSGE model analysis in Ireland (2004) and the discussion of that paper in Juselius and Franchi (2007). These authors replicated the results in Ireland (2004) and tested the assumptions underlying the model used by this author. Essentially all of them were rejected. Even more serious, when the model was reformulated using an alternative approach, the conclusions were reversed.

Given the fact that, in general, economic theories cannot be falsified, they accumulate and remain available inside a large toolbox to be used according to the case under analysis and the practitioner's expertise. Thus, it seems very difficult to find some yardstick that may allow for making a distinction between "right" and "wrong" economic theories. However, orthodox economists usually act as if their economic theory were the right one or the only one and as if economics were as exact of a science as mathematics.

9.5 On the Use of Mathematics in Economics

One of the criticisms of traditional economics has been its (ab)use of mathematics. In the quotation included at the beginning of this chapter, Krugman made the same criticism. A web petition in support of Krugman's criticism collected over 1300 signatures in 2009, most of them from qualified academics. According to Lawson (2009, 130), "the project of mathematical modeling in modern economics has a long history of failure." This issue was broadly discussed in the 1940s and 1950s, although it periodically reappears.

[7] Hicks (1983, 373) maintained that, because economic theories can neither verified nor falsified, economics is a discipline, not a science.

It has been argued that economics suffers from physics envy. However, although physics provides tools to address complex systems, and the economy undoubtedly is a complex system, most of them have been used only marginally in economics. The truth is that what mainstream economics may be found guilty of is not of physics envy but of mathematics envy. Economists have taken physics as the model for science.

Physicists use two basic tools: laboratory experiments and mathematics. However, as laboratory experiments have a very limited application in economics, this leaves mathematics as the main tool for economists to try to mimic physics. Therefore, economists have greatly borrowed the mathematical instruments used by physicists. They have done so to such an extent that, for instance, for the philosopher of science Alexander Rosenberg (1992), economics is not an empirical science at all; for him, it is a branch of applied mathematics.

The general equilibrium theorist and Nobel Prize winner Gerard Debreu (1991, 5) admits that "the use of mathematics imposes certain restrictions on economic theory". The very choice of questions the economist seeks to answer is influenced by her/his mathematical background. Economics may become secondary, if not marginal, in that judgment. Mathematics is a demanding master: it ceaselessly asks for weaker assumptions, for stronger conclusions, and for greater generality. Mathematical models must be manageable and easy to handle. However, this requires drastic omissions and simplifications, often at the expense of the models' ability to capture relevant phenomena. Therefore, in many cases economists conclude with models that exclude everything that is of interest for policymaking.

Mathematics is a language, as Samuelson reminded economists, popularizing Gibbs's sentence. It is no less but no more than *a* language. There is no reason to assert that it is *the* language of economics. The advantage of mathematization is that it prevents logical mistakes. Given the difficulties for experimenting in economics, economic theory is strongly dependent on logical reasoning.

In physics, factual observations and experimental results provide a constant check on its theoretical constructions; this occasionally allows some reasoning to be employed, reasoning that knowingly violates the canons of mathematical deduction. This is not acceptable in economic theory where internal consistency is the only guarantee of rigor. However, is logical rigor necessarily equivalent to using mathematical language? In this respect, we must remember that the most influential texts in economics have been *nonmathematical*. For example, Friedman and Schwartz (1963) proved to be more influential in favoring the monetary approach than many sophisticated econometric models, not to mention, on the opposite side, Keynes's General Theory.

Therefore, it is difficult to share Cochrane's (2009) condemnation of the literary style of exposition in economics as an almost deadly sin. The broad use of mathematics in economics often has more to do with the aim of providing the aesthetic pleasure of a beautiful theorem than to provide new substantive insights. The more impressive the use of quantitative techniques or methods, the more likely it is that a paper will be accepted by the editorial board of an academic journal.

Unfortunately, this premium on quantification has had serious adverse consequences, including a misallocation of research efforts in economics.

One must bear in mind that mathematics is just a tool to guarantee logical consistency. If logical consistency can be assured without mathematics, what is the point of using it? On the other hand, if it allows us to arrive at conclusions that cannot be attained with logical reasoning alone, then why not use it?

In fact, one can be dogmatic with blackboard diagrams and open minded with reams of equations. In general, less mathematics has the advantage of lowering the barrier to critical thinking, but simply getting rid of it would imply disregarding an important tool for economic analysis. Some economic problems require a mathematical approach to assure a rigorous treatment, while others can be approached using a literary style. One should therefore conclude that neither the use nor the nonuse of mathematics in economics can be a necessary condition for judging its scientific standards.

9.6 Health Versus Illness in Economic Analysis

After discussing how to study the economy, the following issue is what to study. The natural answer is, of course, economic problems. This may sound rather obvious, but most of the orthodox economists' efforts are devoted to showing the nonexistence of economic problems. The bulk of their papers are aimed at showing how the market solves any potential conflict or difficulty on its own. If so, there is no economic problem to work on.

Looking at the literature, an overwhelming predominance of papers concerns "well-behaved" models. Most scholars' efforts are devoted to study "health" and very little to analyzing "illness" in economics. However, it is economic illness that causes concern to society. Considerable effort is devoted to showing why the economy works smoothly most of the time and very little effort to the analysis of why, from time to time, the economic mechanism breaks down or—more importantly—what is needed to fix it. However, these failures in the economic mechanism have huge economic and social costs. Economic illness rather than economic health should be the focus of economists' efforts.

Although there has been research on issues that played a central role during the recent crisis, such as liquidity evaporation, collateral shortages, bubbles, crises, panics, fire sales, risk shifting, contagion, and the like, "much of this literature belongs to the *periphery* of macroeconomics rather than to its core", as Caballero (2010, 2) frankly recognizes.

This little effort devoted to the study of economic failures reflects in the poor attention paid to curing economic illness. Thousands of pages have been written to show the benefits of global financial integration, but very few to drawing attention to the risks it involved (Stiglitz 2010). Despite the fact that the contemporary economy has been transformed by the forces of technology and entrepreneurship, little attention has been paid, after Schumpeter, to the economic explanation of the forces behind these changes.[8] It seems therefore that priorities in the economic theory agenda are misplaced. Studying economic pathologies and how to cure them should be more encouraged, while fewer resources should be devoted to merely showing why an economy is in good health.

The 1930 crisis inspired Lord Keynes' main contribution to economic analysis. Chapter 10 of this book is devoted to his ideas and the development of macroeconomics, the branch of economics he founded. Keynes's contribution paved the way for a huge improvement in economic policy. This resulted in a notable moderation of economic fluctuations after World War II. As a paradoxical by-product of this improvement, many economists announced that economic fluctuations and crises were no longer a subject to be studied by economists but only by historians. "The economy of the 1990s suggested to [a new] generation of students that the business cycle was no longer of practical importance" (Mankiw 2006, 37).

Several writers dubbed "the Great Moderation" the remarkable decline in the variability of economic variables that took place during the last part of the twentieth century. However, the validity of this concept as a permanent shift has been questioned by the economic and financial crisis that began in 2007. There have also been some previous signals, such as the 1987 stock market crash, the1998 financial crisis triggered by the failure of Long-Term Capital Management or the bursting of the dot-com bubble in 2000, but their limited effects were considered an argument in favor of the theory that crises were only something of the past. Although such problems as poverty, unemployment, and slow growth have been present even during the so-called Great Moderation, they deserved only marginal consideration by mainstream economists.

To elaborate a new order of priorities for the agenda of economic research, it is important to identify the problems that research should address. Economic fluctuations, financial crises and financial regulation, poverty, unemployment, climate and energy security, food and nutrition security, and sustainable growth seem to be the undisputable candidates. However, Caballero (2010, 4) argues that shifting resources from the current core to the periphery is not necessarily a good idea. Despite that, he recognizes "that if the goal of macroeconomics is to provide formal frameworks to address real economic problems rather than purely literature-driven ones, we better start trying something new rather soon".

9.7 Is There a Unique Economic Theory or a Collection of Economic Theories?

Orthodox economists represent the economy as a stable equilibrium system resembling the planetary one. The concept of equilibrium plays a key role in traditional economics. This approach is useful in normal, stable times, when what happened

---

[8] Baumol (2002) and Baumol et al. (2007) are two of some few exceptions to this assertion.

yesterday is the best guide to what will happen tomorrow. However, it is incapable of dealing with unstable, turbulent, chaotic times.

Heterodox contributions shed much more light on what happens during these exceptional although crucial periods in which a good part of the economy is reshaped; they provide powerful insights toward what policies to follow in those extraordinary circumstances. However, as theories, they remain suitable mainly for those periods of instability and crisis. Thus, heterodoxy and orthodoxy are both a one-way street. Both contain some grain of truth but not the whole truth. The first is useful only when the economy is in trouble and the second for when it is stable. The challenge is to arrive at a unified theory valid both for normal and abnormal times. In this respect, the complexity approach, with its use of nonlinear models, offers the advantage that the *same* model allows to describe stable as well as unstable and even chaotic behaviors.

However, one should bear in mind that up to now not even physics has a unified theory. Moreover, general relativity theory and quantum mechanics are mutually incompatible. Therefore, perhaps, as Elster (2009) suggests, one should be less ambitious with economic theory. It would be important to convince the entire profession that there is nothing like "the" economic theory; all economists should be taught to have a sense of respect for those theories and models they do not share or like. Instead of disqualifying rival theories, it would be better to react by looking at them for worthwhile elements.

Instead of a unique economic theory, there is a collection of economic theories, our collective diversified intellectual portfolio. Some of these are in competition with each other. Just as carpenters choose the proper instrument from their toolboxes according to the tasks they have to complete, practitioners have to choose the appropriate tool to use in each case. What help do they have in choosing among competing economic theories? The main one comes from experience. In economics, although refutation does not come through the empirical tests learned in statistics and econometrics courses, it does come through what I have called "big social experiments" (Beker 2005, 8).

These are the "big events" alluded by Tobin (1996), which discredit ideas and replace them with new ones. The Great Depression in the 1930s, for instance, discredited the idea that full employment of resources could be automatically reached. Today, no reasonable economist in the USA would cast doubts about the role of the Federal Reserve and its monetary policy in stabilizing the economic cycle.

In the same way, for many years the role of monetary policy in inflationary processes was discussed. Moreover, even nonmonetary inflation theories were developed. However, the processes of high inflation in the 1970s and the cases of hyperinflation, such as the Argentinean one in the late 1980s, left no doubt as to the necessary existence of a *monetary* component in these processes and the need to resort to monetary policy to control them.

The 1987 stock market crash persuaded more economists to put aside efficient-market theory than any econometric result. Finally, if we have learned anything from the recent financial crisis, it is that financial markets are too important a matter in economic life to be left unregulated or badly regulated.

9.8 Conclusions

This chapter has been devoted to the analysis of the implications of the recent financial crisis in the field of economic theory. Mainstream neoclassical economic theory has been blamed for not having even considered the possibility of the type of collapse that the subprime mortgage meltdown unleashed.

An analysis of the causes of the recent financial crisis shows that it was, first, a case of massive malpractice. Such a massive case of malpractice exposes deep failures in the regulatory system. The deregulation movement that took place during the 1980s and 1990s was inspired by an almost religious belief in the power of market forces to solve any economic problem. Mainstream neoclassical economics bears the main responsibility in having nourished this belief.

The financial crisis has underlined the need for reform of the financial system's regulatory and supervisory architecture. The importance of this undertaking, and of doing it properly, can hardly be overstated. Some steps have been taken in this direction, as is shown in Chap. 3. Others, especially at the international level, are still pending.

It is urgent to address the broad-based problems of the financial system, chiefly, to eliminate the incentives for the risky bets that necessitated government bailouts. The role of rating agencies has to be redefined so at the very least their fees can no longer be paid by issuers of the securities they are supposed to qualify. To set up a public credit ratings agency may be a second step toward correcting the present perverse incentive system facing private agencies.

The criticism of neoclassical economic theory includes its (ab)use of mathematics. On this issue, it should be kept in mind that mathematics is just a tool to guarantee logical consistency. However, logical consistency may also be warranted without the use of mathematics, depending on the type of problem one wants to solve. The type of problem dictates what method to use, not the other way around. The truth is that the most influential texts in economics have been nonmathematical.

Priorities in the economic theory research agenda are misplaced. Studying economic pathologies and how to cure them should be encouraged, while fewer resources should be devoted to merely showing why an economy is in good health. There is nothing like "the" economic theory. There is a collection of economic theories, some of which are in competition with each other. The process of natural selection defines which survives and which do not. "Big social experiments" discredit certain ideas and replace them with new ones.

References

Akerlof GA, Shiller R (2009) Animal spirits. Princeton University Press, Princeton

Barth JR, Brumbaugh RD Jr, Wilcox JA (2000) The repeal of Glass-Steagall and the advent of broad banking. Economic and policy analysis working paper no. 5. Available via https://www.google.it/webhp?sourceid=chrome-instant&ion=1&espv=2&ie=UTF-8#q=2.+Barth+J.+R.%2C+Jr.+R.+D.+Brumbaugh+and+J.+A.+Wilcox+(2000)%2C+%E2%80%9CThe+Repeal+of+Glass-Steagall+and+the+Advent+of+Broad+Banking%E2%80%9D%2C+Economic+and+Policy+Analysis+Working+Paper+n.+5

Baumol WJ (2002) The free-market innovation machine. Princeton University Press, Princeton

Baumol WJ, Litan RE, Schramm CJ (2007) Good capitalism, bad capitalism and the economics of growth and prosperity. Yale University Press, New Haven

Beker VA (2005) Is economics a science? A discussion of some methodological issues, July. Available via http://ssrn.com/abstract=839307

Blaug M (1992) The methodology of economics. Cambridge University Press, New York

Buiter W (2009) The unfortunate uselessness of most 'State of the Art' academic monetary economics. Vox, Mar 6. Available via http://www.voxeu.org/article/macroeconomics-crisis-irrelevance

Caballero R (2010) Macroeconomics after the crisis: time to deal with the pretense-of-knowledge syndrome. MIT department of economics working paper no. 10–16. Available via http://ssrn.com/abstract=1683617

Cochrane JH (2009) How did Paul Krugman get it so wrong? Sept 16. Available via http://faculty.chicagobooth.edu/john.cochrane/research/Papers/krugman_response.htm

Colander D (2009) Economists, incentives, judgement, and the European CVAR approach to macroeconometrics. Economics 3. http://www.economics-ejournal.org/economics/journalarticles/2009-9/

Colander D, Holt R, Rosser B Jr (2004) The changing face of mainstream economics. Rev Polit Econ 16(4):485–499

Colander D, Föllmer H, Haas A, Goldberg M, Juselius K, Kirmen A, Lux T, Slot B (2009) The financial crisis and the systematic failure of academic economics. Working paper no. 1489, February, Kiel Institute for the World Economy. Available via http://papers.ssrn.com/sol3/papers.cfm?abstract_id=1355882

Coval J, Jurek J, Stafford E (2009) The economics of structured finance. J Econ Perspect 23 (1):3–25

Debreu G (1991) The mathematization of economic theory. Am Econ Rev 81(1):1–7

Elster J (2009) Excessive ambitions. Capital Soc 4(2):1–30, Available via http://www.bepress.com/cas/vol4/iss2/art1/

Friedman M, Schwartz J (1963) Monetary trends in the United States and the United Kingdom: their relation to income, prices and interest rates, 1867–1975. University of Chicago Press, Chicago

Gintis H (2009). Animal spirits or complex adaptive dynamics? A review of George Akerlof and Robert J. Shiller animal spirits, University of Massachusetts. Available via http://www.umass.edu/preferen/gintis/AkerlofShiller.pdf

Hausman DM (1992) The inexact and separate science of economics. Cambridge University Press, Cambridge

Heymann D, Stiglitz JE (2014) Life after debt: the origins and resolutions of debt crisis. Macmillan, Palgrave

Hicks JR (1983) A discipline not a science. In: Hicks JR (ed) Classics and moderns: collected essays on economic theory, vol III. Basil Blackwell, Oxford, pp 365–375

Ireland P (2004) A method for taking models to the data. J Econ Dyn Control 28(6):1205–1226

Juselius K, Franchi M (2007) Taking a DSGE model to the data meaningfully. Economics. Available via http://www.economics-ejournal.org/economics/journalarticles/2007-4

Kehoe T, Prescott E (2007) Great depressions of the 20th century. Federal Reserve Bank of Minneapolis, Minneapolis

Krugman P (2009) How did economists get it so wrong? The New York Times Magazine, Sept 2. Available via http://www.nytimes.com/2009/09/06/magazine/06Economic-t.html

Lawson T (2009) Contemporary economics and the crisis. Real World Econ Rev 50:122–131, Available via http://www.paecon.net/PAEReview/issue50/Lawson50.pdf

Levine DK (2009) An open letter to Paul Krugman, Sept 18. Available via http://www.huffingtonpost.com/david-k-levine/an-open-letter-to-paul-kr_b_289768.html

Mankiw G (2006) The macroeconomist as scientist and engineer. J Econ Perspect 20(4):29–46

Mayer T (1993) Truth versus precision in economics. Edward Elgar, Aldershot

Rajan R (2005) Has financial development made the world riskier? NBER working paper no. 11728. Available via http://papers.ssrn.com/sol3/papers.cfm?abstract_id=842464

Robinson J (1972) The second crisis of economic theory. Am Econ Rev 62(1–2):1–10

Rosenberg A (1992) Mathematical politics or science of diminishing returns? University of Chicago Press, Chicago

Sachs JD (2009) Rethinking macroeconomics. Capital Soc 4(3). Available via http://jeffsachs.org/2012/09/rethinking-macroeconomics/

Schneider F, Kirchgässner G (2009) Financial and world economic crisis: what did economists contribute? Public Choice 140:319–327

Stiglitz J (2010) Risk and global economic architecture: why full financial integration may be undesirable. Am Econ Rev Pap Proc 100(2):388–392

Strauss-Kan D (2010) Economic policy challenges in the post-crisis period. In: Speech at inaugural conference at the institute for new economic thinking by IMF managing director Dominique Strauss-Kahn, Cambridge, UK, Apr 10

Tobin J (1996) Full employment and growth: further Keynesian essays on policy. Edward Elgar, Cheltenham

Chapter 10
Rethinking Macroeconomics in Light of the Great Crisis

Victor A. Beker

10.1 Introduction

The US financial crisis showed that mainstream economics was unprepared to deal with it. There was a widespread belief in the self-correcting power of markets. For Colander et al. (2009, 2), the majority of economists "failed to warn policy makers about the threatening system crisis and ignored the work of those who did." Sachs (2009) underscores that "the operating assumptions of macroeconomics from the 1980s onward are passé, so too is the policy framework that has dominated the US and the world economy for the past 30 years".

Undoubtedly, the recent financial crisis has damaged the reputation of economics, particularly of macroeconomics. So, it is time to question what has gone wrong with it and try to put it right (see also Chap. 1, Sect. 1.6).

Section 10.2 reminds readers of the origin of macroeconomics as a branch of economics; then, I recall the major turn that it experienced under the influence of the "Lucas critique". Section 10.3 is devoted to the origin and widespread use of real business cycle (RBC) models. In Sect. 10.4, I present how the crisis is analyzed from the RBC perspective. The conclusion is that the neoclassical business cycle model contributes too little to the understanding of the recent economic crisis. So, it seems necessary to look for an alternative perspective. In Sect. 10.5, a claim is made to reevaluate Keynes' original contribution to economic analysis and return to Keynes' thoughts, which have been ignored or misstated during the past 40 years. The main contributions made by Keynes are also highlighted. Section 10.6 reconsiders Minsky's long ignored contributions to financial theory. Section 10.7 contains the main conclusions, which point out the need to rebuild macroeconomics as a discipline in which aggregate quantities play an essential role, while prices have only second-order effects.

V.A. Beker (✉)
University of Belgrano and University of Buenos Aires, Buenos Aires, Argentina
e-mail: victor.beker@ub.edu.ar

B. Moro, V.A. Beker, *Modern Financial Crises*, Financial and Monetary Policy Studies 42, DOI 10.1007/978-3-319-20991-3_10

10.2 From Keynes to Lucas

Macroeconomics, as it is now understood, namely, the systematic study of business fluctuations and stabilization policy, was founded by John Maynard Keynes as a distinct field of study within economics. The central contribution of Keynes was to focus attention on the economic aggregates (income, consumption, investment, savings, etc.).

In Keynesian macroeconomics, quantities are related to other quantities, while the role of prices is de-emphasized. This was the quintessence of macroeconomics until Phelps (1970) criticized this approach by arguing that it lacked proper microfoundations. Lucas (1976) argued in the same direction, and this "Lucas critique" had devastating effects on the then dominant approach in macroeconomics.

Macroeconomic theory took a major turn at that point: rational expectations of representative agent models became the only allowable modeling method. The necessity of microfoundations has been taken as a dogma that rejects as nonscientific whichever contribution had a different approach on this basic principle.

However, it is natural to ask how a model that assumes away any agent coordination problems can shed light on macroeconomic phenomena that precisely emerge because of coordination problems. Since in a complex system aggregate behavior cannot be deduced from an analysis of individuals alone, representative agent models fail to address the most basic questions of macroeconomics (Colander et al. 2008, 2). In Harcourt's (2004, 1) words, "Modeling the economy as a representative agent rules out by assumption one of the fundamental insights of Keynes (and Marx), to wit, the fallacy of composition, that what may be true of the individual taken in isolation is not necessarily true of all individuals taken together".

While new classical macroeconomics demands for microfoundations as a conditio sine qua non, other scientific disciplines such as thermodynamics and chemistry do not claim for the need of a micro-theory. All biological creatures are made up of particles. This does not mean that the natural place to start in building biology is to start with particle physics.

Botanists study certain characteristics of the behavior of plants without knowing the exact biochemical mechanisms behind them. Zoologists study anthills without having to resort to the individual behavior of ants. It is well known that relativity theory (macrophysics) and quantum mechanics (microphysics) are mutually inconsistent. They both recognize that the aggregate behavior of the systems of particles, molecules, cells, and social insects cannot be deduced from the characteristics of a "representative" of the population.

In general, microeconomic models usually ignore non-price interactions and consider individuals as isolated entities who take decisions independently of each other. A basic assumption of general equilibrium theory is that the only interactions among economic agents are through the price system. All adjustments are carried out via fully flexible prices, and agents never experience quantity constraints.

Assuming that the preferences and thereby the choices of one individual are influenced by others introduces an important element of uncertainty, which conspires against the possibility of arriving at a stable price equilibrium. So, agents' interactions are discarded at the microlevel, and, at the same time, to be acceptable, macro-models are supposed to be derived from these sorts of micro-models. Not surprisingly, the result is that the most important real economic problems are excluded from economic analysis.

10.3 RBC Theory

Lucas' work started new classical macroeconomics, which was later recast as RBC theory by Kydland and Prescott. It also goes under the names of neoclassical growth theory and dynamic stochastic general equilibrium models.

The RBC research program stems from the assumption that business cycles can be studied in a framework postulating market clearing and agents' optimizing behavior (Lucas 1977). The origins of economic cycles lie in exogenous shocks to the fundamentals, rather than being somewhat intrinsic to the economic system. So, there is nothing inherently bad in business cycles: they are the optimal response of rational economic agents to unexpected changes in the economic environment. Consequently, there is no room—nor need—for stabilization policies implemented by the government (Pensieroso 2009).

Following these ideas, Kydland and Prescott (1980, 1982) developed a framework to analyze business fluctuations based on a representative agent who solves optimization problems to arrive at competitive equilibria that are always Pareto optimal.

This framework was used by Prescott (1986) to study the business cycles in the USA during the post-World War II period. His conclusion was that fluctuations mostly resulted from random changes in the growth rate of business sector productivity. So, he challenged the dominant view that business cycles are caused by monetary and financial disturbances.

The general equilibrium growth model became the workhorse of neoclassical economics. It is the orthodoxy accepted paradigm for studying most macroeconomic phenomena, including business cycles, tax policy, monetary policy, and growth.

As stated above, the original RBC model was calibrated for the post-World War II period. In the 1970s and 1980s, Lucas and Prescott maintained that, because of its exceptional character, an explanation of the Great Depression was beyond the grasp of the equilibrium approach to the business cycle.

However, while Lucas stuck to this view, Prescott changed his mind at the end of the 1990s. RBC theory, he argued, has succeeded in its endeavor to elucidate the Great Depression. The authors credited with this breakthrough were Cole and

Ohanian (1999). After that, a volume studying 12 great depressions in different countries by employing simple applied dynamic general equilibrium models was published in 2007 (Kehoe and Prescott 2007). Finally, Ohanian (2010) published an analysis of the recent economic crisis.

10.4 The Economic Crisis from a Neoclassical Perspective

Ohanian (2010) used a general equilibrium business cycle model to analyze the 2007–2009 recession. So, a model that started out being applied to a relatively stable period in the US economy such as 1954–1982—and for that reason was long considered inapplicable to explain the Great Depression—is now being employed to explain the Great Recession.

What are the conclusions Ohanian arrives at? His main conclusion is that lower output and income is exclusively due to a large decline in labor input. According to Ohanian (2010, 45), "labor input during the 2007–2009 recession in the United States was far below the level consistent with the marginal product of labor". Given the huge level of unemployment the crisis generated, it is not big news to know that the labor input sharply declined during that period.

More surprising is the reason for that decline. According to Ohanian, the marginal rate of substitution between consumption and leisure was very low relative to the marginal product of labor. So, it seems that the crisis was caused by a sudden and mysterious increase in the preference for leisure. American workers suddenly decided to stay at home and watch TV instead of going to work.

Of course, you are forced to reach that conclusion if you start assuming that the recession is an equilibrium outcome for agents who maximize their utilities. We are now again in the pre-Keynesian world where unemployment is always a voluntary decision by workers who have an increased preference for leisure compared with work. Worst of all, this does not contribute at all either to our knowledge of the causes, mechanisms, and consequences of the Great Recession or to the knowledge of the policies to prevent a phenomenon like this from happening again.

In fact, as Ohanian himself recognized, neoclassical economists know little about the specific sources and nature of the shocks, why labor market deviations were so large, why productivity deviations seem to play such a small role in the USA in this period, on how to model real-world financial and policy events in order to determine their impact on the economy, and why macroeconomic weakness continued for so long after the worst of the crisis passed (Ohanian 2010, 63–64). In summary, the neoclassical business cycle model does not contribute at all to the understanding of the recent US economic crisis.

Its main contribution, if any, is that it shows that you cannot analyze crises as an equilibrium phenomenon. Of course, this may sound rather obvious for the naïve observer; however, for mainstream economists, this statement has been considered almost taboo for more than 30 years.

This seems to justify Colander's assertion that "the dynamic 'truth' force pushing for the best idea and method to win out is relatively weak in comparison to other specific institutional forces that have little to do with the truth of the idea or the usefulness of a method in arriving at the truth" (Colander 2009, 6).

In the same direction, physicist Martin Bojowald (2010) stated that if a certain line of research reaches an influential position, either by chance or because of fashion, that position will soon become stronger thanks to money raising and the influence on new contracts to fill vacant positions. So, it generates a cumulative process that sometimes has nothing to do with truth or usefulness.

10.5 Back to Keynes

I have argued elsewhere (Beker 2010, 19) that "it should be economic illness rather than economic health the main object of economists' efforts". So, for example, it is of little help to know that Kydland and Prescott's RBC model gives a good approximation of the events in a stable period of the American economy such as the post-World War II period. What we need first of all are instruments to deal with unstable, turbulent, chaotic times.

As stated above, Keynes founded macroeconomics. It was a reflection of the Great Depression on economic thought. Keynes offered a theory of depression economics that asserted that the market mechanism could not be relied upon to spontaneously recover from a slump. The labor market may fail to clear; so, government intervention might be necessary to reach full employment. A central tenet in Keynes' thought was his stress not only on the possibility of market failure but also on the idea that unemployed resources could exist as an "equilibrium" state not spontaneously eliminated by the market mechanism.

The anti-Keynesian counterrevolution was triggered in the 1970s by the appearance of chronic inflation as an economic problem. Neoclassical economics was considered to be mainstream economics for a long while; however, its failure now opens the way to rethinking macroeconomics, recovering its original aims and methodology. So, it seems reasonable to go back to the *General Theory* itself as a starting point and recover Keynes' real ideas.

Keynesian analysis was a policy-oriented one. Keynes was writing in the middle of the Great Depression and he was mainly interested in advising decision-makers on how to get out of it. His approach was a short-run one, which is relevant for policy decisions: "in the long run, we are all dead", he remarked in his *Tract on Monetary Reform* (1923, 65), where he added that "economists set themselves too easy, too useless a task if in tempestuous seasons they can only tell us that when the storm is long past the ocean is flat again". For example, it is of little use and comfort to know that after 10 years of deflation, full employment would be restored.

The main contribution by Keynes was his concept of involuntary unemployment. Voluntary (classical) unemployment is caused because real wages are above the marginal productivity of labor. The solution lies in reducing wages. On the contrary, Keynes defines involuntary unemployment in the following way: "Men are involuntarily unemployed if, in the event of a small rise in the price of wage-goods relatively to the money-wage, both the aggregate supply of labor willing to work for the current money-wage and the aggregate demand for it at that wage would be greater than the existing volume of employment" (Keynes 2006, 14).

So, involuntary unemployment persists even if real wages are reduced. The level of employment is not defined in the labor market but in the goods market. For Keynes, given the equipment, organization, and technique of an economy, there is a one-to-one relationship between output and employment.

In fact, in the Keynesian model, the aggregate demand function is given by:

$$D(N) = C(N) + I \tag{10.1}$$

where N is the level of employment, $C(N)$ is consumption, and I is investment. The equilibrium in the goods market requires excess aggregate demand to be zero at some level of employment:

$$D(N) - S(N, K_o) = 0 \tag{10.2}$$

where $S(N, K_o)$ is the aggregate supply function. So, employment is determined as the inverse of the excess demand function for given values of investment, namely, the exogenous variable:

$$N = g(I, K_o) \tag{10.3}$$

Given the organization, equipment, and technique of production, the labor demand is a function of the level of investment. In the Keynesian model, the volume of employment is defined in the goods market. In Keynes' words: "The propensity to consume and the rate of new investment determine between them the volume of employment, and the volume of employment is uniquely related to a given level of real wages—*not the other way around*" (Keynes 2006, 27, italics mine).[1]

Given the level of employment, "the wage is equal to the marginal product of labor" (Keynes 2006, 5). If:

$$Q = h(N, K_o)$$

is the aggregate production function, being:

$$S = pQ$$

[1] By the way, this quotation shows how wrong is Colander's (1991, 7) interpretation of Keynes, according to which "there is not a one-to-one relationship between the number of workers used in the production process and the output of those workers".

then:

$$w/p = Q_N(N, K_o) = h_N(I, K_o) \tag{10.4}$$

where w is the nominal wage and p the general level of prices; $Q_N(N, K_o)$ is the marginal productivity of labor for a given level of capital K_o.

In short, the amount of labor employed depends on the amount of output being produced, which depends on the level of investment. The level of employment is not a function of the real wage rate as in the classical model. Rather, the real wage rate is a function of the level of employment or, ultimately, of the level of investment.

For Keynes, it was self-evident that fluctuations in the level of employment were mainly correlated with fluctuations in the level of output. He did not even think he should give an explanation on this.

There are at least two arguments that justify Keynes' approach. Small changes in the real wage rate usually have a second-order effect on firms' profits and they are often offset by the transaction costs of firing or hiring personnel. That is why if there is a small decrease in real wages, the aggregate demand for labor will not change. Only changes in the output can cause first-order changes in employment. So, it makes sense to assume labor demand as solely a function of output. In the real world, a huge decrease in the real wage rate is needed in order to offset the effect on employment of a relatively small decline in output. Such a decrease in wages is usually socially non-feasible and, by contrast, as Keynes himself noted, may have a contractionary effect on output demand and, consequently, on the level of employment.

A second argument is the one developed in Yellen's (1984) efficiency wage theory. If wage cuts harm productivity, then cutting wages may end up raising labor costs. Workers may accept a reduction in real wages but this does not warrant a higher level of employment. Firms will not hire them even at a lower wage because any reduction in the wage paid would lower the productivity of all employees already on the job.

Thus, no self-adjusting mechanism in the labor market ensures full employment. In the Keynesian model, it is not true that real wages and the level of employment are determined by the intersection of the labor demand function with the labor supply function. The level of employment and the real wage rate define an equilibrium point on the labor demand schedule. Workers earn a real wage, which equals the marginal productivity of labor, but it does not necessarily equal the marginal disutility of labor.[2]

[2] This is the main difference between Keynes and Patinkin's definitions of involuntary unemployment. According to the latter, involuntary unemployment appears when producers are forced by insufficient demand to operate in a region in which the marginal product of labor exceeds the real wage rate (Grossman, 1972, 28–9). But Patinkin (1989, 323) admitted he could not find a convincing explanation why then firms did not demand more labor.

The second important contribution by Keynes was to point out that only by chance the market can attain the full employment equilibrium. The most likely situation is one of involuntary unemployment, where labor supply exceeds labor demand.

This is the key difference between Keynes and the different versions of the classics (be it classics themselves, neoclassics, or new classics): in the Keynesian model, the labor market does not necessarily clear. If excess labor supply reduces real wages, the volume of employment does not increase; in such a case, the volume of employment will be given by a point to the left of the labor demand curve at the new reduced real wage rate.[3] That is why, for Keynes, it makes sense for workers to resist any wage reduction.

In Keynes' *General Theory*, there is no reference to real wage rigidity. On the contrary, Keynes argues that workers will usually resist a nominal wage reduction but, instead, they will not resist moderate reductions in real wages because of an increase in prices (Keynes, 2006, 13). Wage rigidity was introduced by those—like many New Keynesians—who claim that otherwise the labor market would clear and no unemployment could exist at all. But, strictly speaking, unemployment because of rigid wages is the (classical) voluntary kind of unemployment. It has nothing to do with Keynes' definition of involuntary unemployment. A reduction in real wages will reduce/eliminate the kind of unemployment in New Keynesian models. This contradicts Keynes' definition of involuntary unemployment as quoted above. Unemployment in New Keynesian models is not very Keynesian.

For Keynes, the huge fluctuations in employment studied by macroeconomics have to do with fluctuations in the level of output, not with the level of real wages. Keynes also disregarded the role of prices in eliminating any discrepancy between aggregate demand and supply. Orthodox economists after Keynes assumed that prices play the key role in reaching equilibrium in the goods market. Keynes did not. And not because he assumed rigid prices as the New Keynesians interpret. For Keynes, the equilibrium in the goods market is attained when demand (consumption plus investment) equals aggregate supply. If there is a general glut, firms would reduce their supply until the equilibrium is attained.

The argument that a supply glut would press prices down until aggregate demand equals aggregate supply was developed after Keynes by the so-called neoclassical synthesis as a way out of his dismal conclusions. As a matter of fact, neither Keynes nor the classics thought there was a close connection between Say's Law and price flexibility as the modern parlance imagine.[4] The classics emphasized that every act of production is an act of potential demand creation. And this was the argument Keynes refuted. Only after Keynes did the neoclassical synthesis

[3] In the efficiency wage case, the demand curve for labor would move to the left, reflecting the fall in productivity caused by the decline in real wages.

[4] See Montgomery (2006, 128) for a well-developed argument on the classics, Say's Law, and price/wage flexibility.

introduce the role of prices through the wealth effect as a way to guarantee the attainment of the full employment equilibrium.

So, it is not surprising that Keynes—interested in rebutting classical theory and particularly Say's Law—did not mention anything on this argument. In fact, it was only in 1943 that Pigou wrote his seminal article on the wealth effect (Pigou, 1943). Let us have a look at this effect and its assumptions.

10.5.1 The Wealth Effect and Price Asymmetry

Keynes never thought that the decline in prices could be a way out of involuntary unemployment. For him, the real balance effect was limited to the money market, the so-called Keynes effect. He admitted that those who believe in a self-adjusting economic system could argue that declining prices and wages would reduce the nominal demand for money and the nominal interest rate, thereby restoring a market economy to full employment. He rejected this argument by pointing out that a decline in prices and wages is analytically equivalent to an increase in money supply and thus subject to the same limitations he pointed out in connection with increasing the money supply as a way to reach full employment.[5] Keynes did not consider the possibility of a real balance effect on the goods market as nobody did before Pigou (1943).

Keynes was a practical-minded economist. In this respect, although he admits wage and price flexibility, he is very skeptical about downward flexibility. That is why he insists that real wages, in practice, can be lowered only by the increase in wage/goods prices, not by the contraction of nominal wages. If so, it is clear why he did not even consider that there could be a significant real balance effect on the goods market capable of leading automatically a market economy to full employment by a reduction in nominal prices.

Moreover, with reference to the recent economic crisis, Krugman (2008) illustrates how small the real balance effect could be in practice. Before the crisis, the US monetary base was about $800 billion. Supposing a 20 % fall in price levels, this would raise the real value of that base by $160 billion. But the housing bust wiped out something like $6 trillion of wealth; there is no comparison with the effects of a drastic fall in the aggregate price level, even if it were feasible.

So, although the wealth effect may be of some use in analyzing inflationary processes, it is of no practical relevance when dealing with recession and unemployment. This highlights the need for different approaches when analyzing an increase in aggregate demand and when analyzing a fall in it.

[5] Mainly, the limitations that the liquidity trap imposes on the reduction in the interest rate and, consequently, on an increase in investment. "If a tolerable level of employment requires a rate of interest much below the average rates which ruled in the nineteenth century, it is most doubtful whether it can be achieved merely by manipulating the quantity of money" (Keynes, 2006, 282).

In fact, as pointed out by Dobrynskaya (2008), "the Phillips curve is empirically found to be convex (Alvarez 2000; Latxon et al. 1999, for the USA; Dolado et al. 2004, for several European countries), implying asymmetric price rigidity, which means that prices are more sticky downwards than upwards. This results in the Phillips curve being steeper for positive changes in inflation than for negative ones. Therefore, as documented by many authors for many countries (e.g., Cover 1992), positive demand shocks give rise to inflation without affecting output significantly, while negative ones reduce output without affecting inflation". The same author in another paper asserts that "Peltzman (2000) studies over 240 markets for consumer as well as producer goods and finds that asymmetries are persuasive, substantial and durable, and exist in periods of low inflation as well as in periods of high inflation. These asymmetries also apply to price indices" (Dobrynskaya 2009, 53. See also Verbrugge 1998).

For the sake of elegance, economics usually assumes symmetric behavior. But reality is seldom asymmetric. In particular, price behavior is not symmetric. Usually, wages and prices are downward inflexible and a lot more flexible upward as illustrated by inflationary and hyperinflationary processes. A variety of evidence suggests that price/wage asymmetries in fact hold in actual economies.[6] Empirical research on wage dynamics has highlighted the presence of downward wage rigidities in a large number of countries.[7]

In his 1972 presidential address to the American Economic Association (AEA), Tobin argued that nominal prices can rise more easily than they can fall. Ball and Mankiw (1994) use a menu cost model to explore a possible explanation for such asymmetry, while other authors simply assume in their models its existence. In this respect, it may be worthwhile recalling Solow's AEA presidential address reflection: "I remember reading once that it is still not understood how the giraffe manages to pump an adequate blood supply all the way up to its head; but it is hard to imagine that anyone would therefore conclude that giraffes do not have long necks. At least not anyone who had ever been to a zoo" (Solow 1980, 7). Although it is, of course, desirable to have an acceptable theory to explain price asymmetry, it seems anyway much more reasonable to assume asymmetric rather than symmetric price behavior, at least for anyone who studies the real-world economy.

10.5.2 The Role of Investment

The third main contribution by Keynes was to identify the key role that investment plays in determining the level of employment. The level of employment is determined in the goods market at the point of equilibrium between the aggregate supply

[6] See, for instance, Ball and Mankiw (1994, 14) for additional references to those mentioned by Dobrynskaya (2008).

[7] See Dickens et al. (2007) and Babecký et al. (2010).

and demand for goods. Given the consumption function—which is increasing in the level of income—it is the volume of investment that defines the equilibrium.

Keynes identifies investment as the volatile component of aggregate demand. Investment depends on expectations: the marginal efficiency of capital is, for Keynes, the expected rate of profit. These expectations are subject to a high degree of uncertainty. Economic fluctuations are exaggerated in degree because decisions are highly dependent on the political and social atmosphere that gives way to waves of optimism or pessimism—the ups and downs of "animal spirits".

As Skidelsky (2011, 2) points out, "Keynes' picture of the economy differs from the classical—as well as the new classical—picture in its stress on the volatility of investment and the weakness of the rate of interest as an equilibrating mechanism". Thus, fluctuations in investment are responsible for fluctuations in aggregate output and thereby in employment. No mechanism guarantees that the level of investment will be the one that leads to full employment. On the contrary, only by chance it will be that particular one.

The neoclassics' and new classics' stories are that market clearing ensures that supply and demand in both the labor and goods markets reach equilibria, which correspond to full employment. So, we come to the fourth main contribution of Keynes: markets do not necessarily clear. For Keynes, equilibrium does not necessarily mean market clearing. If we accept the definition of equilibrium as a state of the world where economic forces are balanced in such a way that in the absence of external influences the (equilibrium) values of economic variables will not change, Keynesian involuntary unemployment is an equilibrium state. Of course, this concept differs from the received view that identifies the equilibrium with the concept of market-clearing solutions. Precisely, Keynes' point of view is that there are no forces in the labor market capable of leading it to a clearing solution.

That is why Barro's (1979, 54) critique of Keynesian involuntary unemployment as implying a failure of agents to realize perceived gains from trade misunderstands the Keynesian concept. Barro argues that "it would be mutually advantageous for workers and firms to determine levels of employment in an efficient manner." But Keynesian unemployment is *involuntary* precisely because it is out of the reach of firms and workers to reduce it. Explicitly, Keynes defines it as a situation where a decline in real wages does not alter the level of employment. So, the simple conclusion is that Barro was not discussing with Keynes but with his own personal interpretation of the *General Theory*.

10.5.3 Keynes on Savings

One of the more shocking aspects of Keynesian doctrine is Keynes' approach to personal thrift, as a drag on the economy because of the reduction in aggregate demand for produced goods and services.

This has to do with the active role that Keynes ascribes to investment, while savings adjust passively to the volume of the former. So, for Keynes, investment leads the way and determines the volume of output and employment. Given the volume of investment, savings equal it, being the level of output the adjustment variable.

Keynes makes clear his thoughts on the subject when, criticizing underconsumption theories, he points out that "a relatively weak propensity to consume helps to cause unemployment by requiring and *not* receiving the accompaniment of a compensating volume of new investment" (Keynes 2006, 339). A "weak propensity to consume" means a high propensity to save. A higher propensity to save demands a higher volume of investment to reach full employment.

It is true that in the long run, output depends upon productive capacity and productive capacity depends upon capital formation, but capital formation does not depend on savings but upon investment. Only at full employment can the volume of savings be a restriction for the volume of investment. Of course, this is the only case that orthodox economics considers.

10.5.4 Keynes on Inflation

The *General Theory*'s main concern was unemployment. Its aim was to show why an economy can be stuck in unemployment and how to get out of it. The appearance of chronic inflation as an economic problem in the 1970s triggered the anti-Keynesian revolution. It was argued that demand stimulus to raise employment would always be associated with higher inflation. Keynesian models—it was said—assumed away the problem of inflation as a possible consequence of excessive aggregate demand stimulus.

"Popular folklore has it that he was largely unconcerned with inflation from the start, that his subsequent preoccupation with unemployment led him to ignore it altogether, and that, as a result, he favored expansionary measures to eliminate unemployment regardless of their inflationary consequences" (Humphrey 1981, 1). As a matter of fact, Keynes (2006, 271) admitted that wages and prices would rise gradually as employment increases: "... we have in fact a condition of prices rising gradually as employment increases" and "an increasing effective demand tends to raise money-wages though not fully in proportion to the rise in the price of wage-goods" (ibid., 275). This was the origin of the idea behind the Phillips curve: there is always a trade-off between alternative levels of unemployment and inflation: the lower the level of unemployment, the higher the level of inflation is. It is up to society to choose the preferred combination of both.

Finally, "when a further increase in the quantity of effective demand produces no further increase in output and entirely spends itself on an increase in the cost-unit fully proportionate to the increase in effective demand, we have reached a condition which might be appropriately designated as one of true inflation" (ibid., 276). So, for Keynes, true inflation sets in after full employment has been reached.

The new classical literature objected that the short-run Phillips curve trade-off could not be exploited because a reputation for doing so would soon lead the public's inflation expectations to change, in a way that would eliminate the apparent gains achieved by the policy. The argument was that the private sector, endowed with rational expectations, would expect the central bank to act in the way that it does, and the expectation of inflationary behavior would shift the short-run trade-off in an adverse direction. This adverse shift in the employment–inflation trade-off would mean higher levels of inflation for each level of unemployment. So, the long-run Phillips curve would be vertical, which means that there would be no trade-off between inflation and unemployment.

However, the argument is valid only if the central bank follows a naïve policy of inflating at any cost without making any commitment on inflation goals. If it does and the commitment is credible to the private sector, there is no reason for a shift in the Phillips curve. By contrast, the good empirical fit of traditional Phillips curve equations is an important argument against new classical objections. The fit would not be as good as it is if the Phillips curve were continuously shifting as actual inflation changes.

Anyway, as stated at the beginning of this subsection, the *General Theory* was mainly devoted to the analysis of unemployment. Anyone interested in knowing Keynes' opinion on inflation and the ways to fight it should refer to his writings between 1913 and 1930 when inflation was a major economic problem in Europe.

10.6 Hyman Minsky's Contribution to Financial Theory

The turmoil in financial markets has brought to prominence the ideas of Hyman Minsky, after a long period of unjust oblivion. Minsky called himself a "financial Keynesian". His financial theory is a distinguished contribution to the analysis of economic instability.

While Keynes identified as a fundamental flaw of the capitalist system the possibility of stable unemployment, Minsky added instability as a normal result of modern financial capitalism. He was convinced that leverage is the Achilles' heel of capitalism. His 1987 analysis of securitization was a prescient study of its nature and perils: "Securitization lowers the weight of that part of the financing structure that the central bank (Federal Reserve in the United States) is committed to protect. A need by holders of securities . . . may mean that a rise in interest rates will lead to a need by holders to make position by selling position, which can lead to a drastic fall in the price of the securities" (Minsky 2008, 3).

He strongly criticized the neoclassical approach: "The neoclassical way of doing economics, which rests upon splitting the financial system off from what is called the real economy, throws no appreciable light on the effect that a financial system has upon the functioning of the economy" (Minsky 1992a, 15).

On the contrary, he thought that the financial system plays a critical role in modern capitalist economies. "Liability structures, which link yesterdays and tomorrows to today, introduce a degree of intertemporal complexity into the economic process beyond that due to the different expected lives of capital assets, the gestation period for investment output and the time it takes to transform a labor force" (ibid., 3). Such complexity may generate time series that can be characterized as incoherent, chaotic, or ones that exhibit hysteresis (ibid.).

He characterized modern capitalism, especially in the USA, as "money manager capitalism." "The evolution has been from a financial structure where external finance was mainly used for trade to an even greater use of market or institution based external funds to finance the long term capital development of the economy" (Minsky 1996, 11).

He maintained that "the financial panic is made possible by the changes in the financial structure that takes place during the long-swing expansion. As a result, the triggering event for a deep depression need not be specially severe…" (Minsky 1964, 325). Financial instability is fostered by three factors: (1) the rise of debts relative to income, (2) the rise in the price of stock market and real estate assets, and (3) the decrease in the relative size of ultimate liquidity (ibid., 325–6).

Minsky held that during expansions, profits accrue disproportionately to firms with the most aggressive financial practices, resulting in an erosion of safety margins. So, over a prolonged period of prosperity, investors take on more and more risk, until lending exceeds what borrowers can pay off from their incoming revenues. When over-indebted investors are forced to sell even their less-speculative positions to make good on their loans, markets spiral lower and create a severe demand for cash—an event that has come to be known as a "Minsky moment."

As pointed out by Randall Wray (2011, 62), "Minsky's view is that the transformation of the economy and its financial structure from robust to fragile is due, not to external market factors like government intervention and regulation, but to the 'normal' operations and incentives of financial capitalism".

Minsky's financial fragility theory classifies the financing of the purchase of large real illiquid investment projects into three categories: hedge finance, speculative finance, and Ponzi finance. Ponzi financing is the most fragile financial system and it is the one most likely to lead to a "Minsky moment".

"The first theorem of the financial instability hypothesis is that the economy has financing regimes under which it is stable, and financing regimes in which it is unstable. The second theorem of the financial instability hypothesis is that over periods of prolonged prosperity, the economy transits from financial relations that make for a stable system to financial relations that make for an unstable system" (Minsky 1992a, 7–8). "Over a protracted period of good times, capitalist economies tend to move from a financial structure dominated by hedge finance units to a structure in which there is large weight to units engaged in speculative and Ponzi finance" (ibid., 8).

He also formulated what he termed his *anti-laissez-faire* theorem: "In a world where the internal dynamics imply instability, a semblance of stability can be achieved or sustained by introducing conventions, constraints and interventions into the environment" (Ferri and Minsky 1991, 20). Apt intervention and institutional structures are necessary for market economies to be successful.

The financial instability hypothesis "holds that business cycles of history are compounded out of (1) the internal dynamics of capitalist economies, and (2) the system of interventions and regulations that are designed to keep the economy operating within reasonable bounds" (Minsky 1992b, 8). "To contain the evils that market systems can inflict, capitalist economies developed sets of institutions and authorities, which can be characterized as the equivalent of circuit breakers. These institutions in effect stop the economic processes that breed the incoherence and restart the economy with new initial conditions" (Minsky et al, 1994, 6).

Although recognizing that Minsky always professed to draw his inspiration from Keynes, Leijonhufvud (2009, 742) argues that Minsky's "upward instability hypothesis stands in stark contrast to the economy's tendency, in Keynes' theory, to gravitate to a state of unemployment equilibrium." However, De Antoni's (2008, 4) interpretation seems more accurate in that "the two authors might be considered as faces of the same coin looking in opposite directions." For this author, while Keynes looked at a depressed economy, Minsky looked at a booming economy. Both share a common approach to economics. "A careful reading of their writing suggests that, whilst both of them are at the mercy of waves of optimism and pessimism, Minsky 'fights' against the upswing while Keynes 'fights' against the downswing" (ibid., 25).

As Minsky did not provide a rigorous formal model, his contributions did not reach the pages of leading mainstream journals, although his analyses were far more illuminating than were many of the elegantly mathematical but often useless models that plagued them. Only after the recent crisis has his name been rescued from oblivion.

10.7 Conclusions

The failure of neoclassical economics opens the way to rethinking macroeconomics. Since its foundation in the 1930s, macroeconomics has developed as a separate branch of economic theory with little connection to microeconomics. Macroeconomics was the realm of aggregate quantities, while prices played a limited or null role in it. Lucas' (1987) program aimed at bridging that gap. For him, macroeconomics should be embedded in microeconomic theory. "The most interesting recent developments in macroeconomic theory seem to me describable as the reincorporation of aggregative problems such as inflation and the business cycle within the general framework of 'microeconomic' theory. If these developments succeed, the term 'macroeconomic' will simply disappear from use and the modifier 'micro' will become superfluous. We will simply speak, as did Smith, Ricardo, Marshall and Walras, of *economic* theory" (pp .107–8). He succeeded but at the cost of making macroeconomics a discipline nearer to science fiction than to a subject that analyzes the issues of interest for policymaking.

So, the first conclusion is that macroeconomics has to go back to its roots and recover its original aims and methodology. Of course, for mainstream economists, a denial that prices always clear markets is felt as tantamount to the abandonment of the explanatory paradigm, so that economic analysis is left with little to say. This is the type of economist that 150 years ago Carlyle caricatured as parrots that only knew the words demand and supply.

By contrast, one should bear in mind that up to now there has been no unified theory in physics. Why should there be in economics? Moreover, general relativity theory and quantum mechanics are mutually incompatible. Why should we demand that the Keynesian theory of unemployment be compatible with Walrasian general equilibrium theory? Perhaps, one should be less ambitious with economic theory.

This is especially so if one takes into account that today there are outstanding physicists such as Stephen Hawking who think that it may not be possible to construct a unified theory and that to describe the various aspects of the universe you have to use different theories. This "is acceptable so long as the theories agree in their predictions whenever they overlap, that is, whenever they can both be applied" (Hawking and Mlodinow, 2010, 117). So, perhaps we should not search for a single theory but for a network of theories in economics, too. Demanding microfoundations for macroeconomic analysis has not proven to be a good idea up to now. If anything, it has led astray macroeconomics.[8]

The first step in rethinking macroeconomics would be to rescue Keynes' original ideas. One of the main Keynesian contributions is the concept of involuntary unemployment as an equilibrium state. The other key contribution of Keynes has been to identify the crucial role of investment in determining the level of output.

Owing to the asymmetric behavior of prices and wages, an increase and a fall in aggregate demand require different approaches in macroeconomic theory. While prices adjust rapidly to excess demand, they do not react at all or are much slower to respond in the presence of excess supply. While in the first case price adjustments play a key role, in the other one quantity adjustments prevail. The search for a unified treatment is the reason for the failure of models that have assumed the symmetric behavior of prices and wages for that purpose.

On the contrary, it seems much more reasonable to consider separately, on one hand, the macroeconomics of inflation and, on the other, the macroeconomics of recession and depression.

This would not be a different situation to the one we have today in physics. According to today's prevalent point of view, "it might be that to describe the universe we have to employ different theories in different situations" (Hawking and Mlodinow, 2010, 117).

One example of this is physicists' approaches to the Big Bang. General relativity theory predicts its existence. But Einstein's theory breaks down at that point: it cannot be used to predict how the universe began, only how it evolved afterward. To describe the origin of the universe, physicists resort to another theory—quantum theory—because it was a very small-scale phenomenon, the kind of phenomenon governed by quantum theory. So, the forces at work were different at and after the

[8] I have also extensively argued this in Beker (2010).

Big Bang. The same happens when aggregate demand moves up or down: the forces at work are different; thus, we need different models for their treatment.

If so, policies to guide the economy to full employment in one case and to stabilize prices in the other should be different chapters of the research agenda. In this respect, let us recall, for instance, the assertion by Blanchard et al. (2010, 9) that "there is a lot we do not know about the effects of fiscal policy, about the optimal composition of fiscal packages, about the use of spending increases versus tax decreases, and the factors that underlie the sustainability of public debts".

Broadly speaking, we still know very little on how to help the economy recover from a recession. This is not strange if the underlying assumptions in traditional economic theory have been that recessions are highly improbable and that in any case markets can fix them.

While Keynes identified as a fundamental flaw of the capitalist system the possibility of stable unemployment, Minsky added instability as a normal result of modern financial capitalism. Minsky held that during expansions, profits accrue disproportionately to firms with the most aggressive financial practices, resulting in an erosion of safety margins. When over-indebted investors are forced to sell even their less-speculative positions, markets spiral lower and create a severe demand for cash—an event that has come to be known as a "Minsky moment".

The currently observed turmoil in financial markets makes it advisable to rescue from unjust oblivion Minsky's illuminating ideas. His contributions together with Keynes' ones should be a starting point to rebuild macroeconomics on a solid basis.

References

Alvarez L (2000) Asymmetries in the capacity-inflation trade-off. UFAE and IAE working paper. Available via http://pareto.uab.es/wp/2000/47000.pdf

Babecký J, Caju PD, Kosma T, Lawless M, Messina J, Rõõm T (2010) Downward nominal and real wage rigidity: survey evidence from European firms. Scand J Econ 112(4):884–910

Ball L, Mankiw NG (1994) Asymmetric price adjustment and economic fluctuations. Econ J 104:247–261

Barro RJ (1979) Second thoughts on Keynesian economics. American economic review, papers and proceedings of the ninety-first annual meeting of the American economic association, May, 69(2):54–59

Beker VA (2010) On the economic crisis and the crisis of economics. Real World Econ Rev 56, March. Available via http://www.paecon.net/PAEReview/issue56/whole56.pdf

Blanchard O, Dell' Ariccia G, Mauro P (2010) Rethinking macroeconomic policy. J Money Credit Bank 42:199–215

Bojowald M (2010) Before the big bang: a complete history of the universe. Random House Mondadori, New York

Colander D (1991) Mr. Keynes and the 'classics' again: an alternative interpretation, Mimeo. Available via http://community.middlebury.edu/~colander/articles/Mr%20Keynes%20and%20the%20Classics%20Again.pdf

Colander D (2009) Economists, incentives, judgment, and the European CVAR approach to macroeconometrics. Econ e-J. doi:10.5018/economics-ejournal.ja.2009-9

Colander D, Howitt P, Kirman A, Leijonhufvud A, Mehrling P (2008) Beyond DSGE models: towards an empirically-based macroeconomics. Am Econ Rev 98(2):236–240

Colander D, Föllmer H, Haas A, Goldberg M, Juselius K, Kirmen A, Lux T, Slot B (2009) The financial crisis and the systematic failure of academic economics. Working paper no. 1489, February, Kiel Institute for the World Economy. Available via http://papers.ssrn.com/sol3/papers.cfm?abstract_id=1355882

Cole HL, Ohanian LE (1999) The great depression in the United States from a neoclassical perspective. Fed Reserv Minneap Q Rev 23:2–24

Cover JP (1992) Asymmetric effects of positive and negative money supply shocks. Q J Econ 107 (4):1261–1282

De Antoni E (2008) Minsky's financial instability hypothesis: the Not-too-Keynesian optimism of a financial Cassandra. Universitá degli Studi di Trento Discussion paper No. 12 [Reprinted In: Zambelli S (ed) Computable, constructive and behavioural economic dynamics: essays in honour of Kumuraswamy Velupillai on the occasion of his 60th birthday. London, Routledge]

Dickens WT, Goette L, Groshen EL, Holden S, Messina J, Schweitzer ME, Turunen J, Ward ME (2007) How wages change: micro evidence from the international wage flexibility project. J Econ Perspect 21(2):195–214

Dobrynskaya VV (2008) Asymmetric price rigidity and the optimal interest rate defense of the exchange rate: some evidence for the US. J Policy Model 30(5):713–724

Dobrynskaya V, Dobrynskaya VV (2009) Optimal monetary policy under incomplete pass-through and asymmetric price rigidity: the empirical evidence from Russia. In: Spanjers W (ed) Monetary policy, trade and convergence: the case of transition economies. LIT, Berlin, pp 49–77

Dolado J, Pedrero RMD, Ruge-Murcia FJ (2004) Nonlinear monetary policy rules: some new evidence for the US. Stud Nonlinear Dyn Econ 8(3)

Ferri P, Minsky HP (1991) Market processes and thwarting systems. The Jerome Levy economics institute of bard college working paper no. 64. Available via http://www.levyinstitute.org/pubs/wp64.pdf

Grossman HI (1972) Was Keynes a 'Keynesian'? J Econ Lit 10(1) (March)

Harcourt GC (2004) The economics of Keynes and its theoretical and political importance. Post-Autistic Econ Rev 27

Hawking S, Mlodinow L (2010) The grand design. Bentam Press, London

Humphrey TM (1981) Keynes on inflation. Econ Rev. Federal Reserve Bank of Richmond, January, pp 3–14

Kehoe T, Prescott E (2007) Great depressions of the 20th century, Federal Reserve Bank of Minneapolis, Minneapolis, March. Available via https://www.google.it/webhp?sourceid=chrome-instant&ion=1&espv=2&ie=UTF-8#q=Kehoe+T.+and+E.+Prescott+(2007)%2C+Great+Depressions+of+the+20th+Century%2C+Federal+Reserve+Bank+of+Minneapolis%2C+Minneapolis

Keynes JM (1923) Tract on monetary reform. Macmillan, London

Keynes JM (2006) The general theory of employment, interest and money. Atlantic Publishers & Distributors, New York

Krugman P (2008) Real balance effects (wonkish). The New York Times, Dec 4

Kydland FE, Prescott EC (1980) A competitive theory of fluctuations and the feasibility and desirability of stabilization policy. In: Fischer S (ed) Rational expectations and economic policy. University of Chicago Press, Chicago, pp 169–198

Kydland FE, Prescott EC (1982) Time to build and aggregate fluctuations. Econometrica 50 (6):1345–1370

Latxon D, Rose D, Tambakis D (1999) The US Phillips curve: the case for asymmetry. J Econ Dyn Control 23(9):1459–1485

Leijonhufvud A (2009) Out of the corridor: Keynes and the crisis. Camb J Econ 33(4):741–757

Lucas RE Jr (1987) Models of business cycles. Blackwell, New York

Lucas RE Jr (1976) Econometric policy evaluation: a critique. In: Brunner K, Meltzer AH (eds) The Phillips curve and labour markets. Carnegie-Rochester conference series on public policy, vol I [J Monet Econ (Suppl):19–46]
Lucas RE Jr (1977) Understanding business cycles, Studies in business cycle theory. MIT Press, Cambridge, pp 215–239
Minsky HP (1964) Longer waves in financial relations: financial factors in the more severe depressions. Am Econ Rev 54(3):324–3335
Minsky HP (1992a) The capital development of the economy and the structure of financial institutions. The Jerome Levy economics institute of bard college working paper no. 72. Available via http://www.levyinstitute.org/pubs/wp72.pdf
Minsky HP (1992b) The financial instability hypothesis. The Jerome Levy economics institute of bard college working paper no. 74. Available via http://www.levyinstitute.org/pubs/wp74.pdf
Minsky HP (1996) Uncertainty and the institutional structure of capitalist economies. The Jerome Levy economics institute of bard college working paper no. 155. Available via http://www.levyinstitute.org/pubs/wp155.pdf
Minsky HP (2008) Securitization. In: The Jerome Levy Economics Institute of Bard College (ed), Policy note. Available via http://www.levyinstitute.org/pubs/pn_08_2.pdf
Minsky HP, Delli Gatti D, Gallegati M (1994) Financial institutions, economic policy, and the dynamic behaviour of the economy. The Levy economics institute of bard college working paper no. 126. Available via http://www.levyinstitute.org/pubs/wp126.pdf
Montgomery MR (2006) The genesis of an idea: classical economics and the birth of monetary disequilibrium theory. In: Koppl R (ed) Money and markets: essays in honor of Leland B. Yeager. Taylor and Francis, Oxford, pp 126–142
Ohanian L (2010) The economic crisis from a neoclassical perspective. J Econ Perspect 24 (4):45–66
Patinkin D (1989) Money, interest and prices. MIT Press, Cambridge
Peltzman S (2000) Prices rise faster than they fall. J Polit Econ 108:466–502
Pensieroso L (2009) Real business cycle models of the great depression. IRES - Institut de Recherches Economiques et Sociales discussion papers. Available via http://www.storep.org/workshopdynamics/Pensieroso.pdf
Phelps E (1970) Microeconomic foundations of employment and inflation theory. Norton & Company, New York
Pigou AC (1943) The classical stationary state. Econ J LIII:343–351
Prescott EC (1986) Theory ahead of business cycle measurement. Q Rev. Federal Reserve Bank of Minneapolis (Fall):9–22
Sachs J (2009) Rethinking macroeconomics. Capital Soc 4(3), article 3. doi:10.2202/1932-0213.1065
Skidelsky R (2011) The relevance of Keynes. Camb J Econ 35(1):1–13
Solow RM (1980) Theories of unemployment. Am Econ Rev 70(1)
Verbrugge R (1998) A cross-county investigation of macroeconomic asymmetries. Economics working paper 9809017. Department of Economics, Virginia Polytechnic Institute and State University, Virginia. Available via http://128.118.178.162/eps/mac/papers/9809/9809017.pdf
Wray R (2011) Waiting for the next crash: the Minskyan lessons we failed to learn. Real-World Econ Rev 58, December. Available via http://www.paecon.net/PAEReview/issue58/whole58.pdf
Yellen JL (1984) Efficiency wages of unemployment. Am Econ Rev 74(2)

Part VI
Current Issues and Conclusions

Chapter 11
Current Issues and Policies

Victor A. Beker and Beniamino Moro

11.1 Introduction

In this chapter we illustrate the more recent problems that characterize the economic and financial situation of the three geographical areas we have dealt with in this book: Argentina, the USA, and Europe. Our analysis is updated until May 2015, and our focus is pointed on current issues and policies promoted in each of these areas, with a special emphasis toward the open problems that still remain unsolved.

The chapter is organized as follows. In Sect. 11.2, the case of Argentina's new debt restructuring in 2005 and again in 2010 is dealt with. Section 11.3 is devoted to an evaluation of the Dodd–Frank Act in the US, and to the need for a global lender of last resort. Section 11.4 deals with current issues and unsolved problems in Europe, particularly in the Eurozone.

Among these, in Sect. 11.4.1 we analyze the EMU's crisis-hit countries assistance programs, while in Sect. 11.4.2 the unsuccessful results of the first two assistance programs in Greece are dealt with. In Sect. 11.4.3 we illustrate some remaining EMU's institutional matters. We also discuss if the ECB can assume the role of lender of last resort for the sovereign debts in Sect. 11.4.4 and the recent quantitative easing monetary policy implemented by the ECB in Sect. 11.4.5. Finally, in Sect. 11.4.6 we conclude with an assessment of the legacy of the Eurosystem crisis.

Anticipating the main conclusion, we share the view that the resilience of the Eurozone in the long run depends on the continuing process of political unification,

V.A. Beker (✉)
University of Belgrano and University of Buenos Aires, Buenos Aires, Argentina
e-mail: victor.beker@ub.edu.ar

B. Moro (✉)
Department of Economics and Business, University of Cagliari, Viale San Ignazio 17, 09123 Cagliari, Italy
e-mail: moro@unica.it

B. Moro, V.A. Beker, *Modern Financial Crises*, Financial and Monetary Policy Studies 42, DOI 10.1007/978-3-319-20991-3_11

which must proceed hand in hand with the creation of a fiscal union. Such a political unification is needed because the Eurozone has dramatically weakened the power and legitimacy of member states' governments and left a vacuum in their place instead of creating a supranational government.

This would also imply the creation of a supranational fiscal risk-sharing mechanism that could insure European countries against very severe downturns like that caused by the Great Crisis.

11.2 Argentina: The New 2014 Default

In 2005 Argentina restructured its debt with a significant reduction which was accepted by 76 % of the creditors and resumed payment to them. In 2010 a second debt swap was offered which was accepted by another 17 % of the creditors. So, only 7 % of the bondholders rejected the terms of the debt exchanges, among them the so-called vulture funds.

Between 2009 and 2011, two of them—NML Capital and Aurelius—together with other individual holdouts, sued in federal court in New York for full payment of 1.3 billion dollars in Argentine bonds that had acquired in 2008 at 20–30 % of their nominal value.

The district judge Thomas P. Griesa ruled that Argentina could not pay the creditors who had accepted its restructuring until it fully paid—including past interest—those who had rejected it. According to him, the country could not pay only those who cooperated with the 2005 and 2010 restructurings and ignore the rest.

However, if Argentina paid 100 % of what the holdouts were owed in principal and accrued interest, as the district court ruled, the bondholders who agreed to the 2005 and 2010 restructurings could invoke the "most favored creditor clause" included in the debt exchange contract and demand the same treatment. This amounted more than USD100 billion—Argentina's Central Bank reserves totaled at that time only USD29 billion. So, in practical terms, the ruling became of impossible compliance until December 31, 2014, when the "most favored creditor clause" expired.

Many lawyers considered that the ruling was surprisingly harsh, marking the first time a US judge had issued such an injunction based on a peculiar interpretation of the so-called "pari passu" clause that states that all bondholders must be treated equally. In this case, the clause has been interpreted by the court as meaning that a debtor cannot make individual payments on a loan unless it is current on all payments under that loan. In an open letter to the US Congress, 100 international economists warned that the ruling "can torpedo an existing agreement with those bondholders who chose to negotiate", thus threatening future debt restructurings.

The US judicial ruling that the holdouts must be paid before bondholders forced Argentina to miss bond payments on July 30, 2014. Although Argentina transferred the payment in question, the US judge ordered the Bank of New York Mellon not to transfer the money to the creditors. This in turn caused Argentina to be declared in selective default by Standard & Poor's and in restricted default by Fitch. Both terms indicate that Argentina had defaulted on one or more of its financial commitments but continues to meet others.

The US court ruling pushed Argentina to a new default on its total public debt. In fact, the judge blocked any payment to bondholders unless the country also paid to the vulture funds favored by his ruling. It was expected this default to be a short one. As of January 1, 2015, an arrangement would be more likely to be made once the "most favored creditor" clause expired. In the meantime it aggravated the country's already bad economic situation.

The default meant that in spite of settling the ICSID arbitral awards against the country which remained unpaid, reaching an agreement to pay Repsol for the expropriation of YPF and with the Paris Club on outstanding debt, Argentina still had no access to international capital markets it badly needed.

After growing by an average of 5.6 % from 2005 to 2013, the rate of growth was negative in 2014. Commercial credit lines were cut off, investment dropped, and access to dollars was further strangled, which will unleash new restrictions on imports. Of course, this was not the sole result of the default. It only worsened existing problems: an increasing use of the inflation tax by the government, growing macroeconomic imbalances and exchange and trade controls which have long made it hard to get hold of primary materials, and stifling production.

However, the fact that less than 1 % of the creditors can put at risk an agreement settled with 93 % of the bondholders calls for international action on this issue.

A Sovereign Debt Restructuring Mechanism is badly needed to avoid this situation to repeat in the future. Another alternative is the creation of a forum for debt renegotiation, along the lines of the Paris Club (for long-term, bilateral government debt of poor countries) and the London Club (for debt owed to banks). A first step in this direction has been for developing countries to include collective action clauses (CACs) into sovereign bond contracts. This clause allows a supermajority of bondholders to agree to a debt restructuring that is legally binding on all holders of the bond, including those who vote against the restructuring.[1]

[1] Edwards (2015) uses data on 180 sovereign defaults to analyze what determines the recovery rate after a debt restructuring process. Why do creditors recover, in some cases, more than 90 %, while in other cases they recover less than 10 %? He finds support for the Grossman and Van Huyk (1985) model of "excusable defaults": countries that experience more severe negative shocks tend to have higher "haircuts" than countries that face less severe shocks. Edwards discusses in detail debt restructuring episodes in Argentina, Chile, Uruguay, and Greece. The results suggest that the haircut imposed by Argentina in its 2005 restructuring was "excessively high." The other episodes' haircuts were consistent with Grossman and Van Huyk's model.

11.3 The USA After the 2007–2009 Crisis

11.3.1 The Dodd–Frank Act

In the USA, one of the main lessons taught by the crisis was the existence of misaligned economic incentives within mortgage securitization transactions as well as the financial system in general. Some steps were taken after 2008 to correct this situation. We list below six of these misalignments and mention the measures (in italics) already taken by the Dodd–Frank Act in order to deal with each of them.[2]

A comment on their limitations is included. A reference is also made to the compensation policies and the need to align them with the goal of avoiding excessive risk taking by financial institutions. Some additional pending issues are briefly mentioned in the following points:

1. The originators and securitizers seldom retained meaningful "skin in the game". These market participants received immediate profits with each deal while assuming that they faced little or no risk of loss if the loans defaulted. As a result, securitizers had very little incentive to maintain adequate lending and servicing standards. Moreover, an active market arose in selling and repackaging equity tranches in collateralized debt obligations, thereby removing all risk of loss from the original security issuer.

   The Dodd–Frank Act, passed in 2010, requires security issuers to retain no less than 5 % of the equity risk, so they have an incentive to more carefully choose the mortgages and other assets they include in the pool. However, asset-backed securities that are collateralized exclusively by residential mortgages that qualify as "Qualified Residential Mortgages" are exempted.
2. Since the servicers of securitized mortgages do not own the mortgages, they lack economic incentives to mitigate losses through effective loan restructuring.

   The Dodd–Frank Act called for banks to retain at least 5 % of the risk in the loans they originate. However, the so-called Qualified Residential Mortgages are exempted from this requisite.
3. Risk migrated into the so-called shadow banking system. For banks, once loans were securitized, they were off the balance sheet and no longer on the radar of many banks and bank regulators.

[2] The Dodd–Frank Act implements changes that, among other things, affect the oversight and supervision of financial institutions, provide for a new resolution procedure for large financial companies, create a new agency responsible for implementing and enforcing compliance with consumer financial laws, introduce more stringent regulatory capital requirements, effect significant changes in the regulation of over-the-counter derivatives, reform the regulation of credit rating agencies, implement changes to corporate governance and executive compensation practices, incorporate the Volcker Rule, require registration of advisers to certain private funds, and effect significant changes in the securitization market. Further comments on the Dodd–Frank Act from an economic point of view are exposed by Acharya et al. (2010).

The Dodd–Frank Act made provisions which go some way toward regulating the shadow banking system by stipulating that the Federal Reserve System would have the power to regulate all institutions of systemic importance. However, the 75 trillion global shadow banking system still remains mostly unregulated.

4. Lack of effective market discipline due to "too big to fail". Policymakers in several instances resorted to bailouts instead of letting these firms collapse into bankruptcy because they feared that the losses generated in a failure would cascade through the financial system, freezing financial markets and stopping the economy in its tracks. These fears were realized when Lehman Brothers filed for bankruptcy.

   With the benefit of this implicit safety net, these big institutions have been insulated from the normal discipline of the marketplace that applies to smaller banks and practically every other private company. This poses a moral hazard issue which has to be tackled by way of regulation.

   The Dodd–Frank Act created the Federal Stability Oversight Council (FSOC), chaired by the Treasury Secretary and made up of the other financial regulatory agencies, which is responsible for designating systemically important financial institutions (SIFIs). SIFIs are subject to heightened supervision and higher capital requirements. They are also required to maintain resolution plans and could be required to restructure their operations if they cannot demonstrate that they are resolvable.

   Banking companies with over $50 billion in assets are automatically considered SIFIs. Additionally the Dodd–Frank Act gives FSOC the authority to design as SIFI any nonbanking financial company that could pose a threat to the financial stability of the USA.

   The Dodd–Frank Act creates a new resolution authority for large financial institutions whose failure could threaten the US economy. This Orderly Liquidation Authority (OLA) replaces bankruptcies for affected financial institutions. The OLA strictly prohibits bailouts. It is expected that with bailout off the table, management will have a greater incentive to bring in an acquirer or new investors before failure, and shareholders and creditors will have more incentive to go along with such a plan in order to salvage the value of their claims.

   However, as the former FDIC's Chairman Sheila Bair (2011) warned, the tools provided by the Dodd–Frank Act will be effective only if regulators show the courage to fully exercise their authorities under the law. Unfortunately, the past experience shows that regulators acted too late, or with too little conviction, when they failed to use authorities they already had or failed to ask for the authorities they needed to fulfill their mission (ibid).

5. Insufficient capital standards. At the height of the crisis, the large financial institutions had too little capital to maintain market confidence in their solvency.

   The international Basel III agreement and Section 171—the Collins Amendment—of the Dodd Frank Act have increased the amount of bank capital with the purpose of ensuring that banks will be able to withstand future downturns.

   Experience will show if these levels are enough to keep financial institutions safe and avoid bank runs in the future.

6. Failures of the credit rating agencies. They were an essential input into the process of manufacturing vast quantities of triple-rated securities with attractive yields which turned out to be highly risky assets.

   The Dodd–Frank Act imposes a new regulatory scheme on rating agencies. It mainly directs the SEC to issue rules implementing the law and authorizes various studies of issues related to credit ratings. In August 2014, the SEC adopted new requirements for credit rating agencies. The new requirements address internal controls, conflicts of interest, disclosure of credit rating performance statistics, procedures to protect the integrity and transparency of rating methodologies, disclosures to promote the transparency of credit ratings, and standards for training, experience, and competence of credit analysts.

Time will tell if these reforms are enough to keep credit rate agencies transparent and free of conflicts of interest. In principle, they not seem to be enough to deal with such a big challenge. Excessive risk taking by financial institutions was a factor that significantly contributed to the incubation of the crisis. Compensation policies can play a useful role in reducing excessive risk taking.

In this respect, there are very interesting proposals by the president and CEO of the Federal Reserve Bank of New York, William C. Dudley. He argues that a well-designed compensation structure can help favorably tip the balance between maximizing benefits and risk taking by effectively extending the time horizon of senior management and material risk takers and by forcing them to more fully internalize the consequences of their actions. For example, as long as deferred compensation is set at a horizon longer than the life of the trade, this can ensure the firm's and the trader's incentives are aligned (Dudley 2014).

However, as Dudley argues, given that unethical and illegal behavior may take a much longer period of time to surface, a decade would seem to be a reasonable timeframe to provide sufficient time and space for any illegal actions or violations of the firm's culture to materialize and fines and legal penalties realized. The goal should be to incent senior management and the material risk takers to focus on maximizing the long-term "enterprise" value of the firm, not just the short-term share price. One mechanism which can contribute to this goal is to increase the relative size of the debt component of deferred compensation as one moves up the management ranks to the senior managers of the firm (ibid).

Dudley also proposes that a sizeable portion of a fine should be paid for out of the firm's deferred debt compensation. In other words, in the case of a large fine, the senior management and the material risk takers would forfeit their performance bond. This would increase the financial incentive of those individuals who are best placed to identify bad activities at an early stage or prevent them from occurring in the first place.

11.3.2 The Need for a Global Lender of Last Resort and the Interest Rate Risk

As we have seen in Chap. 3, the 2007–2009 crisis did not begin in the traditional banking system but instead was centered in the new shadow banking system. This was a quite unregulated system. The Group of Thirty has advanced some proposals to regulate the money market mutual funds, which compete with depository banks without being subject to any prudential regulation (Group of Thirty 2009).

Although money market funding is global, the collapse of shadow banking onto the traditional banking system was local, depending on which particular nationally domiciled bank had the responsibility of rolling over the money market funding of a given shadow banking entity (Mehrling 2014).

As the funding of the global shadow banking system was reliant on the Euro-dollar market, the question of a global lender of last resort was really a question about backstop for that market. The decision in October 2013 to establish permanent unlimited swap lines between the C6—the Fed, the European Central Bank, the Bank of Japan, the Bank of England, the Swiss National Bank, and the Bank of Canada—can be seen as a first step in the direction of creating such a global lender of last resort.

A lender of last resort is needed whenever everyone wants to sell risk exposure but no one wants to buy, even as the price of risky assets continues to fall. Central banks act as lenders of last resort purchasing these risky assets and putting so a lower bound to their quotation. The fact that central banks can help in this way by creating money reflects the fact that financial crisis are mainly a matter of liquidity (see Chap. 1, Sect. 1.2). However, when a solvency issue is at play, liquidity backstop is not sufficient and capital injection is required.

A final consideration is that credit intermediation is essentially the transformation of maturity and liquidity. Maturity mismatch is an inherent by-product of credit intermediation whereby short-term liabilities are transformed into long-term assets. Since the liability side of the bank balance sheet is typically shorter in duration than the asset side, banks tend to be adversely affected by rising interest rates.

During a prolonged period of very low short-term interest rates and a steep yield curve, institutions are tempted to make money by essentially borrowing short and lending long. However, structuring the bank portfolio in this way increases the institution's vulnerability to losses in the event of rising interest rates. This is a threat which looms on the horizon after the extended period of low interest rates that followed the 2008 crisis.

Banks should be induced to match the maturities and reprising dates of their assets and liabilities, keeping away from assuming high levels of interest rate risk. There is a need to limit the size of asset–liabilities mismatch by means of an increase in longer-term liabilities. Banks should be induced to try to mobilize more long-term resources to expand their lending limit for long-term loans.

11.4 Europe: Current and Open Issues

11.4.1 The EMU's Crisis-Hit Countries Assistance Programs

We now turn our attention to Europe. It is an opinion shared by many economists that the Eurozone is an "imperfect currency union" lacking effective mechanisms of fiscal transfer and sufficient levels of labor mobility at the interstate level (Pisani-Ferri et al. 2013; Sapir et al. 2014).

In this context, faced with the risk of a euro breakdown, policymakers adopted austerity measures whose impact in terms of economic growth is highly controversial and risks are pro-cyclical.[3]

We discuss these problems in this section, beginning with the financial assistance granted to the Eurozone crisis-hit countries in exchange of an implementation of an economic adjustment program whose aim was to regain the international competitiveness of these countries.

In May 2010, Greece became the first euro area country to receive financial assistance from the EU and the IMF. The financial assistance was combined with a commitment to implement an economic adjustment program that was designed in discussions between the national authorities and the so-called Troika, consisting of the European Commission (EC), the European Central Bank (ECB), and the International Monetary Fund (IMF).

On November 21, 2010, Ireland became the second euro area country to request financial assistance, followed by Portugal in April 2011. Roughly 2 years later, in March 2013, Cyprus also applied for financial assistance.

What makes all four programs special is the fact that they were undertaken within a monetary union. This had a number of important implications. First, the exchange rate was permanently fixed and no competitive devaluation was possible, in contrast to many IMF programs outside monetary union (Pisani-Ferri et al. 2013, 37). Although potential growth crucially relies on structural competitiveness factors, an initial exchange rate devaluation could have "jump started" the economy of program countries, alleviating the short-term consequences of fiscal retrenchment (Svensson 2001).

Second, the monetary union had led to a large increase in cross border financial integration and capital flows. The large lending flows via the banking system led to the buildup of larger cross border financial exposures and also permitted the financing of extraordinarily large external debt levels. Average external debt levels of close to 100 % of GDP at the beginning of the programs were more than twice as

[3] To end the euro crisis and return the Eurozone countries to healthy growth rates of income and employment, Feldstein (2015) proposes to adopt revenue neutral fiscal incentives by the individual Eurozone countries, while Alesina et al. (2015) show that fiscal adjustments based upon cuts in spending appear to have been much less costly, in terms of output losses, than those based upon tax increases, and the difference between the two types of adjustment is very large.

high as external debt levels in typical IMF program countries. The resulting financial contagion made debt restructuring more difficult.

Third, the common central bank, the ECB, provided large amounts of financing to the banking systems of member countries and thereby prevented that the balance of payment crisis turned into a full-blown funding crisis and a meltdown of the financial system, which eventually would have meant the introduction of a new currency in one or more crisis-hit countries.

Sapir et al. (2014) provide a systematic evaluation of financial assistance for Greece, Ireland, Portugal, and Cyprus. All four programs, and in particular the Greek one, are very large financially compared to previous IMF's programs, because macroeconomic imbalances and the loss of price competitiveness that were accumulated by crisis-hit countries appeared exceptional (see Chap. 5, Sect. 5.5).

Yet programs were based on far too optimistic assumptions about adjustment and recovery in Greece and Portugal. In all four countries, unemployment increased much more significantly than expected. Although fiscal targets were broadly respected, debt-to-GDP ratios ballooned in excess of expectations due to sharp GDP contraction.

The GDP deterioration was due to four factors: larger-than-expected fiscal multipliers; a poorer external environment, including an open discussion about euro area breakup; an underestimation of the initial challenge; and the weakness of administrative systems and of political ownership. The focus of surveillance of conditionality evolved from fiscal consolidation to growth-enhancing structural measures.

The Greek program is the least successful one. Ireland successfully ended the program in December 2013, but problems remain in the banking system. Exit from the Portuguese program in May 2014 was accompanied by a precautionary credit line. It is too early to make pronouncements on the Cypriot program, which only started in May 2013, but it can safely be said that there have been major collective failures of both national and EU institutions in the run-up of the program (Sapir et al. 2014).

The Troika programs stand out compared to typical IMF programs because of their exceptionally long durations and the exceptionally large size of the financial assistance packages. One reason for this is that the buildup of imbalances in all economies at the start of the program was much more significant than in typical IMF program countries. Another one is that, unlike many IMF programs, official assistance entirely substituted markets in the financing of sovereign borrowing needs.

Economic and social hardship remains severe in all countries. However, assessment cannot stop there and has to be based on a comparison between reasoned expectations and outcomes. Against this yardstick, the programs have so far been successful, though subject to risks, in two of the four countries under international financial assistance, Ireland and Portugal, which regained access to financial markets, not yet completely successful in Cyprus, and completely unsuccessful in Greece, which is on a totally different trajectory to the other Eurozone countries.

In the first two countries, Ireland and Portugal, we can say that the programs have been successful in some ways and unsuccessful in others. The main success has been in the current account, with deficits shrinking much faster than expected. Although depending on the country concerned, the reasons for this are either encouraging (an improvement in exports) or discouraging (a collapse of imports because of the recession).

Cyprus has outperformed Greece in implementing reforms and is now on track to exit its €10 bn bailout program ahead of schedule. Anyway, it still faces the threat of nonperforming loans, which are at €23 bn, well in excess of the island's total output of €17 bn. These are seen as the bigger obstacle to financing the local economy. At close to half of banks' total lending and still on the rise, the nonperforming loans are also viewed as the greatest challenge to the Cypriot banking system.

The high level of nonperforming loans remains the major not completely solved problem to address also for Ireland, which has a potential to be the fastest-growing Eurozone country in 2015 (3.9 % according to IMF's spring forecast). The more forthcoming collectively borrowers and the lenders can be in addressing nonperforming loans, the faster the banking sector will restart and the more they can create room on their balance sheet to extend new loans to the economy. Ireland is a country that has been hit extremely hard by the crisis, but it made a lot of efforts and is now starting to reap the fruits of these efforts. It has reaped benefits not only in terms of growth but also in terms of restoring market access and lowering the cost of government funding (Cœuré 2015).

In Greece, early assumptions by the Troika about the ability of the economy to adjust and of the Greek political–administrative system to implement program measures proved unrealistic. By contrast, the Irish and Portuguese programs were based on more realistic assumptions, and implementation of program conditionality was much better.

The four countries under financial assistance have by and large adopted the austerity measures prescribed to them by the Troika. In structural terms they all implemented significant consolidation efforts. They had little choice since lender countries were unwilling to provide more financing. The alternative to austerity would have been debt restructuring.

In the Greek case, earlier restructuring would have been preferable, at least from a Greek point of view. In the Irish case, the bail-in of senior bank bondholders might have been desirable from the Irish point of view. But it would have improved the program's sustainability far less than in Greece, and it could have had significant negative implications for the funding of Irish banks.

In the absence of expansionary measures elsewhere in the euro area, austerity measures in program countries, the loss of confidence in the euro, and the fragmentation of the euro financial system (see Chap. 6, Sects. 6.5 and 6.6) severely depressed growth. The recession was deeper or much deeper than anticipated. Together with the collapse of labor-intensive sectors such as construction, this also implied that unemployment increased far more than anticipated.

Compared to earlier IMF programs, the drop in GDP and the slow adjustment in the real exchange rate in all the four euro area countries under financial assistance were exceptional, but this is also true for Italy and Spain.

11.4.2 The Unsuccessful Results of the First Two Assistance Programs in Greece: Is There a Third Bailout Coming?

In Greece, this situation risks jeopardizing the sustainability of the countries' necessary adjustment. Moreover, even if the Greek debt restructuring was the largest in history, Greece still remains an open problem. In fact, ever since the euro crisis erupted in late 2009, Greece has been at its heart. It was the first country to receive a bailout, in may 2010. It also was the subject of repeated debate over a possible departure from the single currency (the so-called Grexit) in 2011, again in 2012, and once more in 2015, after Syriza, the far-left Populist Party led by Alexis Tsipras, won the political elections in January.

At its root, the problem with Greece is simple but dramatic. Greece does not have enough money to pay its bills. Since the financial crisis began, its economy has shrunk by more than any other Eurozone economy. Between 2008 and 2014, nominal GDP fell by 22 %, much more than any other European country. House prices are down by around 40 % since 2008, and median income fell by 22 % between 2008 and 2014.

After a first bailout it received in 2010 (for a total of €110 bn), Greece received a second one in 2012 (€130 bn). This shifted most of its debts from old private to new public creditors, but, despite losses imposed on some private sector lenders, it did little to lower the whole debt. At the end of 2009, Greece owed €301 bn (127 % of GDP) mainly to private sector. In 2015 it owes €316 bn (175 % of GDP), most of which is now owned by European institutions (€187.5 bn), the ECB (€26 bn), and the IMF (€32.5 bn). Only €70 bn is owned by private sector.[4]

[4] Forni and Pisani (2013) assess the macroeconomic effects of a sovereign restructuring in a small economy belonging to a monetary union by simulating a dynamic general equilibrium model. In line with the empirical evidence, they make the following three key assumptions: first, sovereign debt is held by domestic agents and by agents in the rest of the monetary union; second, after the restructuring the sovereign borrowing rate increases and its increase is fully transmitted to the borrowing rate paid by the domestic agents; and third, the government cannot discriminate between domestic and foreign agents when restructuring. They show that the macroeconomic effects of the restructuring depend on (a) the share of sovereign bonds held by residents in the country as compared to that held by foreign residents, (b) the increase in the spread paid by domestic agents, and (c) its net foreign asset position at the moment of the restructuring. Their results also suggest that the sovereign restructuring implies persistent reductions of output, consumption, and investment, which can be large, in particular if the share of public debt held domestically is large, the private foreign debt is high, and the spread paid by the government and the households does increase.

In 2014, Greece seemed to be on the mend: after 6 years of recession, unemployment appeared to have peaked and the economy had started to grow. But in January 2015 something went wrong, after Syriza won the vote on the promise of a strong anti-austerity program. On the contrary, austerity programs were a condition of the bailouts and for receiving financial assistance from the EU, the ECB, and the IMF (the so-called Troika). Soon after he won the elections, Tsipras applied for a substantial restructuring of Greek public debt and also asked for a substantial debt haircut.

On February 11, 2015, the Eurogroup of financial ministers of the 19 Eurozone countries met in Brussels to find a way out of the latest phase of the Greek crisis. They agreed, in disarray with Tsipras's request, that Greece should have respected the existing assistance procedures and should have applied the Troika of EU-ECB-IMF for an extension of the old assistance program, which was going to expire on February 28.

Even countries like France and Italy, who might otherwise be sympathetic to Mr. Tsipras's anti-austerity message, ruled out debt haircuts, not least because they would lose out themselves. Further, the ECB autonomously decided to cut off its main extraordinary line of support to Greek banks, which meant that Greece in a few days should not have had the money to pay public servants.

Greece's new public creditors (EU, ECB, and IMF) are both generous and demanding. They decided that the country's interest rate paid to them should have been slashed: its total interest rates payments in 2014 were just 2.6 % of GDP, lower than several less indebted European countries.

But the money comes with conditions aimed at stabilizing Greece's finances. These include cuts to Greece's minimum wage and pensions, layoffs of civil servants, and the privatization of various assets, including ports and state-owned buildings. Creditors like Germany hope the package will make Greece more competitive and thus spur economic growth, as well as generating a budget surplus to be used to pay down debt.

Before the old assistance program expired on February 28, Greece agreed to talk to its creditors to find a way out of its international bailout and applied to the Eurogroup for a temporal extension of the old program to agree a new solution to the crisis.

The Eurogroup reiterated its appreciation for the remarkable adjustments efforts undertaken by Greece over the last years and agreed an extension of 4 months of the old program to gain time and prepare for a possible new third bailout of between €30 and 50 bn.

The resolution was approved in exchange of a strong commitment of Greek authorities "to a broader and deeper structural reform process, aimed at durably improving growth and employment prospects, ensuring stability and resilience of the financial sector and enhancing social fairness."

The authorities also committed "to implementing long overdue reforms to tackle corruption and tax evasion, and improving efficiency of the public sector". The Greek authorities should have reiterate "their unequivocal commitment to honour their financial obligations to all their creditors fully and timely". Further, the Greek authorities should "have also committed to ensure the appropriate primary fiscal surpluses or financing proceeds required to guarantee debt sustainability in line with the November 2012 Eurogroup statement".[5]

Finally, the Greek authorities also committed to refrain from any rollback of measures and unilateral changes to the policies and structural reforms that would negatively impact fiscal targets, economic recovery, or financial stability, as assessed by the institutions.

With respect to the electoral promises, it is obvious that Mr. Tsipras could hardly hide from his own radical supporters the fact that he had made a series of painful climb-downs.

First, he had abandoned his Syriza party's preelection pledge to write off a big chunk of Greece's sovereign debt and hence draw a line under 5 years of harsh austerity imposed by the hated "Troika". But he had no choice, because he needed new money to escape default.

Add that Athens bankers were already worried by a steady outflow of deposits: close to €20 bn had been withdrawn in the first 2 months of 2015. If a deal had fallen through, capital controls would have been imposed, bringing a renewed threat of "Grexit" from the euro.[6]

That prospect has receded for the moment, but Greece is still on a knife-edge. Despite the insistence that Syriza's electoral program was still on track, the list of tax, revenue, and structural measures he proposed to "the institutions", as the Troika was renamed to soothe voters, looked familiar with those accepted by the previous center-right government.

There are plenty of obstacles along the way, as Syriza also promised its creditors not to roll back reforms already in place. But sticking to that would mean abandoning plans which are cherished by its voters, such as relaunching collective wage bargaining and raising the minimum monthly wage to €750, the precrisis level.

11.4.3 Some Remaining Institutional Matters

Turning to institutional matters, EU–IMF cooperation clearly played an important role in the design, monitoring, and, ultimately, the implementation of the crisis-hit countries programs.

Though fraught with many potential problems, EU–IMF cooperation to deal with the crisis was inevitable in euro area countries. From the EU side, despite various political misgivings, recourse to the IMF was necessary because the EU lacked expertise on, and experience of, crisis funding and also lacked sufficient trust in its own institutions to act alone.

---

[5] "Eurogroup statement on Greece," approved on 20 February 2015.

[6] "Greece and the euro: Doing the splits," *The Economist*, February 28, 2015.

Despite a number of tensions stemming from their different logic and rules, the EU and the IMF succeeded in cooperating in Ireland and Portugal, much less in Greece. The issue on which Troika members disagreed most was the risk of financial spillovers between euro area countries, which led to divergent views about the Greek debt restructuring and about imposing losses on senior bondholders of Irish banks, two options that the IMF viewed favorably.

Pisani-Ferri et al. (2013) evaluation of the functioning of the Troika reveals a number of problems for each of its members, which give rise to a number of reform proposals.

First, they argue that the European Commission's dual role, as an agent of the European Stability Mechanism (ESM) and the Eurogroup, from one side, and as a European Union institution, from the other, is problematic and can lead to conflicts of interest. Therefore, they propose that, eventually, the role should shift to a European Monetary Fund (EMF), which would replace the ESM and would be a true EU institution. A narrowly mandated agency would also be less exposed to different policy objectives.

Second, the ECB is involved in the Troika in liaison with the European Commission. It does not offer program assistance per se but provides crucial liquidity assistance to banks in program countries. Therefore, ECB participation in the Troika is necessary for it to have access to full information and to retain the ability to voice concerns.

Yet, its role should not be one of a full negotiating partner because of potential conflicts of interest. Currently, the ECB does not publish independent documents on the programs but it does cosign mission statements. Pisani-Ferri et al. (2013) recommend that it discontinues cosigning such statements and behaves as a "mostly silent" participant in the Troika.

Third, the IMF has become much more involved in the euro area operationally and financially than deemed sustainable by its shareholders. Pisani-Ferri et al. (2013) envisage possible evolutions of its role and conclude that it should become a "catalytic lender" whose participation in programs would be desirable, as long as the euro area has not set up an EMF and become a member of the IMF but that could abstain from taking part without putting the whole package in jeopardy.

In concrete terms, this would imply limiting IMF participation to about 10 % of total financing. More generally, Pisani-Ferri et al. (2013) regard EU–IMF cooperation as an important template for future cooperation between global and regional financial institutions. In this respect, the euro area crisis is an important test of the feasibility of such cooperation.

11.4.4 Has the ECB the Role of Lender of Last Resort?

In the European monetary union (EMU), all these major events characterized the evolution of the crisis, not only for those economies that entered in a financial assistance program but also for all the other member states. In fact, the Eurozone sovereign debt and banking crises have exposed the structural weaknesses of the Eurozone. These structural weaknesses are intrinsic to a monetary union and depend on the fact that the EMU countries issue debt in a currency, the euro, over which they have no control.

As a result, when a recession hits and public finances deteriorate, market panic can be set in motion, leading to large surges in the government bond spreads and a sudden stop in liquidity provision, forcing governments of Eurozone countries into quick and intense austerity (see Chap. 1, Sect. 1.3, and Chap. 8, Sect. 8.6). In stand-alone countries, these surges in spreads and sudden stops are avoided because of the existence of national central banks that will provide liquidity in times of crisis (De Grauwe and Ji 2015; De Grauwe 2011).

In this regard, an important side issue of the debate on the tasks usually attributed to central banks is the discussion if the ECB can behave as a lender of last resort. According to De Grauwe and Ji (2015), as illustrated in Chap. 5, Sect. 5.4, the structural weakness of the Eurozone countries arises from the absence of a back-stop, that is, a lender of last resort, in the government bond markets, making sovereign debts in the Eurozone vulnerable to market sentiments of fear and panic.

When these sentiments surge, they can lead to self-fulfilling liquidity crises characterized by sharp increases in the government bond rates, sudden stops in liquidity in the government bond markets, and intense austerity measures. As these crises typically erupt when the economy experiences a downturn, these austerity measures have the effect of switching off the automatic stabilizers in the government budget. As a result, the economic recessions are made more intense and can lead to social and political instability in the countries concerned (De Grauwe and Ji 2015).

Against this dangerous evolution of the crisis, Eurozone countries have successfully taken political as well as technical measures. From a political point of view, as we pointed out in Chap. 6, Sect. 6.5, since 2012 the European Council of the heads of states and governments of the EU approved the creation of a banking union and a unified banking supervision housed within the ECB. They also approved to create a common deposit insurance for households and a common bank resolution rule. Finally, they decided to move toward a fiscal union and more political integration and that troubled countries and their banking systems could directly access to Eurozone rescue funds (EFSF, EFSM, and ESM).

Over the following months, many steps forward have been taken toward an effective governance of the Eurozone in order to guarantee financial stability, through the signature of the Treaty on Stability, Coordination, and Governance (also known as the Fiscal Compact), the Six Pack, and the Two Pack Agreements.

To complement this policy, not less important for overcoming the crisis and stabilizing the European financial markets were the technical measures decided by the ECB. These include first, the approval, between December 2011 and February 2012, of two unconventional long-term refinancing operations (LTRO) for a total of more than €1.000 bn at a fixed rate of 1 %, maturing 3 years later; second, president Mario Draghi's announcement in July 2012 that the ECB would have done "whatever it takes" to preserve the euro and to struggle the crisis; third, the ECB's approval, on September 6, 2012, of the Outright Monetary Transactions (OMT) program, under which the Bank decided to engage in buying in secondary markets unlimited sovereign bonds of troubled countries, with a maturity of between 1 and 3 years; and fourth, the ECB's announcement, on January 22, 2015, to proceed with nonconventional monetary policies yet decided some months before and, among them, to engage in a full quantitative easing monetary policy.[7]

11.4.5 The ECB's Quantitative Easing Monetary Policy

A quantitative easing (Qe) monetary policy was due to combat the increasing risks of deflation in the euro area. In fact, the headline rate of inflation stayed below 1 % throughout 2014, reaching the negative sign of −0.2 % in December and −0.6 % in January 2015, while the bank's goal rate is of almost 2 %. A prolonged spell of "low inflation" which tends to become deflation is bad for the area because many of its member states are weighed down by excessive public and private debt. If outright deflation were to take grip, it would arm borrowers, because when prices fall, the real burden of debt increases.

Furthermore, the ECB could no longer help by cutting interest rates. It lowered its main lending rate in September 2014 to just 0.05 %, while charging banks on deposits they leave with it, through a negative rate of 0.2 %. The ECB had hoped to reverse the shrinking of its balance sheet, after commercial banks reimbursed their 2011–2012 LTROs, through another more extended round of long-term funding operations, providing liquidity until 2018 at a fixed rate of just 0.15 % a year. But the first two of eight ECB's planned lenders have been a disappointment: in September and December 2014, banks borrowed only €212 bn, little more than half the €400 bn available.[8]

So, the only way for the ECB to expand the size of its own balance sheet, which it intended returning at least to the high of €3.000 bn that it reached in early 2012, after the successful two extraordinary LTROs of December 2011 and February 2012 just mentioned above, was to proceed without further delay with Qe. The aim

[7] Friedman (2014) argues that one of the two forms of hitherto unconventional monetary policy that many central banks have implemented in response to the 2007 financial crisis—large-scale asset purchases or, to put the matter more generically, the use of the central bank's balance sheet as a distinct tool of monetary policy—is likely to become part of the standard toolkit of monetary policymaking in normal times as well. As intended, these purchases have lowered long-term interest rates relative to short-term rates and lowered interest rates on more-risky compared to less-risky obligations. Moreover, their introduction fills a conceptual vacuum that has long stood at the heart of monetary policy analysis and implementation. In contrast to the last century or more of monetary theory, which has focused on central banks' liabilities, the basis for the effectiveness of central bank asset purchases turns on the role of the asset side of the central bank's balance sheet. The implications for monetary theory are profound.

[8] Anyway, Neri and Ropele (2015) share the opinion that the accommodative monetary policy stance of the ECB helped to moderate the negative effects of the sovereign debt tensions.

of the Bank is to reach the size of its own balance sheet of €3.000 bn in 2016 and €3.700 bn in 2017.

To reach these aims, the ECB has engaged in an expanded asset purchase program announced on January 22, 2015, which consists of combined monthly purchases of €60 bn each month in public and private sector securities, beginning March 9, 2015, and lasting at least until September 2016. These purchases are intended under the public sector purchase program (PSPP) of marketable debt instruments issued by euro area central governments, certain agencies located in the euro area, or certain international or supranational institutions.

Therefore, the ECB is now engaged in a full Qe monetary policy, which adds the purchase of sovereign bonds to its existing private sector asset purchase programs, in order to address the risks of a too prolonged period of low inflation.[9]

All these decisions are aimed at fulfilling the ECB's price stability mandate, which consists in achieving inflation rates below, but close to, 2 % over the medium term. The EBC is buying bonds issued by euro area central governments, agencies, and European institutions in the secondary market against central bank money, which the institutions that sold the securities can use to buy other assets and extend credit to the real economy. In both cases this contributes to an easing of financial conditions.[10]

There are two main channels through which Qe is likely to work in the euro zone. One is the "signaling" effect that the ECB is sending a clear message to markets and to firms that it is determined to bring inflation closer to 2 %. The other is through the exchange rate. The euro has already been weakening since spring 2014, and it is expected to reach the parity with the dollar, after it reached the exchange rate of 1.08 on March 2015. A sharp drop in the euro is considered very important for recovery in the Eurozone.

In regard to the risk sharing, which implies the sharing of hypothetical losses in the extreme event of a full uncooperative euro breakup (see Chap. 6, Sect. 6.3), the ECB decided that purchases of securities of European institutions (EFSF, EFSM, and ESM), which will be 12 % of the additional asset purchases and which will be purchased by national central banks (NCBs), will be subject to loss sharing.

The rest of the NCBs' additional asset purchases will not be subject to loss sharing. As the ECB will hold 8 % of the total asset purchases, this implies that not more than 20 % of the additional asset purchases will be subject to a regime of risk sharing.

[9] The ECB's Qe program, which will encompass the asset-backed securities purchase program and the covered bond purchase program, both launched in 2014, as just mentioned in the text, will amount to €60 bn monthly. Starting on March 2015, it will be carried out until at least September 2016, for a total of bond purchases of €1140 bn. This figure compensates the ECB's withdrawal of about €1.000 bn out of the Eurozone economy as the result of banks repaying loans they had taken during the last 2 years of the debt crisis.

[10] Further details on the technicalities of ECB's Qe can be found in the articles by Bird (2015), Bird and Pozzebon (2015), ECB (2015b), Lynch (2015), WP (2015).

Until the first months of 2015, the whole ECB's monetary policy decisions have had two main effects: first, the harmonized long-term interest rates calculated by the ECB for convergence assessment purposes,[11] and based on the secondary market yields of government bonds with maturities of close to 10 years, have shrunk in all countries, except for Greece;[12] second, as mentioned above, they have had a significant effect on the exchange rate of the euro.

By increasing the supply of money base with a Qe policy, the ECB will certainly contribute to a further weakening of the euro vis-à-vis other currencies such as the dollar, the pound, and the yuan, thereby increasing exports and boosting inflation.

Can these decisions of the ECB be interpreted as corresponding to the behavior of a lender of last resort for public debts of Eurozone countries? The answer is no, because unlike other central banks (Fed, BoE, and BoJ), the ECB lacks a state: it is forbidden by the EMU's rules to buy public bonds in primary markets and to finance directly public deficits of member states (the no-bailout clause of Article 125 of the EU Treaty).

Anyway, the effects of these decisions on the stabilization and harmonization of European financial markets are very important, because of, at the least, a partial risk sharing among Eurozone countries.

There is much misunderstanding and fear regarding Qe, especially in Germany and some other northern countries. The credit ratings of the EMU countries vary from AAA in Germany to junk in Greece. If the ECB buys government bonds from countries like Greece, German taxpayers risk having to pay the bill if Greek politics sour further.

If Greece defaults, it will create a loss on the balance sheet of the ECB. The other member countries of the Eurozone, especially Germany, will then have to cover the loss. The fear that German taxpayers may be forced to cover future losses of the ECB has become the main reason why the ECB has waited so long to begin with Qe.

In fact, this fear is funded only for the 20 % of the additional asset purchases that will be subject to a regime of risk sharing, while for the remaining 80 % of purchases that will not, each of the NCBs is responsible for the purchases of their

[11] See https://www.ecb.europa.eu/stats/money/long/html/index.en.html.

[12] Some examples are illustrative: Italian bonds long-term interest rates (10-year government bond yields) decreased from 3.87 % in January 2014 to 1.70 % in January 2015, Ireland bonds from 3.39 % to 1.22 %, Spain bonds from 3.79 % to 1.54 %, Portugal bonds from 5.21 % to 2.49 %, France bonds from 2.38 % to 0.67 %, and Germany bonds from 1.76 % to 0.39 %. Only Greece bond yields augmented their 10-year rate of return from 8.18 % to 9.48 % in the same period. Anyway, Turner (2013) advises that an extended period of very low long-term interest rates and high public debt creates financial stability risks. Interest rate risk in the banking system has grown, and some institutional investors face significant exposures. Central banks in the advanced economies now hold a high proportion of bonds issued by their governments, most of which have so far failed to arrest the rise in the ratio of government debt to GDP. Implementing an effective exit strategy will be difficult. According to Turner, current policy frameworks should be reconsidered, with a view to clarifying the importance of the long-term interest rate for monetary policy, for financial stability, and for government debt management.

national government bonds. These are permitted to each NCB in proportion to the economic weight that each country has in the Eurozone (ECB 2015a, b).

Thus, German NCB buys 27 % (of total Qe) of German bonds, French NCB buys 20 % of French bonds, Italy NCB buys 18 % of Italian bonds, and so on. As long as these bonds are kept on the ECB's balance sheet, the governments of these countries pay interest to the ECB, which will then apply the rule of "juste retour", that is, it reimburses the same amounts to each of these governments. So, no fiscal transfers between member states occur. If one government were to default on its bonds, it would stop paying interest, but at the same time, applying the "juste retour" clause, it would not get any interest refund. Again there would be no fiscal transfer among Eurozone member states (De Grauwe 2015b).

In conclusion, the ECB's monetary policy for the time being remains a milestone of the well functioning of the EMU, even if it does not have a full role of lender of last resort. The recovery, since the double-dip recession between 2011 and 2014, has been weak and faltering, while deflation has tumbled.

The ECB has sought to combat deflation through a variety of means, including LTROs and negative interest rates on the deposit facility, to force banks to expand their credit to SMEs. But what it had yet not done was a massive Qe policy, similar to other central banks of most developed countries, which will boost its balance sheet, injecting money into the economy and stimulating activity.

The ECB's final goal is to boost recovery in all Eurozone countries, which remains the main device to regain a smooth and efficient functioning of the EMU.

11.4.6 The Legacy of the Euro Crisis and Conclusions

In a closed-door seminar held in Milan on March 13, 2015, De Grauwe (2015a) summarizes as follows the present state of the EMU: the Eurozone, which was built on the promise of progressive integration and harmonization of countries sharing the same currency, has instead gradually split into creditor and debtor nations. Debtor countries were left with internal devaluation, and this meant higher unemployment and wage shrinking. This, in turn, generated stagnation in the Eurozone as a whole.

Further, austerity meant that the rebalancing imposed on euro area countries was asymmetric: debtor nations had to adopt fiscal tightening, while creditor countries could continue in their "business as usual" model. This asymmetric adjustment mechanism supported a deflationary bias in the Eurozone. This is because, by expecting low economic growth, economic operators also expected low inflation and low interest rates. Moreover, austerity forced debtor countries to increase their savings, and the low level of consumption again pushed inflation downwards.

According to De Grauwe, the most striking feature of the legacy of the euro crisis is that, despite intense austerity programs that have been triggered since 2010, there is no evidence that such programs managed to increase the capacity of debtor countries to continue to service their own debt. On the contrary, deflation or persistently low inflation makes it harder to reduce debt burdens, because the nominal debt level remains very near the real debt level or even increases. At the same time, austerity-induced stagnation in economic growth cannot act through the denominator of the debt/GDP level.

As we have strongly emphasized in the final section of Chap. 6 for Germany, De Grauwe's contention is that a more symmetric fiscal adjustment, in which creditor nations properly stimulate their economies, would have reduced the price periphery countries have to pay to achieve a given improvement in their government budget balances. Therefore, first we need to solve the legacy of the euro crisis, and secondly we need to correct for design failures of the Eurozone.

In the first respect, the legacy of the crisis in the euro area has led to unsustainable debt levels in some debtor countries. According to De Grauwe, debt default and restructuring will be inevitable: the only question, then, is when to do it. A rational solution dictates that creditor nations accept a loss as soon as possible, in order to recover as much credit as possible from a defaulting debtor. The later they agree to do this, the less money they will recover from near-default countries such as Greece.

In fact, with respect to the evidence problem mentioned above, as we pointed out in Sect. 11.4.1 above, the financial assistance programs in crisis-hit countries have so far been successful, though subject to risks, in two of the four countries under international financial assistance, Ireland and Portugal, which regained access to financial markets; it was not yet completely successful in Cyprus, which anyway outperformed Greece in implementing reforms and is now on the track to exit its bailout program ahead of schedule; and it was completely unsuccessful only in Greece, which is on a totally different trajectory to the other Eurozone countries.

As far as the public debt service is concerned and De Grauwe's contention that a restructuring will be inevitable, we think that this is not the right solution, because after a first debt restructuring governments will be induced to over-borrow again and again. In fact, as it will be pointed out in Chap. 12, at the end of Sect. 12.1, the reason why governments tend to over-borrow, with limits set only by the probability of defaulting, is relatively straightforward. Governments' objective function is to maximize votes in the short run (next elections). Votes are positively correlated with public expenditure, because it always benefits some constituency and negatively correlated with taxes.

Therefore, debt is the straightforward way of transferring payments to future generations, and governments have too much incentive to maximize debt, only subject to the restrictions that the market imposes on them.[13]

[13] Fochmann et al. (2014) use a controlled laboratory experiment with and without overlapping generations to study the emergence of public debt. Public debt is chosen by popular vote, pays for public goods, and is repaid with general taxes. With a single generation, public debt is accumulated prudently, never leading to over-indebtedness. With multiple generations, public debt is accumulated rapidly as soon as the burden of debt and the risk of over-indebtedness can be shifted to future generations. Debt ceiling mechanisms do not mitigate the debt problem. With overlapping generations, political debt cycles emerge, oscillating with the age of the majority of voters.

In light of all this, how can we redesign the Eurozone? In this regard, we agree with De Grauwe's conclusion that there is no other alternative than to strongly increase coordination of macroeconomic policy among EMU countries. Ultimately, such coordination should bring about the completion of the banking union and the start of a real fiscal union. This in turn requires a real political union, following the principle of "no taxation without representation."

In the short run, what we need is monetary and fiscal expansion at the EU level. The ECB has started its quantitative easing program, and that is for the better. However, we still need fiscal policy to be managed, or at least coordinated, at the EU level.

To conclude with De Grauwe's words, the resilience of the Eurozone in the long run depends on the continuing process of political unification, which must proceed hand in hand with the creation of a fiscal union (Spolaore 2013). Such a political unification is needed because the Eurozone has dramatically weakened the power and legitimacy of member states' governments and left a vacuum in their place instead of creating a supranational government. This would imply the creation of a supranational fiscal risk-sharing mechanism that could insure European countries against very severe downturns like the last Great Crisis (Furceri and Zdzienicka 2013).[14]

References

Acharya V, Cooley TF, Richardson M, Sylla R, Walter I (2010) A critical assessment of the Dodd-Frank Wall Street reform and consumer protection act. Vox CEPR' policy portal, Nov 24. Available via http://www.voxeu.org/article/dodd-frank-critical-assessment

Alesina AF, Barbiero O, Favero CA, Giavazzi F, Paradisi M (2015) Austerity in 2009–2013. NBER working paper no. 20827, January. Available via http://www.nber.org/papers/w20827

Bair S (2011) Examining and evaluating the role of the regulator during the financial crisis an today, Statement before the house subcommittee on financial institutions and consumer credit. Mimeo Available via https://www.fdic.gov/news/news/speeches/archives/2011/spmay2611.html

Bird M (2015) The ECB just gave a major boost to Europe's growth forecast. Business Insider UK, Mar 5. Available via http://uk.businessinsider.com/european-central-bank-ecb-press-conference-march-2015-2015-3?r=US

[14] According to Guiso et al. (2015), entering a currency union without any political union, European countries have taken a gamble: will the needs of the currency union force a political integration (as anticipated by Jean Monnet) or will the tensions create a backlash, as suggested by Nicholas Kaldor, Milton Friedman, and many others? They try to answer this question by analyzing the cross-sectional and time series variation in pro-European sentiments in the EU 15 countries. They conclude that 1992 Maastricht Treaty seems to have reduced the pro-Europe sentiment as does the 2010 Eurozone crisis. Yet, in spite of the worst recession in recent history, the Europeans still support the common currency. Europe seems trapped: there is no desire to go backward and no interest in going forward, but it is economically unsustainable to stay still.

Bird M, Pozzebon S (2015) Europe's massive quantitative easing scheme just arrived – Here's everything you need to know. Business Insider UK, Jan 22. Available via http://uk.businessinsider.com/ecb-meeting-january-2015-2015-1#ixzz3TW4eChfk

Cœuré B (2015) Interview with the Irish times, Jan 16. Available via http://www.ecb.europa.eu/press/inter/date/2015/html/sp150116.en.html

De Grauwe P (2011) The European central bank: lender of last resort in the government bond markets? CESifo working paper no. 3569. Available via https://www.google.it/webhp?sourceid=chrome-instant&ion=1&espv=2&ie=UTF-8#q=7.+De+Grauwe+P.+(2011)%2C+%E2%80%9CThe+European+Central+Bank%3A+Lender+of+Last+Resort+in+the+Government+Bond+Markets%3F%E2%80%9D%2C+CESifo+Working+Paper+No.+3569

De Grauwe P (2015a) Eurozone in the Doldrums. The legacy of the eurocrisis. Closed-door workshop, ISPI-Milan, Mar 13. Available via http://www.ispionline.it/DOC/lecture_de_grauwe.pdf

De Grauwe P (2015b) The sad consequences of the fear of Qe. The Economist, Jan 21

De Grauwe P, Ji Y (2015) Has the eurozone become less fragile? Some empirical tests. CESifo working paper series no. 5163, Jan 26

Dudley WC (2014) Enhancing financial stability by improving culture in the financial services industry. Remarks at the workshop on reforming culture and behavior in the financial services industry, Federal Reserve Bank of New York, New York City. Available via http://www.ny.frb.org/newsevents/speeches/2014/dud141020a.html

ECB (2015a) Introductory statement to the press conference (with Q&A), Jan 22. Available via http://www.ecb.europa.eu/press/pressconf/2014/html/is140109.en.html

ECB (2015b) Press release: ECB announces expanded asset purchase programme, Jan 22. Available via http://www.ecb.europa.eu/press/pr/date/2015/html/pr150122_1.en.html

Edwards S (2015) Sovereign default, debt restructuring, and recovery rates: was the Argentinean 'Haircut' Excessive? NBER working paper no. W20964, February. Available via http://www.nber.org/papers/w20964

Feldstein MS (2015) Ending the euro crisis. NBER working paper no. W20862, Available via http://www.nber.org/feldstein/w20862.pdf

Fochmann M, Sadrieh A, Weimann J (2014) Understanding the emergence of public debt. CESifo working paper series no. 4820, May. Available via http://papers.ssrn.com/sol3/papers.cfm?abstract_id=2436292

Forni L, Pisani M (2013) Macroeconomic effects of sovereign restructuring in a monetary union: a model-based approach. IMF working paper no. 13/269, December. Available via https://www.imf.org/external/pubs/cat/longres.aspx?sk=41176.0

Friedman BM (2014) Has the financial crisis permanently changed the practice of monetary policy? Has it changed the theory of monetary policy? NBER working paper no. W20128, May. Available via http://www.nber.org/papers/w20128

Furceri D, Zdzienicka A (2013) The euro area crisis: need for a supranational fiscal risk sharing mechanism? IMF working paper no. 13/198, September. Available via http://papers.ssrn.com/sol3/papers.cfm?abstract_id=2342177

Grossman HI, Van Huyk JB (1985) Sovereign debt as a contingent claim: excusable default, repudiation, and reputation. NBER working paper no. 1673 (Also reprint no. r1244), July. Available via http://www.nber.org/papers/w1673

Group of Thirty (2009) Financial reform: a framework for financial stability. Available via http://www.group30.org/images/PDF/Financial_ReformA_Framework_for_Financial_Stability.pdf

Guiso L, Sapienza P, Zingales L (2015) Monnet's Error? NBER working paper no. w21121, April. Available via http://papers.ssrn.com/sol3/papers.cfm?abstract_id=2599387

Lynch R (2015) Quantitative easing imminent as ECB Boss Mario Draghi fires €1.1trn starting gun. The Independent, Mar 6

Mehrling P (2014) Why central banking should be re-imagined. BIS papers N° 79. Available via http://www.bis.org/publ/bppdf/bispap79i.pdf

Neri S, Ropele T (2015) The macroeconomic effects of the sovereign debt crisis in the euro area. Bank of Italy working paper no. 1007, Mar 27. Available via http://papers.ssrn.com/sol3/papers.cfm?abstract_id=2600900

Pisani-Ferri J, Sapir A, Wolff GB (2013) EU-IMF assistance to euro-area countries: an early assessment. Bruegel blueprint series, XIX

Sapir A, Wolf GB, De Susa C, Terzi A (2014) The Troika and financial assistance in the euro area: successes and failures. Studies on the request of the Economic and Monetary Affairs Committee, Directorate General for Internal Policies of the European Parliament, Economic Governance Support Unit (ed), February. Available via https://www.google.it/webhp?sourceid=chrome-instant&ion=1&espv=2&ie=UTF-8#q=4.+Sapir+A.,+G.+B.+Wolf,+C.+De+Sousa+and+A.+Terzi+(2014),+The+Troika+and+Financial+Assistance+in+the+Euro+Area:+Successes+and+Failures,+Studies+on+the+request+of+the+Economic+and+Monetary+Affairs+Committee,+Directorate+General+for+Internal+Policies+of+the+European+Parliament,+Economic+Governance+Support+Unit+(Ed.),+February&spell=1

Spolaore E (2013) What is European integration really about? A political guide for economists. CESifo working paper series no. 4283, June. Available via http://papers.ssrn.com/sol3/papers.cfm?abstract_id=2284804

Svensson LEO (2001) The zero bound in an open economy: a foolproof way of escaping from a liquidity trap. Monetary and economic studies (Special Edition), February. Available via http://www.hkimr.org/uploads/seminars/409/sem_paper_0_94_svensson-paper171202.pdf

Turner P (2013) Benign neglect of the long-term interest rate. BIS working paper no. 403, February. Available via http://papers.ssrn.com/sol3/papers.cfm?abstract_id=2247907

WP (2015) The European central bank: let the show begin. The Economist, Mar 5

Chapter 12
Open Problems and Conclusions

Victor A. Beker

> *Serial default on external debt—that is, repeated sovereign default—is the norm throughout every region in the world, even including Asia and Europe*
>
> (Reinhart and Rogoff 2008, p. 5)

12.1 Introduction

Experience shows that in every debt crisis, responsibility is shared between the debtor and the creditor. Usually, the former underestimates the probability of the worst states of nature occurring. Strikingly, creditors' assessments also have the same bias; not only individual investors but also private bankers have been excessively enthusiastic and insufficiently cautious in their willingness to lend large sums of money even though the prospects for being repaid were extremely doubtful. This reveals a misalignment of incentives with the public interest on both sides of the counter. On the one hand, lenders seem to be incentivized to excessive risk taking; on the other, borrowers are driven to over borrow.

If responsibilities are shared, it is natural to think that when a crisis occurs, the solution should come from efforts shared by both parties in the contract. Of course, the contribution of each party should be proportionate to its opportunity to foresee the result. It is one thing for a bank that can obtain advice and abundant information before taking its decisions; it is quite another for an individual borrower to do so.

In the three cases analyzed in this book—the Argentine crisis, the American financial crisis, and the European economic malaise—a common feature has been a huge misjudgment by investors regarding the risks actually involved. However, in at least two of the three cases, this misjudgment was induced by important actors in the financial world. In the case of Argentina, it was by the IMF backing the Convertibility program; in the case of the subprime mortgages, it was by the rating agencies' ratings.

V.A. Beker (✉)
University of Belgrano and University of Buenos Aires, Buenos Aires, Argentina
e-mail: victor.beker@ub.edu.ar

B. Moro, V.A. Beker, *Modern Financial Crises*, Financial and Monetary Policy Studies 42, DOI 10.1007/978-3-319-20991-3_12

The Eurozone case is a bit more complicated. In principle, there was a general assumption that the common currency automatically meant a common level of risk. With the exchange rate risk having disappeared, investors seemed to assume that sovereign default risks were negligible or that in the event that national situations got worse, governments would be bailed out by other Eurozone countries to forestall a breakup of the euro. In other words, the country-specific bankruptcy risk in Europe was either considered nearly negligible or Article 125, which states that no country or EU entity can assume responsibility for a member country's public debt, was not taken into due consideration by investors or expected to have a soft interpretation, thus allowing an in extremis bailout of debtor countries.

An example of this underestimation of country-specific bankruptcy risk can be found in a comment in a 2004 article. Speaking on cross-country differences in yields among Eurozone countries, the authors candidly qualified them as striking "as a sovereign default of any of these countries within 10 years seems far-fetched, given their economic history since World War 2" (Pagano and von Thadden 2004, 550).

This underestimation of default risks is rooted in two major mistakes. The first is a very common mistake of considering government bonds as nearly risk-free assets. As Reinhart and Rogoff (2009) have shown extensively, throughout history rich and poor countries alike have often defaulted on their public debts. Therefore, the historical evidence does not support that curiously extended belief.

A second mistake has to do with the creation of the Eurozone and its impact on default risk. With a national currency, a government facing a public debt crisis can turn to the central bank and order it to print money and buy up debt. A sovereign default can be avoided at the price of high inflation. In the Eurozone, national governments have transferred monetary sovereignty to the ECB, thereby closing this avenue. The implication is that in a monetary union the probability of a government default is higher—not smaller—than for an isolated individual country's government.

Although in the European case the role of rating agencies has been mainly emphasized in connection with the downgrading of European public debt after the onset of the crisis, for a long time the rating agencies gave overly generous ratings to assets that finally proved to be highly risky and, in the case of Greece, only downgraded them *after* the market has done so; this is the same as in the case of the US financial crisis. For instance, Table 12.1 shows S&P's mid-2006 ratings. The government debt of Ireland, a country where the banking crisis erupted in 2007, was still rated AAA. Greece had an A rating and Portugal was rated AA−.

A key issue for the future therefore is how to protect investors from risk misjudgment.

In each of the three cases that are analyzed in this book, some sort of veil obscured the risks that were really involved. The key issue then is to remove these veils and make financial markets much more transparent and accountable. Financial activity as a whole is a public good: systemic risks to financial institutions are risks for the economy as a whole. However, financial institutions per se have a perverse incentive to engage in excessive risk taking; the most aggressive institutions put

Table 12.1 Mid-2006 S&P rating

Austria	AAA
Belgium	AA+
Finland	AAA
France	AAA
Greece	A
Ireland	AAA
Italy	AA−
Netherlands	AAA
Portugal	AA−
Spain	AAA

Source Manganelli and Wolswijk (2007)

pressure on the rest of them, and just like bad money drives out good, bad financial institutions could drive out good ones. Financial regulation should pay attention to risks that are capable of damaging the financial system as a whole.

In the case of private agents, the tendency to over borrow has been modeled by Bianchi (2011) who shows how optimal borrowing decisions at the individual level can lead to over borrowing at the social level. Agents fail to internalize the general equilibrium effects of their borrowing decisions on prices. This is a pecuniary externality that arises due to the presence of financial frictions.

The reason why governments tend to over borrow is relatively straightforward; governments' objective function is to maximize votes. Votes are positively correlated with expenditures—they always benefit some constituency—and are negatively correlated with taxes. Debt is a way to transfer payments to future governments. Therefore, governments have every incentive to maximize debt subject only to the restrictions that the market imposes on them. In the real world, governments are clearly "debt biased", as Alesina and Tabellini (1990) noted.

Transparency in public accounts is a key issue in regard to monitoring the public debt. In this respect, an independent review agency responsible for conducting performance audits and studies on selected fiscal issues may be a useful instrument to ensure that transparency.

12.2 The Role of the IMF

As stated in Chap. 2 devoted to the Argentine case, the IMF played a key role in restoring confidence in Argentina's payment capacity by capital markets. In fact, the misjudgment by the IMF on the sustainability of the Convertibility regime played a key role in reopening Argentina's access to capital markets. The IMF erred in its assessment of the Argentine economy by underestimating the vulnerabilities of the currency board regime.

Although the IMF was initially reluctant to support the Convertibility regime as it was against the IMF's traditional recipe of a free-floating exchange rate, not only did it endorse it but also later on even advised other countries, primarily in Eastern Europe, to adopt it.

The IMF's continuous support of the Argentine program, even after the Tequila crisis showed the Argentine economy's high sensitivity to external flows, allowed the government to accumulate a huge debt long after it was evident that the currency board regime was quite unsustainable. That support can only be explained by the combination of political and ideological factors: Argentina had become a "star" country that was following most of the policies recommended by the so-called Washington Consensus.[1] It was considered that its free markets, deregulation, and privatization policies deserved the IMF's support despite the inconsistencies of the economic program.

Because of the weight that political and ideological arguments have in IMF decisions, as the Argentine case shows, the IMF is not a reliable source in which investors can be confident. This underlines the need for an independent source of assessment that is not subject to political or ideological influences. Unfortunately, the next candidate—credit rating agencies—delivered similar or even worse results than the IMF.

12.3 The Role of Credit Agencies' Ratings

Investors depend on credit ratings to determine the creditworthiness of the assets in which they invest. In the case of institutional investors, it may be argued that as highly sophisticated investors they have the capacity to produce their own internal risk analysis. If so, a rating agency's rating would be used only to corroborate the conclusions of their own studies.

However, as Keynes already suggested, even professional investment managers have a strong incentive to follow the herd because "it is better to fail conventionally than to succeed unconventionally" (Keynes 2008, 141).

However, there is another reason why it is hard to overstate the importance of the role played by credit rating agencies and their ratings: since the mid-1970s, statutes and regulations in the USA have increasingly come to depend explicitly on credit agencies' ratings and have therefore become regulatory licensors. It was then that rating agencies stopped selling ratings to investors and began charging the companies that issue the debt they rate.

Regulatory dependence on ratings created higher demand for them. However, in several cases ratings proved spectacularly inaccurate. Prominent examples include California's Orange County and Enron Corp., both of which were receiving high credit ratings until just before their filing for bankruptcy protection. Finally, rating

[1] "The IMF yielded to external political and market pressures to continue providing its support despite serious concerns over fiscal and external sustainability" (IMF 2003, 72).

agencies widely certified as nearly risk-free assets securities that were actually highly risky, as the events after 2007 overwhelmingly showed.

In Europe, following the so-called Basel II recommendations adopted in 2005, the Capital Requirements Directive introduced a new capital requirements framework for banks and investment firms. The use of credit assessments by External Credit Assessment Institutions was considered essential to the determination of risk weights.

In essence, it forced European banks and even the European Central Bank itself to rely on standardized assessments of credit risk provided by credit rating agencies. The new rules on regulation of credit rating agencies that were passed by the European Parliament in 2009 allow banks to use the ratings only for regulatory purposes.[2]

The fact that rating agencies are paid by the issuer indicates a conflict of interest. One alternative scheme is investor-pay rating agencies. However, it has been argued that such agencies may also be subject to potential pressure from clients to slide ratings in one direction or another. In any event, the experience provided by the US and European crises proves that to rely only on the self-disciplining role played by reputation makes little sense.

It seems quite clear that the issuer-pay model does not offer any guarantee for investors. Incentives should be better aligned. A credible threat of civil liability would undoubtedly force credit rating agencies to be more vigilant in guarding against negligent, reckless, and fraudulent practices (Partnoy 2009, 14).

Credit ratings should only be part of the mosaic of information considered part of the investment process. For this purpose, more competition in the industry and the development of new tools to evaluate credit risk seem to be necessary.

12.4 Why Do Investors Often Make the Wrong Choice?

In addition to the misjudgment of risks by institutional actors such as the IMF or credit rating agencies, an additional issue is why investors are frequently attracted by riskier assets. It seems that just as there is "money illusion", there is also "profit illusion", i.e., profit is considered without taking into consideration the level of risk involved. Important portions of capital are therefore usually invested in high-yield high-risk sectors such as the stock market, real estate, or assets of dubious quality—from tulip bulb contracts to subprime mortgages to Argentine or Greek bonds.

According to prospect theory as proposed by Kahneman and Tversky (1979), decision makers can become less risk averse and even risk seeking if they find that they are operating below target or aspiration levels. Laughhunn et al. (1980) studied the behavior of 224 managers from the USA, Canada, and Europe and found that the majority of managers were risk seekers when faced with below-target outcomes.

[2] In May 2011, the European Securities and Markets Authority (ESMA) was assigned the registration and supervision of credit rating agencies in the union.

Strikingly, this picture coincides with the type of behavior described 150 years ago by Marx (2007, 294) according to which the fall in the rate of profit pushes capital "into adventurous channels, speculation, fraudulent credit, fraudulent stocks, crises".

Such behavior also agrees with Minsky's description of investors' behavior: "over a protracted period of good times, capitalist economies tend to move from a financial structure dominated by hedge finance units to a structure in which there is large weight to units engaged in speculative and Ponzi finance" (Minsky 1992, 8).

According to Schumpeter, the primary waves of prosperity initiated by entrepreneurial ventures that implement technological innovations inevitably become overridden by larger secondary waves of speculative prosperity. In Schumpeter's words, "many things float on this 'secondary wave', without any new or direct impulse from the real driving force, and speculative anticipation in the end acquires a causal significance" (Schumpeter 1961, 226).

Financial crises result in the elimination of speculative ventures and positions but, unfortunately, also of otherwise sound firms that are denied liquidity by now overly cautious bankers. Schumpeter maintained that "reckless banking" and financial speculation should be separated from the "creative destruction" process of innovation by means of "rational as distinguished from vindictive regulation by public authority" (Schumpeter 1961, 91).

Following Schumpeter's terminology, in the "primary wave", banks create credit to finance entrepreneurial ventures that introduce new products or new processes that increase productivity. However, banks eventually find that investment opportunities run scarce while savings continue flowing into their vaults. The time for "financial innovation" then comes.

One example of financial innovation has been structured finance: in the USA, banks nicely packaged multi-trillion dollar dubious mortgages as "safe" securities and sold them to investors eager for high yields. Another example of "secondary wave" financial speculation and "reckless" banking was the sale of Argentine bonds by Italian banks to half a million naïve Italian retirees in the 1990s.

These mechanisms are favored in the event a veil conceals the real risks those investments involve, which is the role that rating agencies played in the US subprime financial crisis when they assured that those assets were safer than what they really were.

However, financial innovation develops only up to the limits that regulations allow, which is why subprime speculation developed *after* financial deregulation took place in the USA rather than before. For this reason, the "rational" regulation advocated by Schumpeter should put limits on "reckless" banking and speculative excesses.

It is true that financial crises can themselves cause the artificial debt built by financial speculation to burst, but the severity and the social costs of the downturn may be unbearable. Frightened banks would severely tighten credit to businesses, which may mean massive destruction of enterprises and jobs that would otherwise have survived. Alarmed depositors would run to withdraw their money from banks, thus worsening the crisis.

Public authority should therefore intervene through regulation to avoid that "the capital development of a country becomes a by-product of the activities of a casino" (Keynes 2008, 142). However, if this is not enough to avoid a financial crisis, once it explodes government intervention is then necessary to minimize damage. A soft landing is always better than a crash landing.

Somebody may argue that it would be better to let market forces handle financial crisis because government intervention creates a problem of moral hazard. This was the reasoning behind the denial of a bailout for Lehman Brothers. However, this case showed precisely that it is one thing to talk about moral hazard in theory and quite another to put the idea into practice. After Lehman Brothers' failure, the Fed and the Treasury had to step in aggressively to stop a colossal bank run and rescue the financial system.

The argument that troubled banks should not be saved because this would eliminate market participants' incentives to monitor and self-regulate banks' risky behavior proved quite impractical. Given the negative externalities of bank failures due to systemic effects, the social costs of a bankruptcy—particularly in the case of large financial institutions—largely exceed private costs. This places the onus on regulation to minimize the room for moral hazard.

As Keynes (2008, 143) suggested, public access to financial markets should, like access to casinos, be "inaccessible and expensive". This is why he argued that the "introduction of a substantial government transfer tax on all transactions might prove to be the most serviceable reform available, with a view to mitigating the dominance of speculation over enterprise in the United States" (Ibid.). His idea was that throwing some grains of sand into the gears of financial markets might deter financial speculation. However, taxing financial transactions may be only a necessary but not a sufficient condition for that.

As stated above, systemic risks to the financial institutions are risks for the economy as a whole. This is the basic case for regulation of all financial activity. Let us look at some of the issues at stake.

12.5 Some Issues at Stake in Financial Regulation

The first issue to be considered is that any regulation means a restriction on the expected rate of return by lowering the level of risk investors or banks are allowed to take. However, this does not necessarily mean a lower ex post average rate of return; it only means that the riskier bets are excluded or restricted, precisely those that may result in huge losses.

Regulation should restrict the type of products that financial institutions can offer to the public. It should also include the conditions that financial guarantees must meet. Higher transparency of the financial guarantee insurance sector is highly desirable, especially because the assessment of a financial guarantor is further complicated by the presence of an important element of circularity: the values of financial guarantors depend on the values of the securities that they have backed, and, in turn, the values of these assets depend on the financial health of the financial guarantor (Schich 2008, 110).

As stated above, financial institutions have a perverse incentive to excessive risk taking. In fact, it is unwise to play safely while everyone else gambles, which is why banks maximize their correlations to fail when all of the other banks are failing, betting that a bailout will take place when a large number of banks are in distress.[3]

Special attention should thus be placed on those risks capable of damaging the financial system as a whole. This goes beyond the traditional regulatory approach whose primary focus is the safety and soundness of individual institutions and markets in isolation. Systemic significance is not only related to the size of the firm itself but also to its interconnectedness with the rest of the economy. For this purpose, a systemic tax fee—as suggested in Acharya et al. (2009, 284)—on all financial institutions based on their contribution to systemic risk may be a useful tool.

This tax would either dissuade financial institutions from those behaviors that increase systemic risk or make them contribute to a fund to be used in the event of a systemic calamity. As in environmental economics, those who pollute must pay the cost of cleanup. It is a matter of efficiency and equity.

Milne (2013, 20) argues that "macro-prudential tools should be used within a strict rule based framework, in which the impact on the cost and availability of credit can be readily predicted". In this respect, he proposes using "cap and trade" to control aggregate systemic liquidity risk instead of regulation of individual institutions and individual markets. For implementation of "cap and trade", a central register of financial assets and liabilities should be established. The systemic risk regulator periodically determines an amount as the upper limit on short-term liabilities of financial intermediaries; licenses for this amount are distributed to financial institutions.

All short-term liabilities used to finance financial investments, both loans and securities, should be subject to licensing control, including any offshore funding (Ibid., p. 5). Exchange between institutions (the trade of licenses) is allowed to determine the most efficient allocation between institutions. Milne argues that the control over the stock of licenses will limit the amount of maturity mismatch in the entire financial system by preventing rapid increase in the ratio of short-term liabilities to nominal GDP.

12.6 The Case of Public Debt

While regulation can help to reduce the level of investors' exposure to risk in the case of private assets, a different issue arises when public debt is involved. How to minimize investors' risk of being victims of a sovereign debt default?

[3] Farhi and Tirole (2009, 22) state under which assumptions this is the optimal behavior for banks.

A key issue is transparency in public accounts.[4] However, transparency is not just an issue of making large quantities of raw data publicly available. They must be accessible, relevant, and easy for everyone to understand. Otherwise, the public cannot use them to make comparisons and exercise choice. Therefore, the first step is to define the key indicators that give a clear idea of fiscal sustainability and a clear way to present them together with a strict schedule for that. For this purpose, the key indicators should also include relevant quasi-fiscal activities conducted outside the general government as well as commitments and contingent liabilities.

Pressures to engage in nontransparent practices usually appear during periods of fiscal stress. Therefore, once a schedule has been established, its lack of fulfillment or the delay in reporting on some indicators may themselves be a signal of fiscal difficulties. If the difficulties are not too serious, the government will prefer to air them instead of alarming the financial markets.

An important instrument for ensuring transparency in government operations is an independent review agency responsible for conducting performance audits and studies on selected fiscal issues, as stated above. To be effective, such an agency must be endowed with wide investigative and reporting authority over government operations.

Finally, as the recent experiences of Iceland, Ireland, and Spain illustrate, banking crises may be a cause of sovereign debt crises. Therefore, the health of the banking system is also a critical issue in assessing the prospective of a country's public debt. Thus, improvement in financial regulation and prudential supervision are not only important for the financial system itself but may also be an important contribution to lowering the risk of sovereign debt default.

12.7 Rethinking Economics

It has already been stressed in Chap. 9 that mainstream neoclassical economics bears a serious responsibility in the incubation of the financial crisis. Research programs have been more motivated by analytical elegance and mathematical tractability than by a powerful desire to understand how the economy works. However, identifying the flaws in economic theory is easier than defining a way to eliminate them. Some guidelines are outlined below.

Economic illness rather than economic health should be the main object of economists' efforts. Considerable energy has been devoted to showing why an economy works smoothly most of the time, but very little to the analysis of why, from time to time, the economic mechanism breaks down or—more importantly—what is needed to fix it.

[4] Greece manipulated data to become a member of the Eurozone and concealed the real amount of its public deficit for years until 2009.

Researchers should pay more attention to issues concerning the coordination of actors and the possibility of coordination failures. The global financial crisis has revealed severe dysfunctional institutions that need to be adapted, revised, or even abolished. Risks turned out to be strongly mispriced, while new financial institutions and instruments posed a threat to both financial stability and the efficient operation of financial sector functions (Blommestein 2009, 73).

From the point of view of the methodological approach, economists should remember that the main purpose of science is explanation. If a theory explains, it helps in understanding a phenomenon. If, additionally, it predicts, it is twice as useful. When an answer is not available, prediction is the second best alternative, but it is never a first best (Beker 2005, 6).

The choice of the questions to which economists try to find answers should be dictated by economics—theoretical and applied—and not by the possibilities of mathematically modeling the answers. The usefulness of the results should be considered more important than formal aspects such as analytical elegance or economy of theoretical means.

Mathematics is just a tool to guarantee logical consistency. However, logical consistency may also be warranted without the use of mathematics, depending on the sort of problem one wants to solve. The method should be subordinated to the problem, not the other way around. Economists should bear in mind that the most influential texts in economics have been nonmathematical.

There is nothing resembling "the" economic theory. Instead, there is a collection of economic theories, some of which are in competition with one another. The process of natural selection defines which ones survive and which do not. "Big social experiments" discredit some ideas and replace them with new ones. It is the practitioner who has to choose from the economists' portfolio the appropriate tool to use in each case. This is the art of economics, to use the concept introduced by John Neville Keynes.

Economics is not an exact science. Economists should have a sense of respect for those theories and models they do not share or like. Dissenters should not be treated as boring old aunts who always have something to grumble about at family parties (Spaventa 2009, 2–3). Instead of disqualifying rival theories, it would be better to react by looking at them for worthwhile elements.

This also implies that editorial boards of leading journals need to be willing to review submitted research papers that are less conventional, less mathematical, or more critical about the received theory and insist on a serious discussion of other empirical results on the same topic. Journals should also be less closed-shop-like in terms of specific nationalities, universities, and research centers (Blommestein 2009, 73). Journals should encourage authors of empirical papers—or their critics—to test the hypotheses included in them by using new data some time after publication to verify the robustness of results.

Any crisis is also an opportunity. Economic crises are an opportunity to renew economic ideas. New ideas may allow a new course of history to be shaped where crises can be avoided or at least become less costly. Let us hope that this opportunity will not be lost.

References

Acharya VV, Pedersen LH, Philippon T, Richardson M (2009) Regulating systemic risk. In: Acharya VV, Richardson M (eds) Restoring financial stability: how to repair a failed system. New York University, Stern School of Business, New York, pp 283–304

Alesina A, Tabellini G (1990) A positive theory of fiscal deficits and government debt. Rev Econ Stud 57:403–414

Beker VA (2005) Is economics a science? A discussion of some methodological issues, mimeo. Available via http://ssrn.com/abstract=839307

Bianchi J (2011) Overborrowing and systemic externalities in the business cycle. Am Econ Rev 101(December):3400–3426

Blommestein HJ (2009) The financial crisis as a symbol of the failure of academic finance? (a methodological digression). J Finance Transform. Available via http://ssrn.com/abstract=1477399

Farhi E, Tirole J (2009) Collective moral hazard, maturity mismatch and systemic bailouts. Toulouse school of economics working paper. Available via http://www.tse-fr.eu/images/doc/wp/ng/wp_nogroup_52_2009.pdf

IMF (2003) Lessons from the crisis in Argentina, Oct 8, mimeo. Available via http://www.imf.org/external/np/pdr/lessons/100803.pdf

Kahneman D, Tversky A (1979) Prospect theory: an analysis of decision under risk. Econometrica 47(2)

Keynes JM (2008) The general theory of employment, interest and money. Atlantic, New Delhi

Laughhunn DJ, Payne JW, Crum R (1980) Managerial risk preferences for below-target returns. Manag Sci 26(December):1238–1249

Manganelli S, Wolswijk G (2007). Market discipline, financial integration and fiscal rules: what drives spreads in the euro area government bond market? Working paper series 745, European Central Bank. Available via http://www.ecb.europa.eu/pub/pdf/scpwps/ecbwp745.pdf

Marx K (2007) Capital: a critique of political economy, vol III, part 1. Cosimo Classics, New York

Milne A (2013) Register, cap and trade: a proposal for containing systemic liquidy risk. Economics 7:2013–2017. doi:10.5018/economics-ejournal.ja.2013-7

Minsky HP (1992). The financial instability hypothesis. The Jerome Levy Economics Institute of Bard College. Working paper no. 74. Available via http://www.levyinstitute.org/pubs/wp74.pdf

Pagano M, von Thadden EL (2004) The European bond markets under EMU. Oxf Rev Econ Policy 20(4):531–554. Available via http://www.csef.it/pagano/orep-2004.pdf

Partnoy F (2009) Rethinking regulation of credit rating agencies: an institutional investor perspective. San Diego Legal Studies Paper No. 09–014. Available via http://ssrn.com/abstract=1430608

Reinhart C, Rogoff K (2008) This time is different: a panoramic view of eight centuries of financial crises. NBER working paper no. 13882. Available via http://www.nber.org/papers/w13882.pdf

Reinhart C, Rogoff K (2009) This time is different: eight centuries of financial folly. Princeton University Press, Princeton

Schich S (2008) Challenges related to financial guarantee insurance. Financ Market Trends OECD:81–113

Schumpeter JA (1961) The theory of economic development. Oxford University Press, New York

Spaventa L (2009) Economists and economics: what does the crisis tell us? Real World Econ Rev 50. Available via http://www.rrojasdatabank.info/Spaventa50.pdf

MIX
Papier aus verantwortungsvollen Quellen
Paper from responsible sources
FSC® C105338

If you have any concerns about our products,
you can contact us on
ProductSafety@springernature.com

In case Publisher is established outside the EU,
the EU authorized representative is:
Springer Nature Customer Service Center GmbH
Europaplatz 3, 69115 Heidelberg, Germany

Printed by Libri Plureos GmbH
in Hamburg, Germany